WILD BRITAIN

A TRAVELLER'S GUIDE

DOUGLAS BOTTING

INTERLINK BOOKS

An imprint of Interlink Publishing Group, Inc.

NEW YORK

First American edition published 2000 by

INTERLINK BOOKS
An imprint of Interlink Publishing Group, Inc.
99 Seventh Avenue • Brooklyn, New York 11215 and
46 Crosby Street • Northampton, Massachusetts 01060

Library of Congress Cataloging-in-Publication Data
Botting, Douglas
   Wild Britain : a traveller's guide / by Douglas Botting.
      p. cm.
   Includes bibliographical references and index.
   ISBN 1-56656-321-6 (pbk.)
   1. Natural history—Great Britain—Guidebooks. 2.
Great Britain— Guidebooks. I. Title.
QH137.B67   2000
508.41—dc21   99-27835
                                                         CIP

Printed in Hong Kong

EDITOR: SIMON RIGGE

Art Direction and Book Design: Ivor Claydon and Bob
Hook
Assistant Editors: Sarah Bevan, Nicholas Lim, Chris
Schüler
Picture Editor: Karin B. Hills
Researcher: Dominic Cotton
Senior Editorial Assistants: Ruth Bourne and Sam
Thorne
Editorial Assitants: Fenella Dick, Charlotte Lawrence,
Joan Lee, Neil Maclean, Lieta Marziali, James Moss,
Rebecca Skipwith, Laura Smith-Spark, Henrietta
Valder, Sally Weatherill
Production Manager: Hugh Allan
Production Assistants: Helen Seccombe, Zoë Hall,
Marie-Anne Poncet
Maps: Oxford Cartographers
Line Illustrations: Syd Lewis

Front cover caption: The play of sunlight and shadow on
the depression known as the Devil's Beef Tub captures
the essence of the undulating landscape of Lowland
Scotland

To order or request our complete catalog,
please call us at **1-800-238-LINK** or write to:
Interlink Publishing
46 Crosby Street • Northampton, MA 01060
E-mail: interpg@aol.com
Website: www.Interlinkbooks.com

THE AUTHOR
AND GENERAL EDITOR

DOUGLAS BOTTING has travelled to Brazil,
South Yemen, the Sahara, Arctic Siberia and to
many European wild places. His travel books include *One Chilly Siberian Morning*, *Wilderness
Europe* and *Rio de Janeiro*. He has recently written the authorized biography of the author and
conservationist, Gerald Durrell.

CONTRIBUTORS

NEIL FAIRBAIRN, who contributed many of
the fact-packs and smaller exploration zones
throughout the book, is a freelance writer and
bassoon player. His books include *A Traveller's
Guide To The Kingdoms Of Arthur*.

FERDIE McDONALD, who made extensive
contributions to the chapter on Lowland Scotland, is a freelance writer specializing in travel
and guide-books.

DAVID SAUNDERS, who made extensive contributions to the chapter on Wales, is publications officer of the Wildlife Trust West Wales.
Formerly Director of the WTWW, Warden of
Skomer Island and organizer of Operation Sea-
farer, he has written many bird books.

CONSULTANTS

JOHN BURTON is a natural history and
wildlife conservation writer and consultant.
Chief Executive of the World Land Trust and
former secretary of the Fauna and Flora Preser-
vation Society, he co-founded, with Douglas Botting, the Wild Guides series.

DAVID BLACK is a writer and editor who has
worked on many nature books including Gerald
and Lee Durrell's *Practical Guide For The Ama-
teur Naturalist*.

ALLAN MARLES is a map consultant who has
had many years' experience working with the
Ordnance Survey.

CONTENTS

This book is dedicated to the memory of my father,
Leslie William Botting,
who loved the countryside of Britain and all its wild creatures

ABOUT THE SERIES

What would the world be, once bereft
Of wet and of wildness? Let them be
 left,
O let them be left, wildness and wet;
Long live the weeds and the wilderness
 yet.

Gerard Manley Hopkins: Inversnaid

These books are about those embattled refuges of wildness and wet: the wild places of Europe. But where, in this most densely populated sub-continent, do we find a truly wild place?

Ever since our Cro-Magnon ancestors began their forays into the virgin forests of Europe 40,000 years ago, the land and its creatures have been in retreat before *Homo sapiens*. Forests have been cleared, marshes drained and rivers straightened: even some of those landscapes that appear primordial are in fact the result of human activity. Heather-covered moorland in North Yorkshire and parched Andalusian desert have this in common: both were once covered by great forests which were then knocked flat by ancient settlers .

What then remains that can be called wild? There are still a few areas in Europe that are untouched by man — places generally so unwelcoming either in terrain or in climate that man has not wanted to touch them at all. These are indisputably wild.

For some people, wildness suggests conflict with nature: a wild place is a part of the planet so savage and desolate that you risk your life whenever you venture into it. This is in part true but would limit the eligible places to the most impenetrable bog or highest mountain tops in the worst winter weather — a rather restricted view. Another much broader definition considers a wild place to be a part of the planet where living things can find a natural refuge from the influence of modern industrial society. By this definition a wild place is for wild life as well as that portmanteau figure referred to in these pages as the wild traveller: the hill walker, backpacker, bird-watcher, nature lover, explorer, nomad, loner, mystic, masochist, *aficionado* of the great outdoors, or permutations of all these things.

This is the definition we have observed in selecting the wild places described in these books. Choosing them has not been easy. Even so, we hope the criterion has proved rigid enough to exclude purely pretty (though popular) countryside, and flexible enough to include the greener, gentler wild places, of great natural historical interest perhaps, as well as the starker, more savage ones where the wild explorers come into their own.

These are not guide-books in the conventional sense, for to describe every neck of the woods and twist of the trail throughout Europe would require a library of volumes. Nor are these books addressed to the technical specialist — the caver, diver, rock climber or cross-country skier, the orchid-hunter, lepidopterist or beetlemaniac — for such experts will have data of their own. They are books intended for the general outdoor traveller — including the expert outside his field of expertise (the orchid-hunter in a cave, the diver on a mountain top) — who wishes to scrutinize the range of wild places on offer in Europe, to learn a little more about them and to set about exploring them off the beaten track.

One of the great consolations in the preparation of these books has been to find that after 40,000 years of hunting, clearing, draining and ploughing, Cro-Magnon and their descendants have left so much of Europe that can still be defined as wild.

WILD BRITAIN: AN INTRODUCTION

Great Britain boasts some of the most varied landscapes and beautiful coastline in the world. Its wild places embrace a multitude of different terrains and habitats, all the way from the mysterious world beneath the sea to the Arctic tundra of the mountain tops via sand dunes, sea-shore, grassland, moorland, forest and fen, island and tor, bog and lake, waterfall and cave, down and dale — the variety is endless. Few of these wild and empty spots are truly primordial in the sense that parts of the Amazon rain forest or Arctic Siberia are primordial, meaning unaltered by human activity. However, by all but this purest of definitions, there are many parts of Britain that are still wild.

Some of the wild places in Britain — such as the bird rock of Handa, one mile long by half a mile wide — are tiny. Others — such as the Cairngorms, which cover 160 square miles of mountain wilderness — are huge by British standards. Some have survived to the present day because they have been the hunting grounds, royal chase, grouse moors and deer forest of the landed aristocracy which has often helped to keep any disturbance to wildlife and the ecosystem to a minimum. Others have survived because they are out and out badlands and have thus been spared the plough and the housing estate: the great bog wastes of Scotland's Flow Country for instance, although some have disappeared beneath conifers. A few wild places — Wicken Fen in Cambridgeshire, for example — have survived as a result of historical accident. Very many have been saved as oases of natural habitat in a wasteland of agricultural and urban development and commercial reafforestation because of the successful rearguard action fought by conservationists, aghast at the accelerated destruction of the natural environment of the British Isles, especially since the end of the Second World War.

A measure of the scale of the havoc can be gained from the statistics of a typical case like Worcestershire, a rural county in lowland England with few pretensions to wilderness status: 30 per cent of ancient woodlands destroyed, 50 per cent of the ponds, 95 per cent of the marshes and bogs, 99 per cent of the pastures and all their flowers and herbs, and 2,500 miles of hedges — a microcosm of Armageddon in the British countryside. The national picture is as bad or worse.

Lowland England has taken the worst of the bashing. The few wild places cling to the extremities, while the farmed, suburban countryside claims the middle ground all the way from Dover to north of Derby, where the Peak District marks the beginning of upland Britain, which remains the stronghold of the British wilds.

Yet if you take to the air over England, the predominance of countryside is astonishing; an apparently limitless carpet of greenery rolls over the landscape and seems to engulf even the most obtrusive conurbation. This greenery is mostly cultivated land, however. In such a landscape the wild places of southern and central England are simply scattered outposts. By contrast, Scotland and Wales present the reverse image of the English scene, for there it is civilization that holds the outposts in a landscape that is still largely wild — though no longer primordial.

Below the tops of the highest mountains most of the landscape of Britain is man-modified, even man-made. This applies even to those celebrated landscapes we fondly cherish as quintessential British wild places, such as the North York Moors, or even the Norfolk Broads. The latter were originally an extensive tract of bogland which the medieval East Anglians dug up for peat, when their excavations became flooded the artificial wetland world of the present-day Broads came into being.

In compiling this book the difficulty has generally been deciding what to leave out rather than what to include. Very small places I have excluded unless they are very isolated (such as the Monach Isles), unique (such as Wicken Fen) or both (such as North Rona) — or part of a series making up a greater whole (such as the bird reserves of the East Anglian coast). On the other hand, very large places are not included merely because they are very large, which explains why the great expanse of the Monadhliath Mountains in the Grampian Highlands of Scotland cannot be found in these pages. Furthermore, it goes without saying that places of no outstanding wildlife interest are not excluded for that reason if their wilderness value is self-evident (some of Dartmoor and the Peak District, and places like Glen Coe fall into this category).

A lot of places that are wild in winter are not always so in summer. This is particularly the case with some of the more spectacular wintering grounds for wildfowl and wading birds, which may become deserted in summer; and of many of the finest wild places which conversely become overcrowded in summer with human beings.

I have also excluded places of purely natural historical interest, where the human presence is too intrusive (as in the major bird stations at Dungeness and Sandwich Bay, and most harbour estuaries and country parks), but I have included them where it is impermanent or seasonally adjusted (as on the North Norfolk Marshes, which become deserted and bitterly wild in winter).

Of all the world's wild places, those of Great Britain are perhaps the least typical. Some of them, especially in the Scottish Highlands, are pure wilderness. But many, particularly in England, are highly organized, exhaustively studied and minutely described, with way-marked paths and a network of elaborately evolved long-distance tracks. As a consequence in the peak holiday season it may be difficult to get away from it all — even in the furthest back of the British beyond. Even a remote Highland peak such as Stac Polly will have an approach trail blazed across the wild peat moors by the sheer weight of back-packing feet in the busy season, and walkers are being actively discouraged from using some of the most popular long-distance paths such as the Lyke Wake Walk over the North York Moors because the ground is being worn away by sheer over-use. At Loch Garten in the Scottish Highlands the number of people who have come to see the ospreys now exceeds a million; in the Peak District National Park the annual number of visits has reached 22 million.

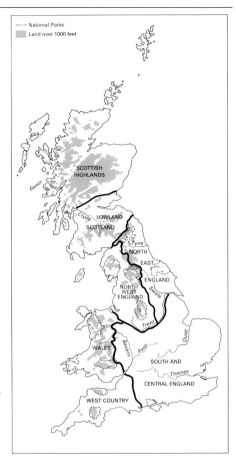

It could be argued that I am making this situation worse by publicizing the wild places in this book. I can only answer that part of my aim has been to instil a respect and love for such places among a wider public, and if this happens it can only be to the advantage of the wilderness areas and nature reserves of Britain. Treat these places with the respect they deserve as a precious natural heritage. Follow the Country Code. Observe the rights of way. Remember the code of conduct in the sensitive ecosystems of the nature reserves: 'Take nothing but photographs. Leave nothing but footprints. Kill nothing but time.' And enjoy yourself.

THE KEY TO BRITAIN'S WILD PLACES

THE SHAPE OF THE WILD

Britain (here meaning England, Scotland and Wales) can be said to consist of a semicircle of islands (700 off Scotland alone) and 7,000 miles (11,200 kilometres) of coastline of immense variety and beauty, enclosing a land roughly divided in two by a diagonal line that runs from the Blackdown Hills in the south-west to the North York Moors in the north-east. Generally speaking, the country to the north and west of this line is Highland Britain, and the country to the south and east of it is Lowland Britain.

Wild places are few and far between in Lowland Britain, and for the most part occupy the periphery where for one reason or another modern farming and development — the scourge of wild places — cannot reach. The few lowland wild places include parts of the coast (such as North Norfolk), some of the islands and the oases of woodland (such as the New Forest), wetland (such as Wicken Fen) and heath (such as Purbeck and Breckland).

It is in the more rugged, bleaker, less easily farmed upland country of Highland Britain that most of the wild places lie: the moorland plateaux of the West Country (Dartmoor, Exmoor and Bodmin Moor); the high fells and moors of the North Country (either strung out along the central spine of the Pennines, like the Peak District, Yorkshire Dales and Upper Teesdale, or rising alongside it, like the North York Moors, Lake District and Cheviot Hills of Northumberland); the great upland mass that occupies nearly all of Wales (the Brecon Beacons, Cambrian Mountains and Snowdonia); and, to the north, the Scottish Highlands and Islands, separated from Lowland Scotland by the Highland Boundary Fault, split in two halves (the Grampians and the North-West Highlands) by the Great Glen and altogether forming the highest and most extensive wilderness area in the British Isles.

Throughout this wide spectrum of landscape types between sea-shore and mountain top, certain broadly distinct habitats recur. Each kind of habitat displays roughly similar land forms and a roughly similar range of wildlife species, allowing for regional variations from south to north. The main habitats of Britain are:

Coastlands and Islands: *cliffs* (e.g. those along the coast of Cornwall, Yorkshire, Shetland and Orkney). Cliff-nesting birds such as gulls, auks, fulmars and cormorants. Salt- and wind-tolerant plants such as thrift, spring squill and samphire. *Dunes* (e.g. Braunton Burrows, Newborough Warren, Ainsdale and Culbin Sands). Many butterflies and flowers, sea holly and sea bindweed on the foredunes, marsh helleborine and the rare natterjack toad in the dune slacks, with marram grass binding the sands. Spits and sand-bars (massive coastal sediment features, e.g. Chesil Bar, the spits of Blakeney Point, Spurn Head and Gibraltar Point). Notable for wide range of plants and nesting birds, especially terns. Also seal-breeding colonies. *Salt marshes and mud-flats* (in sheltered estuaries, bays and sea lochs, e.g. the North Kent Marshes, the Wash, Humber, Morecambe Bay, Solway Firth, Moray and Cromarty Firths). Salt-tolerant plants such as eelgrass, colourful sea lavender, sea aster and sea pink. Important feeding ground for thousands of wintering waders and wildfowl which feed on the salt-marsh plants or the masses of mud-flat invertebrates.

Woodlands: woods cover seven per cent of Britain, but eighty per cent of that is commercial conifer plantation. Hardly any ancient woods left, but notable relics of ancient broad-leaved forest include Anses Wood and Mark Ash Wood in the New Forest and the woods on the cliffs of the Lower Wye. Rich diversity of classic woodland flowers, woodland birds, insects and fungi. Ancient natural pine woods — Caledonian forests — survive only in scattered areas of northern Scotland such as Rothiemurchus, Black Wood of Rannoch, Loch Maree and Glen Affric. Understorey of juniper, cowberry and bilberry, with crossbill and capercaillie, pine marten, wild cat and red squirrel.

Lowland grassland and heaths: open, often man-made (and rabbit-made!) spaces dominated by grasses, heathers and other dwarf shrubs, generally growing on sandy, chalky or limestone soils, mostly in southern England. Notable for their distinctive flora and specialized fauna, including all six British reptiles. *Dry lowland heath* (e.g. parts of the New Forest and the Isle of Purbeck). Specialist flora and fauna, including Dartford warbler and hobby falcon, sand lizard and spider-hunting wasp — all under siege from pasture, plantation and development. Few *chalk grasslands* in Britain (e.g. the downs of Wiltshire, Sussex and Kent) can now be described as wild, and most are much frequented and under threat. The *limestone country* (e.g. the Mendips and the

Derbyshire and Yorkshire Dales) often combines spectacular karst landscape with brilliant richness of flora. The *Breckland* in East Anglia is a large, sandy area of heath and grassland of a type virtually unique in Britain. Very few unimproved natural grasslands; traditional meadows and pastures survive in the lowlands.

Freshwater wetlands: in addition to the lakes, rivers and streams, there are the marshes, broads and fens (e.g. the Insh Marshes, the Somerset Levels, the Norfolk Broads and surviving fens, such as Wicken and Woodwalton). Lush vegetation and a myriad of wetland birds and insects: bittern, reed bunting and bearded tit, many dragonflies and rare butterflies such as the swallowtail.

Uplands: hills, moors and mountains above 800 feet (240 metres). The most extensive land habitat in Britain, and generally the wildest, comprising one-eighth of England and Wales and nearly two-thirds of Scotland. Noteworthy habitat types include *wet upland moor* (e.g. the great uncultivated peat moors of Dartmoor, the Peak, the North Pennines, North York Moors, Upland Wales, Rannoch and the Flow Country). Heather, bilberry and bracken. Red grouse, ring ouzel, merlin and hen harrier. Bogs and mires, with cotton grass, orchids and insectivorous plants. Very high up you come to the *tundra* and *arctic-alpine zone* (e.g. Ben Lawers, the Cairngorms and Upper Teesdale). Notable for their cold, for relict plants from Britain's glacial past (e.g. spring gentian) and specialist fauna which includes the dotterel, snow bunting, ptarmigan and mountain hare.

THE RULES OF THE WILD

The wild traveller should always be prepared for sudden changes in the unpredictable British weather. Mist can come down suddenly (notoriously on Dartmoor); rivers can rise rapidly in spate (as in the West Highlands); clouds can roll over and temperatures drop on the high mountains, where the wind-chill factor may be crucial to survival; winter can turn the green slopes of summer into Yukon blizzard country, so always try to do a weather check. Always take appropriate footwear and clothing, food and necessary gear. Always take the right map and know how to read it. Observe the Mountain Code.

The Mountain Code: learn the use of map and compass. Know the weather signs and local forecast. Plan a route within your capabilities and leave time to get down before dark. Know simple first aid and the symptoms of exposure. Know the mountain distress signals. To give a signal for help, give six blasts on a whistle and/or six flashes with a torch. Wait one minute. Repeat. To answer a signal for help, give three blasts on a whistle and/or three flashes with a torch. Repeat. Take a bearing on the signal and move towards it while continuing to signal. Never go alone. Leave written word of your route and estimated time of return, and report when you get back. Take warm/weatherproof clothing and survival bag. Take map and compass, torch and food. Wear climbing boots. Stay alert all day. Be prepared to turn back if the weather deteriorates or if any member of your party is becoming slow or exhausted. *If there is snow on the hills*, always have an ice-axe for each person. Carry a climbing rope. Know the correct use of rope and ice-axe. Learn to recognize dangerous snow slopes. Lack of space precludes a detailed description of equipment and techniques recommended for travellers in wild places. If in doubt refer to one of the many manuals on the subject.

The Country Code: while you are in the country you should observe the code of behaviour drawn up by the Countryside Commission.

Enjoy the countryside and respect its life and work. Guard against all risk of fire. Fasten all gates. Keep your dogs under close control. Keep to public footpaths across farm land. Use gates and stiles to cross fences, hedges and walls. Leave livestock, crops and machinery alone. Take your litter home. Help to keep all water clean. Protect wildlife, plants and trees. Take special care on country roads. Make no unnecessary noise.

Rights of Way: visitors may not roam off designated rights of way, except in areas of open access. For guidance refer to the most recent OS maps.

PROTECTED WILD PLACES

A number of wild places enjoy some sort of official status and some measure of protection either under the law or from charitable or local conservation organizations such as the RSPB, National Trust or the county Wildlife Trusts.

Officially protected places fall into two categories: those valued for their landscape and those for their wildlife. The principal conservation designation for landscape is the National Park. The first National Parks were established by the government in the 1950s and '60s and there are now ten formally designated parks covering 5,292 square miles (13,706 square kilometres) in England and Wales, such as Dartmoor, Snowdonia and the Lake District, which have a considerable measure of protection. In 1995 National Park Authorities were created to manage the parks and negotiate public access. Areas of Outstanding Natural Beauty, a classification awarded on aesthetic grounds by the Countryside Commission, can also cover large areas, though they are often less well-known to the public than National Parks.

Scotland has, since 1978, had its own conservation designation for landscape: the National Scenic Area. These areas cover around one-eighth of the country and are roughly equivalent in size to the National Parks of England and Wales.

The main wildlife conservation designation, the Site of Special Scientific Interest, was established in 1949 to protect rare or typical plants and animals in their natural habitats. Today there are 6,500 SSSIs in mainland Britain notified by three separate agencies: English Nature, Scottish Natural Heritage and the Countryside Council for Wales. Some SSSIs are also managed by these agencies in the interests of providing public access and demonstrating correct protective procedure; these are known as National Nature Reserves. All protected wildlife sites are designated SSSIs (with the exception of Marine Nature Reserves), but further designations can be added if a site conforms to other specific criteria. For instance, Ramsar sites are internationally significant wetland sites of wildfowl and waders.

After Britain's entry into the EEC in 1973, additional conservation legislation was required. The 1979 Birds Directive and 1992 Habitats Directive led to the new British designations Special Protection Area and Special Area of Conservation respectively, which cover wildlife populations of European importance.

Although conservation campaigners have welcomed the new legislation, they argue that Britain's wild places are still inadequately protected under law. In particular the designation SSSI, though identifying a valuable site, does not prevent damaging agricultural practices or development. A recent report by English Nature stated that almost half Britain's SSSIs were in an 'unfavourable condition' and organizations such as Friends of the Earth continue to campaign for legal safeguards. For more information about threatened wild places, visit the Friends of the Earth web-site: www.foe.co.uk/wildplaces. For a complete list of designations used in this book, see the Glossary on p214

TO THE READER

Organization: Each chapter is divided into exploration zones containing a narrative description, written in the first person singular and illustrated with personal anecdote, followed by a fact-pack which gives practical information on how to get there, when and where to go, where to stay and what to do, backed up with postal, e-mail and web-site addresses, telephone and fax numbers and lists of maps and further reading. This hybrid arrangement avoids cluttering the author's personal narrative with tedious guide-book detail, but at the same time ensures that you can find practical references instantly when you want them.

Eagle symbols: the eagle symbols used in this book indicate the wildness of the exploration zone to which they refer. This scale is based on a number of factors, including remoteness, ruggedness, spaciousness, uniqueness, wildlife interest, natural beauty and the author's subjective reactions. Three eagles is the highest rating, no eagles the lowest.

Maps: at the time of going to press, Ordnance Survey were revising all their British maps, a process which will involve renaming and renumbering. The map references given in this book may, therefore, become inaccurate and we advise you to check the changes with the Ordnance Survey, if you encounter any difficulties.

Grid references: occasionally a grid reference is given if a wild place is otherwise difficult to pin-point. The reference is based on the standard, Ordnance Survey, national grid system.

Updating: information does gradually become outdated. For this reason we would welcome readers' comments and corrections for incorporation in subsequent editions. Please write to The Editor, Wild Guides, Sheldrake Press, 188 Cavendish Road, London SW12 0DA, or send an e-mail to: mail@sheldrakepress.demon.co.uk.

Non-liability: both author and publishers have gone to great pains to point out the hazards that may confront the traveller in certain places described in *Wild Britain*. We cannot under any circumstances accept any liability for any mishap, loss or injury sustained by any person venturing into any of the wild places listed in this book.

CHAPTER 1

The West Country

Some years ago an old acquaintance of mine, the Irish writer Brendan Lehane, spent part of a summer in a remote wooded valley on the edge of the Brendon Hills on Exmoor, as an experiment in post-Armageddon Stone Age living. He brought nothing with him to his valley but a goat, a few hens, a sack of oats, a hammer, an axe, a bucket, two mugs and a wife.

For two months he and his wife lived on what they could squeeze out of their livestock and forage from the surrounding woods and stream. They drank dandelion coffee and buttercup tea; sought solace in whortleberry wine and herb cigarettes; filled their bellies with beechmast cake, roast squirrel, fried grasshoppers and boiled bogweed; washed in home-made sorrel soap and lit their tumbledown hut with the light from a bulrush lamp. They lost weight, looked farouche, grew smelly and slept long. If their green valley had seemed a lush corner of rural England when they arrived, it had become like a wild neck of the New Guinea jungle by the time they left.

The lessons they learned had nothing to do with noble savages or the virtues of self-sufficiency but with the modern civilized world to which they returned. The first town they came to seemed hideously vulgar and brash, the first restaurant meal unbelievably sweet and cloying, the first office-dwellers grotesque caricatures of the consumer society. 'We found the world took some getting back to,' Brendan reported. 'We

The tors of Devon and Cornwall were shaped by the action of wind and water, as all good materialists know, yet few see them for the first time without a disquieting sense of some supernatural force

were thinking of the other side of the hill, and of the peace and freedom from disturbance, the closeness to nature, of putting food, if not in the right place, in a less wrong one; and of a few specially nice moments under the oak trees and stars.' A classic wilderness withdrawal syndrome.

Wilderness is something the West Country has in reasonable proportion. By the West Country I mean the long south-west peninsula of England which juts into the Atlantic west of a line from Bristol to Bournemouth and comprises the counties of Somerset and Avon, Devon, Cornwall and Dorset. This is a very distinctive region, at one and the same time wild and gentle, rugged and lush. Climatically, because of its southerly latitude and warmish sea, it is the most favoured corner of the kingdom; palm trees and subtropical plants flourish on the Cornish and Devon Rivieras, and daffodils bloom in mid-winter on the offshore Isles of Scilly.

Yet there can be few places where the elements rage more violently than along the great Atlantic-facing cliff frontier of Cornwall and North Devon, where gale-swept seas batter the granite battlements of the West Country with a thud that makes the earth tremble; and there is no wilder place anywhere in southern Britain than the bleak upland moorland of Dartmoor, with its sudden mists, its quaking bogs, its vast, unpeopled vistas.

Dartmoor is the largest and highest of a series of granite bosses which, ranged like the knuckles of a clenched fist, form the exposed tops of a gigantic rock-mass, or batholith, underlying the West Country — the others being Bodmin Moor, St Austell, Carnmenellis, Land's End and the Isles of Scilly, which many people think were the legendary long-drowned Cornish kingdom of Lyonesse. Some feel they still are.

Long before Brendan and his wife ran off to the West Country to escape from the pressures of 20th-century living, mainland Britain's granite fastness was a welcome place of refuge. The Celts sought safety there from the Roman invaders, and the Romanized Britons in turn fled there from the incoming Saxons. The exploits of one such Romano-British chieftain, obscured by the mists of this chaotic transitional period and embroidered by later monastic chroniclers, formed the basis of the legend of King Arthur.

The West Country was a cradle of human habitation — and an arena for human conflict — long before Arthurian times, however. Prehistoric peoples left their barrows, hut circles and standing stones on the moors and high places. At Cranbrook, a Dartmoor hilltop more than 1,100 feet (335 metres) above sea level, stands an unfinished hill fort built by Iron Age people, Celts from Brittany and northern France who reinforced this natural strongpoint with ditches, banks and a stone-faced rampart. I first saw this fort by moonlight, when clouds were scudding across the pock-marked face of the moon before a warm, wet south-west wind. Far below this desper-

Some of the small wild flowers that thrive on damp or marshy ground are (from left to right) the bog pimpernel, the ivy-leaved bellflower, both low delicate creepers, and the sturdier bog violet

ate, ancient place I could hear a river gurgling off the moor towards the edge of darkness and the world, and as I stood there a sudden scream echoed through the night — bird or beast, fox or owl, man or phantom of times and peoples past, I never knew.

Like the refugees of times past, the wild places of the West Country hold out on the high ground, the moors and hills of the interior, and the remoter stretches of the sea coast where the islands, estuaries, salt flats, sand dunes, relic heaths and woods form some of the region's finest wildlife sanctuaries and nature reserves.

GETTING THERE

By air: regular scheduled services operate to airports at Bristol, Exeter, Bournemouth, Plymouth, Newquay and the Isles of Scilly (which also has a helicopter service from Penzance).

By sea: visitors from the Continent can travel direct to the West Country on Brittany Ferries, T: (01705) 827701, between Cherbourg and Poole, Roscoff and Plymouth and Santander and Plymouth; and on Condor Ferries, T: (01305) 761551, between St Malo and Poole or Weymouth. A regular ferry service also operates between Penzance and the Isles of Scilly. (For details see under ISLES OF SCILLY.)

By rail: the main towns in the West Country are served by fast, direct and regular train services from London (Paddington), the North-East, Scotland and Midlands throughout the year. Sleeper services to Devon and Cornwall are available on trains from London, and also on trains to Bristol from Glasgow and Edinburgh. Branch lines run local services to many of the smaller towns. For details call National Rail Enquiries, T: 0345 484950, or contact nearest Travel Centre.

By bus: National Express operates a network of coach services to many parts of the West Country from Victoria Coach Station in London. For details contact National Express, T: (0990) 808080.

WHERE TO STAY

The West Country has a multitude of accommodation ranging from *grand luxe* hotels to farmers' barns where you can lay out your sleeping bag. Visitors are advised to get hold of the relevant accommodation guides published annually by the West Country Tourist Board (see below), including the following: *West Country Holiday Homes, Commended Hotels and Guesthouses, Camping and Caravan Touring Map* and *Bed and Breakfast Touring Map*. Tourist information centres can help you find and reserve accommodation. A list of centres is available from the West Country Tourist Board.

Youth hostels: there is an excellent choice of hostels throughout the West Country. For further details and a guide, contact the Youth Hostel Association, Trevelyan House, 8 St Stephen's Hill, St Albans, Hertfordshire AL1 2DY, T: (01727) 845047, e-mail: yhacustomerservice@compuserve.com and, www.yha-england-wales.org.uk.

ACTIVITIES

Walking: the West Country offers some marvellous walking in wild or wildish places. Virtually the entire coastline is circumambulated by the SOUTH WEST COAST PATH, the longest footpath in Britain; another long-distance footpath, the TWO MOORS WAY, links the West Country's two national parks, Dartmoor and Exmoor. Contact the Ramblers Association, T: (0171) 339 8500.

Cycling: the Sustrans West Country Way cycle route, map No. 7, is a spectacular 248-mile (397-km) ride from Padstow to Bristol/Bath. Contact Sustrans for further details, T: (0117) 929 4173.

Climbing: some rock climbing is possible on Dartmoor, and there is spectacular sea-cliff climbing at all grades on the Cornish and Dorset coast. For information contact the British Mountaineering Council (see USEFUL ADDRESSES).

Riding: the riding and pony trekking is excellent on Dartmoor, Exmoor and Bodmin Moor. For list of riding centres contact West Country Tourist Board.

Fishing: the West Country also provides some of the best sea, game and coarse fishing in Britain, from the wild trout of Exmoor and Dartmoor to the mighty porbeagle shark off the Cornwall coast. For further details, request *Get Hooked* from the S.W. office of the Environment Agency, T: (01392) 444000.

FURTHER INFORMATION

West Country Tourist Board, 60 St David's Hill, Exeter EX4 4SY, T: (01392) 425426, F: 420891, www.wctb.co.uk, and e-mail: post@wctb.co.uk.

RSPB South-West Office, 10 Richmond Road, Exeter EX4 4JA, T: (01392) 432691.

Dartmoor

365 square miles (945 sq km) of high granite moorland in South Devon National Park

It was a lovely summer's day on old Dartmoor and the mortar bombs were falling all around me in tight little smoky groups. *Ping*, crump! went the bombs. *Pong*, crump! The rest of my squad were lying flat on their tummies in shallow hollows, tightly clutching their steel helmets to their heads. But in those days I suffered from a pathological lack of physical fear, so I continued to stand and stare about me, not so much out of bravado as indifference.

What an amazing place, I thought to myself — *such* horizons, *such* space, *such* a huge blue bell-jar of a sky. Ahead and a little to the right of me the bare, boulder-strewn slopes of Yes Tor swelled upwards to a hard nipple of dark granite more than 2,000 feet (600 metres) above the sea. On this raddled cone I could just discern a red danger flag flying: a warning to the world that people like me were banging off live ammunition to every point of the compass. I watched in fascination as flickering blue laser-like streaks of tracer looped over the landscape in gracefully undulating arcs of fire, as though fol-

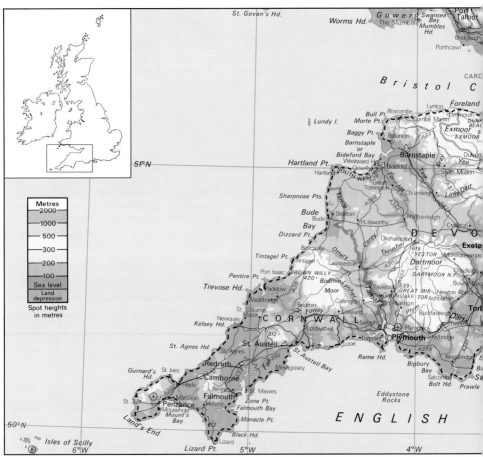

lowing the curvature of the earth.

Then a voice shouted from a hollow in the hill: 'Get down, you fool! Can't you see this place is bloody dangerous?' A blow on the back of my helmet brought me to my senses. Clubbed to the ground by a pick-axe handle wielded by an irate infantry major, I rubbed my nose in the sour peaty soil. 'What are you?' the major, a Korean War veteran, hissed in my ear. 'Some kind of nut? Anyone would think you were here for the *view!*'

It was my first impression of Dartmoor, and my most vivid, for I was there at an impressionable age — one of a squad of infantry and commando officer cadets on a battle course at Okehampton Camp, where

the army had exercised a hotly debated presence on the moor since World War Two. Our days on the highest, wildest land in England south of the Pennines brought saturating rain, obliterating mist, towering cloudscapes and a saucy sun gleaming brazenly out of a pellucid, rain-rinsed sky. There were no trees to shade us, precious few bushes to provide shelter from the wind that slithered over the long curving granite scarp of Corn Ridge. We squelched back and forth across an amphitheatre of blanket bog and waded knee deep down the icy, scurrying streams that fanned out of them like the veins of a leaf. Now and then we holed up for a smoke and a corned beef sandwich inside the stone ruins of a Bronze Age hut, where once people just like us, looking out on a view just like this, had contemplated mortality and the infinite in a fug of peat smoke and steaming cow dung. At the end of the day we yomped home across the wilderness in Indian file while the sunset flickered and flared behind the primordial silhouettes of the blackened tors, like a herd of grazing dragons, and every so often someone behind a rock or a megalith took a pot at us.

Dartmoor is a kind of island continent in microcosm. Its shape is roughly like Antarctica, its pattern of human settlement roughly like that of Australia — a narrow fringe round the circumference of a largely desert interior (of bog and granite moor in the case of Dartmoor). Like Australia, Dartmoor has had its penal colony of convicts, its military comings and goings, its early pioneers, its diggers, mineral claims and mining camps, even its aborigines (Bronze Age Beaker Folk, who vanished long ago). Like the macro island continents of Australia and Antarctica, the micro one of Dartmoor is largely undeveloped because it is still for the most part a wilderness.

Granite is the key to Dartmoor. The broad, rolling uplands of the moor are the highest landmass in Britain south of the Peak District, averaging 1,200 feet (365 metres) above sea level and reaching 2,039 feet (621 metres) at High Willhays, the highest point, and 2,030 feet (619 metres) at Yes Tor. Yet the land surface was once very much higher, rising perhaps to alpine heights. Nearly 300 million years of erosion — the physical and chemical interaction of rock with rain and frost — have reduced the granite mass to its present level and fashioned the unusual landscape we see today. The most noticeable features in the Dartmoor landscape — the fantastic rock-piles, or tors, which crown many of the hilltops on the central moor — are embattled survivors of this continuing process of attrition, the exposed tips of the underlying granite range from which the covering of softer rock has been worn away.

Up to 170 tors have been recorded on Dartmoor, and some 30 are marked on the map, including the best known ones: Hound Tor, Hay Tor, Yes Tor and Great Mis Tor. They top almost every horizon, these still, brooding, apocalyptic rock towers. Cracked by their natural jointing, they look from a distance like man-made edifices, ancient Inca citadels of massive hewn stone on the bleak *paramo* of the high Andes.

The tors differ greatly in size and appearance. Blackingstone Rock (near Moretonhampstead) is shaped like a dome, Shape Tor (near Merrivale) like a series of steeples, Hound Tor like a castle keep with battlements, Bowerman's Nose (near Manaton) like a pile of children's building blocks. The topmost boulders of these tors have been worn round and smooth by the natural process of weathering, and circular rain-filled hollows, called rock basins, like primordial wash bowls and hip baths, have been gouged into their flat tops by the action of freezing water.

Erosion debris, in the form of boulders and large stones known as clitter, is thickly strewn down the slopes beneath the tors, most notably at Hen Tor, near Shaugh Prior. In some parts of high Dartmoor the granite has undergone even greater deterioration and weathered into a gravelly sub-soil called 'growan'. The relative ease with which granite can be rotted accounts for the rolling landscape of the uplands, the gentle slopes, the wide shallow valleys.

Water is the other major factor in the shape and life of the moor. The nearness to the sea, the moist south-westerly winds and the highness of the ground ensure a heavy annual rainfall and a prevalence of saturating mist and hill fog. Most of the interior of Dartmoor is made up of two high plateaux, separated by the two main east-west roads that cross like a pair of scissors at Two Bridges. Blanket bog, consisting of peat 10-13 feet (3-4 metres) thick in places, covers much of the plateaux and acts as a vast sponge-like reservoir where most of the major rivers of Devon, radiating outwards like the spokes of a wheel, have their source: the Teign, the Taw, the Okement (headwater of the Torridge), the Tavy, Meavy, Plym, Yeam, Erme, Avon, Dart and others.

Since Dartmoor is tilted to the south, like most of the south-west peninsula, all but two of these rivers flow southward. In prolonged periods of heavy rain there is a spectacular surface run-off from the granite and saturated peat, and the rivers flood and rise very rapidly. At other times the rivers flow placidly down their shallow wooded valleys till they reach the edge of the granite country.

Here their passage undergoes a dramatic change, for different kinds of rock have been weathered into steeper scarps, deep narrow ravines where the rivers plunge precipitately off the Dartmoor plateaux. At Lustleigh Cleave, Tavy Cleave and Becky Falls, the rivers tumble off the plateau edge in cascades and waterfalls. At the western rim of Dartmoor, the River Lydd plummets into a deep, heavily pot-holed gorge, where it is shortly joined by an exquisitely beautiful tributary waterfall, a 100-foot (30-metre) high skein of tumbling white water known locally as the White Lady. They are lovely places, these Dartmoor streams, water-loud, lush-green and dapple-shaded in summer, haunt of herons stalking in the pools, dippers bobbing on the rocks, dragonflies darting across the shallows — a far cry from the bleak and wind-swept heaths and bogs of the central moors.

The Dartmoor bogs are not everyone's idea of pretty country. Some quake underfoot, some tremble, most can be crossed on foot without sinking further than your knees. Only one is positively dangerous and that is Fox Tor Mire on the southern plateau to the south-east of the disused tin works at

Whiteworks. The only prisoner unaccounted for after escaping from Dartmoor Prison was last seen heading for Fox Tor Mire. There is no firm ground to be felt under this treacherous bog and any walker, or even rider, crossing the moor in its vicinity should give it a wide berth. It was Fox Tor Mire which Arthur Conan Doyle used under the fictitious name of Grimpen Mire for one of the more fearful locations in his Sherlock Holmes story, *The Hound of the Baskervilles* — a trackless waste covered in mist where a man could disappear forever without trace.

Most of the upland bog on Dartmoor would be more accurately described as wet heath. It is a land of silence and isolation, a place for the lover of solitude and the wilds, the seeker of far horizons. Here a raven may address a croak to you, a curlew a babble, a buzzard a pealing cry. Otherwise you are on your own, as circumscribed by the continuous skyline as any hitch-hiker in the Gobi.

The bogs are no place for man or beast and few traces of either are ever found in their acid soil, either present or past. But firm open moorland rings the blanket bog of the Dartmoor uplands and rolls away from tor to tor. This is the country of old men, a world of rock, a land of stone — the natural habitat of Stone Age man and their Bronze Age successors. Few parts of Britain are so thickly littered with monuments of the past. Dolmens, menhirs, cists and cairns, hut circles, stone circles and stone rows, field systems and hill forts. They are everywhere, these testimonies of prehistoric life. 2,000 buildings and several hundred tombs, the earliest dating from about 3000BC.

Relics of the past dominate the moor: no visitor can miss them. More elusive is the wildlife of the moor. Dartmoor is a wild and open place but it is not the Serengeti. There are no red deer here. With luck the casual walker will see a few wild ponies — the tough little native ponies that graze the high moor — and a wheeling buzzard or two, for this is good buzzard country; he may catch sight of a skylark soaring and hear the loud babbling cry of the curlew; he may spy the bright green patch of sphagnum moss which is the tell-tale sign of bog beneath; he will be only too aware of miles of rock-strewn turf,

heather and bracken stretching endlessly before him; but not, at first glance, much more.

The granite tors are virtually lifeless, though their clitter slopes, which are difficult to graze, may shelter a rich growth of plants, including several important relic woods. The wet acid soil, low temperatures and wind exposure of the great blanket bogs of the plateaux severely restrict the range of living things.

The plant cover is dominated by common bog mosses, cotton-grass and rushes, and the bird life is limited to ravens, buzzards, carrion crows, a few snipe and a few curlew, joined by skylark and meadow pipit in the summer. Over the long, rolling expanses of grass and heather moor that stretch away from the central bog country flit stonechats, whinchats and wheatears, and golden plover, dunlin and a few red grouse nest in the remoter reaches.

Numerous woodlands crowd around the edge of the moor and in the river valleys. But there are some, such as Wistman's Wood, Black Tor Copse and Pile's Wood, which are high-level woods of dwarf pedunculate oak where relic fragments of the indigenous woodland of the moor, many hundreds of years old, survive in wind-swept conditions of extreme severity on very steep clitter slopes. Wistman's, an EN reserve, is the most celebrated and least understood of high Dartmoor's woodland pockets. The trees grow in an almost impenetrably tangled copse among massive boulders on a precipitous clitter slope which is extremely difficult to negotiate. They are unbelievably gnarled and contorted: the effect, in all probability, of the relentless wind. The very moist, unpolluted air has encouraged an extraordinarily thick epiphytic growth of mosses, lichens and ferns on the trunks and boughs of the trees, so that the wood looks more like the beard-moss forest high up on Kilimanjaro than a hill-slope on Dartmoor.

'It is a wonderful place, the moor,' recorded Sherlock Holmes's well known side-kick, Dr Watson, in *The Hound of the Baskervilles*. 'You never tire of the moor. You cannot think of the wonderful secrets which it contains. It is so vast, and so barren, and so mysterious.'

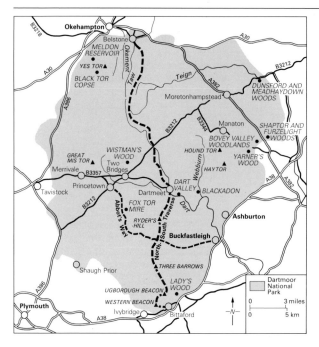

BEFORE YOU GO
Map: Ordnance Survey
1:25,000 Outdoor Leisure
Series, map No. 28.
Guide-books: the Dartmoor
National Park Authority (see
below) publishes *The Dartmoor
Visitor* with details of
accommodation and activities.

GETTING THERE
By car: the M5 feeds into the
A30 and A38, the main ring-
roads around Dartmoor. Most
roads on Dartmoor itself are
narrow, winding, hilly and open
to wandering animals; traffic
can be heavy in summer. Green
signposts indicate national
through roads; black signposts
A or B class roads; blue
signposts medium-sized
vehicles only; brown signposts
cars only; and white indicate
most difficult roads, suitable for
local access only. It is illegal to
drive more than 15 m off the
road on to common land.
By rail: nearest main-line
stations are Exeter (St David's),

Newton Abbot and Plymouth.
A restricted service now
operates between Exeter and
Okehampton station; for
details, T: (01837) 55330.
By bus: National Express
services to Exeter, Plymouth,
Ashburton and Okehampton
on the edge of Dartmoor, T:
(0990) 808080.

WHERE TO STAY
Plentiful accommodation in
towns and villages in and
around the park. The most
comprehensive list is the
Annual Guide produced by the
Dartmoor Tourist Association,
The Duchy Building, Tavistock
Road, Princetown, Devon PL20
6QF, T: (01822) 890567.
Youth hostels: 3 small hostels in
and around the park — Steps
Bridge, T: (01647) 252435,
Okehampton, T: (01837) 53916,
and Bellever, T: (01822) 880227.
Outdoor living: Dartmoor
offers superb opportunities for
camping and caravanning. The
Dartmoor Visitor carries details

of nearly 30 sites. If you are
carrying your own tent, you
can camp on enclosed land
with the landowner's
permission, and on the open
moor provided it is out of sight
of houses or roads and at least
100 m from the road.

ACCESS & CLOSURES
Nature reserves: there are 3
NNRs within the park
boundaries; **Bovey Valley
Woodland:** 646 acres (262 ha) of
coppiced woodland and valley
bog. Permit required off
marked rights of way. **Dendles
Wood:** 125 acres (50 ha) of
upland oak woodland with
lichens, mosses and breeding
birds. Permit required. **Yarner
Wood:** 368 acres (149 ha) of
oak woodland with wood
warblers, hollyblue and white
admiral butterflies. Permit
required off marked trails.
There are 2 forest nature
reserves; **Black Tor Copse:** 72
acres (29 ha) of wooded valley
slope and moorland. Open to
the public. **Wistman's Wood
and Longaford Newtake:** 420
acres (170 ha) of moorland oak
wood. Permit may be required.
There are also 6 Devon Wildlife
Trust reserves; **Dart Valley:** 720
acres (290 ha) of heath and
woodland in one of Dartmoor's
most attractive valleys. Open to
the public. **Lady's Wood:** 7
acres (3 ha) of coppiced
woodland. Open to the public.
Dunsford Wood: 140 acres (57
ha) of mixed valley woodland.
Open to the public. **Mill
Bottom:** 15 acres (6 ha) of
coppiced woodland with
butterflies and otters. Access
only by arrangement with
Devon Wildlife Trust.
Blackadon: 91 acres (37 ha) of
wooded valley slope and
moorland. Open to the public.
Lower East Lounston: 6 acres
(2½ ha) of woodland slope
supporting range of breeding
birds. Open to the public.
Further information from the

Devon Wildlife Trust, T: (01392) 279244, and Dartmoor NPA, who can supply details of the 'Moor Care' initiative. For NNR permits, apply to Phil Page, T: (01626) 832330.

Army Firing Ranges: the Army uses 3 live ammunition firing ranges on the northern part of the moor. Extreme care must be taken in the vicinity — fatal accidents still occur. Firing-range perimeters are marked by red and white posts and by notice-boards on the main approaches. Entry is forbidden when warning signals (red flags by day and red lights by night) are displayed. The National Park Authority distributes a leaflet, *Dartmoor Military Ranges and Training Areas*, including useful maps and timetables for walkers.

ACTIVITIES

Walking: the Dartmoor NPA organizes a range of guided walks; details in *The Dartmoor Visitor*. The 25-mile (45-km) North to South Traverse takes experienced walkers about 14 hours across rough and boggy moorland, beginning at Belstone, just south of Okehampton, and ending at Bittaford. The Countryside Access Group organizes guided walks for the disabled and less mobile; a comprehensive guide *Easy-Going Dartmoor* is available from the NPA.

Riding: there are many riding and trekking stables around

Hay Tor, protruding from a morass of bog cotton is one of Dartmoor's most distinctive granite landmarks

Dartmoor. Contact addresses and telephone numbers in *The Dartmoor Visitor*.

Cycling: cycling suitable for families available on the Plym Valley Cycle Way. Tougher routes include the Sticklepath Cycle Route.

Fishing: fishing allowed on 7 reservoirs in the park and some rivers with permit. Contact Leisure Services, South West Water plc, Roadford Lake, Higher Coombepark, Lewdown, nr Okehampton, T: (01837) 871565.

FURTHER INFORMATION

Dartmoor National Park Authority, Parke, Haytor Road, Bovey Tracey, Newton Abbot, Devon TQ13 9JQ, T: (01626) 832093 and web-site: www.dartmoor-npa.gov.uk.

High Moorland Visitors' Centre, Princetown, Yelverton, Plymouth, Devon PL20 6QF, T: (01822) 890414.

PRECAUTIONS FOR WALKERS

Rights of Way: bridle paths for riders and walkers are marked by blue spots, footpaths for walkers by yellow spots. **Kit**: the moor is often wet and slippery, so rubber boots (ideally classic Wellingtons) or very strong shoes and waterproof clothing are essential. Take a sweater even in summer — cloud and wind can drastically lower the temperature. Take a map and compass and be sure you know how to use them. **Weather**: can change rapidly — you can easily get lost in heavy mists. If you are overtaken by mist while crossing trackless moorland, do not go on but retrace your steps. Beware of rivers flooding during heavy rain. If in doubt 'phone for a weather forecast, T: (0891) 232774 (Devon & Cornwall). **Emergencies**: lone walkers should leave a note of their route and estimated return time. If someone fails to return and there is genuine cause for concern, dial 999 for the police who will alert the Dartmoor Rescue Group. If you suffer a cut, wash the wound with sphagnum moss to guard against infection. **Animals**: if you see sheep grazing, put your dog on a leash, especially in lambing time.

Exmoor

*265 square miles (686 sq km) of Devon
and Somerset moorland
National Park*

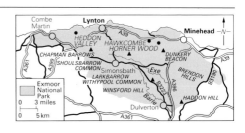

The Exmoor National Park takes in the whole of the main moorland plateau once occupied by the old Royal Forest of Exmoor in the west and centre, together with much of the reclaimed Brendon Hills to the east, the whole of the 32-mile (51-kilo-metre) stretch of sea coast between Mine-head and Combe Martin to the north, and the whole of the high ridge that runs from Dulverton to Shoulsbarrow Common in the south. Though Exmoor has no mountains, much of it lies at 1,200 to 1,500 feet (370 to 480 metres) above sea level. From the high-est point at Dunkery Beacon, 1,706 feet (520 metres) above sea level, one looks out over a broad, level land of heather, bracken and peat bogs, sloping gently to the heads of deep valleys and set amongst a patchwork of beech-hedged pasture.

The core of Exmoor is the old Royal For-est around Simonsbath, once an exclusive hunting ground for the Norman kings. The area is now largely grass moorland, covered in purple moor grass or flying bent, so called because in spring it turns purple and in win-ter its leaves are snapped by the frost and fly about in the wind. On higher grassland areas, such as the desolate wilderness called the Chains, stretches of deer sedge and peat bog three feet (one metre) deep blanket the sodden ground, brightened here and there by cotton-grass, bog asphodel and heath spotted-orchid. The tussocky, sponge-like bogs of the Chains form the source of many of Exmoor's rivers, and more than 70 inches (180 centimetres) of rain can fall here in a year. On the night of August 15th, 1954, during one of the most violent rainstorms ever recorded in the British Isles, more than nine inches (23 centimetres) of rain fell in under five hours on the Chains alone. Later that night, a wall of water 50 feet (15 metres)

high roared down the East Lyn river valley, carrying with it uprooted trees and 40,000 tonnes of boulders. The flood destroyed half the town of Lynmouth, killed 34 people and swept cars, boats and debris far out to sea.

Bordering the 'forest' stretches the open heather moor, a low, dense scrub of ling, bell-heather, bracken, whortleberry, bristle bent and gorse. Though it may not look it, this is a largely man-made habitat, for graz-ing and burning cleared the thin tree cover long ago. The heath now occurs as islands within areas of reclamation and forestry. In high summer it is a marvellous sight, espe-cially on the coastal downs, where the west-ern gorse glows bright yellow and the pur-ple-pink mass of the ling in full bloom is interwoven with the deep purple of the bell heather, and the air is loud with the growling of honey bees.

The upland moors are the haunt of the shaggy-haired Exmoor pony, a tough and agile breed closely related to the wild horses which survived the last Ice Age. Other crea-tures of the open uplands are the adder, common lizard and slow worm, and the birds of prey: the buzzards wheeling majesti-cally with their four-foot wings held stiff and motionless on the thermals that rise from the heath; the kestrels hovering as they quar-ter the ground for prey; the sparrow-hawks in low scurrying flight; a few rare peregrine falcons and the even rarer merlin.

The woodland of Exmoor is confined to the coastal downs and to the 'cleaves', the steep-sided valleys where the streams cut their way to the sea. These are the richest habitat for wildlife on Exmoor and some of the ancient oak woodlands, such as at Horner Wood, Hawkcombe and the Hed-don Valley, which may date back several thousand years, are now nature reserves or

Sites of Special Scientific Interest. The red deer of the valley woods are the largest herd outside Scotland and number around 1,000 heads, direct descendants of the deer that roamed these parts in prehistoric times. During the autumn rut in October the mating stags can be heard bellowing and rattling their horns in fearsome (though rarely lethal) combat. They are wild and elusive creatures: the best times to look out for them are early morning and late evening, when they come out into the open to graze; on open moorland in early summer when the young grass makes good grazing; or on farmland or the edge of the moor in winter.

The very beautiful, very pure, swiftly flowing streams which cascade down through the valley woods support their own characteristic wildlife: plants such as spearwort, fool's watercress, water forget-me-not and water mint; birds such as the dipper, grey wagtail, kingfisher, mallard and heron; insects such as the caddis-fly, mayfly, stonefly, beautiful demoiselle (damselfly) and golden-ringed dragonfly.

Salmon run up the Exe, Barle and East Lyn rivers and can be seen whenever the rivers are in spate at the numerous small falls leaping their way upstream to their spawning grounds. Sea trout occasionally appear in the tributaries of the Taw and in the East Lyn, and rainbow trout and brown trout are common in the larger streams. But otters are scarcer and seldom seen in comparison with the days of *Tarka*.

The sea forms Exmoor's northern boundary. For nearly 32 miles (51 kilometres) it is the highest coastline in England, mostly hog-backed cliffs of long convex slopes reaching almost down to the sea, sometimes descending more than 1,200 feet (370 metres) over a horizontal distance of a mile or so (between Foreland and Porlock Weir), with a few vertical cliff faces falling as much as 800 feet (250 metres) sheer into the water as at Great Hangman.

In more sheltered parts, coastal woods of gnarled and stunted oaks grow right down to the beach and here you can see an unusual mixture of sea and woodland birds — woodpeckers and oystercatchers, fulmars and jays — and sometimes even a red deer on the beach. At Porlock Bay a massive pebble beach has trapped marshes and pools where migrating birds can rest and feed. Elsewhere the cliffs are the domain of guillemot, razorbill, cormorant and shag, kittiwake, fulmar, gannet and jackdaw.

BIRD-WATCHER'S CHECKLIST

The high moor in winter is the preserve of the curlew and the raven, although occasional visitors include the hen harrier, short-eared owl, golden plover, woodcock, common sandpiper, fieldfare and redwing. Spring brings the wheatears and ring ouzels from Africa, and later tree pipits, grasshopper warblers, skylarks, cuckoos, stonechats and whinchats (for which Exmoor is a national stronghold). Wren, dunnock, whitethroat, willow warbler and yellowhammer breed on parts of the moor where grass and heather grow together.

BEFORE YOU GO
Maps: Ordnance Survey 1:25,000 Outdoor Leisure Series, map No. 9.
Guide-books: the Exmoor National Park Authority (see below) publishes *The Exmoor Visitor*; a free annual guide to transport, accommodation, information centres and activities on Exmoor.

GETTING THERE
By car: most visitors will approach Exmoor via Taunton; from here the A358 cuts north to the coast where it joins the A39, and the A361 runs along the the park's southern boundary.

ACTIVITIES
Although Exmoor is a National Park, land is privately owned. You can go almost anywhere, but this is a traditional privilege, not a statutory right. For everybody's sake, observe the Country Code.

Walking: there are 600 miles (960 km) of public footpaths and bridle paths on Exmoor, from gentle to rugged. Most are signposted and many waymarked with coloured squares and arrows. The NPA publishes several guides to *Coastal Walks, Country Walks, Moorland Walks* and *Village Walks*.

Seven basic routes open up the whole of Exmoor: the coast; Dunkery and the Brendon Hills; the moorland

east of the Lynton-Simonsbath road (including Badgworthy and the Doone country); the moorland west of the Lynton-Simonstown road (including the Chains); the Exe valley; the Barle valley; the southern ridge from Dulverton to Shoulsbarrow Common.

The NPA offers a series of guided walks (including special interest walks — birds, archaeology, local history) led by local experts in spring and summer. For details see *The Exmoor Visitor*.

Two long-distance paths traverse the whole of Exmoor along part of their route: east to west along the SOMERSET AND NORTH DEVON COASTAL PATH (part of the SOUTH WEST COAST PATH); and north to south along the TWO MOORS WAY linking Dartmoor and Exmoor. For details see p 30-33 and this page. Another long walk confined to Exmoor itself; the 'Roof of Exmoor', traverses the main ridge of Exmoor between Chapman Barrows and Dunkery Beacon.

Another shorter but popular walk is the 'Doone Valley Trail' from Lorna Doone Farm, Malmsmead, along Badgworthy Water to Hoccombe Combe.

Riding and trekking: you can ride over much of the open moor; bridle paths are signposted and way-marked by the NPA. There are many riding establishments in and around the park, catering for all abilities. For further details see *The Exmoor Visitor*.

Fishing: Exmoor is a paradise for freshwater game, coarse and sea fishing. For further details, including rod-and-line licences, see *The Exmoor Visitor*.

From the summit of Little Hangman in North Devon you look along the line of the South West Coast Path to Great Hangman

FURTHER INFORMATION Exmoor National Park Authority, Exmoor House, Dulverton, Somerset TA22 9HL, T: (01398) 323665.

National Park Visitor Centres at Combe Martin, T: (01271) 883319; County Gate, T: (01598) 741321; Dulverton, T: (01398) 323841; Dunster, T: (01643) 821835; and Lynmouth, T: (01598) 752509.

The Two Moors Way

A long walk of 102 miles (163 km) crossing Devon via both the Dartmoor and Exmoor National Parks

From Ivybridge at the southern boundary of Dartmoor in South Devon the Way heads north over Dartmoor to Drewsteignton on the northern boundary. From there it follows roads and paths across farmland and countryside to West Anstey on the southern boundary of Exmoor to Lynmouth on the North Devon coast, where it links up with the SOUTH WEST COAST PATH.

Before you go *Maps:* Ordnance Survey 1:25,000 Outdoor Leisure Series, map Nos. 113, 114. *Guide-books:* for full details, including outline description of route, sketch maps, bad weather alternatives, transport, overnight camping sites and accommodation known to welcome ramblers, see the official guide, *Two Moors Way* by H. Rowett, which is available from Two Moors Way Association, Coppins, The Poplars, Pinhoe, Exeter, Devon EX4 9HH, T: (01392) 467094.

Bodmin Moor

80 square miles (207 sq km) of granite upland, averaging 800 ft (250 m) above sea level, between Dartmoor and the Atlantic in north-western Cornwall AONB

A lonely landscape of rolling moors, craggy tors, clitter slopes and barren peat-bogs (the source of the rivers Camel and Fowey), the moor is remarkable for its stone relics of ancient peoples. Good, undemanding walking across big open country, with wide, unrestricted views, especially from Brown Willy (1,375 ft/419 m) and Rough Tor (1,312 ft/400 m) — the highest points in Cornwall. Orchids, insect-eating sundews, bog bean and other wetland plants. Wintering wildfowl and waders at the remote and mysterious Dozmary Pool.

Before you go *Maps:* Ordnance Survey 1:25,000 Explorer Series, map No. 109. **Where to stay:** nearest town for accommodation and information is Bodmin. An annual accommodation list for the town and moor is available from the Tourist Information Centre, Shire House, Mount Folly Square, Bodmin, Cornwall PL31 2DQ, T: (01208) 76616.

Access: open all year. Best general base is Launceston, Tourist Office, T: (01566) 772321, or for northern moor only, Camelford, Tourist Office, T: (01840) 212954. Best starting point for southern moor only is village of Pensilva, with path north to Minions, Cheeswring and Twelve Men's Moor.

Activities *Walking:* Bodmin

Tourist Information Centre can provide a list of walking literature. Walks and talks are also organised by Caradon District Council during the summer in connection with the Minions Countryside Project. Contact Martin Eddy, T: (01579) 362350.

The Mendip Hills

From the Welsh *mynydd*, a hill

84 square miles (218 sq km) of limestone hills rising steeply to over 1,000 ft (305 m) and stretching from the Bristol Channel into the middle of Somerset AONB containing several important nature reserves and areas of NT land

The Mendips (or Mendip to the expert) are not wild in the way that Dartmoor can be wild, but they are liberating. The wind from the sea blows sweetly over their open heaths and moors, and although the hills are not high, they rise sheer out of the Somerset levels in a massive, unbroken wall. From the sandstone outcrop of Black Down, at 1,067 ft (325 m) the highest point in Mendip, one can look out over half the West Country to Wales, the Brecon Beacons and the Black Mountains.

The key to this landscape is the relationship between rock and rain. There are no surface streams in Mendip. Rain-water drains through the limestone, dissolving the rock by chemical action and creating a vast underground cave system. Collapses and closed depressions give the landscape a pock-marked appearance.

Mendip supports an unusual range of natural habitats, each with its own particular population of plant and animal life. The intrinsic richness of the limestone flora and fauna of Mendip is further enriched by its nearness to the wetland area of the Somerset Levels. The broad-leaved woodlands of oak and ash, some of them dating back to the original woodland cover of the region, lie mainly on the slopes of Mendip, and in spring they are full of bird-song and wild flowers (including uncommon ones such as herb-Paris).

Grassland covers the limestone plateau, and heathland thrives on the sandstone outcrops such as Black Down. The cliffs of Cheddar and Ebbor Gorges, and their related cave systems, harbour a special range of animals, plants and small organisms, including the rare horseshoe bat and a unique micro-organism in Wookey Hole which is part fungus and part algae.

Before you go *Maps:* Ordnance Survey 1:25,000 Explorer Series, map Nos. 141 (to be renumbered 4) and 142 (to be renumbered 5).

Getting there *By car:* A38 from Bristol; A368 from Bath; A370 from Weston-super-Mare; A371 from Wells. The roads across Mendip are B roads or less. They are narrow — too narrow for comfort for caravans and motor-homes — and parking is difficult except in villages or car parks shown on map. Rural car parks are preferable as they are near best walks and best views.

Where to stay: most accommodation is in the Mendip towns of Wells and Cheddar, or further afield in Weston-super-Mare, though bed-and-breakfast and farmhouse accommodation is more widely scattered. There are two medium-sized caravan and motor-home parks in the Mendip area. Details of all accommodation are in the relevant West Country Tourist Board guides.

Access: free access to Mendip as a whole at all times, but no access to army range (paratroop dropping zone) shown on map in central Mendip. Most nature reserves and Sites of Special Scientific Interest are open to public subject to local regulations. A Warden Service can help and advise visitors: office at Charterhouse Outdoor Activity Centre, contact Les Davis, T: (01761) 462338.

Activities: Charterhouse Centre also organises guided walks and field study courses during the summer. For further details (no leaflets) contact the information department, T: (01761) 462267.

The Somerset Levels and West Sedgemoor

220 square miles (570 sq km) of low-lying, marshy land in the flood plain of the Rivers Parrett, Brue and Axe. One of the most important surviving wetland areas in Britain

Occupying a rough square between Weston-super-Mare, Glastonbury, Taunton and Bridgwater, the Somerset Levels are not a wilderness, nor even a nature reserve or conservation area, but populated farming land which is subject to widespread annual flooding. Once a marsh, now a partly-drained fen, the area is divided into two distinct parts: the levels, a 5-6 mile (8-10 km) belt of slightly raised land along the coast, and the moors, low-lying river valleys further inland. Because the levels are higher than the moors, the rivers have difficulty discharging through them into the Bristol Channel, so that in periods of heavy rain the rivers frequently burst their banks and flood the surrounding meadows over a wide area. The winter flooding and the resulting high summer water table provide a special wetland habitat for a wide variety of birds, plants and animals.

In winter huge flocks of waders (whimbrel, snipe, dunlin, ruff, golden plover, lapwing) and wildfowl (Bewick's swan, mallard, teal, wigeon, shoveler) feed on the abundant supply of invertebrates and plant seeds. Some of these birds (redshank, snipe, curlew, lapwing) stay to breed in summer, when the floods have subsided and the meadows glow with brilliant spreads of wild flowers.

Plants of the Somerset Levels include orchids (marsh, fragrant, frog and green-winged), bog myrtle and bog pimpernel, devil's bit, scabious and adder's tongue fern, and uncommon plants like bladderwort, marsh pea and marsh fern. An extensive network of willow-lined drainage ditches called rhynes provide an undisturbed aquatic environment for water plants like frog-bit, water dropwort, water violet and the flowering rush; for an abundance of fish and invertebrates, and above all for the otter, whose main stronghold in England is here.

Several nature reserves serve as enclaves of unspoilt Somerset Level wetland

Britain's best loved wild mammal, the otter, is seriously threatened by the pollution of its habitats

habitat. The most notable of these is the RSPB reserve at West Sedgemoor. The reserve consists of 740 acres (300 ha) of wet grazing meadows, criss-crossed by drainage ditches and bordered by woods, within a bigger complex of the Somerset Levels covering 3,000 acres (1,200 ha). It is one of the major breeding sites in south-west England for waders and the most important site in Britain for whimbrel on spring migration. Large flocks of lapwing winter here, and redwing and fieldfare may be seen in the daylight hours. There is a heronry, and roe deer also inhabit the reserve. Wetland plants include marsh marigold, marsh orchid, water violet and ragged robin.

Like other wetland areas in Europe, the Somerset Levels are threatened by agricultural improvement and drainage schemes which would wipe out much of their wealth of flora and fauna.

Getting there *By car:* the West Sedgemoor reserve car park is signposted off A378 Langport to Taunton road, near village of Fivehead.

'The loneliness of Mendip is a real loneliness... One is caught as it were in an empty space, a featureless desolation, a solitude that is like no other solitude.'

Edward Hutton:
Highways and
Byways in Somerset

Where to stay: hotel and bed-and-breakfast accommodation is available in Taunton and Bridgwater.
Access: open all year. Also highly recommended is the Somerset Wildlife Trust reserve at Catcott Lows, an excellent site for wintering wildfowl, occupying 127 acres (51 ha) of wet grassland. Viewing is permitted from droves and hides only.
Further information: contact West Sedgemoor reserve, T: (01458) 252805, or RSPB South-West Office, T: (01392) 432691. For Catcott Lows, contact Somerset Wildlife Trust, Fyne Court, Broomfield, Bridgwater, Somerset TA5 2EQ, T: (01823) 451587.

The South West Coast Path

This is the longest official footpath in Britain, running for approximately 613 miles (986 kilometres) from Minehead in Somerset to South Haven Point in Dorset. It encompasses some of the most magnificent coastal scenery in Europe, and in places it is as wild and weather-beaten as anywhere in the British Isles.

I lived on the South West Coast Path once, in a lonely stone farmhouse, a converted medieval barn, high up by the great chalk cliffs of St Alban's Head on the coast of a part of Dorset called the Isle of Purbeck. It was not known even as the South West Way then (its original title), for that was still a dream in the minds of its creators. But the path had been there a long time, an old coast-guard track that teetered airily along the edge of the cliffs, bearing east to Swanage and the sunrise in one direction, and west to Weymouth, Cornwall and the wild Atlantic in the other. From the top of these cliffs, more than 300 feet (90 metres) above the sea, I could look out over a vast, dappled sea to the horizon, and almost vertically down on to the decks of boats passing below. The voices of the people on board, raised above the clamour of the engine and the sea, came up to me clear and sharp on my lofty eminence. 'Look up there!' came the cry. 'There's a dwarf on the top of those cliffs. Doesn't he look *titchy*!'

It was over these cliffs that the weather came: thick white mists that rolled in from the sea and overwhelmed the house as if it was an alpine eyrie; equinoctial gales that shrieked over the headland, tugging at the roof slates and battering at the window panes; rain, rainbows, and opalescent moon; scream of gulls, wail of foghorn and the deep throb of a big ship's diesels.

On paper at least this could not properly pass as a wild place. A fine-weather track wound inland to a village with a general store and a pub. Arable fields reached down to a dry-stone wall enclosing a garden that grew nothing but chives as thick as a lawn.

But the combination of season and weather, health and amenities made even this little corner of the Dorset coast seem as isolated and austere as a Hebridean croft in mid-winter. There was no electricity in the house, only a pot-bellied iron stove, candles and a couple of hurricane lamps. All through the winter months the farmhouse had been deserted and its ancient stone walls had grown as chill and clammy as a tomb; in the flickering candlelight the bare stone glistened with moisture like a cave.

The pocket diary I had brought with me from London indicated that winter was over and spring had begun by the time I arrived. But the season was so retarded that none of the illiterates with whom I shared this simple abode paid any attention to such mathematical niceties. At the beginning of winter the empty house had been taken over by various creatures with varying numbers of legs — 4, 6, 8, 100, 1,000, or no legs at all. Now, though spring had officially begun, all these various slithering, skulking, crawling things were still obstinately asleep in tight little balls and coils and spirals all over the house. Just to open a drawer was an adventure. In a linen cupboard I discovered a solitary mouse out for the count in a perfectly rounded nest fashioned out of a finely shredded *Farmer's Weekly*. Under a wooden fruit box by the scullery door I found a dormant adder as neatly coiled as a liquorice catherine wheel, an exquisite creature which did not move except to raise a glittering eye and stare fixedly back at me.

I was the only creature in the house with two legs. They were the biggest in the place but before long they let me down. In the cold and damp I soon succumbed to a bronchial influenza and lay shivering and sweating on a mattress on the floor by the stove, a candle on one side of me and an axe on the other. When the fire sank low I feebly raised the axe and let it fall with its own weight on to a pile of old orange boxes, and with this wood I fed the fire. All through the night I could hear the melancholy bray of the lighthouse foghorn. All through the day I could watch the mad March hares, like surreal creatures of delirium, cross and re-cross my line of vision as they boxed each

The sheer millstone grit cliffs at Hartland Quay on the North Devon Coast Path overlook the site of a vanished quay financed by the Elizabethan seafarers Raleigh, Drake and Hawkins

other across the lawn of chives. I never knew who won. I never cared. I couldn't tell one March hare from another.

Then one morning the sun came up and stayed out, and I got up and went out — into the sunlight, on to the hill. I was better. And it was spring. The first butterfly spreading its wings in the shelter of a sunny wall. A skylark ascending. The first migrant birds, wheatears among them, flitting across the downland from the Channel cliff. The mouse had gone from the linen cupboard, the snake from under the fruit box. I walked out to the coast path along the cliffs, the sea a blinding silver, a soft warm wind sidling in from the south-west. On the rock ledges below me kittiwakes were shrieking like fishwives in their bird-slum tenements, and fulmars were soaring and gliding over the waves and hovering in the wind-sheer off the

cliff edge. No, not a wild place, perhaps, I reckoned, but a heck of a place to be.

For these West Country cliffs — in some parts 600 feet (190 metres) or more above the thunderous sea — are a frontier, where the elements of earth, air and water are locked in perpetual conflict. Once there was a fourth element, fire, the fiery molten lava forced up from the magma of the inner earth to form the igneous rocks of the great Atlantic-facing cliffs of Cornwall and north Devon. Sea and weather claw and pound at these rocks, gouging out sandy coves, rock arches and long spines of rock jutting out to sea. To walk the South West Coast Path along such a spectacular and varied coast you must pick your way from headland to headland, from cliff to valley, stream, water-fall, rock-pool, beach, river, estuary, mud-flat, back to cliff, plateau, heath and moor, wood and pasture — all the time within sight and sound and smell and feel and even, when the salt spray blows in on the wind, taste of the open, restless sea.

It can be glorious walking, through an ex-

27

ceptional range of habitats, and wildlife of one sort or another is with you most of the way. Grey seals haul out on the rocks and breed in the secluded coves. Sea-birds teem on the cliffs, waders and wildfowl on the tidal estuaries. An immense variety of plants thrives in the warm, damp climate of the maritime south-west and in summer a burst of wildflowers colours the coast with vivid masses of pink, yellow and blue.

The wind is a dominant element here. Trees grow horizontally because of it, and the rocky shore is littered with shipwrecks. Other ruins mark the passage of humankind: Iron Age camps and Bronze Age burial sites on the headlands, the melancholy remains of the Cornish tin and copper mines on the cliffs. Slowly these monuments to mortality are weathered away by the wind and the waves. Walking this magnificent coast you become part of the elemental conflict and the ebb and flow of life on England's south-west frontier, and for a day or a week or a month you can become a frontiersman in your own right.

I have traversed the South West Coast Path three times in its entirety, always in the same direction: anti-clockwise from the Bristol to the English Channel. But I fear I would not qualify for any medal for this apparent feat of derring-do, still less the certificate awarded by the South West Way Association to anyone who has walked the 613 miles of this path from end to end.

The first time I followed the path was in an old Auster Husky monoplane, which toiled in and out along the outline of the coast at the minimum legal altitude of 500

SIGNS OF DISTRESS AT SEA
If you see any of these signs out at sea, dial 999 and inform the Coastguard:
Rocket, parachute flare or hand flare showing red light
Rocket or shell throwing red stars one at a time at short intervals
Smoke signal with orange smoke
Any signal reproducing the words SOS or MAYDAY (from the French *m'aidez*)
Continuous sound from a fog horn
Flames on a vessel from a burning tar barrel
Square flag with a ball below it
Red ensign upside down
Red ensign made fast to upper part of rigging
International distress code signal NC (blue and white chequered flag with 16 squares above a flag striped horizontally — blue, white, red, white, blue)
Clothing fixed to an oar
Human figure slowly raising and lowering outstretched arms

feet or about 150 metres — a wonderful way to see the south-western shore in its geographical context. The second time was in a mahogany-and-brass Owl class sail-and-motor cruiser that had been built on the Clyde in the 1930s and butted the sea and the weather like a tank. The third time was in an ex-army signals truck converted to provide rather tight living quarters for four men and two women on a conservation study of the whole coastline.

The immense panoramic blur left in my mind by these protracted ventures leaves me in no doubt that this is one of the most magnificent wild coasts in the world.

BEFORE YOU GO
Maps: as on any serious walk, you should set out equipped with the relevant maps. These are: Ordnance Survey 1:50,000 Landranger Series and 1:25,000 Pathfinder Series. In the sections that follow the map number refers to the Landranger series.
Guide-books: to walk the whole of the South West Coast Path in one go takes about 7 weeks.

Few people have time for this and must content themselves with walking one or more sections of the path at a time. The South West Way Association publish an excellent guide, *The South West Coast Path*, which provides a comprehensive list of accommodation *en route*, camp-sites, public transport, ferries, tide-tables, maps, publications and sectional

notes on the path, with distances and gradings of physical difficulty. As a complement to this essential compendium, take with you the best of the other available guides: *The South-West Peninsula Coastal Path* by Ken Ward and John Mason (John Bartholomew & Sons, 3 volumes), with excellent maps and commentary, and relevant Path Descriptions, highly detailed accounts of short sections of the path with maps and illustrations, also published by the South West Way Association.

GETTING THERE

For information on how to get to the South West Coast Path by public transport refer to *The South West Coast Path*, available from the South West Way Association (see below).

WHERE TO STAY

For complete up-to-date list of all accommodation available along the 560 miles of the South West Coast Path see *The South West Coast Path*. For further details contact YHA.

ACCESS AND CLOSURES

There is free access to all parts of the coastal path at all times of year. Certain short sections, however, are closed from time to time because of the tides, or closed for army practice. For walkers who wish to take short cuts across tidal beaches and estuaries, annual tide tables are published in *The South West Coast Path* (as well as ferry timetables for crossings at high tide), and daily tide tables are printed in the relevant local papers. Closures by the Army mainly affect the Lulworth stretch of the coastal walk in Dorset: see the DORSET COAST PATH section below.

ACTIVITIES

Walking: in Cornwall especially, the cliffs can be high and rocky and go up and down all day as much as 1,000 ft (305 m) at a stretch. If you are a hardened walker this should be within your capacity. If not, check the relief of the route before you set out and see if there is an escape route or refreshment available *en route*.

Occasionally there are other hazards. Sea mists roll in

One of Britain's most typical inland water birds, the heron, still flourishes despite the loss of many wetlands

without warning and obscure the path ahead and behind. Tides move in swiftly to cut off coves and beaches. Rain can make rocks wet and slippery. Gale-force winds can make it difficult to keep your balance, especially if you are carrying a large pack.

The South West Way Association's official route follows the path anti- or counter-clockwise and this is the order followed here.

For much of its length the South West Coast Path runs through unspoilt coastal scenery. But inevitably some stretches have to wend their way through towns, ports, caravan and motor-home parks and recreation beaches, so not all of the South West Coast Path is of interest to the wild traveller or naturalist. The sections outlined below have been chosen because they are the wildest and finest (and often the toughest) stretches of the sea coast in the west of England. For a rock-by-rock account you must refer to the recommended guides. Nature reserves adjoining the South West Coast Path, and other areas of particular interest such as LUNDY and the SCILLIES, are dealt with alongside the adjacent section of the coast path.

FURTHER INFORMATION

Contact the South West Way Association at the following addresses: Secretary (Eric Wallis), 'Windlestraw', Penquit, Ermington, Devon PL21 0LU, T: (01752) 896237. Membership Secretary (Sarah Vincent), 25 Clobells, South Brent, Devon TQ10 9JW, T/F: (01364) 73859, email: coastpath.swwa@virgin.net.

SOMERSET AND NORTH DEVON COAST PATH

OS 1:50,000 Landranger Series, map Nos. 180, 181 and 190

This section of the South West Coast Path is 112 miles (181 km) long and runs from Minehead on the Bristol Channel in Somerset to Marsland Mouth, overlooking the Atlantic on the North Devon-Cornwall border. The route passes along the coast of the Exmoor National Park and the North Devon Area of Outstanding Natural Beauty. Before starting the walk in this direction, naturalists may want to visit the nature reserves at Brean Down, Bridgwater Bay and Steep Holm Island. The finest section of the walk on the Bristol Channel coast runs from Lynmouth to Combe Martin, and is outlined briefly below.

Walkers who follow the coast round to Bideford Bay will find themselves near the remarkable sand dune reserve at Braunton Burrows. Bideford itself is one point of departure for trips to Lundy Island. I have included the best section along the Atlantic coast, from Hartland Point to Marsland Mouth, under the heading of the Cornish Coast Path, of which it is geographically and logistically a part.

Steep Holm

Nature Reserve (Kenneth Alsop Memorial Trust) SSSI

Small, steep, 50-acre (20-ha), 300-million-year-old limestone island in the Bristol Channel off Weston-super-Mare, Avon. Geologically an outlier of the Mendip Hills, Steep Holm is remarkable for its unusual flora and fauna, and remains of Victorian, World War I and World War II military emplacements. Several rare plants were introduced by Augustinian monks in medieval times, including wild leek, wild peony, henbane, alexander and the caper spurge. A few plants (for example the stagshorn plantain) are found nowhere

else in Britain.

Nesting herring gulls dominate the cliff scene in summer, along with lesser black-backed and great black-backed gulls, cormorants and shelduck. Other notable birds include peregrine falcons, merlins, buzzards and ravens, while the small range of other animals include muntjacs, pipistrelle bats, grey seals and enormous slow worms — a specimen caught in 1984 was 20 in (51 cm) long, a British record.

Getting there *By sea:* from Weston-super-Mare. Day trips Apr-Oct, Saturdays, some Wednesdays and Bank Holidays, tide and weather permitting. Pre-booking is essential; call Mrs Joan Rendell, T: (01934) 632307. **Activities:** 2-mile nature trail round island — time required 2-3 hours. Take sandwiches, waterproofs, stout shoes,

binoculars. No dogs. No swimming (lethal currents). No rock scrambling (dangerous, unstable cliffs and scree). **Where to stay:** accommodation available in Weston-super-Mare. Sadly, for legal reasons, it is no longer possible to stay in the Victorian Barracks on the island. **Further information:** from Warden (Chris Maslen), Kenneth Alsop Memorial Trust, Mellborne Port, Sherborne, Dorset, T: (01963) 32583. **Further reading:** Rodney Legg, *The Steep Holm Guide* (Wincanton Press, 1995).

Brean Down Sanctuary

NT Reserve SSSI

160-acre (64-ha) limestone headland jutting into the Berrow mud-flats of the Severn estuary near Weston-super-Mare, Avon. An outlier of the Mendip Hills, with the island of Steep Holm in front and the Somerset Levels behind. Important landmark for migrating birds and insects. **Access:** via coast road from Brean; open all year. **Where to stay:** variety of accommodation in Weston-super-Mare. **Further information:** contact NT office, T: (01392) 881691.

Bridgwater Bay

EN NNR

The reserve consists of 6,000 acres (2,400 ha) of mud-flats, salt marshes and lagoons in the tidal estuary of the River Parrett, 5 miles (8 km) north-west of Bridgwater on Somerset coast. The main interest is the large number of wildfowl and waders that can be seen there. Thousands of ducks congregate in winter: mallard, shelduck, wigeon, pintail, shoveler and teal, together with the occasional white-fronted goose, and large flocks of waders, including many thousands of dunlin, lapwing and curlew. At migration times dunlin, lapwing, redshank, oystercatcher, black-tailed godwit, knot turnstone and grey plover stop here to feed and rest on passage – a fabulous sight when they take to the air *en masse*. Bridgwater Bay is the only known place in Britain where shelduck gather in large numbers for their midsummer moult.

Access: to shoreline from car park at Steart village but limited to public rights of way and bird hides. Permit required to visit Steat Island and no visitors allowed 1 Nov-31 Mar. Report unexploded bombs to site manager or police. **Where to stay:** accommodation on site, various in Bridgwater. **Further information:** from Site Manager, Dowells Farm, Steart, nr Bridgwater, Somerset TA5 2PX, T: (01278) 652426; leaflet from EN Taunton, Roughmoor, Bishop's Hull, Taunton TA1 5AA, T: (01823) 283211, F: 272978

Lynmouth to Combe Martin

13-mile (21-km) walk along Exmoor coastline

A pleasant introduction to the South West Coast Path, through some lovely Devon greenery and scenery. A gentler stretch than some, and less remote from the haunts of man, though not without its

The jagged pinnacles of the Valley of the Rocks loom above the Bristol Channel on the North Devon coast

rigours and cliff-top palpitations. You could begin this stretch further back at Porlock or Minehead, or better still at Wingate, on the eastern

side of Lynmouth, with a spectacular track to Foreland Point and a view over Lynmouth from a thousand feet (300 m) above the sea. But the 13-mile (21-km) walk back from Lynmouth, along what amounts to the north-west seaboard bounds of the Exmoor National Park, is

probably the finest continuous stretch: marvellous cliff-top views, craggy valleys, tangled woods, green combes, grassy old coach roads, exquisite bays, 600-ft (180-m) cliffs, cliff-top moorlands and, from the highest eminence along the route – the 1,044-ft (318-m) Great Hangman Hill – tremendous panoramas up and down this lovely coast and across the Bristol Channel to Wales.
Distance: 13 miles (21 km).
Grading: strenuous. **Warning:** no pit stops on long stretch from Heddon's Mouth to Combe Martin.

Braunton Burrows

2,400 acres (970 ha) of sand dunes to the north of the rivers Taw and Torridge near Braunton in north-west Devon
Former EN NNR
UNESCO Biosphere Reserve
Candidate SAC

One of the largest sand-dune systems in Britain, Braunton Burrows is internationally famous for its plant and animal life. The reserve offers a wide range of habitats, from the open sands of the beach, through the richly vegetated wet slacks and damp hollows, to the thick scrub of the inland dunes. When the tide is out the beach seems to stretch to the far horizon. Shelducks and oystercatcher shuffle up and down the distant sand bars of the estuary. A flotsam of shallow-water and littoral marine life lies buried along the strand-line of the tidal sands:

hornwrack and heart urchins, egg cases of dogfish and empty shells of shore crab and masked crab, mussels, common whelk and Baltic tellin. At the back of the beach the dunes begin – some static, others mobile, most built of wind-blown sand of marine origin, much of it crushed shell, stretching inland in a series of ridges up to 100 feet (30 m) high. Low-lying slacks separate the dunes, some containing freshwater ponds and winter flood pools.

An immense variety of flowering plants – more than 400 different species – flourish here. In summer, the dunes are cloaked in a wonderful coat of many colours and the sweet fragrance of wild thyme spikes the desert air. At the front line of the dunes, on the upper beach above all but the highest equinoctial tides, specialist plants like prickly saltwort, sea rocket, sea holly, sea bindweed and the rare and lovely sea stock cling to their precarious beachhead. Marram grass binds the sand of the fore-dunes in large tussocks which shelter the rich plant colonies behind them. The wealth of plants attracts many insects; among the butterflies are the dark green fritillary, marbled white, common blue, meadow brown and gatekeeper, while snails thrive on the lime-rich sand which helps build their shells.

Mammals include rabbits (from whose warrens the Burrows derive their name), fox, hedgehog, weasel, mink, wood mouse, common and pigmy shrews, short-tailed and bank voles.

In spring and autumn migrating birds rest and feed here, and flocks of waders congregate on the estuary. In summer shelduck and wheatears nest in disused rabbit burrows and in winter merlins,

harriers and short-eared owls join the kestrels and buzzards to hunt for voles, shrews and other prey.

Braunton Burrows were used in the Second World War to train American troops for the D-Day beach landings in Normandy; this resulted in severe damage to the dunes, but since 1964 EN (then the NCC) has leased the area from the Ministry of Defence and has largely restored it to its pristine state.

Getting there *By car:* turn left down Sand Lane off B323 Braunton-Saunton road, or turn down toll road (Ferry Road) off A361 at Wrafton. 2 free car-parks at boundary of reserve: the north-east one at end of Sandy Lane, the south-east one at Broadsands end of Ferry Road. No transport inside reserve. **Access:** reserve open to public all year, but no access to military training areas in central section of reserve when live munitions are in use; at such times red flags are flown and sentries posted. For other training exercises, the public is requested to keep a safe distance away. Most unexploded missiles have been removed but some may come to the surface in the shifting sands. If you find one, don't pick it up or kick it, mark the spot, run and report it to the army (see warning notices), police or warden (see below). **Where to stay:** there are various types of accommodation in Barnstaple, Braunton and the surrounding villages. **Further information:** Warden, Broadeford Farm, Heddon Mill, nr Braunton, North Devon EX33 2NQ, T: (01271) 812552, will arrange guided tours for groups or educational parties and can supply guides including *Braunton Burrows Ecology Trail Guide* and *Flowering Plant List*.

Butterflies found at Braunton Burrows include (from left to right) pearl-bordered fritillary, silver-studded blue and small copper

Lundy Island

Small granite island 12 miles (19 km) off North Devon coast in Bristol Channel
MNR owned by NT and leased to Landmark Trust

Lundy is a super little lump of rock with fine sea cliffs and tremendous views of England, Wales and the Atlantic. Three miles (5 km) long, half a mile (1 km) wide and up to 400 ft (122 m) high, the island covers just over 1,000 acres (405 ha) of largely uncultivated land and is inhabited by one of Britain's smallest communities.

With more than a whiff of the far horizon about it, Lundy is not always easy to land on, or to leave, on account of wind and weather. I recall having to free-fall from the galley hatch of a heaving steamer into an open boat which rose and fell 20 ft (6 m) with each wave of a huge Atlantic swell off the landing beach on Lundy. No one would be expected to do that in the normal course of events, but you might be delayed until the weather improves.

The island is a haven to wildlife, both above and below sea level, and the waters around it were declared a marine nature reserve in February 1987 — the first such reserve in Britain. Four hundred species of birds have been recorded on Lundy and 40 species nest there, including razorbill, guillemot, fulmar, lesser and great black-backed gull, herring gull and kittiwake, and a few Manx shearwater and puffins (now much reduced in numbers). Mammals include grey seals, wild goats, island ponies, Sika deer, Soay sheep and black rats (on one of their last British outposts on nearby Rat Island). The Lundy cabbage is found nowhere else in the world, nor are the two species of beetle that live on it.

The underwater rocks and sea bed around the island are like a garden in full bloom, with colourful and showy marine invertebrates such as corals, sea anemones, sea fans, sea fingers and sponges, mainly of an Atlantic-Mediterranean distribution. Coastal fish include wrasse and the red-band fish (*Cepola rubescens*), which burrows in the sand.
Getting there *By sea:* the 300-ton MS *Oldenburg* (an experience in itself) departs regularly throughout the year from either Bideford or Ilfracombe, North Devon. Landing on open beach on Lundy, so arrival and departure can be delayed by bad weather. Timetable and reservations through Landmark Trust (head office), Shottesbrooke, Maidenhead, Berkshire SL6 3SW, T: (01628) 825925, F: 825417. Helicopter trips are offered when weather prevents sea crossing, subject to certain conditions. **Where to stay:** day or overnight visits are possible: small hotel (Millcombe House), tavern, restaurant, camp-site, self-catering accommodation and vacation homes in a number of old, romantic and often remote renovated buildings, including the Castle Keep, the Old Light (lighthouse keepers' quarters in the highest light in Great Britain), The Old School (known as the Blue Bung), and the granite-built Admiralty look-out (from whose remote eminence 14 lighthouses can be seen on a clear night), along with more modest quarters in the Cable Station, the Fridge Room and the Radio Room, and communal accommodation for groups. Campers welcome — camp-site large, grassy and sheltered from west by granite wall. Full details and reservations through Landmark Trust. **Access:** unrestricted but rock climbing may be restricted during nesting season (Apr-Aug). No dogs or cats allowed on ship or island; babies only by prior arrangement. Visitors under 16 must be accompanied by an adult. Don't take supplies to the island as this causes problems when embarking and landing. There is a fully stocked shop on the island. **Further information:** in the guide-book *Lundy Island* and regularly updated accommodation availability list available from Landmark Trust.

33

THE CORNWALL COAST PATH

OS 1:50,000 Landranger Series map Nos. 190, 200, 201, 203, 204

The Cornwall Coast Path, the longest continuous section of the South West Way, runs for 290 miles (460 km) from Marsland Mouth on the North Devon border overlooking the Atlantic to Cremyll Ferry near Fowey on the English Channel. Much of the route passes through the Cornwall Area of Outstanding Natural Beauty. Certain stretches of this route traverse some of the most authentically wild places in the West Country, a world of thrusting headlands, plummeting ravines, wheeling sea-birds, windswept moors, vertiginous cliff walls of stark granite, vast views over coastline, ocean, sky and weather, and the exhilaration of standing at one of the great land frontiers on the edge of 3,000 miles (4,800 km) of empty ocean. The sections of the path outlined below contain some of the wildest stretches.

Hartland Point to Pentire Point

Some 50 miles (80 km) of classic Cornish coast

From Hartland Point to Marsland Mouth the path lies in Devon, but it is such an integral point of the long coastal walk round Cornwall that I have included it here. Hartland Point, 325 ft (99 m) above the sea, is the real start of the wild west coast. After 3,000 miles (4,800 km) of ocean crossing the Atlantic swell hits the rocks with a mighty thud. Beyond the point the path follows the sheer cliffs, up and down steep-sided combes and in and out of primordial views. Few parts of the British coastline provide such perfect examples of folded and contorted rocks as this. Approaching Marsland Point the going gets tougher and is not recommended for the unfit

or inexperienced. But the last few miles to Bude are straightforward enough, some of them along the beach.

South of Bude, between Boscastle and Port Isaac, lies some of the best cliff walking in the whole peninsula, with a particularly wild and unspoiled stretch between Tintagel and Port Gaverne. The towering cliffs provide good nesting sites for fulmars, guillemots, razorbills, shags and, on Lye Rock, puffins; and the uncommon rock samphire clings to its foothold on the west-facing rocks.

Beyond Port Isaac, the cliffs are lower, the scenery gentler. Approaching Padstow Bay the sedimentary slates and shales give way to igneous rocks, such as the splendid lava of Pentire Point, the fossilized flow from an ancient submarine volcano. At Pentire you have the best all-round views on the whole South West Coast Path and here you can actually feel the shock of the Atlantic rollers as they burst against the headland. The South West Way

Association breaks this section down as follows (beginning and ending each stretch with nearest towns):
Hartland Quay to Bude.
Distance: 14 miles (22 km).
Grading: severe.
Bude to Crackington Haven.
Distance: 9 miles (15 km).
Grading: strenuous.
Boscastle to Tintagel.
Distance: 5 miles (8 km).
Grading: moderate.
Recommended as short stretch of good cliff walking with transport available at each end.
Tintagel to Port Isaac.
Distance: 8 miles (13 km).
Grading: severe.
Warning: 'From here [Trebarwith Strand] to Port Isaac the path is long and in parts very tough. The descents to the valley streams and up again on the other side are about the steepest on the whole of the Coast Path. Do not leave Trebarwith Strand unless you have food, energy and plenty of time in hand.' (South West Way Association).
Port Isaac to Polzeath.
Distance: 9 miles (14 km).
Grading: strenuous.

St Ives to Mousehole

AONB

Along this stretch of the South West Way, all of it cliff and most of it a Cornwall Area of Outstanding Natural Beauty, you round the toe of England on a trail that crosses a land of solid granite. The first 16 miles (22 km) of Cape Cornwall are the West Country coast at its wildest: rugged, savage, unpeopled, with soaring cliffs to one side and high moorland to the other.

Beyond the desolate grandeur of Cape Cornwall, the landscape seems almost foreign, more like Brittany perhaps, but devastated by old abandoned tin and copper mines. Land's End, the westernmost point in Britain, is a rock wilderness ruined in the high season (though not in the low) by mass tourism. Half a mile further on, turning the corner of western England and starting east, the cliffs are empty again, the orbit of walker and sea-bird and the ceaseless murmuration of the swell.

The path from Land's End to Porthgwarra is generally regarded as the finest stretch of cliff in the West Country, and the going is relatively easy. After Gwennap Head the cliffs grow gentler, the climate warmer, the vegetation lusher. Another superb stretch of secluded coast walking ends at the little Cornish fishing village of Mousehole (pronounced Mouzel). You can, of course, carry on past it, but our next recommended stretch cuts out Penzance and its environs and picks up the Cornwall Coast Path again at Mullion Cove.

The South West Way Association breaks this section down as follows (beginning and ending each stretch with nearest towns):

St Ives to Pendeen Watch.
Distance: 13 miles (21 km).
Grading: severe.
Warning: 'You are now starting on the longest and most deserted stretch of coast on the whole of the South West Way. Therefore think about accommodation. Out of season you will have to walk…22 miles, even in season…17 miles before you find refreshment on the path.' (South West Way Association).

Pendeen Watch to Cape Cornwall.
Distance: 4 miles (6 km).

Grading: moderate.
Cape Cornwall to Sennen Cove.
Distance: 5 miles (8 km).
Grading: moderate.
Sennen Cove to Porthcurno.
Distance: 6 miles (10 km).
Grading: moderate.
Porthcurno to Lamorna.
Distance: 5 miles (8 km).
Grading: strenuous.
Lamorna to Mousehole.
Distance: 3 miles (5 km).
Grading: strenuous.

Mullion Cove to Black Rock

AONB

Some 20 miles (32 km) of scenic grandeur through the Cornwall Area of Outstanding Natural Beauty. By now the granite has given way to new kinds of rocks: schists, slates and shales, serpentine and gabbro. Rock climbers haul themselves up this tortured geology, walkers pick their way across it. The rewards are considerable: vast views from points and headlands like Predannack Head (St Michael's Mount one way, the coast to Tol-Pedn-Penwith the other, the bare moor of the Lizard peninsula behind), extraordinary natural formations like the dramatic sea-filled amphitheatre of Pigeon Ogo, and the marvellous cove at Kynance, with its caves, blow-holes and pinnacles of multi-coloured serpentine rock.

Rounding the Lizard the landscape changes, the cliffs grow gentler, the soil richer and the valleys lusher – and you pass the half-way point along the South West Coast Path. The South West Way Association breaks this section down as follows:

Mullion Cove to the Lizard.
Distance: 6 miles (10 km).
Grading: strenuous.
Very spectacular and enjoyable walking, no superhuman effort required – a good stretch for people who want to sample the best without fearing the worst.

The Lizard to Coverack.
Distance: 11 miles (18 km).
Grading: strenuous in parts.

Brilliant yellow gorse flowers on wasteland below the ruins of the Cornish tin mine of Carn Galver

The Isles of Scilly
Also known as Scillonia, but never the Scilly Isles

An archipelago of small, low islands, a few inhabited, 28 miles (45 km) out in the Atlantic west of Land's End
Strict conservation protection under Duchy of Cornwall
EN nature reserve (bird sanctuary) on Annet

The Isles of Scilly are the southernmost points of land in the West Country. Little granite outliers of the Cornish landmass, these 200 or more islands, islets and named rocks lay untidily strewn across the teeth of the wind and grain of the sea. Their isolation is also their salvation, at least from a natural-history and conservation point of view. Only five of the islands are inhabited — St Mary's (the largest, most developed, with most of the islands' inhabitants in the 'capital', Hugh Town), Tresco (the most urbane, and privately owned), St Martin's (the finest beaches, longest cliffs), St Agnes (the most

The sea holly (a member of the carrot family) uses its exceptionally long roots to reach down to the water lying deep beneath the surface of the sand dunes

oceanic and least developed) and Bryher (the roughest terrain and smallest population) — and only 2,000 people live on them, 1,700 on St Mary's.

Because of the southerly position of the islands the climate is extraordinarily equable. The winter is frost-free, the spring very early, daffodils bloom in December, and sub-tropical plants flourish all the year round. But don't be misled. When the Atlantic winds itself up for one of its wilder blows, the sea almost engulfs the islands, and howling gales raise waves nearly a hundred feet high, almost as high as the islands' highest land, and shift whole beaches with the awesome power of the wind and water.

The Scillies are far enough from the British mainland to remain free from wind-borne and water-borne pollution. The air has a startling clarity and the sunlight a brilliance never found on the mainland. The offshore waters are so pure and clear that even moonlight can illuminate the bottom. Down there the underwater swimmer and marine naturalist can dive on wrecks galore and view a host of remarkable marine creatures such as bristling sea urchins and feather stars on the tidal rocks and sandy bottoms.

Above the surface of this crystal sea, the blinding white granite beaches and the wind-blown dunes, rocky cliffs and inland heaths support a characteristic range of native plant life and a large number of alien species that have colonized the islands or been planted there.

May and June are the best times to see breeding birds, especially on the uninhabited island of Annet, a bird sanctuary with such a dense cover of thrift that hayfever victims are almost asphyxiated in a cloud of pollen dust. The Scillies are world famous for their birds, especially the incredible number of rare and exotic migrants and vagrants from as far away as Brazil and the USA, which bird-watchers flock to the islands to see every October. Among the 374 species recorded here are large colonies of native sea-birds and land birds, many of which are remarkably tame due to an absence of predators: there are no snakes, foxes, badgers, stoats or weasels.

Of the islands' animal population, only the small shrew is unique to the Scillies, a pretty insectivore that has been evolved by island isolation into something slightly different from its mainland counterpart, and can be commonly seen rummaging about the heaths and among the rocks on the shore. Giant basking sharks, porpoises and dolphins can be seen in the sea around Scilly, as well as colonies of grey seals on the outlying rocks.

The Scillies were first settled by Bronze Age people from southern Portugal, rediscovered by the Phoenicians from Asia Minor looking for tin in Cornwall, later used by the Romans as a kind of Devils' Island for Celtic dissidents and deserters from the legions, and by the Vikings as a plunder and pillage base. Today these beautiful little islands are invaded by gentler souls, refugees from post- industrial civilization — the late ex-Prime Minister Lord Wilson was one of them — who come to refresh their spirits amid the space and silence of oceanic island life, and stare out at one of the clearest horizons in the world.

BEFORE YOU GO
Map: Ordnance Survey 1:25,000 Explorer Series, map No. 20 (to be renumbered 101).
Guide-books: *The Standard Guide to the Isles of Scilly* obtainable by mail order from the Isles of Scilly Tourist Information Centre (see below).

GETTING THERE
By air: British International operates a 20-minute helicopter service from Penzance to St Mary's and Tresco throughout the year. Information and reservations from Helicopter Travel Service, British International, The Heliport, Penzance TR18 3AP, T: (01736) 363871. Skybus operates varying numbers of flights to St Mary's from Bristol, Exeter and Land's End throughout the year, and from Newquay and Southampton during the summer season. (Skyrail packages are available from elsewhere in the country.) Advance booking is essential; for more information contact the Isles of Scilly Travel Centre, T: (0345) 105555.
By sea: a 2-hr 40-min ferry service on *Scillonian III* operates Apr-Oct between Penzance and St Mary's. Advance booking is recommended; contact the Isles of Scilly Travel Centre on the telephone number given above.
Inter-island travel: a 'fleet' of inter-island launches operates every day, weather permitting, from the quay at St Mary's to the main inhabited and uninhabited islands. Other islands have their own boats. (St Agnes offers daily trips to other islands on its purpose-built catamaran *Spirit of St Agnes* and some crossings can be made at low tide on foot.)
By car: caravans, motor-homes, trailers and similar vehicles are not permitted on the islands. Private cars are not encouraged — there are only 8 miles of road on St Mary's and taxis and buses serve all visitors' needs. Cars are best left either at Penzance Harbour car park or Heliport.

WHERE TO STAY
There is a wide variety of accommodation on the 5 inhabited islands, most of it on St Mary's. For a complete list of hotels, guest-houses, bed and breakfast, self-catering vacation homes and camping accommodation, get the standard free annual brochure which can be obtained from the Isles of Scilly Tourist Information Centre (see below). Advance reservations in high season are strongly recommended.
Outdoor living: camping is restricted and prohibited on open spaces. Advance reservations are essential. Strict control is kept on the landing of animals. Very few hotels and guest-houses accept dogs, and on Tresco dogs must be kept on leads at all times.

ACCESS AND CLOSURES
Many uninhabited islands are closed during the breeding season 15 Apr-15 Aug. Annet, the most important reserve, is closed all year round. Permits can be acquired out of the breeding season, but visiting is discouraged. The seal breeding season is Sept-Oct and during this time visitors are requested to stay well away from the seals. Further details can be obtained from the Isles of Scilly Environmental Trust, T: (01720) 422153.

ACTIVITIES
Walking: the islands are ideal for walkers; lanes, tracks and cliff and moorland paths abound. There are 2 nature trails on St Mary's: the Lower Moors nature trail starting at Hugh Town, and the Higher Moors nature trail via Old Town. Recommended viewpoints for sunset-watchers on St Mary's: Star Castle, Streval Point, Porthloo, Carn Morval, Buzza Tower and Peninnis Head.

St Agnes in the Scillies is the westernmost inhabited land in England; beyond it lie scattered islets, the Bishop Rock lighthouse and the open Atlantic

Cycling: bicycles can be hired in Hugh Town and High Lanes, St Mary's.

Boating and fishing: pleasure launches leave St Mary's Quay every day for all the inhabited islands and for Bishop Rock Lighthouse and sometimes Samson and other uninhabited islands during non-nesting season. The same boats run evening fishing trips — good fishing for mackerel, pollock, wrasse, plaice. Boats are not usually hired without a boatman, due to many concealed hazards in Scilly waters.

Sailing: good sailing in St Mary's Road for capable helmsmen and in inner harbour for less experienced ones. Visitors are encouraged to bring their own boats and will be made welcome by the local Sailing Club, St Mary's. Further details from Tourist Information Centre.

Swimming and diving: the Isles of Scilly Underwater Centre organizes diving trips for groups of up to 12, May-Oct. Otherwise snorkelling is possible from many beaches.

The only dangerous places are the sand-bars. A code of conduct for divers is displayed at the Town Hall and the Museum. Details from the Underwater Centre, Gunner Rock, Jackson's Hill, St Mary's TR21 0JZ, T: (01720) 422595.

FURTHER INFORMATION
Isles of Scilly Travel Centre, Quay Street, Penzance TR18 4BD, T: (01736) 334230, F: 351223 and www.islesofscilly-travel.co.uk.
  Isles of Scilly Tourist Information Centre, Wesleyan Chapel, Well Lane, St Mary's, Isles of Scilly TR21 0HZ, T: (01720) 422536, F: 422049.

THE SOUTH DEVON COAST PATH

OS 1:50,000 Landranger Series map Nos. 192, 193, 201, 202

This path runs for 93 miles (150 km) from Plymouth to the Dorset boundary, just west of Lyme Regis, through the East Devon and South Devon Areas of Outstanding Natural Beauty. The section outlined below is the one most likely to appeal to the wild traveller, but anyone wanting to stretch their legs over a longer distance could try the 53-mile (85-km) hike from Turnchapel to Torcross, of which the Bolt Tail to Start Point section is a part.

Bolt Tail to Start Point

Heritage Coast

About 15 miles (22 km) of the best coast walking in South Devon round the peninsula that juts into the English Channel between Plymouth and Torquay. The path climbs steeply from Inner Hope and follows the coastline high above the sea to Bolt Head through the longest stretch of National Trust land in England. As far as Start Point this is spectacular walking and you will need to be fit to get up the steep sides of Sloan Mill Cove. The rocks – the cliff face in these parts are metamorphosed mica schists, wrung out by gigantic pressures and populated by shags and fulmars, ravens and buzzards, and wild flowers such as wild thyme, pink thrift and blue vernal quill. From the high cliff top the path winds down through wooded slopes into Salcombe, the most southerly resort in Devon and the largest yachting centre in Britain.
A ferry takes you across the estuary to East Portsmouth,

where the South West Coast Path winds back up to the cliff tops for the stretch to Prawle Point – the loneliest and wildest part of the South Devon Path, with dramatic cliff formations and lung-bursting gradients. In late summer butterflies abound in the more sheltered places: silver-studded blues, small coppers, pearl-boardered fritillaries. And there are all kinds of birds to be seen: sea-birds such as kittiwakes, terns and shearwaters, waders such as turnstones, oystercatchers and dunlins, migrating birds such as warblers, wagtails and wheatears.
After Prawle Point the landscape changes once again, giving way to a flat table of farming land with a raised beach – the original line of cliffs, 300 ft (92 m) high and complete with caves – half a mile inland. Start Point is a nature reserve and a marvellous spot for watching migrating birds in spring and autumn.
The South West Way Association breaks this section down as follows (beginning and ending each stretch with nearest towns):
Hope Cove to Salcombe.
Distance: 7 miles (12 km).
Grading: strenuous.
Some of the finest coastal

walking in South Devon.
Salcombe to Torcross.
Distance: 13 miles (20 km).
Grading: strenuous.
First-class walking as far as Start Point.

Exe Estuary

12 square miles (31 sq km) of open water, mud-flats, salt marsh and sandy spit on the River Exe estuary RSPB Reserve

The most important wetland area in the whole of the West Country, the reserve covers Exminster Marshes and Bowling Green Marsh, south-east of Exeter. Enormous numbers of wildfowl and waders of many species in winter, including less frequent visitors such as avocet, greenshank, spotted redstart, ruff, curlew-sandpiper, purple sandpiper, whimbrel and others.
Access: open all year round, but access is restricted to footpaths and the bird hide at Bowling Green Marsh. **Further information:** contact the reserve on T: (01392) 833632.

Aylesbeare Common

450 acres (182 ha) of lowland heath with valley bog and woods RSPB Reserve, SSSI

Wildlife includes nightjar, stonechat, yellowhammer, linnet, and curlew on heath; tree pipit, marsh tit and great spotted woodpecker in woods.

Raven and buzzard can also be seen but the Dartford warbler is now a rarity following two disastrous winters in the 1960s and 70s. Thirty-two species of butterflies, several dragonflies, roe deer, badger, harvest mouse, adder and wood cricket. Dwarf gorse, pink butterwort, bog pimpernel, royal fern. **Getting there** *By car:* via car park 2 miles (3 km) west of Newton Poppleford on B3052 Lyme Regis-Exeter road. **Access:** open all year but keep to way-marked trail. Best time is spring, early summer. No smoking — fire hazard. **Where** **to stay:** bed and breakfast in Newton Poppleford and surrounding villages. Hotels in coastal resorts (Sidmouth, Budleigh Salterton, Exmouth) and larger towns (Honiton, Exeter). **Further information:** contact the reserve on T: (01395) 567880.

THE DORSET COAST PATH

OS 1:50,000 Landranger map Nos. 193, 194 and 195

The Dorset section is the shortest section of the South West Coast Path. It runs for 72 miles (115 km), or up to a week of steady walking, from Lyme Regis in the west to Shell Bay near Studland in the east. Though never as wild and lonely as the Cornish coast, the Dorset path passes through some of the loveliest and most varied coastal scenery in England — most of it Heritage Coast and Area of Outstanding Natural Beauty.

Axmouth to Lyme Regis Undercliffs

EN NNR

Heavy rainfall and an inherently unstable geological structure causes small landslips every year along this stretch of the chalk and sandstone sea cliffs. Big landslides occur at much greater intervals, and the famous landslide of Christmas 1839 was the biggest of all. A ravine (known locally as the Chasm) was opened up and 15 acres (6 ha) of broken-off land (known locally as Goat Island) was isolated from the mainland.

In due course a wild wood grew up in the Chasm and today this is one of the wildest and most unspoilt tracts of country in southern England. On the windward side of the woods grows a low, wind-pruned scrub; in the shady places the woods are thick with all kinds of ferns.

As many as 120 species of birds have been recorded in the Undercliffs reserve. Roe deer and badgers lurk in the thickets, adders and common lizards bask on the open slopes, and a host of insects throng the flower banks and woodland glades. The Jurassic limestone is famous for fossils, including huge ammonites and nautiloids. The most celebrated of all was a 25-ft (7-m) ichthyosaur, a fish-like reptile found in 1809 by Mary Anning of Lyme Regis. **Access:** by footpath, either at east end from Underhill Farm approach near Lyme Regis, or at west end from stile at top of Bindon Cliff. Permit required to leave right of way or collect specimens. Apply in writing to EN Taunton. **Further information:** leaflet from EN, T: (01929) 556688.

DO'S AND DON'TS FOR FOSSIL HUNTERS

Do keep your collecting to the minimum
Do check the local tide conditions
Do take care on unstable cliffs
Do beware of falling rocks
Don't let rocks fall on other people
Don't collect from walls or buildings
Don't leave dangerous or untidy holes or debris behind you
Don't disturb the wildlife
Don't collect on SSSIs or other protected areas without a permit

Chesil Bank and the Isle of Portland

SSSI, Ramsar, SPA, SAC, AONB

The 5-mile (8-km) storm beach of Chesil Bank is one of the five largest pebble ridges in Europe. Behind it lies a large, shallow tidal lagoon, the Fleet, where mute swans breed at the Abbotsbury swannery and large numbers of wildfowl feed on the rich supply of brackish-water plants in winter. Chesil Bank is an important nesting site for common and little tern.

The Isle of Portland itself is a massive limestone outcrop jutting 6 miles (10 km) into the English Channel and connected with mainland by pebble ridge of Chesil Bank. Bird observatory and ringing station in converted lighthouse. Staging post for migrant birds and marvellous place to watch birds at sea, such as sooty, Manx and little shearwater. Occasional birds of passage have included Egyptian nightjar and pallid swift. **Getting there** *By car:* via A354 from Weymouth, following signposts to Portland. **Access:** all year. **Where to stay:** in small dormitories at Observatory lighthouse, open all year, no food provided but cooking facilities available. Contact Warden, Portland Bird Observatory and Field Centre, Old Lower Light, Portland, Dorset DT5 2JT, T: (01305) 820553. **Activities:** for details of guided walks and events contact the Chesil Bank Warden at the Chesil Beach Centre, Portland Beach Road, Portland, Dorset DT4 9XE, T: (01305) 760579.

Ringstead Bay to Durlston Head

Heritage Coast, AONB, European Diploma

More than 20 miles (32 km) of superb walking over the open cliff tops of the chalk and limestone Dorset coast, with some stiff climbs that bring you up to 550 ft (170 m) above the sea. There is plenty of interest along the way: the great natural archway at Durdle Door; the huge roofless sea cave at Stair Hole; the circular bay at Lulworth Cove, hemmed in by cliffs pierced by a narrow entrance; the magnificent high-level cliff walk along the Purbeck coast around St Alban's Head; the flora and fauna of the cliffs and downs, including rarities like the spider-orchid, the Lulworth skipper butterfly and a vagrant bird more common in the Balkans, the wallcreeper.

Durlston Head itself, which forms the south-east corner of the Isle of Purbeck, is a 261-acre (105-ha) country park run as a wildlife sanctuary by Dorset County Council, an SSSI (geology, wildlife), SAC and recipient of the European Council Diploma for Conservation. Numerous points of interest include great cliff-top views across to Isle of Wight, the Tilly Whim Caves, a 40-ton Portland stone globe and sea-bird colonies on the cliffs.

The South West Way Association breaks down this section as follows (beginning and ending each stretch with nearest towns):
Weymouth to Lulworth Cove. Distance: 2 miles (9 km). **Grading:** moderate to strenuous.
Lulworth Cove to Kimmeridge. Distance: 7 miles (11 km). **Grading:** severe. Fine walk, but tough. **Warning:** route runs through RAC Gunnery School, Lulworth Ranges. Information is obtainable from the Range Control Office, T: (01929) 462721 ext. 4859/4700.
Kimmeridge to Swanage. Distance: 12 miles (19 km). **Grading:** strenuous, then moderate.

Isle of Purbeck

The South West Coast Path ends at shell bay where Poole Harbour meets the Isle of Purbeck in Dorset. Purbeck is not actually an island, but one of the most important areas of lowland heath in Britain. The RSPB reserve at Arne, in the south-west corner of Poole Harbour, boasts 190 species of moths and butterflies, 450 species of plants and all 6 British reptiles.

The Studland NNR, on a promontory between Poole Harbour and Studland Bay, remains an important heathland oasis, a good place for birds, rare reptiles and all 3 British insectivorous plants. Hartland Moor NNR near Wareham shelters Dartford warblers, a number of rare insects and every species of British reptile. Around Kimmeridge Bay, 4 miles (7 km) of coast has been designated a Marine Reserve, while Poole Harbour attracts a good number of wildfowl and waders, which may be viewed from a bird hide on Brownsea Island Reserve.
Getting there: Arne can be approached from Studland village, Brownsea Island by ferry from Poole Quay or Sandbanks Ferry.
Access: all year at Arne and Studland; end Mar-end Sept for Brownsea; permit only to Hartland Moor. Extreme fire risk at Studland; also unexploded bombs. No dogs on Brownsea.
Where to stay: hotel in Studland, various in Swanage, Wareham and Corfe Castle.
Further information: contact RSPB South-West Office, 10 Richmond Road, Exeter EX4 4JA, T: (01392) 432691; or EN, T: (01929) 556688.

CHAPTER 2

South and Central England

There was a time when the whole of Britain from Land's End to John o'Groats, from Orford Ness to St David's Head, was a primordial wilderness of mountain, forest, bog, fen and moor; the haunt of wolves, bears, boars and beavers, where the streams ran pure, butterflies of innumerable species darkened the sun, serried masses of wildflowers dazzled the eyes and the May-time songs of the great choirs of birds in the oak-woods deafened the ear. A land as yet untouched by axe, scythe, plough, shotgun, pesticide or acid rain.

The first colonist farmers to cross the land bridge that then joined Britain to mainland Europe did not like what they saw, and proceeded to knock it flat to the best of their ability. As did all the people who came after them. Over the centuries these land-hungry pioneers laid to waste the woods and wildlife of lowland England, creating the pretty patchwork of yellow wheat fields and green pastures we know as the English countryside.

Any of the great broad-leaved woods that had been preserved as royal hunting forests by the Norman and Plantagenet kings were whittled down when the national need for timber became greater than the royal love of the chase, and today only the New Forest in Hampshire retains a substantial part of its former grandeur. The draining of the East Anglian fens, once one of the major wetland areas of Europe, began

Dew-covered nettles glisten in the morning sunlight on the banks of the Stour in East Anglia, a lushly green corner of lowland England where wildness and wet still hold out

in the 17th century and was virtually complete by the 19th; only a few pockets of Fenland, like that at Wicken in Cambridgeshire, now survive.

Until the turn of the 20th century the last relatively undeveloped wild habitats in lowland England were the heathlands — originally a man-made environment brought about by Bronze Age deforestation and grazing — that covered much of Dorset, East Anglia and Surrey. But 20th-century urban and industrial development have wiped out great stretches of dry heathland. Today only the Isle of Purbeck and the New Forest contain areas extensive enough to support the wildlife which is dependent on this type of habitat.

The wild places are few in southern and central England, and most of them cling on at the extreme perimeters: the North Sea coastal reserves between the Thames and the Humber, wildfowl country *par excellence*, especially along the North Norfolk Coast; the modest outcrop of the Shropshire Hills; and, haphazardly ranged between the two, the woods, heaths and wetlands of the New Forest.

These are not wildly wild places by the standards of the North Country. But they are the best that lowland England offers after the depredations of our forebears. And the New Forest is still big enough and wild enough to get lost in; in an exceptional season the North Sea marshes can offer winter birds and winter blasts on a Siberian scale; and from the top of the Shropshire Hills you peer over a void so vast it encompasses two countries and 12 counties. So let's count our blessings while we may.

BEFORE YOU GO
Maps: OS 1:50,000 Landranger map of any area will be your most valuable guide.
For the scattered parts of England covered in this chapter, no one organization can give comprehensive advice. For details of the county wildlife trusts that manage many nature reserves, contact the Royal Society For Nature Conservation (see below).

GETTING THERE
By rail or bus: contact Train, Bus and Coach National Enquiries, T: (0891) 910910.
By bicycle: Sustrans National Cycle Network, Fakenham to Harwich, map No.1 plots the cycle route through Norfolk and Suffolk. Sustrans map No. 4 (41) follows an easy route through southern England on the Severn and Thames Cycle Route. Contact Sustrans Information Service, T: (0117) 929 0888 and web-site: www.sustrans.org.uk.

ACTIVITIES
Walking: serious walkers may wish to join the Ramblers' Association, London, T: (0171) 339 8500, for details of more challenging walks and local walking clubs and societies. But good gentle walking can be found all over southern and eastern England, with much variety and magnificent clifftop views in the Dorset and New Forest areas.
Cycling: the Cyclists' Touring Club, 69 Meadrow, Godalming, Surrey GU7 3HS, T: (01483) 417217, F: 426994, e-mail: cycling@ctc.org.uk, and www.ctc.org.uk, provides advice on routes and equipment as well as organizing cycling holidays.
Bird-watching: some of the most popular sites are on the East Coast. Northwood Hill is the largest heronry in Britain, with Elmley Marshes in close proximity on the Isle of Sheppey. The wild bird sanctuary at Cley Marshes on the North Norfolk Coast boasts an international reputation as one of the finest bird-watching sites in Britain, and the RSPB reserve at Minsmere is equally renowned. It is open every day 9am-9pm, or sunset when earlier. For additional information on Minsmere contact G. Welch, Minsmere Reserve, Westleton, Saxmundham IP17 2BY, T:(01728) 648281.
Field studies: for those interested in a variety of environmental study courses or summer outdoor activities and holidays, contact the Bradwell Outdoor Education Centre, Bradwell-on-Sea, nr Southminster, Essex CMO 7QY, T: (01621) 776256, F: 776378.

FURTHER INFORMATION
Royal Society For Nature Conservation, The Green, Witham Park, Waterside South, Lincoln, LN5 7JR, T: (01522) 544400.

The New Forest

100 sq miles of woodland, heathland and wetland in southern Hampshire NNR administered by the Forestry Commission and other bodies

I was talking to a head keeper of the New Forest during the course of an abortive project for the Countryside Commission. At the end of our meeting the head keeper remarked: 'And I'll tell you another thing. Some of the people who come here go into the woods and can't find their way out.'

'They get *lost*?' I exclaimed. 'In the New Forest?'

'Town people,' the head keeper explained. 'They can't tell one tree from another and end up spending the night under one. My keepers find them in the morning trudging around in circles dying for a cup of tea.'

Nothing like that, I was sure, could ever happen to my ex-Countryside Commission colleague and myself. After all, between us we had quartered half the earth's unexplored frontiers. We had a map. We even had a compass. We congratulated ourselves that we were old hands at this sort of thing.

It was a hot summer day. A few puffs of cloud floated lazily across the blue sky before a light north-easterly wind. Young foals lay collapsed in the heat on the grass by their mothers. There were no people about and a great silence, an all-pervading, lethargic hush hung over the heath, broken only by the occasional cries of the birds — a cuckoo in the dark wall of trees of the distant forest edge, and a skylark trilling as it soared vertically upward on madly fluttering wings.

The track took us into a subtle, elusive landscape of horizontal planes — the belts of gorse scrub, the low lines of ridges undulating gently one behind the other, the dark wall of conifers (sequoias, good heavens) on the skyline, wobbling in the heat haze — strata of landscape piled one on top of the other and topped by a broad band of sky. Such a profoundly recumbent terrain in-

duced a sense of space and repose, and reinforced an impression of lifelessness.

But when I turned the binoculars on this vast and empty plain, life suddenly jumped out at me from the middle distance: a small group of ponies grazing stilly as if frozen in a Victorian pastoral woodcut, two fallow deer skipping about in a thick gorse copse, a tall pillar of gyrating mayflies suspended above a swampy patch in a valley bottom, a girl with long flaxen hair on a horse ambling down a shallow gulch till the landscape swallowed her up at the valley bend.

We ventured into the woods in a state of heightened curiosity like early Amazon explorers. We came to a glade where the ground underfoot was soft and soggy and covered in green bog moss, and here our ears were beguiled by a very curious and most unnerving sound; an immense, unending hum like a turbine whirring above our heads. It was not until I had sploshed across the mire and turned to face the way I had come that I saw what the cause was. I was now looking into the sun, and high among the branches of the trees a huge swarm of insects, mainly bees, wasps and perhaps a few hornets, invisible before, were now illuminated, each tiny darting form clearly delineated by a golden outline, each contributing its individual insect voice to this raised growl of massed insecthood.

The sundew traps and digests small insects in its leaves

We wandered on as the sun reached its zenith and then passed it. Every forest glade was like a brilliantly lit proscenium where the scenery, like the pastoral backcloth of some 18th-century *folie bergère*, was always changing. We looked out from the darkened auditorium of the woods, now at a tiny sun-lit meadow, now a gently swelling flowerclad mound, sometimes a small stream where the most exquisite electric-blue dragonflies rested on the mossy stones or a brilliant emerald-green spread of marshy ground. In one of the glades my attention was arrested by a

sudden agitated bird cry, and I caught a rare glimpse of an exotic yellow bird, a golden oriole scurrying for cover in the tops of the trees — a sight that was for me the fulfilment of a boyhood ambition.

In our absorption, we forgot the time and neglected to check our bearings. The shadows were much longer and the air distinctly cooler when I asked: 'Where are we?'

And so it was that we found we too were lost in the New Forest. Nothing on the ground tallied with anything on the map and the compass only told us where north was.

©Oxford Cartographers

In a classical beech wood near Holm Hill in the New Forest, shafts of sunlight pierce the cathedral gloom and dapple the bare ground of a forest floor devoid of undergrowth

There were no sounds of civilization to give us a bearing on the outside world, no distinguishable landmarks, just trees, and more trees, and clearings, groves, gullies leading nowhere in particular, and trees again.

For an hour or more we stumbled this way and that, with an increasing sense of urgency and a decreasing sense of humour, and the first star had popped out of a crepuscular violet sky, and we were tired, thirsty, hot and incredulous, when we chanced on a track bearing the marks of horses' hooves leading in one direction. So we were saved from the ignominy of a comfortless night on the forest floor. And we had learnt for ourselves what we had long ago read in books, that the New Forest was big, and that it could also be wild.

The reasons lie in the accidents of history. William the Conqueror transformed the whole area into a royal hunting preserve in 1079. Local farmers were forbidden to fence off their land, as this would interfere with the free run of the king's deer. By way of compensation, the farmers were allowed to graze their domestic animals throughout the Forest. Today their successors, known as Commoners, still exercise this right, and their cattle, pigs, donkeys and famous New Forest ponies can still be seen browsing among the unenclosed woods and lawns.

These animals are the true architects of the landscape. Their browsing has kept the woodland in check, preserving the balance between it and the open heath. This ancient pastoral economy is an integral part of the ecosystem. Elsewhere in the lowlands of Europe it has virtually disappeared but the New Forest survives as it does largely because of this anachronism.

The last king to hunt in the New Forest was James II. Timber became more important than deer and large areas were fenced off by Forest Inclosures to allow new woodlands to grow. Many of these oak and beech woods, now known as Ancient and Ornamental Woodlands, contain some of the most magnificent old trees in the whole of the New Forest.

The New Forest is the largest tract of wild, unsown country in lowland England, six times greater than any other surviving English forest. Parts of it, such as the primary forests of Mark Ash Wood, are the nearest we now have to the ancient Atlantic wildwood that covered two thirds of Britain some 5,000 years ago. A large bird population inhabits the woods. Many of these birds depend on the rich invertebrate fauna to be found there, which in turn depends on the large quantity of dead and decaying wood that is characteristic of natural woodland. At a rough calculation, half of all the insect species of Britain occur in the New Forest, including spectacular beasts like the stag beetle. For many, such as the New Forest cicada, this is the their only home.

The Forest Inclosures today form extensive refuges for the larger mammals of the New Forest: badgers, foxes and the seldom-seen deer. They are also home for many of the large population of birds of prey including merlin and peregrine falcon, which hunt the heathland in winter. The heathland is a mixture of grassland, heather and mire known as lowland heath. All over Europe lowland heath has suffered the same catastrophic losses as ancient woodland. The most extensive tracts to survive in Britain are found in the New Forest, and only here is the complete heathland fauna likely to continue to survive. Fauna that has declined elsewhere in Britain still holds out here: birds such as the Dartford warbler, woodlark and nightjar; reptiles such as the sand lizard and smooth snake; butterflies such as the grayling and silver-studded blue.

The New Forest, in short, is a national treasure house for British wildlife. Because of its size, intact condition and tremendous diversity of habitat the New Forest is a truly unique enclave — a triumph of wilderness over the ravages of human development.

BEFORE YOU GO
Maps: OS Outdoor Leisure Series Map No. 22 or OS Landranger Series map Nos. 195 and 196.
Guide-books: Terry Heathcote, *Discovering the New Forest* (Halsgrove Press, 1997); Forestry Commission, *Explore the New Forest* (HMSO, 1987).

GETTING THERE
By car: via M3 from London, M27 from south-east coast, A34 from the North and Midlands.
By rail: main station and motor-rail terminal for New Forest is Brockenhurst; most Waterloo-Bournemouth trains stop there. Several other New Forest stations — Lyndhurst Road, Beaulieu Road and Sway — are served by local trains. Nearest major rail stations are Southampton and Bournemouth. National Rail Enquiries, T: (0345) 484950.
By bus: National Express London Victoria Coach Station to Southampton service, T:

(0990) 808080. Contact Dorset Passenger Transport Group for rural public transport on T: (01305) 225165.

WHERE TO STAY
Hotels and guest houses: there are plenty in the New Forest, mostly in Brockenhurst or Lyndhurst. A list of accommodation can be obtained from New Forest District Council, Appletree Court, Lyndhurst, Hants SO43 7PA, T: (01703) 282269, F: 284040, or Dorset and the New Forest Office, County Hall, Dorchester, Dorset, T: (01305) 221001, F: 221200.
Youth hostels: full list from YHA, Trevelyan House, 8 St Stephen's Hill, St Albans, Herts., AL1 2DY, T: (01727) 854047 or 855215.
Outdoor living: there is no camping permitted in the Forest except at authorized sites. Complete list of campsites is available from the Forestry Commission, Lyndhurst (see below).

ACCESS AND CLOSURES
Open access all year except on private land or enclosed Forestry Commission plantations, where unauthorized vehicles are not allowed, though walkers or riders may pass through. If in doubt, keep to public footpaths. Most forest bogs (shown on maps as Bog, Flash or Bottom) are impassable.

WHERE TO GO
The Forest can be divided into three main areas representing three main terrains: the high flatland in the north; the central forest; and marshes. Anyone exploring on foot would need to divide the area into smaller units. I found the following break-down into 10 areas, evolved with the help of my friend, Bud Young, formerly of the Countryside Commission, particularly helpful:
  In the *north-west* the area of the Avon's tributaries, with its strong sloping relief and heath-

dominated views south-west to the Avon.

In the *north* the area of the Stoney Cross plateau, aerodrome country pervaded by a sense of height and bordered by major forest edges.

In the *north-east* the area of the King's Garn Gutter — steep land with northern aspects, Scandinavian forestry and alder carr stream bottoms.

In the *east* two adjacent areas of flatland that probably should be dealt with separately: Ashley Rolling Down — heathland with tree-clumps and long-distance landscapes, but close to the Ashburn-Southampton road; and the area of Matley Bog — mixed wet and dry heath, with an overtly boggy centre enclosed by higher land.

In the *south-east* the area of Beaulieu Heath — flat, dark and featureless, with sinuous green seepage lines that are almost brooks.

In the *south* the area of Hinchelsea Moor, a medium-profile landscape with just enough height to set off the horizontals and the soft edges of the deciduous woodland, and just enough relief to emphasize the beautiful curves and shapes.

In the *south-west* the area of Holmsley Red Shoot Bluffs, a Scottish-style landscape, with rounded bluffs, Scots pine and heath, neat narrow gullies and valleys and medium views contained by the forest margin.

In the *centre* the area of the great central woodlands, which occupy a third of the forest area. They can be sub-divided into two adjacent units: the woodland that includes Mark Ash, Gritnam Wood and Boldrewood to the west of the Highland Water; and secondly the woodland that includes Denny Wood and Frame Wood to the east of the Highland Water.

ACTIVITIES

Walking: take a compass. Wear stout walking shoes or boots; even in summer the going can be very wet underfoot. In winter or wet weather, some parts of the Forest, particularly the valleys and wet heaths, can be very difficult to get through.

Cycling: popular cycling area. *Cycling in the New Forest — the Network Map* available from New Forest Visitor Centre, T: (01703) 282269.

Riding: the New Forest is superb riding country. In order to obtain a list of licensed riding schools and stables in the area contact the New Forest District Council on T: (01703) 285000.

Fishing: permits for fishing from the Forestry Commission, T: (01703) 283141.

Natural history: all wildlife, plant or animal, is protected by law. Permission to study or collect specimens for scientific purposes must be obtained in writing from the Deputy Surveyor at the Forestry Commission, Queen's House, Lyndhurst, Hants. SO43 7NH.

FURTHER INFORMATION

New Forest Museum and Visitor Centre, High Street, Lyndhurst, Hants. SO43 7NY, T: (01703) 282269/283914, F: 284404; Forestry Commission, Queen's House, Lyndhurst, Hants. SO43 7NH, T: (01703) 283141, F: 283929; Dorset and New Forest Office, c/o Dorset Tourism, Environmental Services, County Hall, Dorchester, Dorset DT1 IXJ, T: (01305) 221001, F: 221200; New Forest District Council, T: (01703) 282269; EN Dorset Team, Slepe Farm, Arne, Dorset BH20 5BN, T: (01929) 556688, F: 554752.

A poorer spot than this New Forest there is not in all England, nor I believe in the whole world. It is more barren and miserable than Bagshott Heath

William Cobbett:
Rural Rides

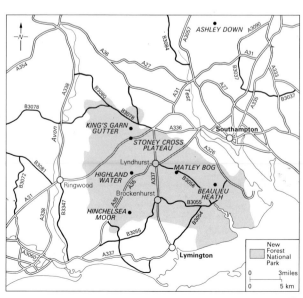

THE SHROPSHIRE HILLS

AONB

Between the Wyre Forest and the Welsh border lie the Shropshire Hills. These parallel ridges of weathered, spectacularly ancient rock — in places as much as 1,000 million years old — grow wilder the nearer they are to the border, where they lift range upon range into Wales.

They offer the best wild walking in the West Midlands, and excellent pony trekking. For the naturalist, and especially the geologist, they are of compelling interest. The Shropshire Hills have one other advantage: the holiday masses tend to pass them by, leaving this sweeping upland landscape to the solitude and tranquillity that is sometimes hard to find in the Cotswolds or the Peak District.

Each of the component parts of the Shropshire Hills has its own distinct geology, landscape and wildlife; but perhaps the most satisfying, from the wild traveller's perspective, are Long Mynd and the Stiperstones.

Long Mynd

NT

Although this broad moorland plateau is only six miles (10 km) from end to end, its great vistas and its remoteness and desolation make it seem an altogether vaster place. All but the southern end is owned by the National Trust.

The Long Mynd is divided into rounded blocks by deep, glacial valleys known locally as hollows or batches. Cardingmill Valley, with the Light Spout waterfall at its head, is the best known, though Ashes Hollow and Minton Batch are just as lovely.

From the trigonometric point crowning Pole Bank, the highest point on Long Mynd (1,695 ft/517 m), you have an unobstructed view to the Malverns and Cotswolds in one direction and to Snowdon and the Brecon Beacons in the other. Buzzards and ravens soar

above the heights, skylarks sing and dippers bob about the lower reaches of the streams, where brown trout lurk in the pools, foraging for the larvae of stonefly, mayfly, dragonfly and caddis fly.

Before you go *Maps:* OS Landranger Series, map Nos 126 and 137. *Guide-book: The Story of the Long Mynd* by Kate Thorne, available at local bookshops. **Getting there** *By car:* the Long Mynd is 3 miles (5 km) west of Church Stretton off the A49 Ludlow-Shrewsbury road. Minor roads lead west from the B4370, connecting with ancient cattle drovers' tracks (trails) leading to the ridge. **Activities:** excellent sail- and hang-gliding; contact Midlands Gliding Club at top of Minton Batch, T: (01588) 650206. **Further information:** leaflets from Tourist Information Centre, Church Road, Church Stretton, Shropshire, T: (01694) 723133; National Trust, Mercia Regional Office, Attingham Park, Shrewsbury, SY4 4TP, T: (01743) 709343.

Range upon range of ridges crest many of the Shropshire Hills on the borders of Wales

The Stiperstones

EN NNR

This desolate, rock-strewn heather and bilberry moorland is dotted with bogs, cut by deep valleys and crowned with hard white quartzite crags. The best known is the Devil's Chair; when cloud is draped over the Stiperstones (as it often is) it is said that the Devil has taken

his seat, and you could well believe it.

Lead was once mined in these hills, but the industry closed down early in the 20th century and only the eerie white landscape of the waste tips and abandoned smallholdings remain, where redstart and tree pipits inhabit the old walls and hedges. Several tracks lead over the hills and there are superb views from the Devil's Chair. **Getting there:** access from A488 (Bishops Castle to Shrewsbury road). **Where to stay:** youth hostels at Bridges and Wilderhope. Inn at Stiperstones village, T: (01743) 791327.

Activities: Field Study Centre at The Bog. **Further information:** TIC, Ludlow, T: (01584) 875053.

Cannock Chase

AONB, managed by SCC and FC

A Royal Forest in Norman times, Cannock Chase is situated in south Staffordshire between Birmingham and the Vale of Trent. This position has made it popular with the inhabitants of nearby Midland cities, reducing its wildness but not its wildlife. The resident species range from deer to rare bog plants, a rich crop of fungi (with expressive names such as blusher, sickener, razor-strop and earthball), butterflies, moths, and birds such as the grasshopper warbler, crossbill, goldcrest and nightjar. **Getting there:** via minor roads off A34, A513 and A460. **Access:** unrestricted. Motor vehicles banned from FC land. **Further information:** Cannock Chase Visitor Centre, T: (01543) 578762, or Stafford Visitor Centre, T: (01785) 240204.

51

THE EAST COAST

North Kent Marshes

Between the Channel and the Humber, the east coast of England contains a number of areas that are remarkable either for the wild quality of their landscape on the edge of the ever restless sea or the range of their wildlife. The east coast follows one of the major bird migration routes of Britain; the North Kent Marshes, parts of the Essex and Suffolk coast, the North Norfolk Marshes and the Wash, and parts of the Lincolnshire coast to the south of the Humber Estuary contain vast stretches of sand flats, mud-flats and marshes with huge views, immense skies and extraordinary congregations of birds.

The North Kent Marshes, which stretch along the south shore of the Thames Estuary from Gravesend to Whitstable, are the best place to watch birds within 50 miles (80km) of London. This bleak Dickensian wilderness is a mere electric train ride from London, but a century away in time; wide, desolate, wind-swept, and bitter in winter. The horizon is unnervingly vast; like a sailor far out at sea, you can see the weather coming from a long way off, and from every direction. It is not a pristine horizon: projecting above it here and there rise the ganglions of encroaching industry; and cargo ships slide eerily along the squelching soft grey edge of the land.

Yet this is, I think, an authentic English wild place, and your spirit will be uplifted by the vast congregations of wildfowl and waders, many of them seasonal refugees from the remotest corners of Eurasia. The major areas for wildfowl include the RSPB reserve at Northwood Hill which is the biggest heronry in Britain; the Medway Estuary, especially around Chetney Marshes; and best of all the Isle of Sheppey, which has two reserves along its southern shore, Elmley Marshes (RSPB) and the Swale (EN NNR).

Pick of the bunch is Elmley, a vast, flat landscape, featureless except for the domes and towers of distant industry, like the lost city of some vanished civilization. Some 216 species of birds inhabit the area, including the highest nesting concentration of redshanks and lapwings in the country. Many birds stop here to feed on their autumn migration; exotic errant birds like the African

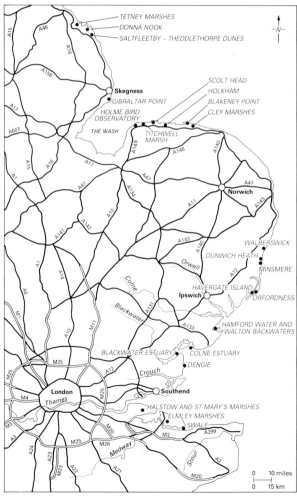

crowned crane and Chilean flamingo have been sighted.

The marsh frog, an outsize defector from Eastern Europe, three times bigger than our native British runt, has successfully found asylum in this reserve and its loud, jubilant croak can be heard over great distances in the early summer. The 140 species of moth recorded here include the rare ground lackey moth, whose eggs can withstand being dried in the sun or drowned in salt water and still hatch normal offspring.

Getting there *By car:* for Northwood Hill, turn off A228 to High Halstow. For Medway Estuary turn north off A2 at Rainham. For Elmley Marshes take A249, then farm track 1 mile off Kingsferry Bridge; park at Kingshill Farm and walk to hides at Spitend Marsh. The Swale can be reached from Shellness Hamlet at end of B2231. **Access:** at all times on rights of way. Permit only for Northwood Hill heronry. **Further information:** RSPB, T: (01767) 680551, or EN, T: (01733) 455000.

Essex Coast and Marshes

'The Essex coast', English Nature rightly claims, 'is one of the most important remaining areas of relatively undeveloped coastal estuarine mud and sand flats.'

Hundreds of thousands of geese, duck, waders and songbirds pass up and down this coast during the spring and autumn migrations. Many thousands more arrive each winter from northern Russia and Siberia. To protect the most important of their roosts

Clockwise from the left are the crane fly (commonly known in Britain as daddy long-legs), golden-ringed dragonfly and the short-lived adult mayfly

and feeding grounds, and the plants and insects that live there, English Nature has established a series of reserves from the Thames to the Stour.

The most important reserves are: the large stretch of almost uninhabited open coast between the mouths of the Rivers Crouch and Blackwater at Dengie; the marshes and mud-flats on both sides of the River Colne, among the best in East Anglia; the drowned and lonesome landscape of Hamford water and the Walton Backwaters, a wetland archipelago of outstanding wildlife interest, but remote and inaccessible except by boat. **Getting there** *By car:* Dengie off B1021. For Blackwater Estuary, aim for Old Hall Marshes from Maldon. For Colne Estuary, turn off B1027 to Point Clear for east shore, off B1025 to beyond East Mersea for west shore. Hamford Water can be reached

by minor roads from B1414 and B1034. **Access:** all year on rights of way, but permit only for St Osyth on east shore of Colne. **Further information:** EN, Colchester Office, T: (01206) 796666, F: 704466.

The Suffolk Coast

AONB

The dynamics of the East Anglian coast are confusing, not to say dramatic. You could once walk to Denmark without getting your feet wet. Now some parts, such as the Wash coastline, are advancing, while others are being eroded. Dunwich used to send an MP to Westminster; now most of it lies under the sea.

Suffolk lies on the major east-coast bird migration route and attracts very many common species and a few rare ones as well. Its six river estuaries are wonderful places to watch birds. So are the reserves,

53

especially the RSPB reserve at Minsmere, possibly the most renowned bird spot in Britain; over 280 wetland species have been recorded here.

Wide, shallow lagoons have been bulldozed in an area of derelict marsh which now bears the name of the Scrape. Many migrant waders can be seen here: osprey, black tern, little stint, spotted redshank, black-tailed godwit, and rarities such as the exotic spoonbill and purple heron, along with the second biggest avocet colony in Britain.

Other important reserves are Havergate Island (RSPB) in the River Ore, which has Britain's largest breeding colony of avocet; an area of coastal heathland known as the Sandlings at Dunwich Heath (NT); and the national nature reserve at Walberswick, an extensive area of reed-beds, mud-flats, woods and coastal heathland overlooking the Blyth Estuary and Westwood Marshes, the largest uninterrupted area of freshwater reed-beds in Britain and nesting site to one of Britain's rarest breeding birds, the marsh harrier. A stone's throw away from Dunwich Heath is Orford Ness (NT), the largest vegetated shingle spit in Europe, home to many rare species and plant communities. **Getting there** *By sea:* for Havergate Island and Orford Ness, by ferry from Orford Quay. *By car:* Orford town is 10 miles east of A12. To Minsmere via B1125 or B1122. To Dunwich Heath off Dunwich-Westleton road. To Walberswick via public footpaths between Walberswick and Bythburgh. Traveline, Suffolk travel advice line, T: (0645) 583358. **Access:** all year on public rights of way, except Havergate (permit only). Guided visits available at

Orford Ness. **Further information:** RSPB Minsmere, T: (01728) 648281; Havergate Island, T: (01394) 450732; NT Norwich, T: (01263) 733471; EN, T: (01284) 762218; Dunwich Heath, T: (01728) 648505; Orford Ness, T: (01394) 450900; Suffolk Coast and Heaths Project, T: (01394) 384948.

The North Norfolk Coast

AONB

The North Norfolk Coast between Sheringham and the Wash has been described as 'the finest complex of sand flats, marshes, shingle ridges and dunes in the country'. And every year it gets finer still. Day in, day out, the North Sea fills the Wash with detritus; equally steadily the eastern shore is added to as tide after tide dumps yet more mud and sand in the shallows.

The Wash itself is a place where land and water often lose their separate identity — and all too suddenly regain it. The immense foreshore dips imperceptibly towards the sea, so that when the tide comes in it does so at tremendous speed. Trying to record this phenomenon for posterity and the BBC, I was once marooned half a mile out to sea before I had shot half a roll of film.

The sandbanks of the Wash are the haunt of the common seal and of enormous flocks of geese, duck and waders. Under

During a harsh winter even welcoming bird sanctuaries like Minsmere in Suffolk can be reduced to icy, inhospitable wild places

these steely, squall-rinsed skies, a multitude of terns and other sea-birds go about their cacophonous business. And not a few bird-watchers, rather more discreetly, go about theirs; even in dead of winter, when the east wind seems keen enough to cut your head off.

A number of nature reserves are strung along the North Norfolk Coast to form an almost continuous single reserve of major importance for both birds and bird-watchers. Some are vast, like the national nature reserve at Holkham, which covers more than 7,500 acres (3,035 ha) of marshes, dunes and mud-flats between Burnham Overy and Blakeney.

Others are smaller but hugely important for migrant birds, such as the NWT reserve at Cley Marshes, which is internationally renowned as one of the finest bird-watching sites in Britain. No less than 325 different species have been recorded here, including rare migrants such as bluethroats and spoonbills, as well as a multitude of wildfowl, waders and sea-birds.

Also notable are the Norfolk Ornithologists' Association (NOA) bird reserve and observatory at Holme; the RSPB reserve on Titchwell Marsh, where you can see an avocet colony, 12 species of duck, 20 species of wader, 40,000 knot and godwits on a single roost when the Wash is flooded, and the remains of an ancient submerged forest (low tide only); the NT/NWT reserve on Scolt Head Island; the NT reserve at Blakeney Point, one of the most important nesting sites in Britain for terns and other shore-nesting birds; and the national nature reserve at Winterton Dunes, the largest mainland dune system on the East Anglian coast and a refuge for many rare species,

including the natterjack toad, adder, hen harrier and rough-legged buzzard.

Getting there: from the A149, though access to the coastal strip is on foot only. Scolt Head and Blakeney Point are best visited by small boat, the former from Brancaster Staithe, the latter from Morston or Blakeney Quays by arrangement with local boatmen. **Access:** at all times, but no access to Scolt Head ternery during nesting season (May-July). **Where to stay:** a range of hotels and bed and breakfasts in villages along the coast, notably in Thornham and Wells-Next-to-the-Sea; some self-catering and vacation homes; camp-sites near Titchwell Marsh at Thornham and Chosely Marsh. **Further information:** RSPB Titchwell Marsh, T: (01485) 210779; NOA, T: (01485) 525406; EN Norfolk, T: (01603) 620558; NT East Anglia, T: (01263) 738000; NWT Norfolk, T: (01603) 625540.

The Lincolnshire Coast

Northwards from the Wash to the Humber stretches the Lincolnshire coast, the most even stretch of shoreline anywhere round Britain, and one which is constantly growing. North of the Humber the whole Yorkshire coast is being eaten away at the rate of seven feet (two metres) a year. Yorkshire's loss is Lincolnshire's gain. The old coastguard station at Gibraltar Point, which was once on the edge of the sea, is now over a mile inland. At Donna Nook, miles of sand continue to push the sea further and further

away from the shore.

From Skegness to Mablethorpe is caravan and motor-home country and the wild traveller will probably want to avoid it. But there are several extensive enclaves of open sand, marsh, sea and birds well worth a visit by anyone who, like the hordes of migrating birds of this coast, happens to be heading north or south at the time. These include the sand dunes and salt marshes of Tetney Marshes (RSPB) near the mouth of the Humber; the six miles (ten kilometres) of flats and dunes at Donna Nook between Grainthorp Haven and Saltfleet, a reserve of the LTNC which also runs the five-mile (eight-kilometre) stretch of dunes, flats and marsh comprising the Saltfleet-by-Theddlethorpe reserve.

Most outstanding of all is Gibraltar Point. This is a national nature reserve and one of the finest coastal reserves in the country, it stretches for three miles from the Wash to south of Skegness, with a rich variety of marsh and dune flora, wildfowl, waders and common seals on the sand-bars.

Getting there: Tetney Marshes, Donna Nook and Saltfleetby-Theddlethorpe can all be reached off the A1031; for Gibraltar Point, take Gibraltar Road south of Skegness. **Access:** all year. Gibraltar Point Visitor Centre: winter, weekends only during daylight hours; summer, daily from 10am. **Where to stay:** there is a hostel for up to 28 people at Gibraltar Point field station and bird observatory. Enquire Warden, T: (01754) 762677. **Further information:** RSPB Tetney Marshes, Lincs., T: (01472) 388109; EN Grantham, T: (01476) 568431; Lincs. Trust for Nature Conservation (LTNC), T: (01507) 526667.

The Norfolk Broads

Contains 117 sq miles (303 sq km) of land with National Park status

The Norfolk Broads consist of some 52 lakes (or 'broads') in the valleys of the Rivers Ant, Bure, Thurne, Waveney and Yare. About a dozen of the broads are linked by these rivers, so that it is possible to travel from one to the other by small boat along 125 miles (200 km) of navigable waterways. The broads are the remains of large-scale peat diggings which flooded as the land began to sink during the 15th century. In time they became one of the great wetland wilderness regions of Europe, and a wildlife paradise.

Today, however, the Norfolk Broads are a ravaged Eden; not so much for the quarter of a million holiday-makers who come here each summer as for the lovers of wild places who know of the wildlife, the peace and the solitude that have gone. Powered boats have washed away the banks, destroying reed-beds and driving away the birds and mammals that inhabited them. Chemical fertilizers have stimulated the growth of algae, turning the water into a pea-green soup incapable of sustaining plant or animal life.

The picture is not entirely gloomy. Conservation measures are taking effect and the broads are now protected by the Norfolk and Suffolk Broads Act of 1988. Although not legally a national park because of its by-laws for navigation, the Broads National Park has the same powers and funding entitlements as other national parks.

The broads are rich in wetland bird life and are the only home in Britain of the swallow-tail butterfly. Some 25 species of freshwater fish live in the Broads, including some very big pike and the large predatory zander, introduced from Central Europe.

Only tiny Upton Fen is like the broads of the past, but access is severely restricted. In the broadland reserves that follow, however, it is still possible to savour something of the mysterious, secretive beauty and wonder of the great Broad wetlands of yester-year, especially if you go out of season.

BEFORE YOU GO
Maps: OS Landranger Series, map No. 134.

GETTING THERE
By car: the A11 to Norwich. From Norwich, A47 to Great Yarmouth, or A146 to Beccles and Lowestoft.
By rail: change at Ipswich or Norwich for local services to Lowestoft and Great Yarmouth.
By bus: regular services to Norwich. For local public transport information, T: (0500) 626116 (Norfolk), or (0635) 583358 (Suffolk).

WHERE TO STAY
Main accommodation centres are Norwich, Great Yarmouth and Lowestoft. The Broads Park Authority publishes a *Where to Stay* guide.
Youth hostels: at Norwich, T: (01603) 627647, and Great

Yarmouth, T: (01493) 843991.

ACCESS
All land adjoining the water is privately owned and trespass laws apply. Walkers are asked to keep to footpaths to avoid damaging banks, shoreline vegetation and marshland.

ACTIVITIES
The Broads Conservation

Volunteers welcome holiday-makers who wish to help preserve the wildlife of the broads by clearing scrub. Contact Maggie Engledow, T: (01692) 582753.

FURTHER INFORMATION
The Broads National Park, Thomas Harvey House, 18 Colegate, Norwich, Norfolk NR3 1BQ, T: (01603) 610734.

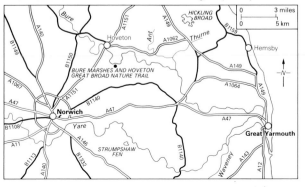

Hickling Broad

EN NNR managed by Norfolk Wildlife Trust (NWT)

Hickling Broad is a large shallow lake fringed by reed swamp, sedge beds, marshes and woodland. This superlative, 1,361-acre (550-ha) broadland reserve is of great floristic and entomological interest, and outstanding for its population of marsh birds.

The reserve is renowned for bittern and bearded tit; and predators such as the great grey shrike and hen harrier, which hunt across the marshes in winter. The butterflies and moths which throng this broad include beauties like the swallow-tail butterfly, the bulrush wainscot moth and winter migrants such as the great brocade. **Getting there** *By car:* 4 miles SE of Stalham, off A149 Yarmouth road. **Access:** Open all year, 10am-5pm daily. Visitor Centre open Apr-Sept. Entry for children free. Entry by permit only; apply to Warden, Hickling Bird NNR, Stubb Road, Hickling NR12 0BW, T: (01692) 598276. Telephone to reserve boat trip to hides and observation tower.

Bure Marshes and Hoveton Great Broad Nature Trail

EN NNR

These 1,030 acres (417 ha) of wet woodland, fen and broads along the middle reaches of the River Bure east of Hoveton form a wide, green, marvellously peaceful area.

Ducks and great crested grebes dot the water and swallows and common terns sweep through the air above the rich banks of sedge, reed, bulrush, milk parsley, yellow iris, bog myrtle, woody nightshade and royal fern. **Getting there:** by boat from Wroxham, just west of A1151. **Access:** weekdays only, May to end Sept, depending on water levels. Dogs must be left on boat. Permit required to visit other parts of Bure Marshes Reserve. **Further information:** leaflet from EN Norfolk, T: (01603) 620558.

Strumpshaw Fen

RSPB Reserve NNR

This 447-acre (180-ha) fen lies on the east bank of the lower tidal reaches of the River Yare. It is one of Britain's most important wetland sites and was designated a National Nature Reserve in 1997. The reserve, which also includes Rockland Marshes on the west bank, offers a wide variety of habitats, from the open brackish waters of the river and broad and the reed and sedge beds of the surrounding fen, to the sallow and alder carrs, the damp woodland, the wet grazing marshes and miles of ditches of the outlying pasture.

More than 80 species of wetland and woodland birds regularly breed here, and recently established breeding species include Savi's warbler, Cetti's warbler, bearded tit and marsh harrier. In summer the reed fens are alive with reed buntings and reed, sedge and grasshopper warblers.

On one of the few surviving Broadland meadow sites yellow wagtails, lapwings, redshank and snipe all breed. Rarities

such as osprey and purple heron pass through here on passage and in winter huge flocks of wigeon and bean geese can be seen down-river on the adjacent Buckingham Marshes. With luck you may also glimpse Chinese water deer, roe and fallow deer, otter, mink, naturalized European green terrapin, grass snakes and swallow-tail butterflies. **Getting there** *By car:* through Brundall off A47, taking Low Road to reserve car-park; then on foot to reception hide. **Access:** open all year. Nature trails and 4 bird hides. **Further information:** leaflet from RSPB, Staithe Cottage, Low Road, Strumpshaw, Norwich NR13 4HS, T: (01603) 715191.

Broadland Conservation Centre

NWT

Half-mile wetland nature trail through Ranworth Marshes on River Bure to floating conservation centre overlooking Ranworth Broad in one direction and Malthouse Broad in the other. Excellent for an encapsulated glimpse of the unusual wildlife environment of the Broads. **Getting there** *By car* to Ranworth village, north of B1140; then on foot from Trust car-park to start of trail at Ranworth Church (wonderful Broadland views from tower). **Access:** open all year. No dogs. **Further information:** leaflets from NWT, T: (01603) 625540.

A channel cuts through Cley Marshes, one of the many fine nature reserves on the North Norfolk Coast, where the bird marshes are among the most extensive in England

THE FENS

In the days of Hereward the Wake, the Fens were a vast, malarial swamp covering most of East Anglia from Peterborough to the Wash; a strange flat land of enormous skies, empty horizons and endless acres of reed and sedge upon a thick rich silt and a blanket of sedge peat. Ignoring the bitter protests of the peasantry who relied on the reeds, fish and wildfowl for their livelihood, the great landowners drained the Fens to make way for farm land. By the end of the 19th century next to nothing was left.

In 1899 a relict area of Fen at Wicken came to the attention of naturalists and was purchased by the National Trust, becoming Britain's first nature reserve. A smaller segment was salvaged at Woodwalton, and an important expanse survives in the Ouse Washes. These few, vital oases provide a marvellous evocation of the lonely, trackless wilderness the Fenland once was.

Wicken Fen

NT Reserve

This square mile of marshland is the last remaining undrained area of the Fenland that formerly covered East Anglia. A windmill, once used to drain the surrounding farm land, now pumps water into the fen, and the vegetation is carefully managed to maintain the widest range of Fenland habitats.

One of the classic sites in early ecological management, Wicken Fen is now a lush green haven of rich scrub and stands of tall herbs: meadowsweet, yellow loosestrife, wild angelica, milk parsley and many others. Pools and ditches are fringed with bulrushes and sedge, spearwort and lesser plantain. The profusion of fenland flora attracts a great variety of butterflies and birds to this temperate English jungle, and the hush of the wilderness prevails.

Getting there *By car:* signposted from Wicken village on A1123. Leave car at NT centre near Wicken Lode and continue on foot along trails across Fen. **Access:** open all year, best in spring and summer. **Further information:** booklet from NT, Lode Lane, Wicken, Ely CB7 5XP, T: (01353) 720274.

Woodwalton Fen

EN NNR

These 520 Cambridgeshire acres (210 ha) encompass a progression of fenland habitats: open water, mixed fen, damp meadows, wet heath and woodland. They shelter unusual plants such as the fen violet, fen wood rush and greater spearwort, and uncommon insects such as the hornet clearwing moth, ruddy sympetrum, large red damselfly and a colony of large copper butterflies, which were reintroduced here from Holland in 1927.

Getting there *By car:* turn off B1040 at Ramsey, drive to Ramsey Heights and continue

on foot. **Access:** permit holders only (permit free, valid for two years). Apply in writing to EN, Beds., Cambs., N'hants. Team, Ham Lane House, Orton Waterville, Peterborough PE2 5UR, T: (01733) 405850. **Further information:** contact Warden, Ramsey Heights, Huntingdon, T: (01487) 812363. Leaflet from EN.

The Ouse Washes

RSPB WT WWT SSSI

The Ouse Washes, which occupy about 6,250 acres (2,530 ha) in a strip half a mile (1 km) wide and 20 miles (32 km) long, are the result of an ambitious drainage scheme undertaken by the 17th-century Dutch engineer, Cornelius Vermuyden. Two parallel channels, the Old and New Bedford Rivers, were cut; when the River Ouse overflowed, it flooded the meadows in between and not the surrounding farmland.

This strip of land is still grazed in summer and usually flooded in winter, and so remains one of few areas in the Fens which is managed in much the same way as it was in the Middle Ages. A profusion of wetland vegetation grows here, including 280 species of flowering plants; bream, perch and roach teem in these waters, and pike and rudd grow to an immense size.

But it is the birds that people come here to see, and with good reason; there are prodigious numbers of wigeon, teal, mallard, pochard and pintail, as well as whooper swans, hen harriers and short-eared owls. Pride of place goes to Bewick's swan; as many as 6,000 (40% of the European population) have wintered here, although the numbers have stabilized now at around 4,500. Conservation bodies own a large percentage of the Washes, but this unique treasure will not be safe from plans to drain it until it is entirely under conservation control. **Getting there** *By car:* the WT and RSPB Reserves at the SW end can be reached from the B1093 or B1098. The WWT Reserve is in the NE corner near the village of Welney on the A1101. **Access:** open every day all year, 10am-5pm. WWT Welney Visitor Centre provides video link and other educational resources. **Further information:** Ouse Washes (WT), T: (01354) 680212, F: 688036, or WWT, Hundred Foot Bank, Welney, Wisbech, Cambs., T: (01353) 860711.

Redgrave and Lopham Fen

NNR

The largest surviving example of the once extensive Fens of the Waveney-Little Ouse Valley, this is a natural oasis for many wetland plants and animals rapidly becoming so rare in East Anglia. It is the only site of Britain's biggest spider, the great raft spider. The three way-marked trails through the fen include all the habitat types: open fen, moorland and open water. **Getting there** *By car:* off B1113, 4 miles (6 km) west of Diss. **Access:** all year. Dogs not encouraged. **Further information:** Suffolk Wildlife Trust, Brooke House, The Green, Ashbocking, Ipswich IP6 9JY, T: (01473) 890089.

BRECKLAND

The Breckland, some 300 square miles (777 sq km) of open heathy countryside between Bury St Edmunds and Swaffham, was once heavily forested. In Saxon times the land was cleared and with the tree cover gone the wind blew away the topsoil. A 14th-century sandstorm buried the medieval farm land, destroying the local economy and creating a treeless desert of sand dunes which soon became a grassy steppe.

Today, the Breckland is a mosaic of developed and undeveloped countryside. There are golf courses, sand and gravel quarries, agriculture and forestry. But large areas remain undisturbed and provide an unusual habitat for snakes, woodlark, nightjar and stone curlew, and many rare plants and insects. Something of the old Breckland can be savoured at the Cavenham Heath and East Wretham Heath.

East Wretham Heath

NWT Reserve

This unusual sandy wild place covers 350 acres (142 ha) of Breckland heath, including grassland with heather and harebell, open scrub of broom and hawthorn, natural birch woodland and a planted hornbeam wood where hawfinch and winter siskin can be found.

Two Breckland meres, fringed with aquatic plants, attract a variety of waders and wildfowl, and also a rare leech. Adders, grass snake and common lizards live on the heath, roe deer, red squirrel and badger inhabit the woods and birds of prey such as the hobby, merlin and hen harrier hunt here. **Getting there** *By car:* 4 miles (6 km) north of Thetford on A1075. **Access:** open all year. Free entry. Nature trails and hide. **Further information:** East Wretham Heath Nature Reserve, Thetford, Norfolk IP24 1RU, T: (01953) 498339; EN, T: (01603) 620558; NWT, T: (01603) 625540.

Cavenham Heath

One of the finest examples of acid Breckland heath, 502 acres (203 ha) in extent
EN NNR

This reserve has lovely sweeps of heather and gorse, sandy areas, woodland and fen. A wide range of plants, insects, birds and mammals includes rarer species such as whinchats and nightjars, and a resident population of roe deer. **Getting there** *By car:* follow along track between Icklingham and Tuddenham, west of Icklingham on A1101. **Access:** main part of reserve open all year; northern part April-July only, or by permit. Beware of adders; fire is a risk. Dogs are not permitted in northern part of reserve; keep them on lead elsewhere. **Further information:** contact Warden, Fen Road, Pakenham, Bury St Edmunds, Suffolk or English Nature Suffolk Team, Norman Tower House, 1-2 Crown Street, Bury St Edmunds, Suffolk IP33 IQX, T: (01284) 762218.

CHAPTER 3

North-West England

This is a cautionary tale of how a latter-day Moley, immured deep inside his heavily mortgaged bunker and bowed down by the cares of the world, took off for the green woods and the high hills. Like the Mole of *The Wind In The Willows*, I had had enough. A year of domestic turmoil had been followed by another half-year of unrelieved toil at a desk. I had become a prisoner, a convalescent, a spiritual malingerer. I had run out of goal, soul and steam. So one day, when I could stand it no more, I broke out of my London penitentiary and fled north, coming to rest that evening beside the tranquil, sunlit waters of Buttermere, in the very different world of the Lake District's Western Fells. Here, in the green stillness and loveliness of the lakes and hills, my transformation from zombie to human being began.

During the night the sweet, ancient smell of straw and cowpat wafted through the window of my room from the stone cattle byre outside. I awoke to a morning of clear skies and dazzling sun like a man reborn. The simplest, most commonplace image or sound in that pastoral landscape now filled me with intense astonishment and delight, unlocking memories of my Yorkshire childhood: lambs bleating in the buttercup fields; the hum of the wind over the swooping swallows' wings and — paradise — a pristine meadow stream flowing swiftly, icily and pure through tangles of reeds and herbs and flowers of

From the summit of Tarn Crags on Blencathra, the wintry view encompasses the peak of Skiddaw which, at 3,054 ft (931 m), dominates the mountains in the northern Lake District

almost tropical luxuriance.

Above the wooded meadows that separated Buttermere from Crummock Water the green hills rose like gigantic mossy stones with sheep embedded in them. To the south-west towered the three linked peaks of the Buttermere Fells: Red Pike, High Stile — the highest at 2,644 feet (806 metres) — and High Crag. By the standards of the world's great mountains these summits were mere hiccups of geology. To me, finding my hill legs after half a year at a desk, they looked huge, almost monstrous. A rough red track, like a ladder of stones, scrambled upwards towards Red Pike, which was out of sight from Buttermere; the path looked like an instrument of torture and I cast about for an easier route, via the highest waterfall in the Lakes, called Scale Force.

The fall lay deep in a cleft on the open hillside high above Crummock Water. You reached it through a wood of an-

The vivid blue flowers of the spring gentian, an arctic-alpine plant, bring a splash of colour to the most inhospitable rock environments in May and early June

cient oaks and a walk over hillsides of sprouting ferns where sheep's wool festooned the gnarled, lichen-scabbed thorns like beard moss. The cleft was enclosed by high, vertical walls of wet rock, where little stunted oaks, hollies and rowan trees clung tenaciously to minute pockets of soil in the crannies. At the end of the chasm, in a dark and horrid gloom, a 172-foot (53-metre) ribbon of white water dropped with fearsome weight and speed into a deep, reed-girt pool — an awesome and killing blow. This was Scale Force.

Lower down, nearer the chasm mouth and the sun, smaller falls busied round rocks and splashed into a brown pool ringed by ferns, foxgloves and green cushions of liverwort. Here lay the body of a sheep that had been swept over the falls to its death. Above the carcass a fluttering bird left a flickering yellow trace in the confined air space between the rock walls. The bird finally came to rest on the dead sheep's tightly convoluted horns, a wagtail of the most intense canary yellow, the quick on the dead; but when the bird opened its bill to sing the sound was drowned by the thunder of the falls.

I climbed up the rim of the gorge, looking for a place where I could peer down at the waterfall from above. Using a dead silver birch tree for support I leaned over the edge, and as I did so, precariously poised between heaven and earth, the air was suddenly rent by the most terrifying tearing sound, and I was so shocked I almost fell. I looked up in time to see a night-black fighter jet, with wings half folded like a stooping falcon, screech over my head, angle sharply left and skim round the bluff of the hill above. At a dull plod I followed the plane, toiling upstream beside the burbling beck that fed Scale Force.

From where I started it was 2,300 feet

(701 metres) of ascent to the highest point of the Buttermere Fell. Most of it now rose before me, a long, unremitting gasper up the convex hump of Red Pike's eastern shoulder. Where the track met the stream I paused to splash my face and drink from the cold, crystal water. I looked at my watch to check my schedule and an inner voice told me: 'Put your watch away, oh busy man! Forget your schedule.'

I sat back. It was a heavenly spot, a soft turfy bank in the sun, blessed with the sweet perfume of rowan blossom, billowing clouds above and a marvellous view down a gap between two fells. And as I paused and looked and dreamed, the cares of the last year fell away. I shouldered my pack and struck up the slope with new-found vigour. Climbing up to the top of Red Pike was like storming Iwo Jima; a steep slope of fine, dark gravel like blood-stained scree, dull red from the syenite in the rock. The view from the summit was majestic. From here I could see five of Lakeland's lakes and many of its highest fells, including the four highest peaks: Skiddaw, Helvellyn, Scafell Pike and its twin summit of Scafell. To the south the sun beat down on Ennerdale, Coleridge's favourite lake, and the wildest of them all.

But in this moment of reaffirmation of life, death suddenly appeared before me in the mountains. As I began to climb up the connecting ridge to High Stile, I heard a strange screeching sound and saw two jet fighter planes swiftly receding from each other, groundwards. A very loud explosion reverberated among the fells, and two narrowly separated large balls of very dark, chocolate-brown smoke drifted up behind Robinson.

The cockpits were still intact when I saw them, but burst open a little, and their innards — the brightly coloured wiring, rods and tubes — lay exposed. From an RAF crane in a field the fuselage of one of the planes hung like the mangled remains of a long-dead shark hauled from the sea. I grieved at the sight of this ill-fated wreckage; but it served only to redouble the *joie de vivre* these Lakeland hills had given back to me.

The route I was following over the Buttermere Fells formed an early stage of the Coast to Coast Walk pioneered by Wainwright between St Bee's Head on the Lancashire coast of the Irish Sea and Robin Hood's Bay on the Humberside coast of the North Sea. I could, if I chose, carry on right through the breadths of the three great national parks that straddle the north country: the Lake District, the Yorkshire Dales and the North York Moors.

But my ambitions were less heroic; I wished to return to Buttermere before the end of the day or the expiry of my stamina, whichever came first. So I carried on, in my own good time, following the long craggy ridge that connects the rugged, battlemented peaks of High Stile and High Crag. From the summit cairn of High Stile, the highest point of these fells, I could see hazy new land across the blue wash of the Irish Sea and the Solway: the Isle of Man in the west, the Scottish hills of Galloway to the north beyond Crummock Water.

It was mid-evening before I got back to my starting point. I had been out on the fells for ten hours, travelling at a ruminative one mile an hour, every mile a revelation, every hour a joy. I rejoiced at the prospect of tomorrow and a long walk over to Ennerdale and back. But before that, before anything, there was a pressing priority: my reward, a pint of real ale — Theakston's Best — and then Nirvana.

©Oxford Cartographers

GETTING THERE
By air: Manchester International Airport, T: (0161) 489 3000, has scheduled flights to major cities worldwide. Leeds-Bradford International Airport, T: (0113) 250 9696, and East Midlands Airport near Derby have flights to major European cities, while Carlisle Airport has a regular London service.
By sea: Belfast Freight Ferries, T: (01524) 855988, operates daily between Belfast and Heysham and Dublin and Liverpool. Norse Irish Ferries, T: (0151) 944 1010, has a daily Belfast to Liverpool service.
By rail: Liverpool and Manchester have rapid rail links to most parts of Britain. Contact National Rail Enquiries, T: (0345) 484950.
By coach: services link all the north-west's principal towns and cities with the rest of Britain. Contact Train, Bus and Coach National Enquiries, T: (0891) 910910.
By bicycle: the Sustrans National Cycle Network, map

No. 7, details a 189-mile (302-km) route, Glasgow to Carlisle.

WHERE TO STAY
Both the region's tourist boards produce free accomodation brochures: Cumbria's *Holiday Guide* and the North West Tourist Board's *Best of the North West*. Both include addresses of local information centres, among them:
Buxton, T: (01298) 25106,
Lancaster, T: (01524) 32878,
Kendal, T: (01539) 725758,
Settle, T: (01729) 825192, and
Penrith, T: (01768) 867466.

ACTIVITIES
The three national parks in this area are popular centres for walking holidays. The Pennine Way starts in the Derbyshire Peak District and passes through the Yorkshire Dales on its way to Scotland.
Information about sports and outdoor activities can be obtained from the regional offices of the Sports Council. For Cumbria, write off for a copy of the excellent *Northern*

Sporting and Recreation Handbook, available from the English Sports Council, Northern Region, Aykley Heads, Durham DH1 5UU, T: (0191) 384 9595. For Lancashire, Cheshire, Greater Manchester and Merseyside, send for a copy of the *Sports Directory* from the Sports Council, North West Regional Office, Fifth floor, Astley House, Quay Street, Manchester M3 4AE, T: (0161) 834 0338.

FURTHER INFORMATION
For general information about Lancashire, Greater Manchester, Merseyside, Cheshire and the High Peak area of Derbyshire contact the North West Tourist Board, T: (01942) 821222. The the rest of the region, up to the Scottish border, is the responsibility of the Cumbria Tourist Board, T: (01539) 444444.
The Yorkshire Dales National Park falls within the authority of the Yorkshire Tourist Board (see Chapter 4).

The Peak District

From the Anglo-Saxon *peac*, meaning knoll or hill

National Park occupying 555 square miles (1,438 sq km) of the southern Pennines

Hen Cloud is a distinctive mass of rock rising 1,240 feet (378 metres) out of the English lowland plain like a mini Rock of Gibraltar. To the traveller heading north this sudden upward heave of the landscape is both exciting and significant. For Hen Cloud is not only a sentinel guarding the approaches to the open and relatively unspoiled territory known as the Peak, but one of the first bastions of Highland Britain. Here you leave the placid plains and gentle

rises of the south and Midlands and enter the starker, more rugged uplands of the north country. The 150-mile (240-km) Pennine spine of England is a geologically complex world of gritstone plateaux, limestone dales, rocks and crags, great moors and vast peat bogs. The Peak District occupies the first 40 miles (64 km) of this upland chain. Here you can find some of the wildest, least tamed landscape in Britain.

The change in the environment is obvious almost at once. Hedges suddenly give way to dry-stone walls, arable fields to rough hill pasture, green slopes to moors and tracts of bog, for as the country climbs the air grows increasingly cooler. The cooler climate in turn brings about changes in the flora and fauna. For lowland plants and animals like the nettle-leaved bellflower and nuthatch, the Peak is the northernmost limit of their range; for highland species like the cloudberry and mountain hare it is the southernmost limit.

The Peak was the first national park in Britain and is still the most popular. Half the population of England are within daytrip distance of it. It is small enough to cross on foot in a day, big enough to get lost in. For the climber it offers hard rock, for the caver an underground wonderland, and for the walker miles of rambling and riding country both on and off the beaten track. For the people of Manchester, Sheffield, West Yorkshire and the Potteries, it is a lung; an escape back to nature, to bird-song and clear skies, the open trail and untrammelled horizon.

There are two kinds of Peak country: the White Peak and the Dark Peak, so called because of the colour of their prevailing rock. The White Peak is limestone country and occupies the southern and central areas of the national park, a dry, porous plateau some 1,000 feet (305 metres) above sea level. It is lighter, brighter, more arcadian countryside than the Dark Peak, and cut through by lovely wooded dales and gorges such as Dovedale, Monsal Dale and Lathkill Dale. These are the famous Derbyshire Dales, renowned for their impressive rock architecture and crystal-clear waters.

For the naturalist the Derbyshire Dales offer the greatest wealth of interest, above all in Lathkill Dale, one of five dales that form part of the Derbyshire Dales National Nature Reserve. It was carved by a torrential river of Ice Age melt-water, Lathkill Dale is a classic White Peak valley which runs through limestone for the whole of its length, a phenomenon which endows it with an exceptional richness and diversity of flora and fauna.

Even today human activity has had little effect on the environment there and many national rarities — most notably, perhaps, the uncommon purple-flowered mezareon — have continued to survive. The ash woods of the Lathkill are among the finest in the country and harbour a tremendous variety of plants. Even on the open rabbit-cropped grassland of the upper dale, 54 species of plant have been recorded in one square yard alone, while down in the dampish bottom of the dale, between the rearing limestone walls of the gorge, another rare flower, the deep blue Jacob's ladder, grows in stands as extensive as any in Britain. Further to the north, beautiful Monk's Dale is just as rich and even less affected by man and change than Lathkill Dale. Both comprise the jewels in the crown of the Peak District's natural history heritage.

By contrast the Dark Peak, which surrounds the White Peak like an inverted horseshoe to north, east and west, is gritstone country, altogether harsher, wilder and more sombre, especially along its dramatic rock edges and on the high heather moors and peat deserts at the more northerly end of the park. The high moors are the kingdom of the red grouse and hardy hill sheep. The hill walker who traverses them needs to be well prepared and well equipped for the unpredictable — and often hostile — weather.

The western edge of the Dark Peak rises sharply for more than 1,000 feet (305 metres) out of the Cheshire Plain, and the rock architecture to be found there provides some of the most spectacular gritstone landscape of the national park. Rock outcrops like the Roaches, Hen Cloud and Ramshaw Rocks, with their rearing towers and serrated pinnacles carved by wind, rain and frost, provide some of the best climbing pitches in the country. Some of them are formidably advanced, with encouraging names like Death Knoll and the Crack of Gloom. One of the few genuine peaks in the Peak District — Shutlingsloe, the 'Matterhorn of the Peak', and 1,659 feet (505 metres) above sea level — is located in this western part of the national park.

West of Sheffield lies the eastern arm of the Dark Peak. Extensive peat and heather moors, the domain of the sheep, the hare and the hill walker, give way to a series of odd-shaped tors such as Crow Stones, Cat Clough and Cakes of Bread and spectacular gritstone rock edges, walls of almost continuous rock which run for miles and descend by steps to the plains below.

Through this impressive landscape flows one of the Peak's great rivers, the Derwent, which rises on the Bleaklow plateau to the north. In its upper reaches, the river has been extensively dammed and forested thereby creating a man-made landscape more like Scandinavia than Derbyshire.

From Edale the high Pennine Moors stretch northwards all the way to the Scottish border. The Pennine Way starts here, aiming straight at the boggy plateau from which rises the Peak's highest point, Kinder Scout (2,088 ft/636 m). This five-square-mile morass of peat bogs and 'groughs', where the water-eroded gullies wind between walls of peat higher than a man, is certainly wild but hardly pretty, and it will appeal more to the dedicated hill walker than the simple country lover, for it is a desolate and monotonous place, climatically temperamental, squelchy underfoot after rain, fearsome in winter.

The name Kinder Scout probably comes from the Saxon *Kyndwr Scut*, meaning 'water over the edge' and referring, in all likelihood, to the tumbling cascade of nearby Kinder Downfall where the nascent Kinder River drops 100 feet (30 metres) over the rocky escarpment of the moorland edge on its headlong course to the west.

The moorland and bog stretch north out of Kinder. There are two major parts to these northern moors: Bleaklow, to the south of the drowned industrial valley of Longendale, and Black Hill to the north of it. It is a matter of personal experience which of these peat deserts is squidgiest, bleakest and most vexing for walkers.

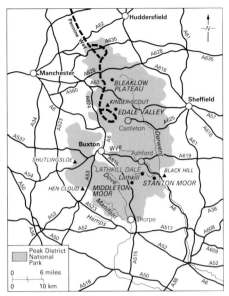

Bleaklow is possibly Britain's only true desert: a semi-tundra of acid peat, once forested, but over the centuries so felled and grazed and burnt and drained that not even the humble sphagnum moss can survive here, and the nodding white heads of the bog cotton grass are virtually the only sign of life. For the wild traveller there are compensations in this desolate state of affairs: solitude, a stark kind of beauty, a sense of grappling with primordiality and the reward of achievement. These are the essential components of any true exploration of wild places.

BEFORE YOU GO
Maps: the Ordnance Survey produces 2 maps covering the entire area in the 1:25,000-scale Outdoor Leisure Series: the Dark Peak (north) and the White Peak (south).
Web-sites: the Peak District National Park Authority's web-site gives a comprehensive guide to the park, at www.peakdistrict.org.

GETTING THERE
By car: the M1 provides rapid access from the north (exits 28 or 29) and south (exit 36).

Main roads through the park include the A515 from Ashbourne to Buxton, the A6 from Matlock to Manchester, the A623 and the A57 from Sheffield to Glossop through Snake Pass.
By rail: the Hope Valley Community Railway, T: (01663) 746377, runs from Sheffield to Manchester with 5 stations inside the park: Edale, Hope, Bamford, Hathersage and Grindleford. Branch lines also run from Manchester to Glossop in the north and Buxton in the south of the

park. For recorded events information, call T: (0161) 242 6296.
By coach and bus: services within the park are listed in the public transport timetable, available from the Peak District National Park Authority (see FURTHER INFORMATION below). For unlimited travel on bus or train, buy a Coast and Peaks 7-Day Rover or a 3-in-7 Flexi Rover (any three days out of seven) ticket from main-line railway stations, individual bus operators or the national park's offices.

Lathkill Dale, one of the gems of the White Peak in Derbyshire, is lit up in August with bright clumps of rose-bay willow-herb

WHERE TO STAY

Hotels and bed and breakfast: Bakewell and Castleton are the principal accommodation centres. Ashbourne, Matlock, Buxton and Glossop, on the fringes of the park, absorb many more visitors. Contact the park authority (see below)for its annual list of accommodation.

Outdoor living: the park authority publishes a list of approved sites. It also runs camping barns — stone farm buildings converted into cheap, basic accommodation.

Youth hostels: at Bakewell, T: (01629) 812313; Buxton, T: (01298) 22287; Castleton, T: (01433) 620235; Crowden, T: (01457) 852135; Dimmingdale, nr Oakamoor, T: (01538) 702304; Edale, T: (01433) 670302; Eyam, T: (01433)

630335; Eyam Edge, T: (0114) 288 4541; Hartington, T: (01298) 84223; Hathersage, T: (01433) 650493; Ilam, T: (01335) 350212; Langsett, nr Peninstone, T: (0114) 288 4541; Matlock, T: (01629) 582983; Millers Dale, T: (01298) 871826; Quarnford, T: (01260) 227625; Shining Cliff Woods, nr Ambergate, T: (01629) 650394; Youlgreave, T: (01629) 636518.

ACCESS AND CLOSURES

Restricted to roads, footpaths and bridle paths in southern park; a special agreement allows visitors to ramble freely over much of the northern moors, except for a few days each year during grouse shoots and when there is a high risk of fire. These periods are posted at park information centres and advertised in the local press.

ACTIVITIES

Walking: the park authority produces a number of leaflets

describing circular walks; it also runs a series of short guided walks, details of which are published in *The Peakland Post*, the annual information sheet available from visitors' centres. The long-distance walker will head for Edale, conveniently located on the Hope Valley Railway, where the PENNINE WAY (see p88) begins its long route across the park's highest hills — Kinder Scout, Bleaklow and Black Hill in the Dark Peak.

The Peak District is so close to a densely populated industrial region that visitors tend to forget that conditions can be harsh. Before setting out on a long walk, check the weather forecast and make sure you are adequately equipped.

Riding: the south offers steep wooded bridle paths, greenways and lanes; exposed and ancient pack-horse routes cut across the bare moors of the northern Dark Peak. The park authority's leaflet *Riding and*

Trekking lists a number of centres which organize trekking and holidays and vacation packages.

Climbing: both the limestone hills in the south and the gritstone cliffs to the east, west and north are popular training grounds. For names of climbing clubs, contact the British Mountaineering Council, 177-179 Burton Road, West Didsbury, Manchester M20 2BB, T: (0161) 445 4747.

Caving: the hollow limestone of the White Peak has fascinated cavers since Edwardian times. This is a potentially dangerous activity and even experienced cavers should seek the advice of a local caving club before going underground. A cave rescue service is available by dialling 999. For information on caving in the region, contact the Derbyshire Caving Association, c/o the English Sports Council, East Midlands Regional Office, Grove House, Bridgford Road, West Bridgford, Nottingham NG2 6AP, T: (0115) 982 2586. Several show caves give the visitor a tempting if touristy glimpse of this otherwise closed world. Blue John Cavern and Mine, T: (01433) 620638, Speedwell Cavern, T: (01433) 620512, and Treak Cliff Cavern, T: (01433) 620571 – all near Castleton – are open daily all year round. For opening times contact the individual caves.

Cycling: quiet roads, bridle paths and disused railway tracks offer many suitable routes. Leaflets describing them are available from the park authority's cycle-hire shops at: Ashbourne, T: (01335) 343156; Bakewell, T: (01629) 814004; Derwent, T: (01433) 651261; Parsley Hay, T: (01298) 84493; Waterhouses, T: (01538) 308609.

Fishing: the waters once fished by Izaak Walton are still popular with anglers. The

'A howling wilderness... the most desolate, wild and abandoned country in all England.'

Daniel Defoe (1725)

Rivers Dove, Wye and Derwent are good grounds for brown and rainbow trout, while several reservoirs are open to the public. Tackle shops issue rod licences and permits and are the best sources of advice on local fishing. The park authority's leaflet, *Fishing*, gives useful information about trout fishing in the park.

Field studies: courses in the natural history and archaeology of the park are offered at the Peak District National Park Authority Study Centre at Losehill Hall, Castleton, Hope Valley, Derbyshire S33 8WB, T: (01433) 620373.

FURTHER INFORMATION

Peak District National Park Authority, Main Office, Aldern House, Baslow Road, Bakewell, Derbyshire DE45 1AE, T: (01629) 816200. For all park authority literature.

English Nature, Manor Barn, Over Haddon, nr Bakewell, Derbyshire DE45 1JE, T: (01629) 815095. For information on Derbyshire Dales Nature Reserve.

National Trust, East Midlands Regional Office, Clumber Park Stableyard, Worksop, Nottinghamshire S80 3BE, T: (01909) 486411, for literature on the NT's substantial holdings in the park.

Derbyshire Wildlife Trust, Elvaston Castle, Derby DE72 3EP, T: (01274) 567697. The Trust's holdings include more than 10 small reserves within the park.

The park information centres at Bakewell, T: (01629) 813227, Castleton, T: (01433) 620679,

Edale, T: (01433) 670270, and Fairholmes, T: (01433) 650953, are open year-round. Other centres are at Torside and Langsett, but remain closed during the winter.

Forest of Bowland
From the Celtic *buland*, a cattle pasture

AONB

A western outlier of the Pennine chain, the Forest of Bowland must be one of the least spoiled and least publicized wild places in England. Once a royal hunting forest and wilderness refuge for Tudor dissidents, it has long since lost its tree cover; today it consists mostly of open heather moor and fell country, 312 square miles (808 sq km) of grandeur and isolation.

This terrain is broken by limestone knolls and gritstone crags, rising to 1,839 feet (560 metres) at Ward's Stone, 1,827 feet (557 metres) at Pendle Hill and 1,786 feet (544 metres) at White Hill, providing the walker with tremendous views towards the Irish Sea, Snowdonia, the Pennines and the Lake District.

The area is privately owned and managed primarily for grouse; few people live here and only one minor road crosses the central area. However, there are a number of public footpaths for the hill walker wishing to explore the high, bracken-covered fells or the steep, tree-lined river valleys.

Merlin and hen harrier hunt over the fells, curlew and plover call on the moors, dippers bob and flit about by the peaty, swiftly flowing streams and

71

waterfalls, redstarts and pied flycatchers nest in the valley woods and some 20,000 pairs of lesser black-backed gulls breed in a huge gullery on Mallowdale Fell.
Getting there: via M6 (exits 32 and 33), then by unclassified roads. Buses run from Lancaster to Abbeystead and Wray in the north and from Preston to Chipping and

Clitheroe in the south. For further information, contact the Lancashire County Council public transport enquiry line, T: (01257) 241693. **Where to stay:** bed and breakfast at Garstang, Chipping, Slaidburn, Dolphinholme, Bolton-by-Bowland and Wray. Youth hostel at Slaidburn, T: (01200) 446656. YHA camping barns at Chipping, Downham, Hurst

Green and Quernmore. Leaflet and booking details from The Bowland Barns Reservation Office, 16 Shawbridge Street, Clitheroe, Lancs BB7 1LY, T: (01200) 428366. Lancaster Tourist Information Centre, T: (01524) 32878, issues accommodation lists. **Access:** few rights of way, but free access in 2 large areas; details from Lancaster TIC.

The Yorkshire Dales

680 sq miles (1,761 sq km) of limestone hills and dales in the central Pennines, one-third of which is National Park

I have a particular fondness for the York-shire Dales, for I was brought up in them; and what I am I owe in part to them, and to the Second World War. My explorations during those formative years were for the most part limited to how far I could travel in a day by bike or bus; but what they lacked in range they made up for in intimacy, for I ex-perienced the world then in a way that would probably be impossible now, and was part of the natural world to an extent that most people find difficult in adulthood.

A large part of my free time was spent in a fragment of the ancient Forest of Knares-borough, a wood of beech and fir, oak, holly and tangled rhododendron thickets border-ing the open rolling dales, where the lap-wings cried and the bluebottles huzzahed in the cowpats and the dipper bobbed in the beds of the stream and I could roly-poly through fields of cowslips that stretched from one end of the known world to the other.

In that vestigial wood I learned the ways of the forest, learned to stalk, climb trees, forage for mushrooms, berries, crab apples, hips and haws, beechmast and hazelnuts, wild horseradish and the young fresh leaves of the hawthorn (which we called bread and

cheese, and ate). Here I first heard the sum-mer oratorio of the birds' dawn chorus, first set eyes on badgers, weasels and shrews, learned to tell the different birds apart, cut my hand on razor grass, and became aware, with the close proximity that only a child can know, of all the smells and feels and shapes and colours and movements of all the different wild things of the forest. For me that wood was a natural sanctuary.

I went to other places too. At Fountains Abbey I was reduced to silence by the ghosts and echoes of times and people past that crowded round me in that green and haunt-ed place. On the weirdly weathered contor-tions of Brimham Rocks I learned to clam-ber around the awkward eructations of geology, and at Scar Beck I learned to fall off them. But in my mind's eye it is to one small spot in Nidderdale that I return time and again. Call it Becksthwaite: a small grey limestone village and a small grey limestone bridge over a little chunk of paradise. The River Nidd ran clear and cold and fast and shallow here and you could go minnowing and sticklebacking with baited jam jars and feel the fish nibbling your toes and lie back and watch the clouds billowing past and the hot summer sun glinting through the branches of the overhanging trees like a star shell.

A year ago I went back to Becksthwaite. It had not changed at all in the intervening years, and it was still paradise. But the boys were not boys like the boys when I was a boy. 'Can you still get sticklebacks down in the river?' I asked one local lad by the bridge. He shifted nervously from foot to foot and glanced uneasily at his chum.

'Never heard of anything like *them*,' he replied at last. 'Can't get nowt like that down't river now.'

One boy's paradise, perhaps, is another's purgatory. But for the right person, the Yorkshire Dales are a blessed patch. Part of the Pennine chain, the dales are formed of carboniferous limestone which reflects the light so that, on sunlit days, they positively gleam.

Nowhere in Britain will you find more spectacular examples of limestone scenery. At Gordale Scar and Malham Cove it takes the form of sheer cliff faces of bone-white rock up to 300 feet (91 metres) high. At Southerscales Scars and Scales Moor, as well as Malham Cove, it takes the form of extraordinary limestone pavements, jointed and fissured by millions of years of rain and dirty weather. Or it is dissolved by underground rivers to form an immense network of caves far below the surface. There are 50 major caves in the Yorkshire Dales, including Britain's largest underground cavern, the 350-foot (107-metre) Gaping Gill.

It is the dales, scoured by Ice Age glaciers and cleared, farmed and populated by man, that determine the ground plan of the park. 'Dale' is a Norse word for valley, and there are some 50 of them in the park, the few major ones establishing the layout of its landscape.

Swaledale, to the north, is narrow, lovely and haunted by the relics of its industrial past. Wensleydale, which runs a parallel course to the south, is the most pastoral of the dales, the gentlest and least wild. It is also the heart of waterfall country; among the many falls (or forces) is the 90-foot (27-metre) drop of Hardraw Force.

To the south, Bishopsdale leads towards Wharfedale, which rises in wild country at the heart of the dales and flows serenely through the most sylvan of all the valleys. To the south-west of Wharfedale, in the bone-bright Great Scar limestone country, Malhamdale and Ribblesdale wind through a land of gleaming cliffs and scars, while Yorkshire's 'Three Peaks' — Ingleborough, Whernside and Pen-y-ghent, all of them over 2,000 feet (610 metres) in height — peer distantly down over Ribblehead.

There are a score of summits above this height, with high grass and heather moorland fells between the valleys. These Pennine uplands rank among the last wilderness areas of England, where there is only the call of the curlew to keep you company, and the cry of grouse and sheep. It is in the water-logged peat of the high fells, tumbling and tinkling downhill via the innumerable small tarns and becks, falls and gills, that the rivers in the dales below have their origin.

There is a great range of plant and animal habitats in the park, the products of soil and climate, which are in turn a product of altitude. On the highest ground above 2,000 feet (610 metres) a sub-alpine pasture of moor grasses, heathers, bilberry and crowberry prevails. One zone down, vast areas of the wetter, western Pennine uplands above 1,400 feet (430 metres) are covered in black, sombre, squelchy peat, up to 90 feet (27 metres) deep in places. In this hostile, wild environment, the fluffy white cotton-grass is almost the only plant that can survive.

Between 1,000 and 1,400 feet (305 and 430 metres), enormous stretches of the upland dales are covered by heather moorland. Carefully managed for grouse and sheep, the moors are best seen in August when the heather is in bloom. In bygone times birch woods covered the moors, but now they are confined to the gills, becks and streams which cut ravines on the steep hillsides out of reach of grazing animals. One of the finest gill woods in the park is Ling Gill, a small national nature reserve in a limestone ravine in upper Ribblesdale east of Ribble-

Spring is the best time for spotting adders, when they have just emerged from hibernation and are doing their best to warm up in the fitful April sun

head, where the dominant trees are ash and hazel and the rich ground flora includes giant bellflower, herb Paris, melancholy thistle, mountain everlasting, marsh hawksbeard, globe flower and ferns of all kinds.

The limestone country has most of the flowers in the dales. They are everywhere, burning bright or coyly winking, on grassland and rocks, chinks in walls and fissures in limestone pavements. The surface of these pavements is mostly bare rock and there is no soil to support plant life; but in the damp, dark fissures — or 'grykes' — there is not only soil but shade from the heat of the sun and protection from grazing animals, and here a classic English woodland flora flourishes: hart's tongue fern and herb Robert, green spleenwort and dog's mercury, wood anemone and wood sorrel. At Colt Park Wood, a national nature reserve near Ribblehead, there is a rare example of a tree-covered limestone pavement, with one of the best native scar ash woods in Britain and a

ground flora totalling more than 150 species.

If the limestone country has more to offer botanists, it is the moors and fells which are likely to be of greater interest to ornithologists, with sandpipers and black-headed gulls round the tarns, ravens, buzzards, merlins, peregrines and kestrels soaring and swooping over the hunting grounds and meadow pipits everywhere between the high fells and the rough grazing. And in the streams that chatter down the gills and dales the dippers dip and the wagtails wag and the kingfishers catch fish in spurts of bright blue and flashing orange flame.

The Yorkshire Dales are a very special and very lovely part of the world. The landscape is remarkable for the harmony between the world of nature and the world of man, his villages, farms and domiciles. The rambler and hill walker, naturalist and fisherman will find peace and beauty wherever they go in the dales: so go.

BEFORE YOU GO
Maps: OS Outdoor Leisure Series Map Nos. 2 and 30.
Guide-books: *Yorkshire Dales* (AA/OS) is very informative on a general level, and full of excellent maps. Four mini-guide leaflets with tourist attractions, local events, contact addresses and telephone numbers for each area of the dales, are available from Yorkshire Tourist Board, T: (01904) 707961. The Yorkshire Dales National Park's annual information sheet, *The Visitor*, includes a complete list of addresses, guided walks, special events and is available free at park information centres or by sending a self-addressed envelope to Yorkshire Dales National Park Authority, Grassington, Skipton BD23 5LB, T: (01756) 752748.

GETTING THERE
By car: from M6, take A65 (exit 36) for southern dales;

A684 (exit 37) for Garsdale and Wensleydale; exit 38 for Kirkby Stephen and Swaledale. From A1, take A59 from Harrogate for Skipton and east of park. Try to use public transport whenever possible, as travel by car is generally not encouraged in the area.
By rail: the Leeds-Lancaster line serves the south of the park, with stops at Skipton, Gargrave, Hellifield, Long Preston, Giggleswick and Clapham. The spectacular Carlisle-Settle line, one of England's most scenic railways, traverses the western side of the

park stopping at Settle, Horton, Ribblehead, Dent, Garsdale and Kirkby Stephen.
By bus: the Darlington-Richmond, Leeds-Skipton, Lancaster/Kendal-Sedbergh coach services all stop at towns on the periphery of the park. Within the park, bus services are often infrequent, but certain routes along the principal dales are well served. Schedules available from park centres (see FURTHER INFORMATION below).

WHERE TO STAY
The park authority's

CAUTION TO WALKERS

Where there are dales there are hills, and potentially treacherous weather. Before setting out on any upland walk, check the 24-hour weather service, T: (0891) 232787 (W & S Yorkshire & Dales), or www.meto.govt.uk. In emergencies, ring 999 and ask for 'fell rescue'.

Disused lead mines are a hazard in some parts of the park, and open pits still exist near Grassington, Arkengarthdale and Swaledale. Consult a park information centre (see BEFORE YOU GO) for details of any such pitfalls along your projected route.

Many lovers of the Yorkshire Dales consider the undulating limestone scenery of Wharfedale the finest, with its woods, moors and pasture

accommodation guide, available by post from the central office, gives details of camp-sites and other accommodation. The 6 park centres, local information points and Yorkshire Tourist Board offices (see below) will provide assistance with booking.
Youth hostels: at Aysgarth, T: (01969) 663260; Cowgill, nr Dent, T: (015396) 25251; Ellingstring, T: (01677) 460216; Grinton, T: (01748) 884206; Hawes, T: (01969) 667368; Ingleton, T: (015242) 41444; Keld, T: (01748) 886259; Kettlewell, T: (01756) 760232;

Kirkby Stephen, T: (017683) 71793; Linton, nr Grassington, T: (01756) 752400; Malham, T: (01729) 830321; and Stainforth, T: (01729) 823577. For more information about hostelling in this area, contact YHA Northern Region, PO Box 11, Matlock, Derbyshire DE4 2XA, T: (01629) 825850.

ACCESS AND CLOSURES
Except for Bardon Moor near Bolton Abbey, where access has been negotiated, walkers must stay on rights of way specified on OS maps. If in doubt, enquire at a park centre.

ACTIVITIES
Walking: fingerposts and colour coding — yellow for walkers only, blue for riders and cyclists — identify the

numerous rights of way. These provide opportunities for walkers of all abilities, from endurance tests across high fell country to guided ambles among lowland farms. The park authority offers a summer programme of over 100 guided walks, each led by an expert in some aspect of the area's natural history or archaeology: details are published in *The Visitor*.
  The long-distance walker may be tempted by The Pennine Way which winds northwards along high ground through Malham, Hawes and Keld (see THE PENNINE WAY, p88). The Dales Way, which angles up Wharfedale on its way from Ilkley to Bowness, is described in Colin Speakman's *The Dales Way* (Dalesman, 1994). The 22-

Britain's smallest falcon, the merlin, hunts over high moorland in summer, but in winter prefers the easier pickings of coastal marshes

41244. Contact individual caves for opening times.

Cycling: the park authority promotes a 130-mile (208-km) circular cycleway; free leaflet from park information centres.

Ballooning: for the unique opportunity of gliding over the park in a wicker basket, contact Black Sheep Balloons, Gargrave, nr Skipton, T: (01756) 748106, or Airborne Adventures, Rylstone, nr Skipton, T: (01756) 730166. Both operators fly daily, weather permitting.

Field studies: Malham Tarn Field Centre is ideally situated for the study of plant and animal ecology, geology and bird life. It offers 20 3- to 7-day courses between May and September for students of any level and age. Information from Malham Tarn Field Centre, Field Study Council, Settle, North Yorkshire BD24 9PU, T: (01729) 830331, F: 830658, e-mail: fsc.malham@ukonline.co.uk.

mile (35-km) Three Peaks Walk takes in the summits of Pen-y-ghent, Whernside and Ingleborough. This itinerary has become such a cult that in places the peaks are seriously eroded. *The Three Peaks Map and Guide* (Stiles Publications) is one of several descriptions of the route.

Climbing: few long climbs, but challenging cliffs at Malham, Gordale and Kilnsey. *Yorkshire Limestone*, a booklet describing these and other climbs, is available from the Yorkshire Mountaineering Club, P. Scott, Secretary, 11 Southview Drive, East Brierley, Bradton, West Yorkshire. Climbing holidays are organized by the park's own

centre at Whernside (Yorkshire Dales National Park Outdoor Recreation and Study Centre, Dent, Sedbergh, Cumbria, T: (015396) 25213) and by the Dales Centre, Grassington, North Yorkshire BD23 5AU, T: (01756) 752757.

Caving: with more than 125 miles (200 km) of cave and tunnel already explored, the park is a centre for enthusiasts. For further information, experienced cavers should consult the Whernside Centre, or refer to *Northern Caves* (Dalesman, 5 volumes), a publication devoted exclusively to the caves of the Dales. Three show caves allow casual visitors a glimpse of the park underground: Ingleborough Cave, Clapham, T: (015242) 51242; Stump Cross Caverns, Grassington/Pately Bridge, T: (01756) 752780; White Star Caves, Ingleton, T: (015242)

FURTHER INFORMATION
For publications and enquiries, contact the Yorkshire Dales National Park Authority, Grassington, Skipton BD23 5LB, T: (01756) 752748. There are 7 park information centres, open Apr-Oct, daily 10 am-5 pm, at Aysgarth Falls, T: (01969) 663424; Clapham, T: (015242) 51419; Grassington, T: (01756) 752774; Hawes, T: (01969) 667450; Malham, T: (01729) 830363; Reeth, T: (01748) 884059; and Sedbergh, T: (015396) 20125.

For regional information, contact the Yorkshire Tourist Board, 312 Tadcaster Road, York Y024 1GS, T: (01904) 707961, web-site: www.ytb.org.uk. They have centres at Leyburn, Richmond, Settle, Skipton, Bentham, Ingleton and Horton-in-Ribblesdale (the last three are closed during the winter).

THE NORTH PENNINES

The North Pennines are England's last great tract of un-protected moorland — wild, remote country wedged between the Yorkshire Dales, Lake District and Northumberland National Parks at the northern end of the Pennine chain. The region is crossed by the Pennine Way and contains the two largest nature reserves in England, as well as the sensational chasm of High Cup Nick and the Pennines' highest summit, Cross Fell (2,930 feet/893 metres), where snow can lay into summer.

Important areas include the following:

Upper Teesdale

EN NNR

Most visitors to this moorland reserve in Durham come to admire the dramatic waterfalls at Cauldron Snout or High Force, to picnic by the great man-made lake of Cow Green reservoir or to walk one of the barest and grandest stretches of the Pennine Way. But this tundra-like moorland has an extra importance: for more than two centuries it has been recognized as one of Europe's unique wild places, a plant community almost unchanged in 10,000 years.

Several habitats thrive in this living museum of post-Ice Age vegetation: small woodlands, riverside pastures and peat-bog uplands. The most unusual and fertile are the grasslands that cover Teesdale's sugar limestone, so called on account of its granulated surface. Rare Ice Age relict plants include artic-alpines such as spring gentian, alpine bartsia, bird's-eye primrose and Scottish asphodel.
Getting there: via unclassified road off B6277, 7 miles (11 km) north-west of Middleton.
Where to stay: Langdon Beck

Youth Hostel, T: (01833) 622228. **Access:** stay on rights of way, which are unaffected by firing ranges south of reserve at Cronkley Fell. **Further information:** leaflet and trail guides can be obtained on site or from English Nature , Archbold House, Archbold Terrace, Newcastle-upon-Tyne, NE2 1EG, T: (0191) 281 6316.

Moor House

EN NNR

It is said that on a clear day one can see the summit of Cheviot, 40 miles (64 km) to the north, from Great Dun Fell in the Moor House reserve. One is more likely to see low clouds and featureless moor, for it rains or snows here an average of 290 days a year.

Moor House in Cumbria is the largest reserve in England and also one of the poorest in terms of higher plant and animal life. A layer of peat averaging 6 feet (1.8 metres) in depth covers 85% of the area, turning this part of the Pennines into a vast black sponge. Few plants can survive in such an environment; heather, cotton grass,

sphagnum moss, moor rush and mat grass are the dominant species.

It is only in the lower plants that the reserve is particularly rich: 260 mosses, 75 liverworts and 120 lichens have been recorded. Few birds and mammals thrive here. Red grouse, curlew, golden plover, snipe, mallard, dunlin, teal, wigeon, ring ouzel and dipper are among the nesting birds. Fox, rabbit, field vole, mole and shrew are also residents, though the black-faced Swaledale sheep is the only mammal you are likely to encounter.
Getting there: take footpath from village of Knoch to Great Dun Fell or join the Pennine Way at nearby Dufton — a longer route. Carry a compass.
Further information: leaflet from English Nature, T: (015394) 45286.

Asby Scar

EN NNR

Situated on the watershed between the Rivers Eden and Lune in Cumbria, the desolate landscape of Asby Scar is a spectacular lesson in the power of water over rock. The limestone pavement of this bare plateau — great slabs known as clints — is deeply notched with fissures, known as grykes, where the rock has literally been dissolved by millennia of rainfall. In this apparently barren world of rock and grass, a few wind-twisted hawthorns are the tallest living things.

But below the surface of the pavement, sheltered from both weather and sheep, an abundant plant life flourishes within the grykes. Of particular interest are the ferns: green spleenwort, brittle bladder fern, limestone polypody and rigid buckler fern. Other plants to

Bird's eye primrose and wood anemone flower below an outcrop in alder and birch woodland on the banks of the Tees

note include mountain melic, lesser meadow rue, hairy rock cress, herb Paris and hart's

tongue. There are even communities of stunted trees in the wider grykes, sunken coppices of sycamore, ash rowan, hazel and elder (see also GAIT BURROWS, p86).
Getting there: half a mile east of Orton on B6261, take

unclassified road north to Broadfell and Scar Side. A track from Scar Side leads up the fell and through the reserve. **Access:** unrestricted. **Further information:** leaflet from English Nature, T: (015394) 45286.

The Lake District

The largest National Park in Britain, covering 885 sq miles (2,292 sq km) of Cumbrian lakes, dales, fells and coast

In few other parts of England are visitors more immediately aware of the geological structure of the land than in the Lake District. The mountains heave up out of the flat plains to greet them. Under their feet lie hard rocks against which they stub their toes, loose scree on which they curse and slide, endless inclines and declines which give them blisters. Beneath their gaze still, deep waters stretch away between the steep slopes of the fells.

Everywhere you look you see geology. The different kinds of rock produce different kinds of scenery, an immense variety of it; and it is old, older then the Alps and the Himalayas, older than almost everything in the world.

Skiddaw is not only the fourth highest mountain in England at 3,053 feet (930 metres), but arguably the oldest mountain in Europe. It is formed of the most northerly of three bands of different rock types that make up the core of the Lakeland fells, a great dome of slates rent by volcanic lavas and covered by later slates and limestones. The name of this rock is Skiddaw Slate, laid down as mud in a shallow sea some 500 million years ago. Most of northern Lakeland, from Blencathra and Skiddaw round via Derwentwater to Buttermere, Crummock and Loweswater, is composed of this dark blue or black slate, which weathers into rounded hills and placid skylines.

The second rock band, in the central Lake District, was formed by a volcanic cataclysm which took place at about the time the Skiddaw slates had been laid down. These Borrowdale volcanics, as they are called, are coloured red, pink and green. Weathered by millions of years of rain, frost and ice, they have produced some of the most fiercely dramatic mountain landscapes of the Lake District: craggy peaks, plunging buttresses, deep chasms, a complex maze of high ridges and crooked valleys across the whole area from Wastwater to the Borrowdale Fells, including the peaks of some of the highest mountains in England, such as Scafell Pike (at 3,210 feet/978 metres, the very highest point in England), Scafell (3,162 feet/964 metres), Helvellyn (3,118 feet/950 metres) and Great Gable (2,949 feet/899 metres).

The third band of rock, running across southern Lakeland, consists of Silurian slates laid down after the volcanic eruptions had created the central mountains. This rock is blue-grey or black, generally soft and easily eroded and produces a gentler landscape of rounded hills and lush woods — the lovely, green, seductive Lakeland countryside of Windermere, Esthwaite Water, Coniston Water, Grizedale Forest, the wooded hills and dales to the east of Broughton, the woodlands of the Furness Fells, the Winster Valley and Hawkshead.

Over millions of years, earth movements raised, buckled and crushed the original rock formations. Rivers cut through the surface, forming the pattern of today's fells. The Ice Ages scooped out the mountain tarns, carved out the peaks and razor-edged ridges, shattered the standing rock into long slopes of scree and deepened the valleys. The smaller side valleys were left stranded and hanging, so that today their streams spill spectacularly over the steep walls of the main valley. These waterfalls (or forces) such as Sour Milk Gill at Buttermere, Taylor Milk Gill at the head of Borrowdale or Aira Force near Ullswater have a wild beauty that has drawn Lakeland travellers since Victorian times.

When the ice at last retreated, life began to return to the stark bare landscape. First came alpine and tundra vegetation, followed by a scattering of birch and pine, and then a luxuriant oak forest into which moved the elk, the bear, the wolf and all the classic fauna and flora of the north European woods — and finally man.

Stone and Bronze Age farmers began to clear the great forest to pasture livestock and plant crops. Here and there they left mysterious stone henges and circles of unknown significance, like those at Castlerigg, east of Keswick, or at Swinside, near Black Combe, and Long Meg near Penrith. In due course, the native Celt was clobbered by the Romans and then by the Anglo-Saxons, and again by the Viking Norsemen, who came down the west coast from Scotland and Ireland, colonized Lakeland and left their language in many of the place names: dales (from *dalr*), fells (*fjall*), becks (*bekkr*), tarns (*tjorn*), force (*foss*, meaning waterfall), thwaite (meaning clearing or meadow) and how (meaning hill).

And so, as the centuries waxed and waned, the tumultuous landscape of the Lake District was settled according to the pattern of scattered farm and village we see today. The earliest fell walkers, the shepherd and sheep-farmer, traversed every inch of the high fells and bestowed their vivid, home-made names upon every nook and cranny: Little Lad Crag and Pots of Ashness, Green Crag Gully and Dollywaggon Pike, Grike, Yoke and Starling Dodd, Beck Head and Windy Gap, White Napes and Green Gable, Base Brown and Tom Blue, Hell Gate Pillar and Eagle's Nest Ridge, Raise, Strands and Steeple.

Until the Romantic movement changed the public's perception of wild places, no one

in their right senses ever went near the fells unless they had to. During the early years of the 19th century William Wordsworth and his circle of Lakeland poets helped to change that. Besides immortalizing the Lakes in his poetry, Wordsworth also wrote one of the best Lakeland guide-books, *Guide to the Lakes* (1835). But it was Coleridge who was the first true recreational fell walker. With his many hair-raising ascents, he pioneered a sport that was to blossom in Victorian times.

The great attraction of the Lakeland fells is that you don't have to be a mountaineer to get up them. The wild traveller will avoid the most popular peaks such as Scafell Pike, Helvellyn and Skiddaw at the height of the summer season, when you may have to wait to get up to the final cairn. They are preferable in winter, especially on a clear day, when the snow is crisp and the sky is blue and with a bit of luck you can have the mountains to yourself. Scafell is a long, slow climb, but not a difficult one. Skiddaw is very easy. Helvellyn is the best of the 3,000-foot (915-metre) peaks, with the finest views and the steepest and most exciting summit, but in poor weather conditions a degree of caution is needed; there are more accidents on Helvellyn than on any other mountain in the Lake District.

The biggest and best known lakes are not ideal places to get away from the madding crowd. Windermere is essentially a summer playground, crowded both on land and water. The same can be said of Coniston Water, Derwentwater and Grasmere, which have busy roads alongside them and heavy tourist traffic in season. This is not to say that they are not immensely beautiful or that one cannot find some measure of peace and seclusion on the quieter sides of these lakes, away from the roads.

But perhaps the wild traveller should turn towards the remoter, less grand lakes such as lonely Haweswater, the most isolated of the lakes; or Wastwater, the gauntest and, at 250 feet (76 metres), the deepest; or Ennerdale, one of the least developed lakes and the only one with no road round it.

I walked to Ennerdale the day after I had slogged over the Buttermere Fells; a gentle, balmy day of complete peace and almost total solitude, as I recorded in my notebook: 'Warm, sunny day, with a wind from the sea. My walk along the edge of Ennerdale is like a stroll by the Med — soft lapping of waves, rich cover of plants, brown fritillaries fluttering, light, sun and sparkling water. On my left, the Buttermere Fells of yesterday. Ahead, Great Gable. On my right, the gaunt wild north face of Pillar, and the 600-foot (188-metre) vertical cliff of Pillar Rock — the Cumbrian Eiger, the tallest vertical crag in England.

'Over a stone bridge and across a wide greensward to the southern side of the lake. See a pied wagtail on a nest deep inside a chink in a dry stone wall. Almost tread on a male wheatear in the hummocky grass. Why did it wait so long before flying off? A hole in the stones revealed no nest — a cobweb across the entrance precluded that.

'The river is dead — no reeds, no fish, no birds. This is because the water, fed straight from the hard rock of Great Gable, is so pure that it contains insufficient nutrients to sustain animal life. The conifer forest is dead, too — too dark for anything much to grow under the dense cover of the closely compact trees, except where they have cut some of the trees down and suddenly let in the light. Round the stump of one felled conifer I saw an extraordinary explosion of vegetable life — an exquisitely beautiful giant tussock of mosses — emerald, leaf green, black and gold — and foxgloves and rushes and sycamore seedlings and tiny pine saplings all springing in a sudden *feu de joie* out of the very stump itself.

'5pm: sky clouding up and signs of rain.'

In fact, Ennerdale is not entirely lifeless. It boasts a unique freshwater shrimp by the name of *Mysis relicta*, trapped here since the Ice Age but rarely seen since it feeds at night and spends the day deep in the lake. Other glacial relicts in the Cumbrian lakes include white fish and char, a deep-water trout living in Windermere and other deep lakes. A very rare fish called a schelley, like a freshwater herring, swims in shoals in Ullswater, Haweswater, and Red Tarn on Helvellyn; and another rare fish, the vendace, like a schelly with a pointed head, is found in Bassenthwaite Lake and Derwent Water and nowhere else.

From sea-shore to mountain top, Lakeland offers an unparalleled wealth and variety of wildlife: sparrow-hawk, redstart, red squirrel and pine marten in the woods; peregrine, raven and golden eagle over the moors and mountains; alpine plants on the mountain tops; meadow and woodland flowers in the gentler, more luxuriant environment of the dales; terns, toads and sea lavender in the dune landscape at the edge of the Irish Sea. Winter is the best time for birds on the lakes: gulls, ducks, various grebes and divers, and — pride and joy of the Lakeland birds — the wonderful wild whooper swan.

BEFORE YOU GO
Maps: OS Outdoor Leisure Series, map Nos. 4, 5, 6 and 7. **Guide-books:** the National Park Authority produces two guides, *The Lake District* and *The Lake District National Park,* and a *Visit Planner.* For books, maps, exhibitions, films, food and family entertainment call at the Brockhole Visitors' Centre, on the A591 between Ambleside and Windermere, open Apr-Oct, 10 am-5 pm, T: (015394) 46601, F: 45555. Alternatively, the Keswick Centre is open daily all year round, T: (017687) 72645.

Contact any tourist information centre to obtain a copy of the park's quarterly magazine, the *Lake District Guardian,* or of their yearly *Events Guide.*
Web-sites: check the park authority's home page at www.lake-district.gov.uk, or the award-winning Cumbria Tourist Board page at www.cumbria-the-lake-district.co.uk.

GETTING THERE
By car: the M6 passes just east of the park, providing easy access from the Midlands and South. For Kendal and the southern lakes, take exits 36 or 37; for Keswick and the North, take exit 40. From Scotland, the A74 and A7 — from Glasgow and Edinburgh respectively — and join the M6 at Carlisle. Motorists from the east have a slower drive across the Pennines, approaching on the A69 from Newcastle or the A66 from Darlington.
By rail: mainline trains between London (Euston) and Scotland stop at Oxenholme, Penrith and Carlisle. From Oxenholme a branch line connects to Windermere. From Carlisle

change for the splendid West Cumbrian Line to Whitehaven; where trains run to Lancaster with stops including St. Bee's, Ravenglass and Barrow-in-Furness.
By bus: National Express, T: (0990) 808080, operates daily services from London, Birmingham and Manchester to Whitehaven via Windermere, Ambleside and Keswick. Otherwise, Carlisle, Penrith and Kendal are principal stops for long-distance buses.
By bicycle: follow the Sustrans Cycle Route, map No. 7, from Glasgow to Carlisle.

WHERE TO STAY
Bowness, Windermere, Keswick and Ambleside are the principal overnight centres, but all grades of accommodation are available throughout the park. All information centres provide details, and most offer a telephone reservation service.
Outdoor living: dozens of camp-sites of varying standards are listed in an inexpensive leaflet, *Caravan and Tent Guide*, published by the park authority and available from bookshops or visitors' centres. The NT operates 3 tent sites, at Great Langdale, nr Ambleside, open all year round; at Low Wray Farm, nr Ambleside; and Wasdale Head, nr Seascale, open Easter to October.
Youth hostels: there are youth hostels in all the park's towns and principal villages, as well as several that are very remote. For more information about hostelling in this area contact YHA Northern Region, PO Box 11, Matlock, Derbyshire DE4 2XA, T: (01629) 825850.

ACTIVITIES
Walking: there are two long walks within the area. The Cumberland Way is an unstrenuous 80-mile (128-km) low-level walk through the

---

CAUTION TO WALKERS
Unlike some parks, the Lake District does not menace visitors with gaping mine shafts or unexploded bombs, but it does have more fatalities each year than any other national park, a statistic caused partly by the extremely variable weather. Before heading for the hills, check the weather forecast, T: (0891) 232789 (Cumbria & Lake District), or www.meto.govt.uk, then set out prepared for the worst - and it probably won't happen.
Enjoy the Fells in Safety, a leaflet published by the park service, gives basic safety advice. Also worth considering are some of the park's courses, which provide instructions in navigation techniques. Details in the *Lake District Guardian*.

Lake District from the Irish Sea to Appleby. OS Landranger Series, map Nos. 89, 90, 91, 96. See *The Cumberland Way* by Paul Hannon (Hillside Publications). The Cumbria Way is a 70-mile (112-km) low-level walk running south to north through splendid scenery in the national park from Ulverston to Caldbeck or Carlisle via Coniston Water, Borrowdale, Derwentwater and High Pike. OS Landranger Series, map Nos. 85, 90, 97. See *The Cumbria Way* by John Trevelyan (Dalesman 1981). For more routes see also the inexpensive *Best Walks in the Lake District* (Bartholomew) or *Best Walks in the Lake District* (Constable). THE COAST TO COAST WALK (see p89) starts in Lakeland at St Bee's Head.
Cycling: the National Cycle Network Sea to Sea route from Whitehaven or Workington to Sunderland or Newcastle (Sustrans, map No. C2C) traverses the Lake District before climbing into the Pennines. It runs roughly parallel to THE COAST TO COAST WALK (see p89).
Riding: especially on the lower fells, pony trekking is very popular; the solitude and excitement of the high country is also accessible to experienced riders. For enquiries about bridle-ways and riding conditions in the Lakes,

contact Mrs T. P. Fell, Cumbria Bridleways Society, White Gate, Backbarrow, Ulverston LA12 8PA, T: (015395) 31459.
Climbing: there are many areas which are able to provide suitable rock faces, although Wasdale, Langdale and Borrowdale are the most popular. For advice about routes and local clubs contact George Fisher, Borrowdale Road, Keswick, T: (017687) 72178, or The Climber's Shop, Compston Road, Ambleside, T: (015394) 32297.

FURTHER INFORMATION
There are Cumbria Tourist Board information centres in Ambleside, Cockermouth, Kendal, Keswick, Penrith, Ravenglass, Whitehaven and Windermere. The Cumbria Tourist Board's main office can be found at Ashleigh, Windermere, Cumbria LA23 2AQ, T: (01539) 444444. For information about National Trust land in the Lake District, contact the National Trust, North West Region, The Hollens, Grasmere, Ambleside, Cumbria LA22 9QZ, T: (015394) 35599, F: 35353, website: www.nationaltrust.org.uk.

The three peaks rising above Wasdale Head at the north end of Wastwater in the Lake District are (from left to right) Yew Barrow, Great Gable and Lingmell

THE NORTH-WEST COAST

Between the Solway Firth, which separates the north English coast from the Scottish coast, and the River Dee, which separates it from the Welsh coast, stretches a shoreline of swirling mud and sand. Amid the great tidal flats and shifting dunes lie the popular resorts of Blackpool and Morecambe, old industrial centres such as Workington and Whitehaven, sprawling ports and docklands such as Liverpool, and the nuclear power station at Sellafield.

Not promising stuff for the wild traveller, you might think; an endless string of coloured light bulbs, belching steam, atomic leaks and derelict jetties. Not so, however. Some of the most important wildlife habitats in northwest England lie along this coast, as well as some of the finest wild seascapes. The Lake District coast of Cumbria between St Bee's Head and Haverigg can be as fine as anywhere, and the enormous estuarine mud-flats and salt marshes of Morecambe Bay and the Rivers Wyre and Ribble in Lancashire and Dee in Cheshire provide internationally important feeding grounds for huge flocks of wildfowl and waders. The most important sites on this coastline are given here in south to north order.

sanctuaries for thousands of waders and sea-birds such as oystercatcher, ringed plover, grey plover, knot, sanderling, purple sandpiper, dunlin and turnstone.

Autumn and spring bring vast numbers of migrants; the Hilbre Bird Observatory, which rings over 1,000 birds annually, has recorded more than 200 species. Hilbre is frequently visited by grey seals and, at low tide, by foxes. **Getting there:** at low tide, the islands are a short walk across rocks and sand from West Kirby. To be safe, set out at least 3½ hours before high tide, when they get cut off, and follow the route in the official leaflet. **Access:** permit only from Wirral Country Park, T: (0151) 648 4371. **Further information:** leaflet from Wirral Borough Council, T: (0151) 647 7000.

Gayton Sands

RSPB Reserve

The tide has long since ceased to wash against the red stone sea wall at Gayton Sands on the Cheshire side of the Dee Estuary. A vast expanse of estuarine plants — sea club rush, common reed, sea milkwort and sea arrow-grass — seems to stretch unbroken to the Welsh shore.

This ocean of vegetation, together with the mud-flats beyond, is one of Britain's richest feeding grounds for wintering waterfowl. Pintail and shelduck, along with oystercatcher, grey plover, knot, bar-tailed godwit, redshank and dunlin are among the many species to be observed here.

The outsider is advised to wait for storms or spring tides when

these birds are driven close to shore. The salt marsh is deeply scored with muddy tidal creeks, making the going difficult and at times dangerous. **Getting there:** turn off A540 on to B5135 (Boathouse Lane) to park gate. Turn right at Boathouse Restaurant for reserve car park. **Further information:** RSPB Warden Colin Wells, T: (0151) 336 7681.

Hilbre

Wirral Borough Council Bird Sanctuary

Like most islands once favoured by medieval monks, Hilbre and its two companions in the Dee Estuary, Little Hilbre and Little Eye, are now

Ainsdale Sand Dunes

EN NNR

The coastal dunes of Ainsdale appeared over three or four centuries, and could easily disappear at the same rate; efforts are continually being made to preserve this volatile environment. Particularly vulnerable to change are the 'slacks', the damp depressions between dunes that harbour a number of important plant and animal species, among them the rare natterjack toad.

The dunes themselves are loosely anchored with marram grass and a variety of other plants including common stork's bill, lesser hawkbit, biting stonecrop, sand sedge and rest-harrow; rarities include dune and pendulous

helleborine.
The pine woods were planted in the 1920s to stop sand blowing on to the nearby railway. Natural or not, they are a valuable habitat for the embattled red squirrel. **Getting there:** from A565 2 miles (3 km) north of Formby, take the coastal road to Ainsdale-on- Sea. Reserve is to the left beyond railway line. **Access:** restricted to official footpaths. **Further information:** leaflet from EN North West Team, T: (01942) 820342, F: 820364.

Ribble Marshes

EN NNR

Like so many areas beloved of sea-birds, the salt marshes and mud-flats that flank the mouth of the River Ribble are singularly unfriendly to man. Greenmarsh, a rough plain of salt-marsh grass scored by deep muddy gutters, gives way to featureless mud-flats and, imperceptibly, to the sea.
This is the wintering ground for 15 to 20,000 wigeon and pink-footed goose, pintail and teal. Waders arrive in even greater numbers during the autumn migration: 50 to 80,000 knot, dunlin, bar-tailed godwit, oystercatcher and redshank, many of which remain for the winter. **Getting there:** from coastal road (Marine Drive) off A565 north of Southport, or footpath along sea wall from Crossens pumping station near Banks. **Access:** free to all areas except marked sanctuary zone. Stay off mud and out of gutters unless you are a wader. Beware of high tides. **Further information:** leaflet from EN, T: (01942) 820342.

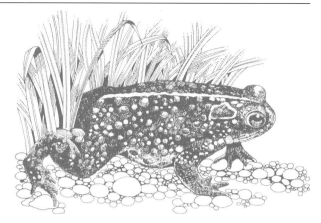

The natterjack toad, Britain's most endangered amphibian, still thrives in the Ravenglass Dunes on the Cumbrian coast

Morecambe Bay

Includes RSPB Reserve

Anyone travelling from Lancaster to the Lake District before the coming of the railway would have set off at low tide, on foot or by stage-coach, across the sands at Hest Bank. The turnpike, though safer, added several miles to the trip.
Today this wide and treacherous highway is the undisputed domain of Morecambe Bay's most numerous pedestrian, the wader; indeed, these 120 square miles (310 sq km) of tidal mud and sand form the largest and most important area for winter waders in Britain. Huge flocks of bar-tailed godwit, knot, oystercatcher, turnstone, dunlin, redshank and curlew feed on the living sands, roosting at high tide on the coastal salt marshes where greylag geese and wigeon graze.
These marshes, furrowed by muddy channels, are the breeding grounds for meadow pipit, skylark, wheatear, lapwing, oystercatcher and redshank. Even non bird-watchers, to whom a wader is no more than a long boot, can marvel at the way a few dozen strides from the illuminations and performing dolphins of Morecambe Marineland bring one to a wilderness of sand and water. **Getting there:** accessible from many points on Lancashire and Cumbria coast. **Access:** do not venture across the sands unguided. 'Those who do, don't come back,' says the official sand pilot and Queen's guide; Cedric Robinson. He conducts fortnightly weekend excursions from Arnside, May-Sept, T: (015395) 32165. **Further information:** Lancaster Tourist Information Centre, T: (01524) 32878.

Leighton Moss

RSPB Reserve

A potent combination of shallow meres, reed beds, marsh and woodland brings together a veritable *Who's Who* of British wildlife in the limited confines of Leighton Moss, near Morecambe Bay. Chief among the celebrities are the dozen or so pairs of breeding bittern, the bearded tit, the water rail, garganey and gadwall. Pochard, teal, shoveler and a large community of mallard also nest here.

In winter, the reserve is a haven for finches, starlings and huge flocks of wildfowl, while migrants may include osprey, goshawk, merlin and harrier, black tern, whimbrel, bar-tailed godwit and ruff. Both red and roe deer may be found here and otters thrive in eel-rich waters. The wide variety of plant life harbours 24 species of butterfly and more than 300 types of moth. **Getting there:** from A6 via Yealand Redmayne. The reserve is just east of Silverdale. **Access:** open daily 9 am-9 pm (or dusk) all year. Small charge for non-members. **Activities:** car-park, visitor centre (open daily 10 am-5 pm all year), 8 bird hides. Public bird hide on causeway off Yealand Redmayne-Silverdale road always open. **Further information:** leaflet from RSPB, or contact the Warden, J. Wilson, Myers Farm, Silverdale, Carnforth LA5 OSW. For information about the full range of activities contact the reserve shop, T: (01524) 701601.

Gait Barrows

EN NNR

One of the finest areas of limestone pavement in Britain has been preserved within Gait Barrows. The flat, unbroken sheet of stone that covered the ground after the last Ice Age is now fissured, fragmented and grooved. This is the work of water, not man, but the unscientific eye might be excused for seeing here, and in many other parts of the Yorkshire Dales and the North

Pennines, the shattered city pavement of some long-destroyed civilization (see also ASBY SCAR, p77).

Where there is enough soil in the fissures (or 'grykes') between the limestone slabs ('clints'), a wealth of plant life has appeared. Stunted trees, mainly ash, yew and hazel, find just enough root space to survive, but it is the flowers, ferns and small woodland plants that truly flourish in these grykes: lily of the valley, herb Robert, biting stonecrop, tutsan, shield fern and the unusual angular Solomon's seal and rigid buckler fern. **Getting there:** via unclassified road between Beetham on A6 and Silverdale. **Access:** permit only off the 2 rights of way. Reserve closed, except for rights of way, 8 days each winter for shooting. **Further information:** leaflet from English Nature, Pier House, Wallgate, Wigan, Lancashire WN3 4AL, T: (01942) 820342, or Warden, Rob Petley-Jones, 3 Challan Hole Mews, Silverdale, Lancashire LA5 0UH, T: (01524) 702181.

Roundsea Wood and Mosses

EN NNR

The reserve consists of two distinct habitats, the wood and the mosses. Roundsea Wood is situated in the main area, surrounded on three sides by a final meander of the River Leven as it carries the waters of Lake Windermere into Morecambe Bay.

The wood encompasses two low ridges, each with its own distinct ecosystem. The slate-based west ridge encourages plants that thrive on acidic soil: rowan, hazel and birch among

sessile oaks, with hair grass and bracken on the forest floor. The limestone east ridge supports ash and oak, wild cherry, lime and yew, above a carpet of lime-loving flowering plants: lily of the valley, early purple orchid, bird's-nest orchid, giant bell-flower, columbine and false brome.

To the east of the reserve are the mosses; some partly drained by peat cutting and now overgrown with birch, rowan and Scots pine, others still undisturbed beneath primeval carpets of sphagnum moss. The mosses are particularly favourable habitats for moths and butterflies, including the large heath butterfly and clouded ermine moth.

Ellerside Moss, though part of the same reserve, is nearly a mile south-east of the Roundsea Wood area. **Getting there:** take B5278 south from A590 through Haverthwaite village and turn right immediately after bridge over River Leven. **Access:** one right of way; for other paths a permit is required. Apply to EN. Reserve is closed a few days each year during deer-hunting season. **Further information:** leaflet from EN, or apply to the Warden, Peter Singleton, 7 The Croft, Flookburgh, Grange-over-Sands, Cumbria LA11 7NF, T: (015395) 31604.

Walney Island

North Walney EN NNR and South Walney Cumbria Wildlife Trust Nature Reserve

Although Barrow-in-Furness has long since spilled across the Walney Channel to colonize the centre of Walney Island, the

The Pennine Way and a dry-stone wall follow the contours of the moorland below Pen-y-ghent, a grand natural belvedere for the Yorkshire Dales

extreme ends of this sandy strip 10 miles (16 km) long by 1 mile (1.6 km) wide have so far been left to nature. The dune slacks of North Walney are home to the natterjack toad, one of Britain's rarest amphibians.

But the noise and excitement is all in the south, where vast numbers of herring gull and lesser black-backed gull wheel and squabble above their nesting sites on the dunes. An estimated 40,000 pairs breed in South Walney. Rich pickings from the corporation dump supplement the food they glean from the sea and beaches.

Other birds managing to breed alongside the overbearing gulls include

lapwing, mallard, shelduck, oystercatcher, common tern, little tern and the west coast's southernmost colony of eider. In autumn and winter Walney becomes home to dunlin and oystercatcher, turnstone, knot, teal and wigeon.

In the varied terrain of North Walney, over 300 species of plant have been recorded, ranging from sundew and marsh cinquefoil in the marshy heath to lady's bedstraw, wild pansy and the 'Walney geranium' in the dunes. In the southern reserve henbane, viper's bugloss, mullein and yellow horned poppy are a particular attraction to moths and butterflies.

Getting there: cross the bridge from Barrow-in-Furness, turn left on the Promenade for South Walney, right for North Walney. **Where to stay:** cottage for rent on South Walney

Reserve, sleeping up to 8 people. Contact Warden. **Access:** North Walney: unrestricted access all year; free. South Walney: open all year 10 am-4 pm (5 pm Apr-Sept) except Mon (excluding Bank Holidays); small admission charge. **Activities:** North Walney: no official guided trail. South Walney: nature trails and 5 bird hides; leaflet with details on entry to reserve. **Further information:** *For North Walney:* the Warden, North Walney EN NNR, Honeysuckle Cottage, 4 Long Row, Marshside, Turby-in-Furness, Cumbria LA17 7UP, T: (01229) 889192. *For South Walney:* the Warden, 1 Coastguard Cottages, South Walney Nature Reserve, Barrow-in-Furness, Cumbria LA14 3YQ, T: (01229) 471066.

Ravenglass Dunes

*Cumbria County Council
Nature Reserve*

The full title of this reserve —
Ravenglass Dunes and Gullery
— is now a sad irony, for
although the dunes are still a
distinguishing feature, the
gullery is not. In 1985 the birds
decided that the level of
radioactive pollution from
nearby Sellafield had reached
unacceptable levels, and the
huge colony of black-headed
gull and the four species of
breeding tern — Sandwich,
common, arctic and little — all
departed.

This is not to say that Drigg
Dunes are dead, only much
quieter than before. Plover,
oystercatcher, shelduck, red-
breasted merganser, wheatear
and skylark still nest here.
Growing on the dunes
themselves are bloody crane's-
bill, carline thistle and field
gentian, while the ponds and
slacks harbour all six British
amphibians.
Getting there: by lane from the
village of Drigg, 1½ m (2 km)
south-east of Seascale on
B5344. Drigg is a railway
station on the West Cumbrian
Line. **Access:** unrestricted in
and around the reserve. Local
libraries hold definitive maps of
public footpaths. **Further
information:** from English
Nature, Pier House, Wallgate,
Wigan, Lancashire, T: (01942)
820342, F: 820364.

The Pennine Way

The north of England is upland
England. From Derbyshire to
the Scottish border the

Pennines run through the
middle of the North Country
like a 150-mile (240-km) spine.
Here can be found some of the
highest, wildest and most
ruggedly beautiful landscape in
England.

A lone, gruelling but
rewarding footpath called the
Pennine Way traverses almost
the entire length of the chain.
Although at least one guide has
been written describing the
route from north to south, for
most walkers the Pennine Way
begins at Edale on the high
moors of the Peak District and
ends at Kirk Yetholm, just over
the Scottish border. This allows
you to walk with the sun and
prevailing wind at your back
for most of the way: 250 miles
(400 km) as the boot plods.

It must be assumed that
anyone walking the entire
Pennine Way will be reasonably
fit and properly equipped;
prepared, that is, for long hauls
in cold, uncomfortable weather
over steep and rough terrain.
Someone in the party must also
be a reliable navigator, able to
take compass bearings and fold
maps in driving rain.

The toughest stretch comes
near the start, over the squelchy
north Peak moors between
Kinder and Stanledge; it is not
to be taken lightly by beginners.
By the time you reach the 750-
foot (229-metre) BBC
transmitting tower at Holme
Moss near Black Hill, which
sticks out like a whaler's
harpoon through a Leviathan's
head, the least inspiring parts
of the walk are over. Ahead lie
the dryer, brighter beauties of
the Dales, the rugged eminence
of Hadrian's Wall and the long
trek over the Cheviots into
Scotland.
Before you go: OS Landranger
Series, map Nos. 3, 74, 80, 86,
91, 98, 109, 110. These 8 maps
are indispensable, and will help
you find *a* Pennine Way, but
not necessarily *the* Pennine

Way, as the precise route in
some areas is nearly impossible
to read, lost in a tangle of
footpaths, contour lines and
other topographical symbols.
The larger-scale OS Leisure
Series shows the route more
clearly, but covers only a
fraction of its distance. From
south to north the relevant
sheets are: No. 1, The Dark
Peak Area; No. 21, South
Pennines (highly
recommended); and Nos. 2 and
30 for the Yorkshire Dales.
Even the best maps cannot give
the sort of detail you may need
along the way, so a guide-book
would be useful. The National
Trail Guides, *Pennine Way
South* and *Pennine Way North*,
both by Tony Hopkins (Aurum
Press, co-published with
Ordnance Survey and the
Countryside Commission),
contain blow-by-blow
descriptions of the route,
divided into one-day sections
and accompanied by extracts
from the relevant OS 1:25,000
maps. The Pennine Way
Association web-site is at
www.pennineway.demon.co.uk.
Getting there: Not everyone
wishes to walk the entire
distance. A number of towns
and villages on or near the
route allow one to join the
Pennine Way or escape from it
at convenient points:

Edale, Derbyshire: trains from
Manchester and Sheffield.

Marsden, West Yorkshire:
A62; buses from Huddersfield
and Manchester; trains from
Leeds.

Todmorden, West Yorkshire:
A646; buses from Burnley and
Halifax; trains from
Manchester.

Hebden Bridge, West
Yorkshire: A646; buses from
Burnley and Halifax; trains
from Leeds or Bradford.

Cowling, North Yorkshire:
A6068; buses from Keighley
and Burnley.

Thornton, North Yorkshire:

A56; buses from Burnley and Keighley.

Gargrave, West Yorkshire: A65; buses from Skipton and Settle; trains from Leeds.

Malham, North Yorkshire: buses from Skipton and Settle.

Horton in Ribblesdale, North Yorkshire: B6479; buses from Settle.

Hawes, North Yorkshire: A684; buses from Kendal and Leyburn.

Middleton in Teesdale, Durham: B6277; buses from Barnard Castle.

Alston, Cumbria: A686/689; buses from Penrith and Carlisle.

Haltwhistle, Northumberland: A69; buses and trains from Carlisle and Newcastle.

Bellingham, Northumberland: B6320; buses from Hexham.

Byrness, Northumberland: A68; buses from Newcastle and Edinburgh.

Kirk Yetholm, Borders: B6401; buses from Kelso.

Where to stay: accommodation is not a problem along the route, but in peak periods it pays to make reservations ahead, especially in the national parks. The *Pennine Way Accommodation and Camping Guide* is published by the Pennine Way Council and available from youth hostels and bookshops along the route, or from John Needham, 23 Woodland Crescent, Hilton Park, Prestwick, Manchester M25 8WQ. The Ramblers' Association annual guide also gives details of many useful bed and breakfast establishments. *Youth hostels:* there are 19 along the way, allowing you to walk the route at low cost and in short stages, except for the last — 27 miles (43 km) over the Cheviots from Byrness to Kirk Yetholm. Planning a hostelling holiday along the Pennine Way is simplified with the Pennine Way Central Booking Service's free information pack; send a

large self-addressed envelope to YHA Northern Region, PO Box 11, Matlock, Derbyshire DE4 2XA, T: (01629) 825850. *Camping*: carrying a tent allows greater freedom in route planning; the price is extra weight and discomfort. Many camp-sites are along the way, and a number of youth hostels allow members with tents to use their facilities at half price.

The Coast to Coast Walk

This long-distance path, running right across the north of England from St Bee's Head to Robin Hood's Bay, was pioneered by the veteran walker Alfred Wainwright. It is 190 miles (304 km) long and crosses

three national parks: the Lake District, Yorkshire Dales and North York Moors. The walk has a truly satisfying beginning and end, in whichever direction you choose to walk.

This is not an 'official' Countryside Commission route, marked by expensive signposts. In places the way will be difficult to follow or even obstructed; it is, in fact, more an idea for a route than a path to be followed literally, step by step.

Before you go: Paul Hannon gives a description of the route in his *Coast to Coast Walk* (Hillside Publications). The relevant maps are the OS Coast to Coast, map Nos. 33 and 34.

Where to stay: beds are scarce along some parts of the route, so get information in advance from the YHA (see THE PENNINE WAY) or other relevant National park information centres (see separate entries).

CAUTION TO WALKERS

The Pennines are among the wettest and windiest parts of Britain. High and treeless, they can subject a walker to what may seem like winter conditions in mid-July. The problem is compounded by tussock grass and peat bog underfoot, a tiring terrain when you are battling with the elements.

For this reason, make yourself familiar with escape routes to towns or sheltered valleys before setting out along a difficult stage. You gain nothing by sticking to the high path in bad conditions and you can often find a pleasant alternative at a lower level. The path has a number of official alternative routes, which are well worth considering if the weather is uncertain.

Parts of the way that may need particular attention in bad weather are, from south to north:

Kinder Scout, Derbyshire: high, boggy land criss-crossed with confusing gullies, or 'groughs'. Consider official alternative.

Bleaklow, Derbyshire: easy to stray off course.

Black Hill, Derbyshire: avoid high route with its boggy terrain.

Birkdale to *High Cup Nick*, Durham: route finding can be confusing for these 4 miles (7 km).

Cross Fell, Cumbria: flat, featureless summit. Prepare to use compass.

Cheviots, Northumberland: long rugged stage. Plan escape routes in advance.

CHAPTER 4

North-East England

I first came to the north-east by sea, putting out of Grimsby through the fierce tide race of the Humber estuary for the long haul to the Pentland Firth and the waters of the north Atlantic. The first patch of *terra firma* I set foot on was the wild and wind-blown sand and pebble spit of Spurn Head. It was not a tremendously satisfactory landfall. The Spurn peninsula is a nature reserve run by the Yorkshire Wildlife Trust, an organization as resolute and worthy as its county-cricket counterpart. Then as now you needed a permit to visit the seaward tip of the reserve. I had barely moved the length of a fast bowler's run-up over the low and stony ground when a kind of binoculared nature policeman sprang up from behind a buckthorn thicket.

What was I doing here? he asked. Had I made prior arrangements? Where were my credentials? Sadly, reprehensibly, I had none. In vain I protested my *bona fide* interest in the wildlife and good works of the reserve. Did I realise, the official enquired, that a clumsy size-11 Wellington boot like mine could crush a whole clutch of eggs in a shallow tern scrape in the pebbles? The terns that screamed about my head joined in the remonstrations. Like an illegal immigrant I was escorted back to the edge of the sea. Next time make prior arrangements, I was told. Permit only means permit only.

From the huge chalk arrowhead promontory of Flamborough Head to

The vast stretches of sand at Bamburgh are typical of a shoreline that varies little along many miles of Northumbrian coast, one of the longest dune systems in England

Redcar the boat butted the sea beneath some of the highest cliffs in England. For most of their length these soaring battlements form the eastern boundary of the North York Moors National Park, whose rolling hills and heather-covered plateaux stretch mile after mile westward into the northern English interior. Here and there, in a chink in these coastal ramparts, a fishing village has gained a footing, sometimes a precarious one. At the old smuggling haunt of Robin Hood's Bay the cliffs were being eaten away so fast you could almost see them eroding. At some of the cliff-top dwellings you could absent-mindedly put the cat out by the kitchen door and it would free fall to a four-point landing on the rocks several hundred feet below. At one house I saw the morning milk bottle on the doorstep, but the step itself hung over an airy void, with nothing beneath it but the beach far below. A great sea wall now protects Robin Hood's Bay from further disintegration, but it is still a spectacularly atmospheric place.

Far to the north, beyond the sprawling industrial seascape of Teesmouth and Tyneside, the coast undergoes a complete change. Between Amble and Berwick in Northumberland stretches one of the longest dune systems in Britain. On a great knoll of volcanic rock at the heart of this linear Sahara lies the soaring edifice of the great restored medieval castle of Bamburgh.

It was here that I most recently set foot on Northumberland. It was mid-summer night. Above the crescent of the sea horizon a false sunset glowed a dull red in the north-east. As black clouds gathered across the darkening sky I collected driftwood from the tide wrack and with two friends made a great camp-fire in a sheltered hollow in the sand dunes.

In every lover of wild places there beats the restless and anarchic heart of a nomad. In every wild traveller, as in every prisoner, there lies the urge to break out of the confining bonds, actual or metaphorical, of four walls. In those flickering, firelit dunes there were no walls, no roof, no burden of possessions, no agents of bureaucracy yelping like a guard dog at one's heel: only the roar of the distant surf, the occasional splinter of raindrops in the flames, the fitful wind stirring the shadows on the sand, and a deeply satisfying, if briefly won, sense of fellowship and freedom. 'Happy summer solstice!' we mumbled as we raised a toast (in Bulgarian red) at midnight.

There is a village at Bamburgh, a golf course, a fishing port and a small holiday resort called Seahouses just down the road. It is therefore not wild in the sense of being far from the haunts of man. But on the brink of that wildest of wild places, the sea, this coast can in certain moods or weather assume the wilder aspect of some far-flung *terra incognita*. Like Lindisfarne bay in midwinter, with a knifing wind and lowering sky, when wildfowl and waders in their thousands settle over the vast mud-flats to feed at low tide, and there is not a soul in his senses to be seen. Or like the great desert beach of Goswick Sands under an unclouded late-June sun. Look north from the dunes of the Snook and the world seems reduced, like some ultimate expression of abstract art, to its simplest residual parts: cobalt blue sky, ochre yellow sand, and nothing else at all.

Or like the Farne Islands on a morning of mist and rain. Only two miles or so separate these bird rocks from the fish and chips and naughty plastic souvenirs of Seahouses, but those two miles are like a time warp in deep space; after a quarter of an hour at sea you reach an outpost of the primordial era. On the rocky skyline of these cracked dolerite crags, cormorants stand motionless, with wings outstretched like ptero-dactyls. Creatures with rudimentary an-imal shapes — inflated bags fitted with eyes and fins — bask on the jagged rocks or float vertically with only their soft humanoid eyes peering above the waves.

In higgledy-piggledy chaos, living embodiments of Darwinism crowd to-gether in messy, intimate and unembar-rassed squalor in the fantastic bird ten-ements of Scale Island. A row of sulking guillemots sit wing to wing on a narrow rock ledge with their backs to the world: from the throat of one of them pro-trudes the rear end of a wriggling sprat. A green shag rising from its mountain-ous nest of seaweed and ordure defe-cates spectacularly over a black-headed gull standing four feet behind it. For a moment the nonplussed gull masquer-ades as an un-black-headed gull and sloshes through the midden with faint squawks of protest. Young birds take food by burrowing their heads deep down their parents' throats. Puffins, ful-mars, kittiwakes, shags and gulls alight and take off, swoop and dive, preen and poke about, sleep, stand and stalk about in a dizzying confusion of random movement. Over the yellow-lichened, white guano-caked rocks a handful of human visitors, reduced by the elemen-tal environment to basic primate status, shuffle gingerly over the slippery fis-sured rocks.

Until recently I had never ventured away from the coast into the Northum-brian interior, one of the least populat-ed areas in England. The Cheviot Hills form the northern mass of the Northumberland National Park and Hadrian's Wall its southern perimeter. A footpath undulates along the top of

Ralph's Cross, emblem of the North York Moors National Park, is also known as Young Ralph to distinguish it from its even more ancient neighbour (see p96)

the wall, emerging in a westerly direc-tion from a wood of oaks.

From this wood I saw a lone figure, bowed under a heavy backpack, strid-ing towards me amid the screeching of hundreds of roosting starlings. He was a Yorkshireman with a bushy Edwardian moustache and legs knotted from miles of thumping turf and rocky tracks.

'Where the bloody hell's this?' he asked me in his Yorkshire voice as he drew near.

I told him: 'Vercovicium Fort on the Roman Wall.'

'Bloody hell, is it?' he replied, 'I'm supposed to be on t' Pennine Way. I don't suppose there's anywhere round here I can get a cup of tea, is there?' There wasn't, and he wearily turned round with a sad 'ta ra' and thumped back the way he had come, vanishing like some lost legionary amongst the trees and the screeching birds, his knot-ty legs bearing him over the Cheviots towards the heather and haggis at jour-ney's end beyond the Scottish border.

93

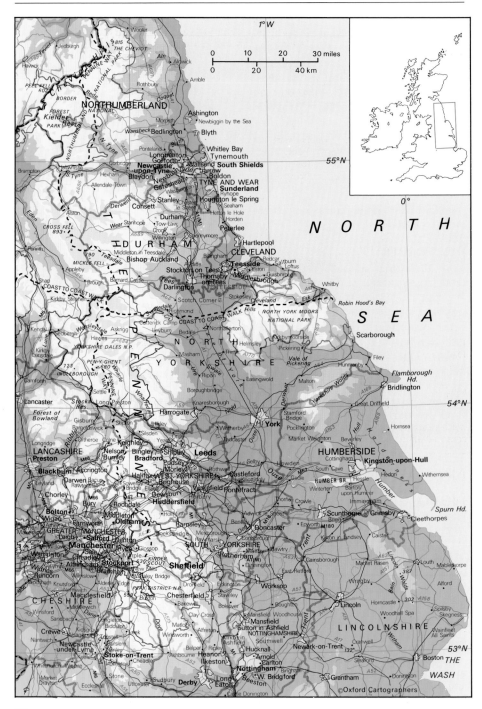

GETTING THERE

By air: Newcastle Airport,T: (0191) 586 0966, provides the nearest access to Northumberland National Park; Teeside Airport, near Darlington, serves Durham and North Yorkshire. There are regular flights from Amsterdam and Scandinavia, as well as from many points within the British Isles.
By sea: Scandinavian Seaways, T: (0990) 333000, operates services to Newcastle-upon-Tyne from Amsterdam, Gothenburg and Kristiansand (Norway) and from Hamburg during the summer. Crossings between Zeebrugge and Rotterdam and Hull are operated by P&O North Sea Ferries. Contact Hull Docks Tourist Information Centre, T: (01482) 702118.
By rail: high speed services operate between London and Edinburgh, stopping at York, Darlington and Newcastle-upon-Tyne. For York, connect via Birmingham from the south-west. The trans-Pennine Tyne Valley line links Newcastle with Carlisle and the north-west. For further details, contact National Rail Enquiries, T: (0345) 484950.
By bus: Newcastle-upon-Tyne, Darlington, York and Hull are principal stops on the National Express coach network, T: (0191) 232 3300.
By bicycle: the Sea to Sea route (Sustrans map No. 7) provides access from the west, running between the Lake District and Newcastle-upon-Tyne; the White Rose Cycle Route (Sustrans map No. 65) runs between Hull and Middlesborough, providing access from the south.

WHERE TO STAY

Visitors will have little problem finding accommodation in and around the national parks. For other areas, the Northumbrian Tourist Board's *Official Holiday Guide* and the Yorkshire Tourist Board's *Holiday Guide* provide useful lists of places to stay, from hotels to camp-sites. These publications also include full lists of tourist information centres.

For information about youth hostels, contact YHA Northern Region, PO Box 11, Matlock, Derbyshire DE4 2XA, T: (01629) 825850.

ACTIVITIES

Walking: the north-east offers superb and often remote expanses of moorland and hills. See the separate national park entries for further information, or contact the Ramblers' Association, T: (0171) 339 8500, for the addresses of their area offices.
Other activities: the English Sports Council provide regional directories giving details of local organizations. Contact the English Sports Council North, Aykley Heads, Durham DH1 5UU, T: (0191) 384 9595, or the English Sports Council Yorkshire, Coronet House, Queen Street, Leeds LS1 4PW, T: (0113) 273 6443.

FURTHER INFORMATION

For Cleveland, Durham, Northumberland and Tyne and Wear, contact the Northumbria Tourist Board, Aykley Heads, Durham DH1 5UX, T: (0191) 375 3000, F: 386 0899 and www.ntb.org.uk. The remainder of the area is covered by the Yorkshire Tourist Board, 312 Tadcaster Road, York YO24 1GS, T: (01904) 707961, F: 701414, web-site: www.ytb.org.uk.

North York Moors National Park

Note: North *York*, never North Yorkshire, Moors

Upland moors, hills, dales, woodland and North Sea cliff coast covering 554 square miles (1,436 sq km) of north-east Yorkshire

The North York Moors are one of the classic paradoxes of the wild countryside in Britain today. Their heather-clad plateaux and smoothly contoured hills and dales are loved by many, and fiercely defended by conservationists; yet this landscape is only semi-natural, essentially man-made.

Bronze-age settlers hacked down the prehistoric forest of oak, elm, lime and yew that once covered the North York Moors, just as the Brazilian pioneers are laying waste to the Amazonian rain forest today. With the tree cover gone, the heather that now covers 35 per cent of the park took over. This is the largest and finest stretch of heather moor in England and much loved as such by the eight million visitors who come each year.

Few national parks are more easily defined by their physical boundaries than this one, a compact upland which stands on its own above the surrounding lowlands and the sea: its eastern and north-eastern boundaries are marked by 26 miles (42 kilometres) of truly magnificent North Sea coastline between Saltburn-by-the-Sea and Scalby Ness, Scarborough. The wild and rolling heather-clad Cleveland Hills, reaching 1,489 feet (454 metres) above sea level at Botton Head, form the natural ramparts of the northern boundary, looking across to the distant Cheviots. The steep scarp of the Hambleton Hills, rising up to 1,000 feet (305 metres), presents a distinctive physical frontier in the west. Along the southern boundary, the narrow limestone belt of the flat-topped Tabular Hills rises gently from the Vale of Pickering, then drops away abruptly in a steep north-facing escarpment that yields impressive 'sudden views' over the moors and dales of the park interior.

It is from the high ground of this grand interior, along the east-west watershed of the moors, that the main rivers drain. To the north a few short streams plunge down small, deep dales to the River Esk; to the south a series of longer tributaries drain off the central moors along the larger valleys of Bilsdale, Bransdale, Farndale, Rosedale and Newtondale, cutting deep narrow valleys through the limestone scarp of the Tabular Hills before flowing into the river system of the Derwent. It is a country of great scenic variety: wild moors and moorland bogs, pastoral dales, native woods, conifer forests, clear-flowing rivers and a coastline of soaring cliffs fronting the broad and restless waters of the North Sea.

The main attraction of the North York Moors is the sheer quantity of open space they provide. You can walk 40 miles (64 kilometres) from one side to the other without obstruction from natural barriers or concentrations of humanity. There are over 1,000 miles (1,600 kilometres) of footpaths and bridle paths in the park, and although 80 per cent of the land is privately owned, access is virtually unlimited provided you follow the public rights of way. You don't have to be a Himalayan expeditionary; the ground is level or at worst gently undulating and the springy turf helps put an extra bounce into every stride. In August and September the heather bursts into bloom, so that the moor walker strides through a purple froth of 3,000 million tiny purple blossoms to each

square mile; that is 120,000 million tiny blossoms for the whole 40-mile crossing.

A wide variety of walks have been evolved, long, short and middling, with wonderful vistas and a lot of sky and space. The official long-distance walk for the North York Moors is the Cleveland Way, which follows a U-shaped route from Helmsley, at the south-west corner of the park, north across the Hambleton Hills, then along the Cleveland Hills to Guisborough and the North Sea coast, where it turns south along the cliffs to Whitby, Scarborough and Filey. A 'link' walk through the Tabular Hills from Scarborough back to Helmsley means that the entire national park can be circumnavigated on foot.

The most popular long-distance walk, now becoming seriously eroded, is the Lyke Wake Walk, a 40-mile (64-kilometre) route across the spine of the Moors between Osmotherley on the western border of the park to Ravenscar on the coast. This walk, which takes its name from the old dialect verse, *Lyke Wake* [corpse watch] *Dirge*, follows the trail of the early settlers who buried their dead on the central moor.

There are a number of other ancient tracks over the moor, humbler affairs known as trods or causeways or panniermen's tracks, which were built in the Middle Ages by the local monasteries to enable pack ponies to carry goods across the moorland. The monasteries were also responsible for setting up stone crosses to guide travellers across the featureless moors. More than 30 still stand; the 7th-century Lilla Cross, near Ellerbeck Bridge on Fylingdales Moor, is probably the oldest Christian monument in northern England, while Ralph Cross, in the heart of the moor, has been adopted as the emblem of the park.

Wildlife is probably not what draws most visitors to the park, although the wide variety of habitats provides a home for a corresponding variety of flora and fauna. The heather and grass moor is varied with bracken, bell heather, crowberry, bilberry and cloudberry on the dry parts, and cranberry, bog myrtle, bog rosemary and other bog plants in the wet parts. This is the haunt of the red grouse — grouse shooting is a major source of livelihood on the moor — of golden plover, curlew and meadow pipit and predatory birds such as the merlin, a tiny falcon the size of a blackbird: the moor is its British stronghold.

The broad-leaved woods contain the greatest range of animal, bird and plant life: fox, badger, rabbit, red deer, roe and fallow, otter and stoat; carpets of bluebells and wood anemones, the archetypal species of the classic English woods. By contrast the limestone country in the south of the park is a botanist's hunting ground, where uncommon plants such as bird's eye primrose, globe-flower, white bog-bean and a variety of orchids make notable finds.

Of the ten nature reserves in the North York Moors, two are national nature reserves (Forge Valley Woods in the extreme south-east corner of the Park and Dunscombe Park, near Helmsley), eight are managed by the Yorkshire Wildlife Trust and can be visited by permit only, while the eleventh, in Farndale, is a nature reserve which protects one of the most spectacular phenomena in the park, an immense colony of wild daffodils. Every spring they spread like a brilliant yellow prairie along the banks of the River Dove and its tributaries.

For many people the sea coast is the North York Moors' greatest glory. The eastern flank of the park is part of a spectacular seaboard of hard jurassic limestone rocks stretching from Flamborough Head to the Tees. In places these cliffs tower 600 feet (180 metres) above the sea; and Boulby Cliff, the second highest sea cliff in England, is 700 feet (210 metres) high. The North Sea continues to chew this coast away at an average rate of three inches a year, even up to three feet a year in some places, and the tidal drill bears the detritus south to the Wash and North Norfolk coast. Fossils abound in these sedimentary rock cliffs, especially ammonites. Living plants and birds are relatively few, though there are always petrels to be seen, swooping and soaring above the fearful void, as well as kittiwakes and gulls.

Access to the edge of the sea is difficult. The roads down to the scattering of picturesque old fishing villages such as Staithes and Robin Hood's Bay are steep, and yet congested in summer. For the wild traveller a better bet is to get to the water's edge down one of the wykes, or wooded cloughs, running down to the sea, such as Hayburn Wyke, a narrow, almost impenetrably wooded valley (and nature reserve) where a fast-flowing beck tumbles down to the sea via a series of pretty waterfalls.

BEFORE YOU GO
Maps: Ordnance Survey Outdoor Leisure Series, map Nos. 26, Western Area and 27, Eastern Area.
Guide-books: much essential information is included in *The North York Moors Visitor*, available for a small charge from information centres or from North York Moors National Park Authority (NPA), The Old Vicarage, Bondgate, Helmsley, York YO62 5BP, T: (01439) 770657. *North Yorks Moors* (AA/OS) provides good maps and popular information. The park authority produces a range of leaflets on accommodation, transport, activities and natural history as well as full publications list.

GETTING THERE
By car: the A1 provides easy access to the park via York on the A64, Sowerby on the A168

or Northallerton on the A684. The A171 Scarborough to Guisborough road skirts the northern and eastern borders

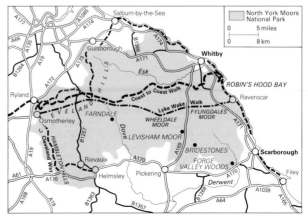

97

The sparkling water of Eller Beck will soon be turned a muddy brown when the stream plunges down to meet Murk Esk

of the park, giving access to the coast. The A170 from Scarborough to Thirsk follows the park's southern border through Pickering and Helmsley.

By rail: Scarborough has rail links with York and Hull. Whitby is the terminus of the scenic Esk Valley railway from Middlesborough, where a rail link connects with the main line at Darlington.

By bus: regular coach services run to Middlesborough, Scarborough and York from many major cities. Moorsbus, the NPA bus service, runs through the summer from major cities in the area and between smaller destinations in and around the park. The NPA produces a leaflet, *Moors Connections*, available from the

above address, or ring the NPA on the above number for details of services.

WHERE TO STAY
Accommodation is available in villages and on farms, mainly near Pickering, Kirkbymoorside and Helmsley in the south and near Whitby in the north-east. The NPA produces an accommodation guide free with the annual Moors newspaper as well as information for the disabled, details of camping barns, youth hostels and accommodation along the Cleveland Way National Trail. Youth hostels in or near the park: Boggle Hole, T: (01947) 880352; Helmsley, T: (01439) 770433; Lockton, T: (01751) 460376; Thixendale, T: (01377) 288238; Scarborough, T: (01723) 361176.

WHERE TO GO
Nature reserves within the park include:

Bridestones: heather moorland with remarkable weathered outcrops of rock; NT. Take minor road north from Thornton Dale, 2 miles (3 km) east of Pickering. Access on foot to Bridestones from Staindale car-park on Dalby Forest Drive, a Forestry Commission toll road.
Farndale: famous for wild daffodils; SSSI managed by national park, 8 miles (13 km) north of Kirkbymoorside.The NPA provides a Moorsbus link to ease congestion caused by volume of traffic.
Forge Valley Woods: semi-natural woodland; EN NNR. Access by road or footpath from West Ayton, 4 miles (6 km) south-west of Scarborough on A170.
Levisham Moor: moorland and wooded valleys managed by national park committee. Access by footpath from Levisham Station on the North York Moors railway or from

A169, 7 miles (11 km) north of Pickering.

ACCESS AND CLOSURES
As in other national parks, most of the North York Moors is privately owned. Visitors may not roam off designated rights of way, except in areas of open access. For guidance refer to the most recent Ordnance Survey maps.

ACTIVITIES
Walking: the park has 925 miles (1,490 km) of public footpath. The Ordnance Survey Outdoor Leisure maps provide the necessary information for experienced walkers; other visitors will appreciate the park service's inexpensive 'Way-Mark Walk' leaflets, which describe around 30 walks of between 2 and 5 miles, and their more detailed guides to long-distance walks including the Cleveland Way and the Link through the Tabular Hills Walk.
Cycling: great opportunities for cycling in the park. The NPA produces a number of guides including *Six Bike Tracks*, which describes routes around Sutton Bank. Part of the National Cycle Network, the White Rose Cycle Route (Sustrans map No. 65), takes in some steep paths in the park.
Other activities: canoeing, gliding, riding, climbing and fishing also available; see *The Visitor* for details.

FURTHER INFORMATION
The park has 2 information centres: The Moors Centre, Danby, Whitby, Yorks. YO21 2NB, T: (01287) 660654, and Sutton Bank National Park Centre, Sutton Bank, Thirsk, Yorks. YO7 2EH, T: (01845) 597426. Yorkshire Tourist Board, 312 Tadcaster Road, York YO24 1GS, T: (01904) 707961, F: 701414, web-site: www.ytb.org.uk.

Spurn Peninsula

Yorkshire Wildlife Trust Reserve

This narrow promontory extends three miles into the mouth of the Humber and encompasses 280 acres (113 ha) of dunes, pebble beach and mud-flats. The first bird observatory on the British mainland was established here in 1946. Today it is one of the best places to see migrants, especially rarities. Large numbers of wildfowl, waders, terns and smaller birds pass through here, and their 'falls' are sometimes prodigious: 6,000 blackbirds in a single day, for instance.
Getting there *By car:* along B1445 to Easington, then minor road to Kilnsea and Spurn. Car-parks by bird observatory and information centre at landward end of peninsula or at the tip. **Access:** unrestricted all year. Use of bird hide for observatory residents. No dogs allowed.
Where to stay: basic accommodation at observatory for around 17 people. Write to Spurn Bird Observatory, The Warren, Spurn National Nature Reserve, Kilnsea, Hull HU12 0UG. **Further information:** send self addressed envelope and £1 to YWT, 10 Toft Green, York YO1 7JT, for information on Spurn and other nature reserves.

Bempton Cliffs

RSPB Reserve

Three miles (5 km) of magnificent chalk cliffs — at 400 ft (122 m) the highest chalk cliffs in Britain — run north-west from Flamborough Head, Humberside. They are the most southerly of the sea-bird cliffs on the east coast of Britain, containing the only nesting colony of gannets on the mainland (2,420 pairs in 1998). In the breeding season the cracks and ledges are packed with nesting birds, including 80,000 pairs of kittiwakes and many thousands of auks and other birds.
As many as 160 bird species have been recorded here, many of them, such as terns, skuas, shearwaters, merlins and bluethroats, on migration.
Getting there *By car:* along cliff road from Bempton village, the B1229 Flamborough-Filey road. **Access:** at all times to cliff-top path, where 4 safe observation barriers give excellent views of sea-bird colonies. Visitors must keep to footpath and observation points, as the cliffs are very high and extremely dangerous.
Further information: leaflet from RSPB Warden (Trevor Charlton), 11 Carlton Avenue, Hornsea, North Humberside HU18 1JT, T: (01262) 851179.

THE LYKE WAKE WALK

The Lyke Wake Walk is one of the most popular long-distance walks on the North York Moors. This is the Lyke Wake Dirge. Repeated *ad infinitum* it grows on you after the first few miles:

'This yah neet, this yah neet,
Ivvery neat an all
Fine an fleet an cannle leet
An' Christ take up thy soul.'

Northumberland National Park

398 square miles (1,030 sq km) of hills and moorland between Hadrian's Wall and the Scottish border

The Northumberland National Park is frontier country. For centuries it was a lawless border land where cattle rustlers, border reivers and moss men, whose deeds are vividly recalled in Scottish Border ballads and the historical romances of Sir Walter Scott, raided and skirmished.

It is still the most sparsely populated part of the most sparsely populated county in England. There are few settlements here, just isolated stone farmhouses in the valleys; there are hardly any roads and industrial centres are far away. When one stands by the Roman Wall and peers northward towards the bare, abandoned hills that recede wave upon wave into the interior, one feels one is staring at a fearful void, 'England's empty quarter', as it has been called, where the only sounds to be heard are the wind in the heath, the curlew's desolate cry and the distant bleat of the white-faced Cheviot sheep.

Most of the park is upland country more than 1,000 feet (305 metres) high, formed by volcanoes and shaped by ice. The sombre, smoothly contoured hills and moors rise steadily towards the rounded boss of the Cheviot, a wide, bare upland heath and grass moor where the wild goats and the blue hares run. At 2,674 feet (815 metres) it is the highest point in the Cheviot Hills which are themselves the most elevated part of the national park. They form the core round which the landscape revolves in concentric circles: farmed land on the lower, softer rocks alternating with ridges and crags of harder rocks such as the Simonside Hills, with the long volcanic escarpment of the Great Whin Sill, where the Romans built their wall, forming a natural barrier at the outer edge to the south.

The park is made up of five main parts. In the north-west are the Cheviots, which stretch down the western side of the park as far as the Border Forest; in the east lie Coquetdale and the Simonside Hills, only 1,444 feet (440 metres) high but more rugged than the Cheviots; in the centre is the softer, more pastoral valley of the Rede; south of the Rede, the farmed valley of the North Tyne and along the southern border, Hadrian's Wall country.

Locals divide the country more simply into the Black Country, meaning the dark sandstone slopes of the Simonside Hills, and the White Country, referring to the light granite of the Cheviots. Though the Simonside Hills offer outstanding walking, most visitors head for the two most outstanding features of the park, the Cheviots at one end and the wall at the other.

The Roman wall is not the only manmade feature to be seen in the park — there are older prehistoric hill forts such as Lordenshaws as well as more recent fortified houses and villages — but it is certainly the most sensational. This long stone battlement sealing off the north-west frontier of the Roman Empire is one of the most impressive remains of antiquity north of the Alps. Constructed between AD122 and 130 on the orders of Emperor Hadrian, it crossed the whole breadth of northern England from the Tyne estuary on the east coast to the Solway Firth on the west.

One of the best-preserved stretches of the wall runs for 15 miles through the Northumberland National Park between Chollerford and Gilsland. Here the great grey stone barrier follows the line of the natural north-facing rampart on which it is built, the basalt scarp of the Great Whin Sill. The well-preserved fort at Vercovicium (now Housesteads), which could garrison some 1,000 infantry, and the milecastle at Cawfields, with accommodation for 30 troops, give a good idea of the solidity of Roman military engineering and the purposefulness of the Roman occupation of Britain. Altogether some 13,000 infantry and 5,500 cavalry manned this last outpost of empire, most of them colonial auxiliaries from Germany, France and the Middle East. It would have been a bleak and dour posting. The view would not have been much different from today's and Gore-Tex clothes and boots would not have been included in the kit that was handed out to them.

The Romans pulled out at the beginning of the 4th century AD. Their wall remains. A foray along its foot, up and down the switchback crest of the Whin Sill ridge, offers as intriguing a walk as can be had in any national park in Britain, strong in its sense of remoteness, especially along the best sections between Sewingshields Crags and Peel Crag, or at Winshields with its vast views towards the Cheviots, Pennines, Solway Firth and Lake District, and over the loughs, or glacial lakes, which dot the landscape north of the wall.

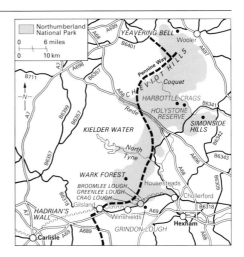

After being an outpost of Rome, Northumbria became an outpost of Christianity. Through the centuries that followed the land was fought over by Scots, Vikings and Saxons in endless turbulent frontier raids. In the Middle Ages Northumberland remained a virtually independent kingdom, and the havoc years of the border reivers only ended with the Union of England and Scotland in 1603. The legacy of centuries of frontier fighting is everywhere in the form of fortified farms and dwellings known as peles and bastles.

It is the modern works of man which have made the biggest and least welcome impact on the park. The British army has taken over where the Roman army left off and turned one fifth of the park — 90 square miles (233 sqare kilometres)of the middle portion between Redesdale and the Coquet valley — into the principal military training area in northern England. For 10 months of the year the sounds of battle rise incongruously from the centre of the national park and the bird-watcher or hill-walker who innocently approaches the firing ground is welcomed with signs that read: 'DANGER. MILITARY TARGET. DO NOT TOUCH ANYTHING. IT MAY EXPLODE AND KILL YOU.'

Elsewhere the Forestry Commission (FC) has installed regiments of a different kind: rank upon rank of conifers that make up the largest man-made forest in Europe. This vast plantation, centred on Kielder and dubbed the Border Forest Park, spreads into the national park, where it is called the Wark Forest. Additionally, a rocket testing site has been established on the western margin of the park, though plans for an atomic waste dump were successfully resisted.

The country north of the Roman wall is probably the most varied in Northumberland. Moorland, woodland, farmland and the wetland of the glacial lakes, upland streams, bogs and basin mires provide the main habitats, together with the mountain habitat of the rocky ravines high up in the Cheviots. Most of the heather moorland lies in Coquetdale and the Simonside Hills, where it is managed as grouse moor, while the slopes of the Cheviots to the north are predominantly green and grass-covered. The hub of the Cheviot Hills, the Cheviot, and the ridges radiating from it provide superb walking and marvellous views in all directions. Like Dartmoor, the high plateau of the Cheviot Hills is covered in blanket bogs of deep acid peat where granite tors protrude out of the vegetation mantle. Deep valleys run off these hills and swift-flowing streams dive over tumbling waterfalls (such as the beautiful waterfall of Harthope Linn) and then broaden out into winding rivers that glide, crystal clear and primordially pure, over pebble and boulder beds.

Ravens and buzzards soar among the hills, and merlins still nest in the deep heather. A regular breeding species on the moors is the short-eared owl, which increases in number during years when the field vole undergoes one of its periodic population explosions. Ring ouzels occupy the higher ground, nightjars favour the birch- and bracken-sheltered slopes, and red grouse and curlew call loudly from the heather moors and fells. Rabbits and brown hares are the most commonly seen animals on the upland pastures, and wild goats graze contentedly in small herds on the Cheviots. Badgers and foxes breed in the valleys and on the high moors; adders, grass snakes, common lizards and slow worms can also be found here.

The high rocky ravines of the Cheviot — Dunsdale, the Bizzle and the Henhole — shelter typical mountain or arctic-alpine plants. These survivors of the arctic tundra world of post-Ice-Age Britain include alpine willow herb, alpine club moss, rose root, starry saxifrage, hairy stonecrop and the rare dwarf cornel. In the valleys, rocky outcrops have weathered to deposit a rich brown earth on the cliff ledges, supporting a tall herb community of plants like rose burnet, foxglove, bluebell, golden rod, wild angelica and wood cranesbill.

On the lower slopes of ravines and the steeper valleys, especially in the Coquetdale and Simonside areas, scattered fragments of the prehistoric forest that once covered much of the region survive. They are mostly sessile oak, with birch, hazel, alder and ash supporting a rich ground layer of primrose, bluebell, meadowsweet, foxglove and enchanter's nightshade, along with an abundance of ferns and fungi such as the fly agaric. One of the best of the old woods can be seen in the valley of the Grasslands Burn, separating the Simonside and Harbottle Hills. Two other fine relict woods, Holystone North Wood and Holystone Burn Wood, are managed as nature reserves by the Northumberland Wildlife Trust.

The wetland habitat of the park takes various forms. Bog is one form: the blanket bog of the upland Cheviots, and the raised bogs of the country to the west of the North Tyne, in the middle of the park. Most notable of these are the Irthinghead Mires, situated in the prairie landscape of the Wark Forest at

the extreme west of the park, far from any roads. Many of these bogs, known locally as mosses or flothers, are of tremendous ecological importance because of the delicate balance of their plant communities: most of them have been designated as SSSIs, and one of them, Coom Rigg Moss, is also a national nature reserve, the only one within the park. These remote, undisturbed and little-visited wild habitats support a wide range of typical bog plants including bog moss, the beautiful bog rosemary, bog asphodel and the round-leaved sundew and rare long-leaved sundew, two unusual plants that supplement the scanty nutrients of their habitat by trapping and digesting small insects in their sticky leaves.

Another kind of wetland found in the park is that of the shallow glacial loughs or lakes that occupy the basins gouged by the ice between a series of basalt ridges stretching northwards from the Great Whin Sill to Simonside, Coquetdale and beyond. Some of the most important loughs are visible to anyone walking along Hadrian's Wall: Broomlee, Crag Lough and Greenlee Lough to the north of the wall, and Grindon Lough, the smallest and shallowest to the south. Some of the loughs, such as Grindon, are still open water; others are in various stages of filling up with vegetation, evolving from reed swamp and fen to raised bog and willow carr, and growing a profusion of tall marshy herbs such as meadowsweet, skullcap, marsh marigold, water mint and ragged Robin. The loughs are popular feeding and breeding sites for waterfowl and waders.

The upland streams provide yet another kind of wetland habitat in the park. These are fed either by water from the loughs or by the rain-water from the hills, and they can be torrential at times, filling the valleys with the busy tumult of their headlong rush. The most commonly seen creatures of the streams are the dipper and grey wagtail, along with the water rat in the slower streams. The otter, which still clings on here, is seldom seen.

As Hadrian's Wall extends eastwards through the Northumberland National Park past Cuddy's Crags and Housesteads, walkers can measure their progress when they reach Milecastle 37

BEFORE YOU GO

Maps: OS Outdoor Leisure Series, map Nos. 16, 42, 43.

GETTING THERE

By car: from the east Midlands and south-east England the A1 provides rapid access to Newcastle-upon-Tyne. For Wooler and the Cheviots, continue north from Newcastle on the A697; for Redesdale take the A696/68 Jedburgh road; for Hadrian's Wall and the southern region of the park, drive west along the A69. From the west and south-west of England leave the M6 on the A69 (exit 43) for Haltwhistle and Hexham. There is easy access from Edinburgh on both the A68 and A697.

By rail: Newcastle-upon-Tyne and Carlisle are linked by the scenic Tyne Valley Line, which stops at Hexham, Haltwhistle and other stations along the park's southern border. Contact National Rail Enquiries, T: (0345) 484950.

By bus: there are regular daily services from Newcastle to Rothbury and Hexham. For Wooler travel via Alnwick, and for Bellingham change at Hexham. Many villages within the park are on bus routes, but services are often infrequent. *The Northumberland Public Transport Guide*, a comprehensive listing of all bus services, is available from information centres and most post offices. For further information contact the Public Transport Department, Northumberland County Council, County Hall, Morpeth, Northumberland NE61 2EF, T: (01670) 533000, F: 533035, e-mail: transport@northumberland.gov.uk.

WHERE TO STAY

Most accommodation is to be found in or near the towns and villages on the western fringes

of the park: Wooler for the Cheviot Hills; Rothbury just north of the Simonside Hills; Hexham and Haltwhistle for Hadrian's Wall in the south. The Northumbria Tourist Board's annual *Official Holiday Guide*, available at information centres, includes a list of accommodation.

Outdoor living: 2 caravan and motor-home parks near Hexham: Brown Rigg, ½ mile south of Bellingham, T: (01434) 220175; Fallowfield Dene, near Hadrian's Wall, T: (01434) 603553.

Youth hostels: Acomb, T: (01434) 602864; Bellingham, T: (01434) 220313; Byrness, T: (01830) 520425; Greenhead, T: (01697) 747401; Once Brewed, T: (01434) 344360; Wooler, T: (01668) 281365.

WHERE TO GO

Nature reserves in the park include:

Coom Rigg Moss: EN NNR. One of the few areas of peat bog to have survived the reafforestation of Wark Forest, 10 miles (16 km) north of Haltwhistle. No rights of way or access except by permission

> '*Over the heather the wet wind blows,*
> *I've lice in my tunic and a cold in my nose.*
> *The rain comes pattering out of the sky,*
> *I'm a Wall soldier, I don't know why.*'
>
> W.H. Auden:
> '*Roman Wall Blues*'

of English Nature.

Grindon Lough: NWT reserve. Important wintering site for waterfowl south of Hadrian's Wall: no access to shore but entire lake can be observed from roadside. From B6319, ½ mile (1 km) west of Fourstones, take unclassified Newbrough Road. Grindon Lough is on right after 5 miles (8 km).

Harbottle Crags: NWT reserve. An area of beautiful open heather moorland with sphagnum moss, ½ mile south-west of Harbottle village. Part of Harbottle Moss SSSI. No permit required, but access confined to Drake Stone area

---

MOORLAND SAFETY

The benign face of moorland on a sunny day can change swiftly and treacherously. Before setting out on a long walk, telephone the weather service, T: (0891) 232788 (NE England), and make sure that someone knows your planned itinerary. Be prepared to alter your plans if the forecast is very discouraging.

Walkers along the beach below coastal cliffs must anticipate a more predictable natural phenomenon - the tide, which can transform an afternoon's outing into a terrifying race against the clock. Before any such expedition, learn the time and the extent of the next tide; tide tables are available from newsagents or tackle shops.

Adders, which thrive on the moor, will generally escape long before you see them; if not, keep a respectful distance. You are less likely to encounter an unexploded bomb, but they do still exist; treat any suspicious object with caution and contact the police.

when shooting is in progress.
Holystone Reserve: NWT.
Broad-leaved and coniferous
woodland, interspersed with
bog and heath. 7 miles (11 km)
west of Rothbury. From
Holystone village, take
Campville road. Visitors to
North Woods (upland oak,
birch) can use FC car-park.
Holystone Valley: NWT
reserve. Sessile oak, juniper
scrub and heather moorland ½
mile west of Holystone village.
Continue past car-park and
leave cars in lay-by where road
leads downhill. SSSI managed
in partnership with Forest
Enterprise. No permit required.
Falstone Moss: NWT reserve.
Blanket bog within the Kielder
Mires SSSI, ¼ mile from Tower
Knowe Visitor Centre. Permit
required for cars.
  For more information contact
English Nature, Archbold
House, Archbold Terrace,
Newcastle-upon-Tyne NE2
1EG, T: (0191) 281 6316, F:
281 6305, or Northumberland
Wildlife Trust, The Garden
House, St Nicholas Park,
Jubilee Road, Newcastle-upon-
Tyne NE3 3XT, T: (0191) 284
6884.

ACCESS AND CLOSURES
Much of the land is privately
owned, and visitors must stay
on public roads or rights of
way except where otherwise
specified on most recent OS
maps. There are 3 areas where
walkers have free access:
Breamish Valley in the vicinity
of Ingram, Harthope Valley
south-west of Wooler and the
land immediately surrounding
Housesteads Fort on Hadrian's
Wall. Access to the College
Valley is by permit only, from J.
Sale and Partners, Glendale
Road, Wooler, T: (01668)
281611, but limited to 12
vehicles a day and closed for
lambing 10 Apr-1 Jun.
  One great obstacle can be the
Ministry of Defence's

Otterburn Training Area
between the Rivers Rede and
Coquet, north-east of the A68.
No access when red flags are
flying, up to 290 days a year.
During lambing (14 Apr-15
May), from Christmas to New
Year and on public holidays the
range is always open.

ACTIVITIES
Walking: countless tracks and
paths meander across the
park's interior. Be prepared for
some serious map and compass
reading: this is easy country in
which to get lost. Equip
yourself as you would for any
demanding hill-walking
expedition; then add another
chocolate bar.
  Hadrian's Wall has now been
designated an official long-
distance footpath. The best
section is between
Sewingshields and Greenhead.
Both can be reached on the
seasonal Hadrian's Wall Bus:
details from Northumberland
National Park, T: (01434)
605555.
Climbing: there is good
climbing in the Simonside Hills,
the Cheviots and at Peel Crags.
Access is rarely a problem, but
make sure that you have the
landowner's permission before
beginning a climb. For further
information contact Mr N.
Jamieson, Northumbrian
Mountaineering Club, 52
Angerton Avenue, Shiremoor,

Newcastle-upon-Tyne NE27
0TU, T: (0191) 253 2703.
Cycling: attractive, if tough,
routes on minor roads
throughout the park. Off-road
cycling available in the Border
Forest Park.
Fishing: the River Coquet is
among the best in
Northumberland for trout.
Good fishing is available
elsewhere in the park. Rod
licences can be obtained from
Northumbrian Water
(Recreation Dept.), Abbey
Road, Pity Me, Durham DH1
5EZ, T: (0191) 383 2222.
Fishing permits are available
from local post offices.

FURTHER INFORMATION
The park runs information
centres in Ingram, T: (01665)
578248; Rothbury, T: (01669)
620887; and Once Brewed, T:
(01434) 344396. It also operates
a centre jointly with the

*'Peace, everywhere
serenity, and a
marvellous freedom from
the tumult of the world.'*

*St Alfred of Rievaulx
Abbey, 1143*

Alpine plants of the English
Pennines include: (from left to
right) alpine lady's mantle, grass of
Parnassus, yellow saxifrage and
sweet Cicely

Northumbrian Water
Authority at Tower Knowe on
Kielder Water, T: (01434)
240398.
 Forestry Commission, Forest
Enterprise, Kielder Forest
District, Eals Burn, Bellingham
NE48 2AH, T: (01430) 220242.

National Trust, Regional
Office, Scot's Gap, Morpeth
NE61 4EG, T: (01670) 774691.
 The Northumbria Tourist
Board, Aykley Heads, Durham
DH1 5UX, T: (0191) 375 3000,
F: 386 0899, web-site:
www.ntb.org.uk.

Northumberland Coast

AONB

Northumberland has one of the finest coastlines in England, with one of the longest sand dune systems. Buffeted by the North Sea, it can be an exhilaratingly wild place, and scattered along it are several remarkable wildlife reserves and bird islands.

The Farne Islands

*NT EN NNR AONB
Heritage Coast*

The Farne Islands, two to four miles (three to six kilometres) off the coast between Seahouses and Bamburgh, are the most easterly forms of the volcanic outcrop known as the Great Whin Sill, along the inland stretch of which the Romans built Hadrian's Wall. The 28 small islands are mostly low-lying, and only 15 of them are visible at high tide. A few, however, boast high stacks and cliffs, reaching 70 ft (21 m) near the Inner Farne lighthouse, which provide ideal nesting sites for many species of sea-bird.
 The fishing-boat trip out to the islands is always a little adventure, long enough to give you the feel of the swell and salt-water tang, short enough not to feel seasick. The islands, none of which are permanently

inhabited, enjoy sanctuary status as a National Trust Nature Reserve and English Nature National Nature Reserve, one of the most important in Britain and, indeed, in Europe. The public can land on only two of them: Inner Farne (the largest) and Staple Island. Even so, they remain among the most easily accessible and enjoyable bird islands of the British coast.
 More than 250 species of bird have been recorded on the Farne Islands, including puffins, guillemots, kittiwakes, lesser black-backed and herring gulls, arctic and Sandwich terns, eider, cormorants, shags, fulmars, black-headed gulls and common terns; a good number of oystercatchers, ringed plovers and meadow pipits; some score of razorbills and a few roseate terns. Most of the terns breed on Inner Farne and if you land there you will need to protect the top of your skull or the irate terns will give you a sharp peck on the head.
 There have been grey seals on the Farne Islands for more than

800 years. They are not hard to see, particularly on the nursery islands of North and South Wamses and Northern Hares.
 Hermits and monks lived on Inner Farne for nearly 900 years, the most famous of them being the 7th-century prior, St Cuthbert. Subsequently the

only inhabitants have been lighthouse keepers, including William Darling and his famous daughter, Grace, on Longstone. For a bracing foray on the ocean wave and an intimate view of teeming bird life at close quarters on an almost desert island group, the Farne Islands are hard to beat. **Getting there:** all sailings from Seahouses, 3 miles (5 km) south of Bamburgh on B1340. Various round trips and journeys to and from the islands are available. Contact boatmen direct for details: Hanvey's, T: (01665)

The stacks of Staple Island, one of the Farne Islands, form desirable detached columns for guillemots and other sociable sea-birds

720388/720258; Jack Shiel, T: (01665) 720825/721210; Billy Shiel, T: (01665) 720308. **Where to go:** around the islands for the

107

best viewing of grey seals. Inner Farne for nesting colonies of puffins, terns and eiders. Staple Island for vast colonies of kittiwakes, also shags, guillemots and puffins. **Access and closures:** Inner Farne and Staple Island closed 1st Oct-31st Mar. Apr, Aug and Sept both islands are open 10.30 am-6 pm; 1st May-31st Jul Staple Island open mornings only, Inner Farne open afternoons only. Dogs are not permitted on islands, but can be left with boatmen. For Inner Farne, take a hat for protection against tern pecks. **Amenities:** information centre and public lavatories on Inner Farne. **Further information:** National Trust Information Centre, 16 Main Street, Seahouses, Northumberland NE68 7RQ, T: (01665) 721099, for annual bird report, colour guide and leaflets, or contact Head Warden (John Walton), T: (01665) 720651.
108

Lindisfarne
(or Holy Island)

EN NNR

The largest reserve in north-east England, these 8,100 acres (3,300 ha) of dunes, salt marsh and mud-flats extend from Holy Island north to Goswick Sands and South to Budle Bay. They are internationally famous for their large winter flocks of divers, grebes, wildfowl and waders.

The inter-tidal flats of the broad Lindisfarne inlet are sheltered by the natural breakwater of Holy Island, a low hump which can be reached at low tide by a causeway from the mainland village of Beal. Behind this natural shelter, enormous flocks of wintering birds congregate to feed when the

flats and marshes are exposed by the receding tide.

Lindisfarne is the only regular wintering ground in Britain for the pale-bellied Brent goose, which flies down from Spitzbergen when the polar ice covers its summer nesting grounds. Lindisfarne is also the most important coastal site for wigeon (peaking at 10,000) and the place where the largest wintering herds of whooper swan in England are to be found. The huge swirling flocks of waders include internationally important numbers of knot, dunlin and bar-tailed godwit, as well as many other wader species, rare passage migrants and regular birds of prey such as the peregrine, merlin and short-eared owl.

All this is in winter, when the sub-polar climate at the edge of this northerly sea may well shiver your timbers, so to speak. In summer, bird life is much less evident, still less so when the tide is in and the mud-flats are covered by the sea. On the other hand, the summer wild flowers of the dunes can be a reward, especially the marsh orchid, common spotted orchid and marsh helleborine. And of course there are always the beautiful ruins of the 11th-century priory, originally founded in 635AD by St Aidan from Iona and considered the birthplace of Christianity in Britain, or Sir Edward Lutyens' marvellous restoration of the 16th-century castle perched on a high rock above the sea. **Getting there** *By car:* 8 miles (13 km) south of Berwick-upon-Tweed on A1, an unclassified road leads to Lindisfarne via the village of Beal. The causeway to the island is impassable from 2 hours before until 3½ hours after high tide; check tide-tables at causeway. *By bus:* buses run from Berwick

to Beal with connecting services to the island dependant on the tide. Contact Berwick-upon-Tweed bus station, T: (01289) 307283.
Where to stay: there are four hotels on the island: Lindisfarne Hotel, T: (01289) 389273; Crown and Anchor, T: (01289) 389215; North View, T: (01289) 389222; The Ship, T: (01289) 389311. No caravans, motor-homes or tents are allowed, but there are camp-sites nearby at Berwick.
Access: free access to reserve, but permits from EN required for field work. Parking off causeway at low tide only.
Further information: contact Site Manager (Phil Davey), Beal Station, Berwick-upon-Tweed, Northumberland TD15 2SP, T: (01289) 381470.
English Nature, Archbold House, Archbold Terrace, Newcastle-upon-Tyne NE2 1EG, T: (0191) 281 6316, F: 281 6305.
Lindisfarne Priory and Museum, T: (01289) 389200.
The Northumbria Tourist Board, Aykley Heads, Durham DH1 5UX, T: (0191) 375 3000, F: 386 0899, web-site: www.ntb.org.uk.

Coquet Island

RSPB Reserve SSSI

A low, flat-topped island some 16 acres (6.5 ha) in extent with rocky or shingle shores. Officially it is not possible to land on this small island off the Northumberland coast, for fear of disturbing the nesting birds. I would not have included it in this book were it not for the fact that I once spent a jolly afternoon on the island in the company of the lighthouse keeper and a few friends; so obviously it is possible for the serious observer to make visiting arrangements with the relevant authorities. I recall landing through choppy seas in a rubber boat and stepping ashore amid a mass of birds' nests on the flat ground under my feet and an even bigger mass of jittery, abusive terns hovering excitedly above my head.
Unless you are a real enthusiast it is probably easier to hire a boat in Amble and view the bird colonies during a sea trip round the island. They include large colonies of Sandwich, arctic and common terns, a small but very important population of roseate tern, Britain's most threatened sea-bird, and large colonies of puffins and eider ducks. Arctic skuas and bonxies come raiding in late summer.
Getting there: island is 1 mile

Among the common sea-birds of the north-east coast are: on the cliff tops (from left to right) guillemot, fulmar and cormorant, all highly successful breeders on crags, cliffs and stacks; and in the air a kittiwake and a common tern, which has a much poorer breeding record, not least because its colonies are in exposed locations on the ground

(2 km) offshore from Amble, which is on A1068. Nearest railway station is Acklington.
Access: no landing permitted, but round-the-island trips from Amble can be arranged with Davey Gray, T: (01665) 711975.
Further information: contact RSPB North of England Office, 4 Benton Terrace, Sandiford Road, Newcastle-upon-Tyne NE2 1QU, T: (0191) 281 3366.
The Northumbria Tourist Board, Aykley Heads, Durham DH1 5UX, T: (0191) 375 3000, F: 386 0899, web-site: www.ntb.org.uk.

CHAPTER 5

Wales

Wales would be guerrilla country if it ever came to it. It was into this great mountain fastness in the west that the early Celts beat a permanent strategic withdrawal from the invaders of lowland England, there to lick their wounds and nurse their language, and live their own peculiarly Welsh kind of Celtic life. Few were inclined to pursue them over the wind-swept upland moors, the black bogs and bristling mountains of the wild Welsh heartland. For centuries the line of English castles along the Welsh Marches marked the beginning of a no-man's land, beyond which there was only Merlin, wizardry and red dragons, a dark stocky tribe of proud defiant hill people and an upland wilderness, the haunt of red kites and the swooping falcon, where even angels and Angles feared to tread.

Wales has had a rich history. There were cave dwellers like those who lived in the classic sites at Cae Gwyn in Flintshire and Paviland on Gower. In the heart of the Welsh uplands to this day there are folk who, in their physical appearance and their blood groups, are akin to some of those early peoples — an indication of the wild remoteness of these regions which later invaders like the Normans never quite overcame. For the historian, Wales seems well-blessed with ancient ramparts, hill and promontory forts, and castles; not just the great Norman and Edwardian strongholds, but Welsh castles like Dinefwr, proud on its limestone crag guarding a crossing of the middle Tywi.

Not all that much has changed. The red dragons are no more and the red

The tranquillity of this sunset over St Bride's Bay on the Pembrokeshire coast is deceptive; the sea here is often tempestuous

kites are reduced, but much of the wilderness remains, and to anyone approaching Wales from the lowland English plain the country seems to be an impenetrable mountain fortress, as it has always done. In no other part of Britain is the landscape so solidly and uniformly mountainous. The uplands extend north and south from coast to coast, and east and west from the Marches to the sea. Wales is literally stuffed with mountains, from the great ramparts of Snowdonia in the north-west — containing the highest mountain in all England and Wales — to the wide sweep of the Brecon Beacons in the south-east, while the highland plateau of the Cambrian Mountains that occupies the middle of the country, though less dramatic than the spectacular rock piles to the north and south, is as remote and solitary as anywhere in Britain: the only sounds to be heard on a still summer afternoon are the mewing of the buzzards and the distant bleating of the sheep.

Numerous rivers branch out to the sea from the highland interior, though a few — notably the Dee, Severn and Wye — drain in the opposite direction, down to the English border. Some of these rivers meander in slow and stately fashion across the flood plains, as if wishing to delay their arrival at the sea. Others dash in a wild, headlong charge through narrow, boulder-filled defiles, where the sound of water is never stilled.

It is an invariable axiom of wild Britain that where there is high ground there is also wilderness, and this is indubitably true of Wales. This is the playground — if dangling from a rock pinnacle or snow-bivouacing in a sub-zero icefield can be described as play — of the hard rock buff, the long-distance backpacker who eats granite for breakfast. Being so near to the main centres of population of Britain, there are more

wild travellers per square mile of scree, cwm and glacial moraine in high Wales than any other part of the country, except perhaps the Lake District.

However, Wales is not exclusively upland. In Anglesey in the north and along the Bristol Channel coast in the south there are large tracts of low-lying land. The long stretches of cliff coast, particularly in Pembrokeshire in the far south-west, are amongst the liveliest and most varied in Britain, and at times the most wind-swept. There is no grander sight than the view from Wooltack Point in the aftermath of a westerly gale, when the great rollers surge across St Brides Bay, or send plumes of spray high over the aptly named Mad Bay on Skokholm Island. Along the western reaches of the south Wales coast you can find places where, at very low tides, the remains of sunken forests are still visible, trees that once flourished on dry rolling lands several thousand summers ago. It is also along this coast that you can see many of the most spectacular gatherings of birds in Wales, especially in the estuaries with their vast expanses of mud-flats and salt marsh, on Pembrokeshire's bird islands and on the freshwater lakes which abound in the interior. Some of these are reservoirs, while others were first filled by the melt-waters of the Ice Age glaciers that once gripped the uplands of Wales, and contain in their depths relict fish peculiar to Wales, such as the gwyniad of Llyn Cedig (Lake Bala) and the freshwater char of Llanberis.

For the naturalist Wales provides a mixed bag; Wales has only 1,100 native plants compared with 1,600 in Britain as a whole. The high proportion of moisture-loving plants such as ferns reflects the rain-laden climate. In compensation, Wales harbours some animals and birds which are either extinct or extremely rare elsewhere in Britain, such as the polecat, the pine marten, the revitalized red kite, the chough, a moth called Weaver's wave and a beautiful beetle, found only on a small area of Snowdon, which rejoices in the name of *Chrysolina cerealis*. Throughout Wales a wide variety of habitats ensures a goodly abundance of species, and off the south-west coast there is the added bonus of a breathtaking cavalcade of marine creatures. Much of the natural heritage and beauty of Wales is contained within the generous boundaries of its three national parks, Snowdonia, the Brecon Beacons and the Pembrokeshire Coast. Much more can be found in the several Areas of Outstanding Natural Beauty, the many nature reserves and along the long-distance paths. Even outside these areas there are wide tracts of unspoiled landscape, as wild and remote as anything you could hope to find in Britain.

GETTING THERE

By air: Cardiff International Airport, T: (01446) 711111, has flights to most major British cities, as well as services to Paris, Amsterdam and Brussels. Charter flights are available from the USA and Canada (from Orlando and Toronto). Manchester and Birmingham airports are convenient for North and Mid-Wales.

By sea: 5 ferry routes link Wales with Ireland. Irish Ferries, T: (0990) 171717, operates between Dublin and Holyhead, and Rosslare and Pembroke Dock; Stena Line, T: (0990) 707070, between Dun Laoghaire and Holyhead, and Rosslare and Fishguard; and Swansea-Cork Ferries, T: (01792) 456116, between Cork and Swansea.

By rail: services run from London Paddington to Newport, Cardiff and Swansea, and from Euston to Bangor and Holyhead. Otherwise, change at Chester for stations along the north coast and at Shrewsbury for trains to Aberystwyth, Pwllheli and other destinations in Mid-Wales. For more information on local rail services, consult *The Wales Bus, Train and Tourist Map & Guide*, available at tourist information centres; alternatively, contact National Rail Enquiries, T: (0345)

484950, or Train, Bus and Coach National Enquiries, T: (0891) 910910.

By bus: National Express, T: (0990) 808080, operates services from major centres in England to the principal towns in Wales. Regular services to Cardiff from London Victoria Coach Station, Birmingham and Manchester. There are also services to Aberystwyth (daily) and Bangor (twice daily), though trains are a better bet for Mid- and North Wales. For more information, again consult *The Wales Bus, Rail and Tourist Map & Guide*.

WHEN TO GO

The weather in Wales is at its most welcoming in summer, but it is wise to avoid the congested

The polecat thrives in the dunes of the Welsh coast, where prey such as rabbits abound

roads and booked-up accommodation in August and on bank-holiday weekends. The Cambrian Mountains in Mid-Wales, on the other hand, are relatively neglected by tourists and can still offer peace and space even in midsummer. Bird-watchers will often choose spring and autumn to visit coastal Wales in order to observe migrating wildfowl and waders. Mountaineers find Wales an exciting challenge year-round, especially Snowdonia, where several centres organize winter climbing holidays.

WHERE TO STAY

Brochures are available from the Wales Tourist Board (see below) and tourist information centres, which contain lists of possible accommodation. The WTB publishes 3 reasonably priced *Where To Stay* guides:

Wales — Hotels, Guest Houses and Farmhouses; *Wales — Self-catering*; and *Wales — Bed and Breakfast*.

Individual tourist information centres generally print lists of local accommodation, including camp-sites. They all operate a bed-booking service (sometimes for a small fee) for accommodation locally and further afield. There are also 3 freephone holiday booking hotlines: for South and West Wales, T: (0800) 243731; for Mid-Wales, T: (0800) 273747; for North Wales, T: (0800) 834820.

ACTIVITIES

Walking: Wales offers some of the best and most accessible walking in Britain. There are few places where you cannot find an attractive, impromptu walk within minutes of stopping your car or getting out of a train. For those who need more structure to their outings, the WTB publishes *Walking Wales*, which contains a catalogue of guides to the hundreds of walks they recommend. Another possibility is to get in touch with the Ramblers' Association in Wales, T: (01978) 855148. The 3 National Parks also produce leaflets of walks within their boundaries. *The Welsh Peaks* by W. A. Poucher (Constable, 1997) is considered the classic guide for the mountain walker.

The Forestry Commission has substantial plantations in Wales, all of them criss-crossed with footpaths. For leaflets with recommended forest walks, contact Forest Enterprise (who are agents of the Forestry Commission) at Victoria House, Victoria Terrace, Aberystwyth, Dyfed SY23 2DQ, T: (01970) 612367.
Riding and trekking: riding centres abound, particularly in the Brecon Beacons and the

Cambrian Mountains. *Activity Wales*, available at tourist information centres, lists all accredited equestrian centres. Alternatively, contact the Wales Trekking and Riding Association, c/o Standby Secretarial Services, 9 Nevill Street, Abergavenny NP7 5AA, T: (01873) 858717, or the British Horse Society, T: (01926) 707700.
Cycling: Wales offers hundreds of miles of beautiful cycling routes. *Cycling Wales*, available at tourist information centres, provides details of possible routes, cycle-hire outlets, accommodation and further useful publications. There are two Sustrans routes in Wales, map Nos. 8 and 8(42), from Cardiff/Chepstow to Builth Wells and from Builth Wells to Holyhead. Contact Sustrans Information Service, T: (0117) 929 0888.
Climbing: the principal centre for climbing in Wales is Plas y Brenin, the National Centre for Mountain Activities in Betws-y-Coed, T: (01690) 720214 (see SNOWDONIA). There are also numerous climbing centres outside Snowdonia. *Activity Wales* contains a list of accredited centres.
Fishing: there are good opportunities for game and coarse fishing throughout Wales, as well as excellent sea angling. To prepare yourself for Welsh waters, consult *Fishing Wales*, available at tourist information centres, which contains a list of Welsh fishing organizations. The Environment Agency, T: (01222) 300500, also offers helpful advice and publishes a comprehensive guide entitled *Fishing the Rivers of Wales*.
Caving: there are many natural cave systems throughout Wales, especially in the south, and 62 caving clubs. Anyone who has acquired a taste for caving is urged to seek the advice of a

local club. *Activity Wales* lists some caving centres. For a more comprehensive list of clubs, contact the Cambrian Caving Council, White Lion House, Ynys Uchaf, Ystradgynlais, Swansea SA9 1RW, T: (01639) 849519.
Ballooning: balloon trips offer an exciting alternative way of viewing Wales' rugged landscapes. Contact Balloons Over Wales, 14 Swansea Road, Penllergaer, Swansea SA1 4AQ, T: (01792) 899333.

FURTHER INFORMATION

Wales Tourist Board, Davis Street, Cardiff CF1 2XU, T: (01222) 499909, and www.tourism.wales.gov.uk, for general information on where to go and where to stay in Wales.

If you are in London, pop along to the Britain Visitors' Centre, 1 Regent Street, London SW1Y 4NS, T: (0171) 808 3838. The Welsh desk will provide you with brochures and advice about Wales.

The WTB publishes 12 guides to holiday areas in Wales, containing useful information about the different regions. Try also North Wales Tourism, T: (01492) 531731, in Colwyn Bay; Mid-Wales Tourism, T: (01654) 702653, in Machynlleth; Tourism South and West Wales, T: (01792) 781212, in Swansea, or; T: (01437) 766388, in Haverfordwest.

Sports Council of Wales, Sophia Gardens, Cardiff CF1 9SW, T: (01222) 300500.

Countryside Council for Wales (CCW), Plas Penrhos, Ffordd Penrhos, Bangor, Gwynedd LL57 2LQ, T: (01248) 370444.

Festival of the Countryside, Frolic House, 23 Frolic Street, Newtown, Powys SY16 1AP, T: (01686) 625384, publishes an excellent magazine with information about events in the Welsh countryside.

©Oxford Cartographers

CARDIFF-WALES

Pembrokeshire

Includes the 225-square mile (580-sq km) Pembrokeshire Coast National Park

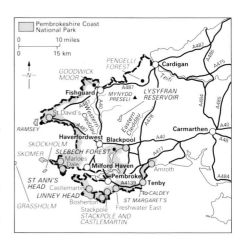

Pembrokeshire, the most south-westerly part of Wales, is a maritime county of wind-swept headlands, of islands large and small and of superb beaches; some of which are very public, but many others secluded and secret. Nowhere is further than 16 miles (25 kilometres) from salt water, for the great waterway of Milford Haven, a valley drowned when sea levels rose at the end of glacial times, wends its way some 21 miles (33 kilometres) inland. The entrance is guarded by the old red sandstone cliffs of St Ann's Head where a lighthouse now fulfils the function of the beacon that long marked the dangers to mariners.

These dangers became all too apparent in 1996, when the *Sea Empress* oil tanker ran aground off St Ann's Head, spilling 72,000 tonnes of crude oil into the sea, contaminating miles of coastline and killing thousands of sea-birds. Fortunately the accident happened in February. If it had come one month later it would have affected thousands more birds, effectively wiping out a whole generation. Pembrokeshire's sea-birds have recovered quickly from the initial devastation but the long-term effects on smaller marine organisms will not become apparent for some time. Although no visible signs of the disaster remain, it serves as a salutary reminder of the vulnerability of Britain's coastline.

Thankfully the local flora has survived intact. The cliff-top flowers here — and indeed all along the Pembrokeshire coast — are superb, especially in early summer: scurvy grass with white flowers and fleshy green leaves, sea campion, thrift, spring squill, kidney vetch and wild carrot, to mention but a few. It was at St Ann's that I first encountered fulmars, on a wild March day when one could barely stand on the cliff top. Despite the weather, these magnificent sea-birds swept effortlessly past the cliff face, dropping down with a quick twist of the wings over the Atlantic swells.

Ideally, one should sail here; that is the most rewarding way to explore inland to the head-waters of the Western Cleddau at Haverfordwest, where the castle guards the first ancient crossing of the river. Alternatively, follow the Eastern Cleddau to Blackpool where the old mill has been restored, and where in most years a pair of dippers nest within a few feet of the wheel shaft. Herons can always be seen along the estuary together with shelduck and Canada geese. From September to March large numbers of wildfowl and waders gather, and the estuary takes on a special importance during severe weather. Sea aster turns some of the saltings mauve during late summer, following on from carpets of sea lavender. At several points the stately marsh mallow can be found; its roots were once used to make the sweets that have taken its name.

Leave the coast and the waterways, and you will find south-west Wales equally enchanting. In the north Mynydd Preseli rises to 1,535 feet (468 metres); it was from here that early inhabitants are said to have taken the famous 'blue' stones to Stonehenge. This land is an archaeologist's and historian's dream; you cannot go far without seeing earthworks, cromlechs and castles.

The lower slopes of Mynydd Preseli, especially the great sweep above Brynberian, are of special interest to naturalists. In spring, botanists can search here for insectivorous species such as pale and common butterworts and long-leaved and round-leaved sundews. In late summer the tiny bog orchid may be revealed by a hands-and-knees search, so be prepared for wet legs. In the same location you may well encounter one of Britain's rarest dragonflies, the southern damselfly, a delicate species with beautiful azure blue segments.

The fragments of lowland heath surviving in the agricultural lands between Fishguard and St David's contain more treasures for the naturalist. These wind-swept areas are a blaze of colour in late summer, when three species of heather contrast with the saffron of western gorse. On the footpaths you can find special plants such as three-lobed water crowfoot early in the year and yellow centuary towards the end. More conspicuous will be the lesser butterfly orchid, bog asphodel and devil's bit scabious, a food plant for the often scarce marsh fritillary butterfly. In days gone by Montagu's harriers nested here; now, alas, they are rare visitors. Hen harriers, by contrast, regularly stop over here in winter, when you may be lucky enough to see several of these fine raptors going to roost in a patch of willow scrub.

BEFORE YOU GO
Maps: Ordnance Survey Landranger Series, map Nos. 145, 157, 158.
Guide-books: *Birds of Pembrokeshire* by Jack Donovan (Dyfed Wildlife Trust, 1994), *Pembrokeshire Coast Path* by Brian John (Aurum Press, 1997) and *A Guide to the Pembrokeshire Coast Path* by C. J. Wright (Constable, 1989) are recommended.

GETTING THERE
By car: the M4 brings the visitor to within an hour of south-west Wales, where the main routes are the A40 to Fishguard, A477 to Pembroke and A487 to St David's. Most people approaching from the north will do so by the A487 from Aberystwyth through Cardigan and Fishguard to St David's. There are a number of B roads, but most other roads are unclassified and many are narrow. There are good car-parking facilities at most points.
By rail: services run from London Paddington, changing either at Cardiff or Swansea for trains to Milford Haven, Tenby and Pembroke to the south and, less frequently, Fishguard to the north.

By bus: buses run from London Victoria Coach Station, with links from other centres, to Haverfordwest, Milford Haven, Pembroke and Tenby. Consult *The Wales Bus, Rail and Tourist Map & Guide* (see p114) for information about local services.

WHERE TO STAY
Major accommodation centres outside the Pembrokeshire Coast National Park are Fishguard, Haverfordwest, Milford Haven and Pembroke; within the park, St David's in the west and Tenby in the south. A telephone bed-booking service run by the Wales Tourist Board is available for a small charge at all tourist information centres, including Tenby, T: (01834) 842404; Haverfordwest, T: (01437) 763110; and Fishguard, T: (01348) 873484. Alternatively, contact the West Wales Booking Bureau at St David's, T: (01437) 720345. **Youth hostels:** at Poppit Sands, T: (01239) 612936; Newport, T: (01239) 820080; Pwll Deri, T: (01348) 891233; Trevine, T: (01348) 831414; St David's, T: (01437) 720345; Penycwm, T: (01437) 720959; Broad Haven, T: (01437) 781688; Marloes Sands, T: (01646) 636667;

Lawrenny, T: (01646) 651221; Manorbier, T: (01834) 871803; Pentlepoir, T: (01834) 812333. **Outdoor living:** tourist information centres will provide lists of camping, caravan and motor-home sites, with which the park is well provided. *Coastal Path Accommodation*, published by the National Park Authority, is a comprehensive list of camp-sites and bed-and-breakfast establishments, indispensable for the long-distance backpacker.

ACCESS
Much of the Castlemartin Peninsula is an MOD tank gunnery range. Access to Range West is possible only on the National Park Authority's escorted visits, while the coastal path through Range East from Elegug Stacks to St Govan's is open only at weekends.

ACTIVITIES
Walking: the coastal path and its adjacent routes offer several hundred miles of walking. Much of Mynydd Preseli is open common land, and there are some special routes such as that around Lysyfran Reservoir, or through the conifers at Slebech Forest. A programme of walks is

117

organized by the National Park Authority. Full details are given in the free publication *Coast to Coast*, which appears annually in April. For the 168-mile (269-km) Pembrokeshire Coast long-distance path from Amroth to the Teifi estuary, see *A Guide to the Pembrokeshire Coast Path*. **Climbing:** some of the sea cliffs, especially in the south, offer striking and varied climbs. Seasonal restrictions apply in certain areas to safeguard nesting sea-birds, details of which can be found in a leaflet published by the National Park Authority. *Rock Climbing in Wales* by Ron James (Constable, 1982) contains much useful information.
Fishing: the rocky coastline, sandy beaches, rivers and reservoirs of south-west Wales offer many opportunities for angling. Consult *Fishing Wales*, available at tourist information centres; alternatively, try the Pembrokeshire Anglers Association, T: (01437) 763216, or enquire at fishing tackle shops. Sea fishing is catered for from ports such as Tenby and Milford Haven.

FURTHER INFORMATION
The National Park operates 3 visitor centres: at Haverfordwest, T: (01437) 760136; Newport, T: (01239) 820912; and St David's, T: (01437) 720392. The headquarters is at Wynch Lane, Haverfordwest SA61 1PY, T: (01437) 764636: postal enquiries should be sent here.
The Wales Tourist Board publishes *Pembrokeshire*, which contains lists of available accommodation and activities in the region.
Another source of information is Tourism & Leisure Services, Pembrokeshire County Council, 19 Old Bridge, Haverfordwest, Pembrokeshire SA6 12EZ, T: (01437) 760980.
118

Pembrokeshire Islands

Grassholm and Ramsey NNR, RSPB Reserves; St Margaret's and Skokholm WTWW Reserves; Skomer WTWW NNR, MNR

The islands of Grassholm, Skokholm, Skomer and Ramsey are without compare, for they support some of the most spectacular seal and sea-bird colonies on the coast of Britain. Part of the Pembrokeshire Coast National Park, they are noted not only for their sea-bird and grey seal colonies but also for maritime flowers and, in the case of Skomer, an indigenous sub-species of bank vole found nowhere else. Lonely Grassholm — a bare cone of granite rock in the wild Atlantic — is home for 34,000 pairs of gannets, the third largest colony in the world. It is the most difficult island to reach; the boat journey can be well over an hour in duration and landings are now prohibited. With so many birds, however, the views from the sea are spectacular.
Skokholm — site of the first bird observatory to be established in Britain — and Skomer, a national nature reserve, are of world-wide importance for their sea-birds, especially the nocturnal Manx shearwater of which the two islands support over 140,000 pairs, and some 6,000 pairs of storm petrels which come ashore to breed on Skokholm. The WTWW have a video link to a camera in a Manx shearwater burrow so that day visitors can now see this elusive species. Razorbills, guillemots and puffins are much more readily sighted, while the

garrulous kittiwakes endlessly call their name from the cliffs.
Flowers include not just the maritime species one might expect on offshore islands, but two surprises: vast acres of bluebells and equally dramatic sweeps of red campion, with a few foxgloves standing nobly along the old walls for good measure.
Choughs apart, Ramsey is disappointing for birds because brown rats, possibly survivors from some long-forgotten shipwreck, have severely diminished the numbers of burrow-nesting sea-birds. This is the place to observe seals, however, for Ramsey has the most important grey-seal breeding colony in Wales. There can be few more dramatic sights than the west coast of Ramsey viewed from a boat; seals watch from cave entrances or lie sprawled on offshore rocks as you pass by.
The inshore waters around Skomer and Marloes Peninsula are now protected as a Marine Nature Reserve.
Getting there *By sea:* the islands can be reached between April and October, when the weather is favourable. Dale Sailing Company, T: (01646) 601636, operates boats to Skomer, Skokholm and Grassholm from Martin's Haven, a rocky beach west of Marloes. Boats run 6 days a week (not Mondays) to Skomer, on Mondays to Skokholm and Thursdays to Grassholm. Eleven boats operate daily to Caldey from Tenby Harbour (not Sundays), T: (01834) 844453/842296. Landings are not permitted on St Margaret's. Thousand Islands Expeditions, T: (01437) 721686, operates boats to

This Ramsey Island beach makes a pleasant sun trap for grey seals, all spent bulls and non-breeding cows

Ramsey daily (not Tuesdays) from St Justinians. **Access:** to all these islands is controlled by WTWW and RSPB. **Activities:** guided walks on Skomer and Skokholm are available through the WTWW, T: (01646) 636234, although they are run only from June to August. Accommodation on Skomer and Skokholm islands is managed by the WTWW: you will need to book well in advance, T: (01437) 765462. **Further information:** leaflets from the RSPB, T: (01686) 626678, and the National Park Authority, T: (01437) 764636; Wildlife Trust West Wales, 7 Market Street, Haverfordwest, Pembrokeshire SA61 1NF, T: (01437) 765462.

Stackpole and Castlemartin

Part of the Pembrokeshire Coast National Park
CCW NNR

The limestone coastline running all the way from Stackpole Quay to Linney Head is one of the finest stretches of the Pembrokeshire Coast National Park. In the east there are nearly 2,000 acres (800 ha) of dunes, rabbit warrens, cliffs and the freshwater lakes at Bosherton. The lakes were formed nearly two centuries ago when the valleys were flooded after the construction of several dams. Now this is one of the best areas in lowland Britain for aquatic flora, the most striking of all being the huge rafts of white water lilies. In winter many ducks may be seen; rarer visitors include bittern and the North American ring-necked duck. The cliffs at Stackpole, with their caves, stacks and wave-worn arches, are noted for their flowers and nesting sea-
120

birds, and even a few pairs of puffins, though you will have to look hard for them. You may see choughs and peregrines and also guillemots, whose Welsh name is *elegug*. At four limestone stacks midway along the Castlemartin Peninsula is a large colony, certainly the most easily viewed in Wales, if not in the whole of Britain.
Getting there *By car:* well signposted south from Pembroke. Stackpole Quay is to the east, Bosherston village and Broad Haven directly to the south and Elegug Stacks to the west. **Access:** Castlemartin is a tank range and access to Range West is possible only on one of the Sunday visits organized by the NPA, T: (01437) 764636. The footpath through Range East is open at weekends. The road to the Stacks is frequently closed on weekdays when the tank range is operational, but is always open at weekends and on bank holidays. **Where to stay:** Pembroke and Freshwater East have a wide range of accommodation. **Activities** *Walking:* short walks at Elegug Stacks and Bosherston lakes. For the more energetic there is a 4-mile (6½-km) cliff walk from Elegug Stacks to St Govan's. **Further information:** leaflets available from CCW, West Area, Aberystwyth, T: (01970) 828551.

Pengelli Forest

NNR, WTWW Reserve

The most extensive remaining ancient woodland in south-west Wales, Pengelli Forest covers 163 acres (66 ha). According to a local Elizabethan historian, who left behind some fascinating information about the forest, it was much larger in medieval times. The forest consists mainly of sessile oak, with a range of other species, including midland hawthorn.
Polecats, and dormice too, may be found here although, like the white-letter hairstreak butterfly which has also been recorded, they are extremely elusive. Woodland birds include sparrow-hawk, redstart and pied flycatcher.
Getting there *By car:* from Velindre on the A487, take a secondary road to Trewilym. Entry to the forest is through a gate about 1 mile (1½ km) down this road on the right. **Access:** open all year on marked paths only. **Activities:** 4 nature trails. **Further information:** TIC, Fishguard, T: (01348) 873484; leaflet from WTWW, T: (01437) 765462.

The Skomer vole is an evolutionary rarity found only on the Pembrokeshire island from which it takes its name

SOUTH WALES

South Wales is bounded in the west by the wild limestone cliffs of Gower, and in the east by the Severn estuary with its vast brown tidal mud-flats and even browner water. Running northwards from the estuary is the Wye valley, the frontier with England; and what a superb frontier it is, this steep, wooded valley with its natural defences augmented by the ancient fortifications of Offa's Dyke.

Between these extremes lies the industrial heart of Wales, though it beats less strongly than in earlier days: the mining valleys, the great works, the docks, marshalling yards and power stations. The casual observer speeding west might think that nature had passed the area by, but there is much to explore and many delights to savour.

There can be few greater contrasts than that which exists between the tiny pools in the heart of Gower and the vast lowland fen of Crymlyn Bog (paradoxically situated in the industrial heartland of Swansea). But the key to it all is water, whether it be river, lake, reservoir or sea; it is water that makes South Wales so rich in bird life and such a joy to naturalists and ornithologists.

Gower Peninsula

AONB, NT Reserves, CCW NNRs, GWT Reserves

This delightful peninsula, barely 5 miles (8 km) wide, extends 20 miles (32 km) westwards from the outskirts of Swansea. Virtually every habitat, except for uplands and mountains, is represented here, though in a coastal area such as this the range of maritime habitats is the dominant feature.

At the extreme south-west is Worm's Head, which takes its name from the Saxon word for 'dragon', on account of its reptilian shape. It is rich in maritime flora and has the only sea-bird colonies of note in Glamorgan, including kittiwakes, razorbills and guillemots; there may even be a few pairs of puffins. Choughs have recently begun to nest on the south Gower cliffs,

indicating a welcome change in their fortunes, which will hopefully extend throughout south-west Wales. To the east of the Worm the cliffs are a botanist's paradise, rich in uncommon species such as the yellow whitlow grass, which grows nowhere else in Britain, spring cinquefoil, white rock rose, hoary rock rose, spiked speedwell and clary.

Two rather special insects may also be found here. One of these is the marbled white butterfly, the other the great green bush cricket, restricted in Wales to a few areas on the south and south-west coasts. This massive beast, over 1½ in (4 cm) in length, is more often heard than seen, though its strident note, which it emits until well after dark, is too high-pitched for some naturalists to hear in the evening of their years.

Oxwich National Nature Reserve is a mosaic of fen, marsh, open water, sand dune

and woodland. The aquatic habitats are exciting: bitterns are regular winter visitors and in some years remain to breed in abundance, while small numbers of Cetti's warbler have nested here since 1985. Adder, grass snake and slow worm inhabit the drier slopes.

In the north the Burry Inlet, flanked by nearly 9 miles (15 km) of salt marshes and guarded by the large sand-dune system of Whiteford Burrows NNR, is one of Britain's major estuaries for wildfowl and waders. Of particular importance is the only regular flock of wintering Brent geese in Wales; the resident eiders are also worth attention, since this species normally breeds no further south than Cumbria. **Before you go** *Maps:* Ordnance Survey Landranger Series, map No. 159. **Getting there** *By car:* the A4118 leaves Swansea and traverses south Gower to Port Eynon, beyond which the B4247 carries on to Rhossili. In the north, the B4271 and B4295 both terminate at Llanrhidian; then it is unclassified roads all the way to the remote north-west. *By bus:* regular services from Swansea to Rhossili. **Where to stay:** there are plenty of hotels and guest-houses in Mumbles and west towards Caswell Bay, beyond which there are bed and breakfasts and a number of camping, caravan and motor-home sites. **Access:** generally unrestricted access to the dunes and woodland paths all along the coast. For conservation reasons, visitors are urged to keep to footpaths or designated nature trails along the coastal reserves. Worm's Head is only accessible for 2½ hours at low tide; visitors are requested not to visit this important nesting site from March to July. **Activities:** there is a National Trust visitor information centre at Rhossili, T: (01792) 390707.

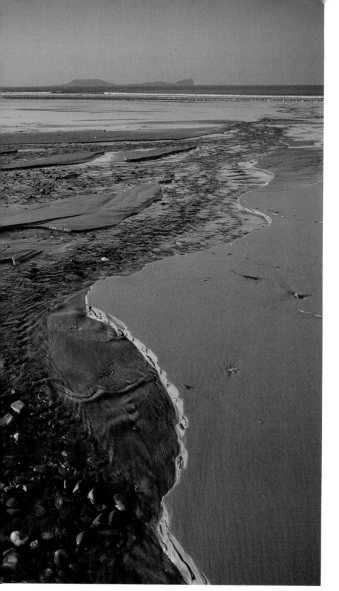

Crymlyn Bog

CCW NNR

The largest lowland fen in Wales, Crymlyn Bog is a remarkable example of a fast-disappearing type of habitat with a wealth of rare plants and birds. Although the great sundew has vanished, both the round- and long-leaved sundews are still found here. In midsummer, the yellow of bog asphodel, great spearwort and yellow sedge make a splendid show. Reed and sedge warblers are numerous in summer, while Cetti's warbler is a more recent arrival. Crymlyn Bog is one of the few places in the extreme south of Wales where snipe can still be heard 'drumming'. Strangely situated in the heart of industrial Swansea, the bog is continuously threatened but somehow, miraculously, it still survives.

Getting there *By car:* via the A4217 in east Swansea. **Access:** permit from CCW required off marked footpaths. **Amenities:** car-park and information centre on Dinam Road, south of Pentre Dwr. **Further information:** leaflet from CCW, T: (01792) 390707. TIC, Swansea, T: (01792) 468321.

Kenfig Pool and Dunes

CCW NNR

These 2,525 acres (1,022 ha) of dunes, flanked on the seaward side by the expanse of Kenfig Sands, contain a large, reed-fringed, dune-slack lake called Kenfig Pool in the middle. Long recognized for its wealth of flowering plants (more than 500 species have been recorded), the reserve also boasts a variety of birds,

The long spine of Worm's Head emerges in the dawn light of Rhossili Bay

Both the CCW, T: (01792) 771949, and the Glamorgan Wildlife Trust, T: (01656) 724100, produce leaflets and organize walks in the many nature reserves. Advice is available at Rhossili on rock climbing and sea fishing. The

CCW owns a substantial collection of books and scientific papers, which can be viewed on appointment. **Further information:** see the *Swansea* guide produced by the Wales Tourist Board for details of accommodation and activities. There are TICs at Mumbles, T: (01792) 361302; and Swansea, T: (01792) 468321.

including uncommon species such as purple heron and bittern. Great crested grebe, tufted duck, and occasionally garganey, all breed here. Several hundred tufted duck and pochard gather in winter, together with smaller numbers of wigeon, gadwall, teal and mallard.

Small numbers of sea-birds pass offshore in late summer and can be observed by those who watch patiently from Sker Point. Among the dune plants are carline thistle, viper's bugloss and even primrose, while the slacks support several species of orchid. **Getting there** *By car:* signposted from Pyle and Porthcawl; junction 37 from the M4. *By bus:* regular bus services from Porthcawl and Bridgend. **Access:** open all year. Several footpaths. **Activities:** lectures and guided walks regularly scheduled by Kenfig Reserve Centre. **Further information:** leaflets available from Kenfig Reserve Centre, Ton Kenfig, Bridgend CF33 4PT, T: (01656) 743386. TIC, Porthcawl, T: (01656) 786639.

The Wye Valley

CCW NNR, GWT Reserves

The River Wye rises at 2,000 ft (600 m) on Plynlimon not far from the sea in Cardigan Bay, but like its near neighbour, the Severn, it chooses an easterly course to the Bristol Channel where eventually the waters mingle. For the last 21 miles (35 km) of its journey the Wye forms the boundary with England, and here it has carved a meandering course through a magnificent gorge from just downstream of Monmouth to the sea at Chepstow.

The gorge contains much fine woodland — among the few ancient woods left in Britain — with oak, beech, ash, wych elm and field maple. A number of scarce species occur, including small-leaved lime and those curiosities of the British flora, the rare whitebeams, of which several species have been recorded here.

The whole area is renowned for its invertebrates, the butterfly fauna being especially rich; nearly half of all the species in Britain can be found here. The riverside cliffs contain caves, which provide a winter hibernation site for greater horseshoe bats, one of Britain's rarest mammals.

Shelduck breed on the lower reaches of the river, while cormorants and grey herons are always to be seen. Look out for the common sandpiper in the summer months. This delightful wader has a nervous disposition, or so it seems as it bobs its way along the water's edge, attracting attention with its shrill 'willy-wicket' song. One wonders whether sandpipers worked the river banks when the monks from Tintern Abbey fished these waters 800 summers ago. **Before you go** *Maps:* Ordnance Survey Landranger Series, map No. 162. **Getting there** *By car:* the A466 (Exit 2 on the M48, at the Welsh end of the Severn Bridge) clings to the banks of the River Wye for its last 18 miles (29 km) from Monmouth to the Severn. From the Midlands and North, turn off the M5 at exit 8 and take the M50 to where it ends near Ross-on-Wye, 12 miles (19 km) from Monmouth. *By rail:* Chepstow is on a direct line between Cardiff and the Midlands. **Where to stay:** plenty of accommodation along the valley, with Chepstow and Monmouth at either end offering a wide range of

overnight stays. Book ahead at tourist information centres in Chepstow or Monmouth. *Youth hostels:* 3 youth hostels are evenly spaced along the valley at Welsh Bicknor, T: (01594) 860300; Monmouth, T: (01600) 715116; and St Briavels Castle, T: (01594) 530272. **Activities** *Walking:* both banks of the river are criss-crossed with footpaths and rights-of-way. Map packs and leaflets are available from tourist information centres and Monmouthshire County Council, T: (01633) 644865.

The Wyndcliff Nature Trail is operated by the FC. About 3 miles (5 km) north of Chepstow, turn left off the A466. The trail leads from the FC car-park. Spectacular views from the Eagle's Nest on cliff top. From there, a path (including 365 steps) descends to the Wye.

Cleddon Bog and Cleddon Shoots (GWT), areas of ancient woodland, are both accessible from the village of Trellech. Take the Llandogo road off the B4293, 5 miles (8 km) south of Monmouth.

Trails for the less able at Lower Whitestone, operated by FC (leaflet available). **Access:** Lady Park Wood open to permit holders only. Apply to CCW. Cars not permitted on FC roads; riding permitted on FC bridleways. **Further information:** *Wye Valley and Vale of Usk* guide available from tourist information centres. TICs in Monmouth, T: (01600) 713899, and Chepstow, T: (01291) 623772. Booklet on reserves from Gwent Wildlife Trust, 16 White Swan Court, Monmouth, Gwent NP5 3NY, T: (01600) 715501. Further details about FC holdings, T: (01639) 710221 (for the Welsh side of the river), T: (01594) 833057 (for the English side). County Council Tourism Officer, T: (01633) 644847.

Brecon Beacons

National Park extending over 519 square miles (1,350 sq km) of mountains and valleys in southern Wales

One of the finest views in all of Wales may be obtained from the A470 just northeast of Brecon. Look south, and you can see the high peaks of the Brecon Beacons, encompassing all the beauty and majesty of the region. At times they are covered by winter snow, at others shrouded in mists that leave only the foothills visible. Whatever the conditions, the Brecon Beacons are always a lure, a reminder that there are still uplands to be walked and less accessible valleys to be followed.

This huge tract of land stretches nearly 40 miles (64 kilometres) eastwards from the corrie cliffs of the Carmarthen Van in the west to the Black Mountains on the border with England. To the south is industrial Glamorgan, to the north more high ground, the Mynydd Eppynt, the southern end of the central spine of Wales.

The westernmost section of the park is known, confusingly, as Black Mountain. From the youth hostel at Llanddeusant, at the base of its northern slopes, the two main peaks of this spectacular region, Bannau Sir Gaer, 2,460 feet (750 metres), and Fan Brycheiniog, 2,366 feet (721 metres), are a popular challenge.

To the east of Black Mountain lies Fforest Fawr, once a hunting reserve for the Lords of Brecon. It is less frequented by hikers than its towering eastern neighbours, the glamorous Beacons — a fact that may make it more attractive to solitary walkers.

Much of the park is composed of old red sandstone; in its eponymous heartland, the Brecon Beacons themselves, it rises to 2,907 feet (886 metres) at Pen y Fan, the highest point in South Wales. There are two lesser peaks hard by: Corn Du, 2,863 feet (873 metres), and the pointed summit of Cribyn, 2,608 feet (795 metres). If you make your way up the path from Storey Arms, you may

be surprised to come across a memorial obelisk commemorating the death from exposure in August 1900 of young Tommy Jones, a local boy who lost his way on a short walk after dark. It serves as a salutary reminder that the high ground can be dangerous, even in midsummer, for those who come ill-prepared.

The park contains many reservoirs, lakes and waterways. The numerous reservoirs provide water for South Wales, while among the natural lakes are Llyn-y-Fan Fawr and Llyn-y-Fan Fach lying below the 650-foot (200-metre) cliffs of Bannau Sir Gaer. The latter is renowned for the folk-tale of the Lady of the Lake, a beauty who lived beneath its wind-flecked waves. Her father allowed her to marry a local farmhand with the catch that if she was touched three times by a cold iron, she would return to the lake, taking her dowry with her. This fateful event came to pass and she was plunged back into the ice-cold waters for all eternity. Further legend has it that one of her sons became the first of the physicians of Myddi, a village a few miles to the north, and you can still see the graves of the last of these healers.

Just south of Llangorse is Llangorse Lake, the largest area of natural fresh water in the southern half of Wales. Famous as a breeding ground for wetland birds, it has unfortunately lost some of its natural history interest as water sports and agricultural pollution have taken their toll. The number of breeding birds has dropped, but there is a good range of wildfowl in winter. Pochard and tufted duck are the most numerous, while small parties of Bewick's and whooper swans are regular visitors. Certain plants have vanished, though several scarce species remain including some which reach the southern limits of their range here. The best time to visit is in late July, when the pale lilac flowers of water lobelia dance in the wavelets and family parties of raven cavort happily overhead.

The park contains several notable reserves such as the one at Craig-y-Ciliau, where the densely wooded limestone cliffs and screes contrast sharply with the open moorland above. Bordering the River Enig near Talgarth is Pwll-y-Wrach, a Brecknock

Wildlife Trust Reserve, which encompasses a rich woodland containing dog's mercury, enchanter's nightshade, woodruff and wild strawberry.

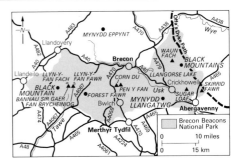

At the southern edge of the park the sandstones give way to millstone grit and carboniferous limestone. This is a dream land for the geologist and the caver. There are more swallow holes per square mile than in any other part of Britain. Like bomb craters they litter the southern boundary. The rivers and streams are in confusion: some vanish below the ground to reappear after a short distance, others pass through gorges and over waterfalls, none more classic that at Henrhyd where there is a 100-foot (30-metre) drop, or at Sgwd yr Eira on the Hepste where you can drive a herd of sheep behind the cascade.

If you really wish to go behind water, to follow its ancient routes, then visit the Dan-yr-Ogof show caves in the upper reaches of the Tawe. The system was first explored in 1912 by the Morgan brothers and their friends, first on a raft and then by coracle. What better way to explore a Welsh cave than by Welsh coracle? For the experienced caver there are numerous other systems in-cluding that at Agen Allwed, where over nine miles (15 kilometres) of underground passages penetrate into the heart of Mynydd Llangatwg, and the cave system at Ogof Ffynon Ddu National Nature Reserve, one of the deepest in Europe and the only cave national nature reserve in Britain.

The park comes to a dramatic conclusion in the east where it reaches OFFA'S DYKE PATH (see page 140) and the daunting peaks of the Black Mountains. Waun Fach, at 2,660 feet (811 metres) is the highest, but Sugar Loaf, 1,955 feet (595 metres) and Skirrid Fawr, 1,595 feet (486 metres), set apart to the south of the main range, are equally inspiring to the hill-walker.

BEFORE YOU GO

Maps: except for its extreme western and south-eastern corners, the Brecon Beacons National Park fits obligingly into two Ordnance Survey Landranger Series maps; Nos. 160 and 161. The serious walker, however, is better equipped with Nos. 12 and 13 of the OS Outdoor Leisure Series, which give the entire park in 1:25,000 scale (about 2½ inches to the mile).

Guide-books: a good introductory guide-book is *Brecon Beacons* by Andrew Davies (Cicerone Press, 1995).

A good place to start any visit is the Brecon Beacons Mountain Centre, 5 miles (8 km) south-west of Brecon. The largest of the park's 5 information centres, it is open every day except Christmas.

GETTING THERE

By air: Cardiff, the principal airport in South Wales, has regular flights to London, Birmingham and Glasgow, and a limited international service.

By car: from the south and east, the M4 brings motorists to within 20 miles (32 km) of the park's southern boundary. Take the A4042 from exit 26 at Newport for Pontypool and Abergavenny. From exit 32, take the A470 for Brecon. From the Midlands and the North, the M50 (exit 8 on the M5) leads to Ross-on-Wye. Continue on the A40 for Abergavenny in the east of the park. The A40 angles north-west across the park to Brecon and from there due west to Llandovery. Most of the major roads, however, run roughly north-south: the A4069 over Black Mountain, the A4067 through Fforest Fawr, the A470 through the Brecon Beacons and the A479 to the west of the Black Mountains. The access route to Llangorse Lake is well signposted from the A40 at Bwlch, the pass that crosses a low shoulder of the Black Mountains.

By rail: at Newport and Cardiff – stations on the London main line – change respectively for Abergavenny and Merthyr Tydfil. Abergavenny also connects via Crewe with cities in the Midlands and North. The beautiful Heart of Wales Line from Swansea to Shrewsbury serves both Llandeilo and Llandovery and connects via its termini to points throughout Britain. National Rail Enquiries, T: (0345) 484950.

By bus: at major coach stations in Newport and Cardiff change for local buses to points within the park. Stagecoach, T: (01633) 266336, and National Express, T: (0990) 808080, operate regular services to Brecon. Train, Bus and Coach National Enquiries, T: (0891) 910910. For more information on local services, consult *The Wales Bus, Train and Tourist Map & Guide*, available at tourist information centres.

WHERE TO STAY

The park has within or just outside its boundaries a number of towns which offer a wide range of self-catering and serviced accommodation. Brecon, with a population of just over 7,000, is the largest community in the park; Hay-on-Wye, Crickhowell and Talgarth are also centres for accommodation and information. Outside the park, Abergavenny to the south-east, and Llandovery and Llandeilo to the west are the principal dormitory towns for tourists. Equally convenient, though less tourist-orientated, are the industrial 'heads of the valleys' to the south, Merthyr Tydfil being the largest among them. Bed-booking services are available from the tourist information centres at Abergavenny, T: (01873) 853254; Brecon, T: (01874) 623156; and Llandovery, T: (01550) 720693.

Outdoor living: the National Park Authority issues a fact sheet listing camping and caravan and motor-home sites within or near the park, which is available from the 5 information centres. Camping elsewhere, even on common land, requires the owner's or tenant's permission. Motorists towing caravans are urged to avoid minor roads which may not be wide enough to accommodate two vehicles.

The FC, T: (01685) 723060, operates several camping sites for walkers only. Further information from the National Park information centres.

Youth hostels: there are 5 youth hostels within the park: Capel-y-Ffin, T: (01873) 890650; Llanddeusant, T: (01550) 740619; Llwyn-y-Celyn, Libanus, T: (01874) 624261; Ty'n-y-Caeau, Groesffordd, T: (01874) 665270; Ystradfellte, Aberdare, T: (01639) 720301.

ACCESS

The unfenced uplands of the park seem to invite ramblers to walk where they will, but remember that most of the open country is common land, used for grazing by the local 'commoners'. In practice, there is rarely a conflict between visitors and commoners, but when in doubt concerning your rights, stick to signposted paths or to rights-of-way indicated on the OS maps.

The Forestry Commission, which has a substantial presence in the park, generally welcomes well-behaved walkers along its many trails. Its 4 major forests are Coed Taf, 5 miles (8 km) north of Merthyr Tydfil; Talybont, just west of the village of that name; Mynydd Du, in the heart of the Black Mountains; and Coed y Rhaiadr — with its spectacular waterfalls — bordering the park to the south of Fforest Fawr. For complete information about FC forests and amenities, visit the Garwnant Visitor Centre, T: (01685) 723060, 5 miles (8 km) north of Merthyr.

For access to nature reserves which are not served by rights-of-way or signposted nature trails, contact the CCW, T: (01873) 857938; or the Brecknock Wildlife Trust office, T: (01874) 625708. Most of the park lies in Powys, but Dyfed, Gwent and Glamorgan nibble at its corners.

ACTIVITIES

Walking: despite the relative proximity of all the major peaks to main roads and the comforts of civilization, the walker in the park should remember that the high ground here is as exposed and the weather as unpredictable as anywhere in Britain. Plan your route carefully and equip yourself for rough terrain, then set out to enjoy some of the most accessible and beautiful hill walking in the country.

With the aid of the OS maps it is an easy park in which to improvise an attractive expedition. Some of the standard routes, however, are hard to beat. From Crickhowell, for instance, you can take in all the major hills of the Black Mountains on the way to the youth hostel at Capel-y-Ffin. From Brecon there is a circular ridge walk which includes as many of the highest Beacons as you have the energy to encounter in a single day. For less strenuous excursions, try stretches of the tow-path by the canal between Brecon and Pontypool, or visit the Forestry Commission plantations, with their well-established network of forest paths.

The National Park Authority issues several booklets suggesting walks of varying distances throughout the park; guided walks are also available.

Cycling: the Sustrans Cardiff/Chepstow to Builth Wells cycle route, map No. 8 (42), passes through the Brecon Beacons. Contact Sustrans Information Service for details, PO box 21, Bristol, BS99 2HA, T: (0117) 929 0888.

Riding: in a land so full of ponies, it is no wonder that pony trekking is such a popular activity. *Factsheets: Pony Trekking*, a leaflet issued by the National Park Authority, contains a comprehensive list

Winter emphasizes the remoteness of Brecon at Pen-y-Fan, the highest of the Beacons

of riding centres, mainly in the Black Mountains, from which you can ride — or learn to ride. Most trips are either half-day or full-day treks.

For further information write to Wales Trekking and Riding Association, c/o Standby Secretarial Services, 9 Nevill Street, Abergavenny NP7 5AA, T: (01873) 858717. *Activity Wales*, available at tourist information centres, also contains information about riding centres.

Caving: in the narrow strip of limestone that extends across the park's southern boundary are some of the longest and deepest caves in the country. From west to east, the principal caving areas are: the Tawe Valley and Black Mountain;

the Nedd, Mellte, Hepste and Sychryd valleys; the Nant Glais valley north of Merthyr Tydfil; and the Llangattock escarpment and Clydach gorge south of Crickhowell.

Caving is an enthusiast's sport and not for the adventurous novice. If you are a caver, contact one of the many clubs whose members have experience in the Brecon underground. The National Park Authority issues a leaflet which lists some of the region's caves and caving clubs. For further information contact the Cambrian Caving Council, Hon. Secretary F. S. Baguley, White Lion House, Ynys Uchaf, Ystradgynlais, Swansea SA9 1RW, T: (01639) 849519.

Non-cavers should content themselves with a visit to the spectacular Dan-yr-Ogof and Cathedral show caves in the Tawe valley.

Climbing: the crumbling red sandstone that lies beneath so much of the park makes it a treacherous playground for the rock climber. Although some climbing is possible on limestone quarry faces in the south of the park, these hardly justify a special visit.

FURTHER INFORMATION
Information centres within the park: Brecon Beacons Mountain Centre, nr Libanus, Brecon, Powys LD3 8ER, T: (01874) 623366, open all year; Monmouth Road, Abergavenny, Monmouthshire NP7 5ER, T: (01873) 853254; Kings Road, Llandovery, Carmarthenshire SA20 0AW, T: (01550) 720693; Cattle Market Car-Park, Brecon, Powys LD3 7BA, T: (01874) 623156; Craig-y-Nos Country Park, Pen-y-Cae, Swansea Valley SA9 1GL, T: (01639) 730395.

CENTRAL WALES

The gateways to Central Wales are the valleys of the Twyi and Teifi in the south, Ystywth and Rheidol in the centre, and Dyfi in the north. Each is a superb route into the heart of Wales, the last refuge for some species, notably the red kite. Eight centuries ago the last beavers in Britain were building their lodges on the Teifi; Hywel Dda the Law Giver valued their skins at six score pence, five times that of marten skins and ten times that of any other animal.

All five westerly flowing rivers, and the Severn and Wye which travel east, rise in the great moorland massif of Central Wales, the Cambrian Mountains. Some 500 square miles (1,280 square kilometres) in extent, this is one of the most remote and sparsely populated areas south of Scotland; a land of open wind-swept hills and deeply incised valleys with thickly wooded slopes where the sound of the axe is rarely heard any more. The real threat to the wilderness here is forestry. There are some, usually those with vested interests, who claim that ugly blocks of alien conifers support more birds than the open grouse and heather moor. No one who truly loves Wales would wish to exchange the hill-top call of red grouse for that of the conifer wood-pigeon, the song of the golden plover for that of the blackbird, or the dashing merlin for the dunnock. Each has its place, but the moorlands are for moorland birds.

Upper Twyi Valley

RSPB Reserves, WTWW Reserves

Llandovery was described by the 19th-century travel writer George Borrow as 'about the pleasantest little town in which I have halted in the course of my wanderings'. It is an ideal base from which to explore the Twyi valley. Hard by the town is Poor Man's Wood, given to the town three centuries ago by Vicar Pritchard with a stipulation that the poor people could remove such dead wood as they could carry. Few, if any, now avail themselves, but the wood remains, still owned by the townsfolk.

If you go to Llyn Brianne Reservoir at the head of the valley, you will arrive at the borders of Carmarthen, Ceredigion and Brecon. A huge conifer plantation extends north for a further 10 miles (16 km) but beyond the trees lie the open uplands. Here you can enjoy the wide open spaces, apparently yours alone until a low-flying aircraft on a training mission sweeps by and, depending on your inclination, you either marvel at or curse the jet engine.

Two miles (3 km) below the great rock and clay dam of Brianne, the RSPB have their Dinas Reserve. Here, a nature trail passes round the base of a conical wooded hill almost encircled by the rushing Twyi and its tributary the Doethie.

The red kite retreated to these two river valleys around the end of the 19th century. Central Wales still remains its principal home, although it has been introduced into other parts of Britain recently. Efforts over the last ten years have allowed the once tiny, fragile population to grow significantly here, the number of breeding pairs increasing from 111 in 1994 to 164 in 1998.

Getting there *By car:* leave the A40 in Llandovery and choose any of the unclassified roads which follow the river north to Rhandirmwyn village and beyond. *By rail:* the Heart of Wales Line from Shrewsbury to Swansea stops at Llandovery.

Where to stay *Youth hostel:* Bryn Poeth Uchaf at Hafod y Pant, Cynghordy, Llandovery, T: (01550) 750235. **Further information:** TIC, Llandovery, T: (01550) 720693; leaflet from Dinas RSPB Nature Reserve, Troedrhiwgelynen, Rhandirmwyn, Llandovery SA20 0PN, T: (01550) 760276.

Dyfi Estuary

Includes CCW, NNR and RSPB Reserves

The Dyfi Estuary marks the border between Central and North Wales. To the south lie the rolling hills of Ceredigion, to the north the ramparts of Cader Idris and Snowdonia. Few estuaries can encompass such a range of habitats, and there can be few better places to start an exploration than at the Ynyslas Dunes NNR. The dune slacks are worth inspecting closely because they house some botanical treasures, particularly orchids.

To the south-east, trapped by the coastal ridge, is another great mire of Central Wales, Cors Fochno. It is part of Ynyslas NNR and one of the largest raised bogs in Britain, rich with myrtle, rosemary, cranberry and royal fern.

The estuary narrows as it

twists its way inland. On its southern shore is Ynys Hir, an RSPB reserve with habitats ranging from saltings to woodland and bracken-clad hillsides, and consequently a wide variety of birds. **Getting there** *By car:* easily accessible from the A487 Aberystwyth to Machynlleth road. For Ynyslas, take the B4353 9 miles (14 km) north of Aberystwyth. Ynys Hir is signposted near the village of Eglwsfach on the A487, 7 miles (11 km) from Machynlleth. **Access:** the dunes and shore at Ynyslas are open at all times. Ynys Hir is open daily 9 am to 9 pm or sunset, when earlier, and on weekends only Nov-Feb. There is an entry charge for non-RSPB members. Access to the rest of the estuary reserve, including Cors Fochno, is by permit issued by CCW, Aberystwyth. **Activities:** visitor centre, bird hides, guided walks (take rubber boots) at both Ynyslas, T: (01970) 828551/871640, and Ynys Hir, T: (01654) 781265. **Further information:** contact CCW, Plas Gogerddan, Aberystwyth, Dyfed SY23 3EE, T: (01970) 828551. Further details about Ynys Hir from RSPB Wales Office, Byrn Aderyn, The Bank, Newtown, Powys SY16 2AB. TIC, Machynlleth, T: (01654) 702401.

Cors Caron

From the Welsh *cors/gors,* meaning bog

CCW NNR

This huge upturned saucer of peat, in places 30 ft (9 m) thick, rests on the bed of a lake formed in glacial times and is one of the largest and best preserved raised mires in western Europe. It lies immediately north of Tregaron, surrounded by low hills, which are the haunt of the raven and

The kite is now a rare spectacle away from Central Wales

buzzard. This is one of the best places to see the red kite, especially in winter, as well as whooper swans and other wildfowl, which you can watch from a tower-hide reached after a 1-mile (1½-km) walk along the disused railway line. **Getting there** *By car:* access from the B4343, 1½ miles (2½ km) north of Tregaron, 15 miles (24 km) south-east of Aberystwyth on the A485. *By bus:* bus services run from Aberystwyth to Tregaron. **Access:** limited road-side parking on the B4343; public access only along nature trail — including observation tower — which follows disused railway. Permit required for other areas. **Further information:** contact the Warden, CCW, Neuaddlas, Tregaron, Ceredigion SY25 6LG, T: (01974) 298480.

Lake Vrynwy

RSPB Reserve

The largest man-made lake in Wales, nearly 5 miles (8 km) long and with a perimeter of 11 miles (18 km), has supplied water to Liverpool for nearly 100 years. The reserve extends through the superb woodlands right on to the upland

catchment at the southern edge of the Berwyns. Here birds such as hen harrier, merlin and short-eared owls breed, while other species that are scarce in Wales, such as the golden plover, may also be encountered. In the woods there are woodcock and even the elusive long-eared owl, best located early in the year when its characteristic triple hoot may be heard. The breeding goosanders are probably the highlight among the waterfowl. **Getting there** *By car:* located 20 miles (32 km) north-west of Welshpool. From Welshpool, take the A490 to Llanfyllin, then continue to Llanwddyn on the B4393, which encircles the lake close to the shoreline. **Where to stay:** the Lake Vrynwy Hotel provides bed and breakfast, as do a number of local farms. **Access:** unrestricted. Some of the best views are from the B4393. **Activities:** the RSPB operates a visitor centre, T: (01691) 870278, and provides information on an extensive range of activities. Nature trails, 4 bird hides (one wheelchair-accessible), guided walks and teaching programmes. **Further information:** RSPB leaflets and guides at centre. Tourist information centres at Lake Vrynwy, T: (01691) 870346; and Welshpool, T: (01938) 552043.

NORTH WALES

The hills and mountains of North Wales tower to the north of the Dyfi and west of the Shropshire and Cheshire plain. The Welsh princes once held sway in these fastnesses, high above the coastal regions, which heard the remorseless tramp of many an invading army. After the death of Llywelyn ap Grufydd, a 13th-century prince who led a rebellion against the English, Edward I had a series of magnificent fortifications erected at key points such as Flint, Conwy, Caernarfon, Beaumaris and Harlech, proud on its rock high above the sea; a sea now receded over half a mile to the west.

The Snowdonia National Park covers half of North Wales, but there are many delights beyond its boundaries. Anglesey, separated from the mainland by the lovely shores of the Menai Straits, is a land of broad, flat-topped ridges and shallow valleys, of superb beaches, cliff headlands and lakes thronged in winter with Siberian waterfowl. One visitor has said that 'all the softness of Anglesey has marched down to the edge of the water', and the spot is 'not only one of the fairest in Britain but in Europe'.

Further west lies the narrow peninsula of Lleyn, its hills sloping gently down to the sea. With its quiet countryside, narrow roads and tiny coves, it is an area much underrated and worthy of exploration. Beyond it lies Bardsey Island, now a bird sanctuary, but formerly a religious one; in days gone by three journeys to Bardsey were considered equal to one to Rome.

Bardsey Island

Bird Observatory and Nature Reserve

Some 1½ miles (3 km) off the tip of the Lleyn Peninsula, Bardsey is the legendary burial ground of 20,000 saints, a place where fact and legend are inextricably interwoven. It has a long ecclesiastical history, for a holy man called Einion Frenchin had a cell here early in the 5th century, as did St Cadfan about 100 years later.

Unlike the Pembrokeshire Islands, Bardsey was once cultivated by a thriving farming community. Only one family still farms the island, but many of the old houses remain in good condition. The Bardsey Bird Observatory now operates in one of them and others are used as holiday and tourist accommodation.

The island is renowned for its bird migration, partly because in certain conditions following a new moon large numbers of birds are killed by flying into its infamous lighthouse. A mouth-watering list of rare vagrants has been recorded on the island and includes honey buzzard, sora rail, bee-eater, tawny pipit, penduline tit, yellow warbler and grey-cheeked thrush. Ten species of sea-bird also breed here, as do a few pairs of the rare chough.

Getting there *By sea:* the Bardsey Island Trust Ltd operates regular boat services from Pwllheli and Porthmeudwy. Depending upon weather conditions and demand, there are up to 2 daily services from Porthmeudwy and 1 from Pwllheli. Journey time approximately 2 hours. Day trips or longer stays. Contact the Trust Officer, Coed Anna, Nanhoron, Pwllheli, Gwynedd LL53 8PR, T: (01758) 730740. **Where to stay:** the Bardsey Island Trust rents out self-catering cottages to groups or individuals willing to share; a booking service, T: (01758) 760667, operates June-Aug. The Bardsey Bird and Field Observatory runs residential courses. For enquiries and reservations, contact The Booking Secretary, 46 Maudlin Drive, Teignmouth, South Devon TQ1 8SB, T: (01626) 773908. **Further information:** *Bardsey, Its History and Wildlife* is available from the Bardsey Island Trust. Nearest tourist information centre is in Pwllheli, T: (01758) 613000.

Newborough Warren

CCW NNR

Newborough Warren, the site of one of the finest sand-dune systems in Britain, was once threatened by conifer planting; fortunately, the plan was abandoned before it was too late, and nearly 1,605 acres (650 ha) of coastline were declared an NNR in 1955. In addition to the dunes there is a freshwater lake, the Cefni estuary, a beach and the rocky islet of Ynys Llanddwyn, an island only at high tide. In the extreme west, at the head of the estuary, is

Carnedd Llywelyn looms giddily south-east of Bethesda near the North Wales coast

Malltraeth Pool, made famous by the bird artist Charles Tunnicliffe who lived here from 1947 until his death in 1979.

In winter various waterfowl, including red-throated and great northern divers, pintail, wigeon and goldeneye frequent the bay. Montagu's harriers used to breed here, but sadly no longer do so, although marsh and hen harriers can still be seen in passage.

Getting there *By car:* signposted access from A4080 in village of Newborough. **Access:** open access on the beach, otherwise restricted to footpaths.
Activities: the CCW runs an information centre on Ynys Llanddwyn Island, T: (01248) 373100. **Further information:** the WTB's *Anglesey* brochure is available at tourist information centres. Local TICs in Bangor, T: (01248) 352786; Holyhead, T: (01407) 762622; and Llanfair Pwllgwyngyll, T: (01248) 713177. For further information, contact the reserve, T: (01248) 372333, or the FC, T: (01492) 640578, which runs Newborough Forest. Leaflet from CCW, North Wales Region, Hafod Elfyn, Ffordd Penrhos, Bangor, Gwynedd LL57 2LQ, T: (01248) 372333.

The Manx shearwater, which spends most of its life skimming the Irish Sea, nests on Skokholm and Skomer

South Stack

RSPB Reserve

At the most westerly extremity of the island of Anglesey soars a 2-mile (3-km) stretch of cliff, which is a popular challenge for climbers. Sharing parts of the cliffs that are out of bounds to climbers during the breeding season are large numbers of sea-birds, including up to 3,000 guillemots and smaller numbers of razorbills, puffins and kittiwakes.

Peregrines nest here and choughs can usually be seen, often close to Ellin's Tower, the observation room and information centre. The heaths behind the cliffs boast some superb late summer flowers, including such specialities as the field fleawort and spotted rock-rose.

Getting there *By car:* secondary road signposted to South Stack from Holyhead leads out to cliffs; several nearby car-parks. **Access:** many footpaths around the reserve. Walkers are advised not to leave the paths because the cliffs are dangerous.
Activities: Ellin's Tower Sea-bird Centre (open Easter to September), T: (01407) 764973, has displays on bird life and fine views from first floor. **Further information:** leaflet from RSPB. TIC, Holyhead, T: (01407) 762622.

'There are, as perhaps the reader knows, no jaguars in Wales - nor pumas - nor anacondas...What I feared most was lest, whilst my sleeping face was upturned to the stars, some one of the many Brahminical-looking cows in the Cambrian Hills might poach her foot into the centre of my face.'

*Thomas de Quincey,
Confessions of an
English Opium Eater*

Anglesey's Offshore Islands

Two small islands on opposite sides of Anglesey have something to offer bird-lovers and island-goers alike. On the west coast the offshore islets at Rhosneigr support the largest roseate tern colony in Britain, as well as summer populations of common, arctic and Sandwich terns, and passage waders such as whimbrel in winter. On the east coast the small, green, whale-backed cliffs and grassy slopes of uninhabited Puffin Island provide nesting sites for numerous sea-birds, including razorbills, cormorants, shags, guillemots and, of course puffins. The island also boasts an old telegraph station, once used to signal news between Holyhead and Liverpool.
Getting there *By car:* Rhosneigr is on the A4080. For Puffin Island, follow an unclassified road north-east of Beaumaris to Penmon. **Further information:** tourist information centres in Holyhead, T: (01407) 762622; and Bangor, T: (01248) 713177.

Great Orme

Nature Trail

This massive headland, jutting out into the Irish Sea to the north of Llandudno, is a botanist's paradise, with a profusion of maritime flowers and scarce species such as goldilocks aster, spotted cats-ear, Nottingham catchfly and spiked speedwell. Five bushes of a cotoneaster not found elsewhere in Britain cling on here. Great Orme is also notable for its butterflies and a fine sea-bird colony, including fulmars, kittiwakes, guillemots and razorbills on the cliffs. **Getting there:** from Marine Drive (toll road) in Llandudno, or by tramway to the centre summit and then on foot. **Access:** public nature trails along cliffs. **Further information:** Conwy RSPB Nature Reserve, T: (01492) 584091, will give details of nature trails and the best bird hides. Local tourist information centre, 1-2 Chapel Street, Llandudno LL30 2YU, T: (01492) 876413.

Dee Estuary

Ramsar, RSPB Reserve at Point of Ayr

The Dee Estuary, the third most important in Britain for its waders and wildfowl, straddles the border of England and Wales. In mid-winter up to 100,000 waders and 20,000 wildfowl are resident, using the rich feeding areas on the sands and mud-flats and retreating to the salt marshes and coastal fields at high water. Among the wildfowl the winter flock of up to 5,000 pintail is the largest concentration in Europe.

The estuary also provides a popular refuge for a herd of

The puffin, one of Britain's most distinctive sea-birds, is easily distinguished from its relatives, the auks, by its colourful bill

grey seals. The sight of up to 200 animals hauled out on the West Hoyle Bank is memorable. They are some 150 miles (240 km) from their nearest major breeding area, the Pembrokeshire coast.

Like many other estuaries, the Dee is constantly under threat from development but is now recognized as internationally important for its 11 species of waders and wildfowl. The estuary is the winter home for flocks of black-tailed godwit, oystercatcher, curlew, redshank and pintail, which migrate here from their Arctic breeding grounds. **Getting there** *By car:* from Chester the A548 North Wales coastal road runs along the shoreline from Connah's Quay to Point of Ayr. On the Wirral side, a number of towns and villages, all linked by the A540, give access to the shoreline. *By rail or bus:* trains and buses run from Chester to Flint and

Prestatyn, which are close to the estuary. **Where to stay:** Chester is one of the major tourist centres in Britain. The North Wales coastal towns of Rhyl and Prestatyn are popular holiday resorts. **Activities:** opportunities for bird-watching on both shores. Two nature reserves on the Welsh side of the estuary: at Connah's Quay, 4 miles (6 km) south-east of Flint on the A548, and at Point of Ayr, at the mouth of the Dee on the Talacre turn-off from the A548. **Access:** Connah's Quay: a number of public open days — generally Sundays — each year; otherwise access is by application to the North Wales Wildlife Trust, 367 High Street, Bangor, Gwynedd LL48 6LF, T: (01766) 770274. Point of Ayr RSPB Reserve, T: (01352) 780527: no restrictions, but visitors are asked to be careful so as not to disturb roosting waders. **Further information:** nearby tourist information centres are at the Town Hall, Chester, T: (01244) 317962; and the Offa's Dyke Centre, Prestatyn, T: (01745) 889092.

133

Snowdonia

National Park comprising 838 square miles (2,170 sq km) of Welsh mountain terrain

🐾🐾🐾

'Horrible with the sight of bare stones' John Leland wrote of Snowdonia in the mid-16th century. Other early visitors also made disparaging remarks about the terrain and, not surprisingly, about the weather, for the high Snowdonia peaks may receive as much as 200 inches (5,080 mm) of rainfall in a year. They are rugged and often wet, but do not be put off, for this is the wildest region in central Britain, a place to savour and to explore, and it does not rain every day. The heights may be mist-shrouded on occasions, but then the blue sky appears, with white clouds passing behind the ridges and peaks. Climb to the high ground and it seems as though you can see to the ends of Wales, with no hint of the valleys hidden away among the folds.

This is upland Britain at its very best. Snowdon, or Yr Wyddfa as it is known in Welsh, soars to 3,557 feet (1,085 metres), making it the highest mountain in England and Wales. It forms the centre of the North Wales massif, a great sweep of moor and mountain that includes 13 other peaks above 3,000 feet (900 metres), stretching from high above the Conwy valley southwest to the Rhinogs, Cader Idris and the Dyfi. The park contains many deep and narrow valleys, through which the main routes pass, together with some 22 miles (35 kilometres) of coast, the sandy shore of Merioneth running south from Harlech to the Mawddach estuary.

For the geologist, for those interested in land forms and the shaping of the countryside, Snowdonia is the greatest classroom in Britain. Early geologists came here to describe the classic sites, and their interpreta-

The picturesque countryside of Crawcwellt is overshadowed by the silhouettes of the Rhinogs, rising grimly away to the west

tions still enlighten our visits today. One of the most dramatic sites is at Cwm Idwal, the first NNR in Wales, a magnificent bowl gouged by ice out of the surrounding crags with a glacial lake at its base. Above the lake, in the cliff cleft of Twill Du, the Devil's Kitchen, can be seen the base of the great rock fold of the Snowdon syncline, a feature very rarely revealed elsewhere.

To the south of the main Snowdonia uplands, spread across the tranquil Vale of Ffestiniog and bounded by the beautiful Mawddach Estuary, are the craggy uplands of the Rhinogs. A rough landscape with massive ledges and block screes makes this one of the most intractable places in Wales. One visitor to the highest peak, Rhinog Fawr, claimed that it extracted more perspiration to the yard than any other climb in Snowdonia. Only ancient trackways and footpaths cross this region, including at one point the so-called Roman steps in the defile of Bwlch Tyddiad. These great slabs of stone are more likely to have been laid by medieval hands than by those of the Romans, but the name persists.

At the south-western extremity of the park, on the peninsula that lies between Barmouth Bay and the Dyfi Estuary, soars Cader Idris. Although this impressive 2,928-foot (893-metre) peak is not, topographically speaking, part of Snowdonia proper, it falls within the boundaries of the National Park and has a nature reserve on its slopes. The ascent to the summit of Cader Idris is spectacular but often rugged; be prepared for treacherous weather and carry a map.

Snowdonia is not all open hill. Fragments of ancient woodland cling to some valley sides, while modern forestry has created some extensive wooded tracts, none more so than the Gwydyr Forest Park, which extends for over nine miles (15 kilometres) from above the Conway valley to the south of Betws-y-Coed. Visitors are well catered for with several forest walks and picnic sites for the short-distance walker, and there are plenty of opportunities for those who require more arduous journeys. Don't miss Coed Aber, a valley running inland from the coast just west of Llanfairfechan, which provides an access to the uplands by way of a footpath past the spectacular Aber Falls.

Snowdonia has long attracted naturalists, one of the most famous being Edward Lhuyd, described by John Ray as 'very learned not only in the matter of plants, but also of all Natural History'. Lhuyd has given his name to many rare species, including *Lloydia serotina*, the Snowdon lily. Found on a few limestone cliffs in Snowdonia and nowhere else in Britain, this arctic-alpine plant flowers briefly in early June.

The upland birds are a little disappointing, however. The golden eagles have long since disappeared, but there are still ravens, peregrines, merlins, ring ouzels and choughs. In South Wales the chough is restricted to the coast, but here it ranges high into the mountains and some 30 pairs nest, mainly in quarries and mine shafts. For me, a party of choughs feeding on the grazed turf and then taking flight, their screaming calls fading into the distance as they cross a valley to fresh ground, is one of the great moments of any visit to Snowdonia.

BEFORE YOU GO
Maps: all of Snowdonia National Park is contained in 4 of the OS Outdoor Leisure Series maps: Snowdon; Conwy Valley; Harlech; Bala and Cader Idris/Dovey Forest. With a scale of 1:25,000 (about 2½ inches to the mile) these are an essential first purchase for the serious walker.
Guide-books: a good book to start with is the *Landranger Guide-book to Snowdonia,*

Anglesey and the Lleyn Peninsula, published by the OS and generously illustrated with full-colour maps.
The weather in Snowdonia is notorious, even by Welsh standards. 'Phone for a regularly updated regional forecast, T: (0891) 500449.

GETTING THERE
By car: from the south-east, take the M1 and M6, then the M54 (exit 10A) to where it ends

near Wellington. From there, follow the A5 to Betws-y-Coed and the north of the park, or take the A458 from Shrewsbury – generally a quieter route – to Dolgellau and the park's southern region.
Motorists from the north should leave the M6 at junction with the M56 (exit 20), then follow the A55 to Colwyn Bay. From there, take the A470, the main north-south route through the park. Alternatively,

continue westward on the A55
to junction with the A5, or
drive on to Caernarfon, where
the A4085 and A4086 head
south-east into the park's most
mountainous region.
By rail: a fast service operates
from London to Holyhead in
Anglesey; change at Chester for
minor stations along the North
Wales coast. The beautiful
Conwy Valley Line runs south
into the park from Llandudno
Junction to Blaenau Ffestiniog.
Access by train to Aberdyfi,
Harlech, Barmouth and other
towns along the park's south-
west coast is from Shrewsbury
in Shropshire. Contact
National Rail Enquiries, T:
(0345) 484950.
By bus: National Express, T:
(0990) 808080, operates coach
services to Llandudno, Bangor,
Caernarfon and Porthmadog
from London and Manchester.
Crosville Wales, T: (01248)
351879, runs the 'Traws
Cambria' service from South
Wales to Dolgellau,
Porthmadog, Caernarfon and
Bangor. For further
information, *The Wales Bus,
Rail, Tourist Map and Guide* is
available from tourist
information centres.
Alternatively, 'phone Public
Transport Services in
Gwynedd, T: (01286) 679535;
or the Conwy area, T: (01492)
575414.

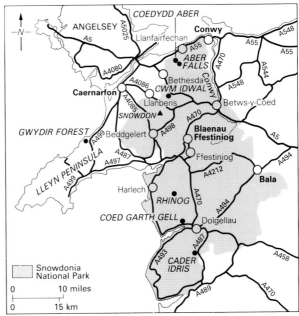

WHERE TO STAY
Snowdonia's principal towns
provide a full range of self-
catering and serviced
accommodation. Llanberis,
Bethesda and Conwy lie just
outside the park's northern
boundary. Blaenau Ffestiniog
and Betws-y-Coed serve the
central area, while Harlech,
Dolgellau and Bala are among
the southern centres for
accommodation. *Wales —
Where to Stay* guides,
published by the Wales Tourist
Board, include useful sections

on Snowdonia. In conjunction
with the Wales Tourist Board,
National Park information
centres produce lists of local
accommodation, including
camping, caravan and motor-
home sites; they also operate a
telephone bed-booking service.
'Phone the freephone booking
line, T: (0800) 834820; or
contact one of the 5 National
Park information centres in the
area: at Betws-y-Coed, T:
(01690) 710426; Blaenau
Ffestiniog, T: (01766) 830360;
Dolgellau, T: (01341) 422888;
Harlech, T: (01766) 780658;
and Aberdyfi, T: (01654)
767321. Alternatively, contact
one of the numerous tourist
information centres in the area.
Youth hostels: there are 15
hostels within the park or just
outside its boundaries at
Bangor, T: (01248) 353516;
Bryn Gwynant, T: (01766)
890251; Capel Curig, T:
(01690) 720225; Conwy, T:
(01492) 593571; Corris, T:
(01654) 761686; Cynwyd, T:
(01490) 412814; Idwal Cottage,

T: (01248) 600225; Kings, T:
(01341) 422392; Llanbedr, T:
(01341) 241287; Llanberis, T:
(01286) 870280; Llangollen, T:
(01222) 396766; Lledr, T:
(01690) 730202; Pen-y-Pass, T:
(01286) 870428; Rowen, T:
(01492) 650089/593571; and
Snowdon Ranger, T: (01286)
650391. For an accommodation
guide and further information,
contact YHA, Trevelyan
House, 8 St Stephens Hill, St
Albans, Hertfordshire AL1
2DY, T: (01727) 845047.

WHERE TO GO
Snowdonia has no obvious
centre. It falls into several
regions, each with its own
attractions, which are most
conveniently approached from
the following towns:
  Beddgelert: at junction of the
A498 and A4085 to the south
of Snowdon. Forest walks and
climbs to 2,566-ft (783-m)
Moel Hebog and summit of
Snowdon. Can be congested
with traffic in summer.
  Bethesda: slate-quarrying

137

town on the A5, just outside northern boundary of park. Good access from here to the Carneddau Range and Carnedd Llewelyn, at 3,484 ft (1,062 m) the park's second highest mountain.

Betws-y-Coed: major centre at the junction of the A5 and A470, 21 miles (34 km) south of Llandudno Junction. Extensive walks and beautiful waterfalls in the surrounding Gwydyr Forest Park. Information, T: (01690) 710426.

Dolgellau: on the A470, 10 miles (16 km) east of Barmouth. Centre for climbing Cader Idris, for the Coed y Brenin Forest, 6 miles (10 km) to the north, and the craggy Arans to the east. Information, T: (01341) 422888.

Harlech: west-coast town on the A496. Access from here to the Rhinog Range and the coastal flats. Information, T: (01766) 780658.

Llanberis: 7 miles (11 km) south-east of Caernarfon on the A4086. Principal centre for climbing Snowdon itself, by rail or by the gentle, 5-mile (8-km) Llanberis Path to the summit. Also convenient for access to the Glyder Range immediately to the east. Information, T: (01286) 870765.

Nature reserves in Snowdonia include:

Cader Idris: CCW NNR, best visited on the Llyn-y-Cau route from Minffordd village, 7 miles (11 km) from Dolgellau on the A487. CCW permit required to visit enclosed woodland on reserve.

Coed Garth Gell: wooded river gorge; access on footpath off the A496, 3½ miles (6 km) from Dolgellau. Excellent displays on local natural history at Penmaenpool Information Centre, 1 mile south across Afon Mawddach.

Coedydd Aber: wooded river valley; access from Aber village

on the A55, 5 miles (8 km) east of Bangor; nature trail. Permit required for areas off rights-of-way. CCW leaflet.

Cwm Idwal: cliffs and glacial lake; access from footpath running south from Ogwen Cottage Mountain School on the A5, 5 miles (8 km) south of Bethesda. Nature trail. CCW leaflet.

Rhinog: craggy, heather-covered moorland and mountain 5 miles (8 km) east of Harlech. Access on footpaths leading off unclassified roads in Cwm Bychan or Cwm Nantcol. CCW leaflet.

ACTIVITIES

Walking: the independent mountain walker will be in expert hands if he adds a copy of W. A. Poucher's *The Welsh Peaks* to the 4 OS Outdoor Leisure maps that cover the park. There are many other useful guides, however, including *Walking Wales*, published by the WTB, and leaflets on individual routes produced by the park information service. The FC also produces leaflets for walkers. Contact the District Forest Office in Dolgellau, T: (01341) 422289; or the visitor centres in Ganllwyd, T: (01341) 440666, or Llanrwst, T: (01492) 640578. *Guided walks:* during July and August the Park Authority offers a number of undemanding day and half-day guided walks, starting at various centres throughout the park. Full details are published in the *Eryri Snowdonia*, the park's newspaper-style information sheet — or 'phone the park information service, T: (01766) 770274.

Climbing: Snowdonia offers some of the most challenging and popular climbing in Britain. The inexperienced mountaineer should associate himself with a climbing centre which will provide equipment

Glyder Fach rises above the waters of Llyn Bochlwyd amid a jumble of frost-shattered boulders

and expert instruction: details can be found in *Activity Wales*, available at tourist information centres. Contact Plas y Brenin National Centre for Mountain Activities, Capel Curig, Betws-y-Coed, Gwynedd, T: (01690) 720214. The largest climbing

138

centre in Britain, it offers year-round courses in hill walking, orienteering and mountain leadership, as well as in rock climbing.

Fishing: there is good fishing, both coarse and game, to be had in many of Snowdonia's lakes, rivers and reservoirs. Only Llyn Cedig (Lake Bala), the largest natural lake in Wales, is controlled by the park authority. It contains 14 species of fish, with perch, roach, pike and trout frequently taken. For further information and a descriptive leaflet, contact the information centre in Bala, T: (01678) 521021; or the Bala and District Angling Association, T: (01678) 520626. For fishing in other waters, enquire at local tackle shops, consult *Fishing Wales*, available at tourist information centres, or contact the Environment Agency, T: (01222) 770088, which publishes *Fishing the Rivers of Wales*.

Field studies: Snowdonia National Park Study Centre, Plas Tan-y-Bwlch, Blaenau Ffestiniog, Gwynedd LL41 3YU, T: (01766) 590324/590334. Courses include natural history and ecology, geology, photography, painting, mountain walking and archaeology. Open 50 weeks a year.

FURTHER INFORMATION
Snowdonia National Park Office, Penrhyndeudraeth, Gwynedd LL48 6LF, T: (01766) 770274, for information about activities organized by the National Park Authority.
  Snowdonia National Park Visitors' Centre, Y Stablau, Royal Oak Stables, Betws-y-Coed, Gwynedd, T: (01690) 710426. The largest of the park's information centres, Y Stablau features displays and

acts as an agent for the Wales Tourist Board.
  The Forestry Commission, Victoria House, Victoria Terrace, Aberystwyth, Dyfed SY23 2DQ, T: (01970) 612367, for information and leaflets on Gwydyr and Coed y Brenin Forests.
  The National Trust, Llewelyn Cottage, Beddgelert, Gwynedd, T: (01766) 890293, for general information and leaflets on the NT's substantial holdings within the park.
  Countryside Council for Wales, North-West Area, Bryn Menai, Holyhead Road, Bangor, Gwynedd LL57 2EF, T: (01248) 373100, for

information and advice on access to nature reserves in Snowdonia.

Offa's Dyke Path

Offa, whose name is as grandly stamped on the pages of Britain's early history as those of Alfred and Canute, was King of Mercia from AD757 to 796. He commanded a bank and ditch to be built along the 149 miles (238 km) from Prestatyn in the north to the Sedbury cliffs on the Severn shore in the south, in order to mark the frontier between the Saxon kingdom of Mercia and the mountain hide-outs of the cattle-raiding Welsh tribes. Offa's Dyke is the longest earthwork in Britain, and closely follows the present-day border between England and Wales, a region known as the Marches
  The word 'march' comes from the Anglo-Saxon '*mearc*', meaning boundary. William the Conqueror created the positions of Earl of Chester, Shrewsbury and Hereford to guard this frontier and these Norman barons left their legacy in the form of a series of 11th-century motte-and-bailey castles, many of which can be seen not far from the dyke.
  Offa's Dyke Path was the fourth long-distance footpath in Britain, opened in 1971 by Lord Hunt of Everest. The 177 miles (285 km) of path along or close to the dyke are way-marked by signposts bearing an acorn insignia. Even so, you will need a compass for some sections of the route. This is no lowland ramble; prepare as you would for any rugged mountain

---

WALKING IN SNOWDONIA

The uplands of Snowdonia offer a great variety of walks, most of which are well marked.

  Make sure you are properly equipped, for there are few places in Great Britain where the hill walker experiences such rapid changes of weather as in Snowdonia, where a fine sunny dawn may be replaced in a few hours by torrents of wind-lashed rain or shrouds of mist and low cloud.

  Preparation is essential, and this includes obtaining local weather information from Weathercall, (0891) 232785 (Gwynedd & Clywd). Be sure to have suitable footwear and clothing, maps, compass, whistle, food and drink.

  Temperatures drop considerably at an altitude where snow can remain in some gullies until July. Wind speeds are much greater on the high exposed ground. Of further assistance are the information boards at the start of the main routes, while the National Park visitor centres will be pleased to provide advice.

  A visit to Plas y Brenin, the National Centre for Mountain Activities at Capel Curig is a must for the walker, both novice and more experienced.

  Be prudent and prepared, for in the often quoted words of Edward Whymper, 'negligence may destroy the happiness of a lifetime'.

  Lastly if you do experience difficulties, or see others in trouble, ring 999 and ask for the police.

trip. Although the border country is not as spectacular as Snowdonia or as spacious as the Cambrian Mountains, it does offer access to one of the least-known parts of Wales, one which most visitors pass through all too rapidly.

It is a dream land for geologists, a land of fossil beds laid down in an equatorial heat, of limestones now extensively quarried, of coal measures, Silurian mudstones, bands of Ordivician rock and pre-Cambrian grits. Such variety is reflected both in the scenery and the botanical gems to be found along the route, especially on the Breidden Ridge with its monument to Admiral Rodney, who campaigned successfully against the French for control of the West Indies, and at Corndon Hill, Long Mountain and Llanymynech, all close to where the Severn makes its massive bend east into England. Here plants like herb paris, parsley fern, hound's tongue, spring cinquefoil, blue-eyed grass and various orchids can be seen, as well as three rarities: the western spiked speedwell, the sticky catchfly and the rock cinquefoil.

Before you go: the entire length of Offa's Dyke Path is covered from south to north by 7 OS Landranger Series maps, Nos 162, 161, 148, 137, 126, 117 and 116. As there is no discernible track along certain sections, the extra detail of the 1:25,000 scale series is useful. Alternatively, the Offa's Dyke Association (see **Further information**) publishes 9 strip maps of the entire route at 1 inch to the mile, increasing the scale to 1:25,000 where necessary. *Offa's Dyke North* and *Offa's Dyke South*, both by Ernie and Kathy Kay and Mark Richards (Aurum Press, 1994), provide detailed maps and background information.

The mountain spiderwort or Snowdon lily is found only in Snowdonia

Getting there: the path can be joined at any road crossing its route. Towns from which one could start to walk a section of the path are, from south to north:

Chepstow and Monmouth (Gwent), for the scenic Lower Wye Valley (see page 123).

Hay-on-Wye (Powys), 20 miles (32 km) west of Hereford on B4350; approach on A438; easy access for section of path crossing the Black Mountains immediately to the south.

Knighton (Powys), on A488, 17 miles (27 km) west of Ludlow (Shropshire); also a station on the Heart of Wales Railway from Shrewsbury to Swansea. Largest town on route; convenient for Radnorshire Hills to south and Shropshire hills to north.

Llangollen (Clwyd), on A5, 11 miles (17 km) north-west of Oswestry (Shropshire). Path leads north along splendid cliffs on way up to Clwydian Hills.

Prestatyn (Clwyd), 5 miles (8 km) east of Rhyl on A458; station on North Wales Railway from Chester. Clwydian Hills nearby.

Where to stay: the Offa's Dyke Association publishes a *Where*

to Stay guide, which contains extensive information about accommodation and other amenities along the path. The guide is also distributed through the Ramblers' Association, Welsh Officer, Ty'r Cerddwyr, High Street Gresford, Wrexham, Clwyd LL12 2PT. *Youth hostels:* 6 hostels along the path are (from south to north) St Briavel's Castle, T: (01594) 530272; Welsh Bicknor, T: (01594) 860300; Capel-y-Ffin, T: (01873) 890650; Clun Mill, T: (01588) 640582; Tyndwr Hall, Llangollen, T: (01978) 860330; and Maesham, in Mold, T: (01352) 810320.

Further information: headquarters of the Offa's Dyke Association is at the Old School, West Street, Knighton, Powys LD7 1EN, T: (01547) 528753. More information can be obtained by sending a self-addressed envelope to the Correspondence Secretary. There are tourist information centres along the route that include (from south to north): Chepstow, T: (01291) 623772; Abergavenny, T: (01873) 857588; Presteigne, T: (01544) 260650; Knighton, T: (01547) 528753; Welshpool, T: (01938) 552043; Oswestry, T: (01691) 662753; Llangollen, T: (01978) 860828; and Prestatyn, T: (01745) 889092.

CHAPTER 6

Lowland Scotland

Crossing into Scotland from the Cheviot Hills of Northumberland recently, I was struck by how quickly and perceptibly the feel of the country changed. The differences between England on one side of the border and Scotland on the other were subtle, and they were to be found as much inside one's own head as in the lie of the land. As an Englishman, I very soon felt as if I were in a different country; as indeed I was.

Sitting on top of a hill that had once been a defensible Iron-Age camp not far from the Roman army commando training base near Woden Law in the Scottish Lowland county of Borders, I tried to take my bearings among all those lonely green rolling hills and twisting valleys. This was Teviotdale; sheep country, and fox country too, with trout in the little streams and ring ouzel in the upper burns. The odd thing was that, though I was quite obviously to the north of the Cheviots, I now felt myself quite firmly in southern country. In the Cheviots my orientation had been instinctively towards London and the south. Here in the Borders it was towards the north, to Edinburgh and to the great rearing mass of the Scottish Highlands beyond.

The Lowlands of southern Scotland stretch from the border northwards to the great Highland Boundary Fault, which runs diagonally across the country from the Firth of Clyde in the west to Stonehaven on the east coast. Beyond that line lies the grandly wild and rugged world of the Highlands and the Islands — the most extensive wilderness areas in Britain, from one point of view,

The play of sunlight and shadow on the depression known as the Devil's Beef Tub captures the essence of the undulating landscape of Lowland Scotland

and a neglected and underdeveloped colonial outpost from another.

Compared with lowland England, the Scottish Lowlands are high hill country. The Southern Uplands stretch across much of the area south of the valley between the Firths of Clyde and Forth. In the eastern half of these uplands, in the border country dominated by the River Tweed and its tributaries, the hills are smooth and round and grassy. In the western half, especially in Galloway where the mountain called the Merrick rises to 2,764 feet (842 metres), the hills are more rugged and more Highland in character. The Southern Uplands offer delightful hill walking through forests and over moors in weather that is generally finer than in the higher mountains to the north.

Though the interior of the Lowlands is really Scotland *sotto voce*, a curtain-raiser for the great show that booms out further north, the coastal perimeters are fine places in their own right, and of

special interest to bird-watchers. To the west, the Solway Firth provides a haven for wildfowl in great numbers, best seen at the superb wildfowl reserve at Caerlaverock. To the east, a succession of bird places are strung up the coast along the line of one of the major bird migration routes between Scandinavia and the Continent. These start at the great sea-bird colonies at St Abb's Head in Borders, where you will find the highest cliffs in eastern Scotland, and end with the sand flats and long shingle bars of Culbin Sands along a remote stretch of coastline on the Moray Firth in the Highlands, where seaduck, greylags and wading birds hole up for the winter in their thousands, and the north wind will have your guts for garters.

By all means set your sights on the wild splendours of the Highlands and Islands. But do give the Lowlands a whirl on your way there. They are worth every moment of the wild traveller and ornithologist's time.

GETTING THERE
By air: Edinburgh, Aberdeen and Glasgow International Airports all have regular services to centres in the UK, Europe and North America. **By sea:** 4 ferry services operate from Northern Ireland. P&O sails from Larne to Cairnryan, T: (0990) 980777; Stena Line, T: (01232) 747747, and Seacat, T: (0345) 523523, provide a service from Belfast to Stranraer; and for a more leisurely journey, Argyll and Antrim Steam Packet Company runs a seasonal ferry from Ballycastle to Campeltown, T: (0345) 523523. **By car:** Edinburgh is served from the Midlands and south by the A1; Glasgow by the M6 as far as Carlisle, then the A/M74. The M8 connects Glasgow with Edinburgh. **By rail:** regular services to

Glasgow and Edinburgh from major English and Welsh stations. Contact National Rail Enquiries, T: (0345) 484950. **By bus:** National Express, T: (0990) 808080; and Scottish Citylink Coaches, T: (0990) 505050, operate services between all major towns. Scottish Citylink run connecting services within Scotland. For local bus services, check tourist information centres in the area where you wish to travel.

Another way to get around is by postbus, generally a 4-seat van or an 11-seat mini-bus that carries passengers — as well as the post — to relatively isolated communities throughout the country, giving you a chance to rub shoulders with the locals. The *Scottish Postbus Timetable* is available free from local post offices or TICs.

WHERE TO STAY
The Scottish Tourist Board publishes 4 useful guides under the general title *Scotland — Where to Stay: Hotels and Guest Houses, Bed and Breakfast, Self-Catering* and *Camping and Caravan Parks.* These guides are available by post from the STB (see below).
Self-catering forest cabins can be rented from the FC, who also run well-provided camp, caravan and motor-home sites. Contact the FC, 231 Costorphine Road, Edinburgh EH12 7AT, T: (0131) 334 0303, for general information; or T: (0131) 314 6100, for holiday accommodation queries.
Youth hostels: full details from *SYHA Handbook* and *Touring Map of Scotland*, available from SYHA, 7 Glebe Crescent, Stirling FK8 2JA, T: (01786) 891400.

Outdoor living: Scotland has many camping, caravan and motor-home sites, but the walker may well find himself far away from such amenities. Remember that even in the wildest terrain, you are almost always on private land. Wild camping is not allowed on FC property, on National Trust for Scotland land or in nature reserves. On private estates try to seek the landowner's permission – it will rarely be refused. Where this is not practicable, treat the land with consideration; leave no litter, carry a stove and use it with care.

ACCESS AND CLOSURES

Land trespass is not an offence in Scotland, but most land is owned or tenanted by people who try to earn a living from it. To prevent damage or disruption, access is controlled in the following seasons: deer stalking, 1 Sep-20 Oct; grouse-shooting, 12 Aug-10 Dec; lambing Apr-May (no dogs should be taken on to grazings). If in doubt, enquire at local estate or nearest farmhouse. Your courtesy will be much appreciated and if access is restricted for that day you may be offered another route.

Unrestricted access to National Trust for Scotland land. Many major cross-country routes in Scotland are safeguarded as public rights of way under common law but are not designated as such on OS maps as they are in England and Wales.

ACTIVITIES

Cycling: Sustrans publish a map of The Scottish National Cycle Route (No.7) which covers a 402-mile (643-km) stretch from Inverness to Carlisle, T: (0117) 929 0888, and www.sustrans.org.uk. Scottish Cycling Holidays also offer a selection of routes

The crested tit, which feeds and breeds only in pine woods, welcomes the works of the FC

throughout Scotland with accommodation suggestions to suit all budgets. Contact Scottish Cycling Holidays, 87 Perth Street, Blairgowrie PH10 6DT, T: (01250) 876100, e-mail: 106412.3500@compuserve.com.
Outdoor activities: The Scottish National Sports Centre offers both accommodation and internationally acclaimed instruction in outdoor sports. Contact them at Glenmore Lodge, Aviemore, Inverness-shire PH22 1QU, T: (01479) 861256 and web-site: www.GlenmoreLodge.org.uk.

Kindrogan Field Centre in Perthshire, run by the Scottish Field Studies Association, offers natural history courses. For more information on the courses available contact Kindrogan Field Centre, Enochdhu, Blairgowrie, Perthshire PH10 7PG, T: (01250) 881286, e-mail: Kindrogan@btinternet.com.
Fishing: salmon, trout, arctic char and pike are found in lochs throughout Scotland's lowlands and highlands. One place boasting all five is Loch

Insh, where sailing, water-skiing and wind-surfing are also available through Loch Insh Watersports, Kincraig, Inverness-shire PH21 1NU, T: (01540) 651272. The STB (see below) publishes a brochure *Fish Scotland* detailing fishing sites all over the country.
Riding and trekking: for a comprehensive guide to riding centres consult *Trekking and Riding*, published by the STB.

FURTHER INFORMATION

Scottish Tourist Board, Central Information, 23 Ravelston Terrace, Edinburgh EH4 3EU, T: (0131) 332 2433, web-site: www.holiday.scotland.net/os.

Scottish Natural Heritage, 12 Hope Terrace, Edinburgh EH9 2AS, T: (0131) 447 4784, for information on national nature reserves in Scotland.

The National Trust for Scotland , 5 Charlotte Square, Edinburgh EH2 4DU, T: (0131) 226 5922.

RSPB, 17 Regent Terrace, Edinburgh EH7 5BN, T: (0131) 557 3136.

The Scottish Wildlife Trust, Cramond House, Kirk Cramond, Cramond Glebe Road, Edinburgh EH4 6NS, T: (0131) 312 7765.

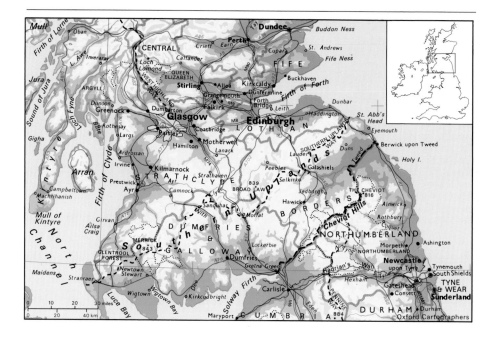

The Solway Coast

Along the shore of Galloway and Dumfries I came across an unexpected, unique corner of Scotland: a sunny south-facing coast with huge luminous skies, their light reflected on the calm waters of the Solway Firth, or at low tide on vast stretches of shining wet sand. I remember one bright spring day I stood for an hour watching the shadows of tiny clouds as they raced across the glistening flats, momentarily confusing the flocks of dunlin at the water's edge. But turn inland and you realize that typical Scottish scenes of moor and mountain are close at hand; the detritus of the glaciers which formed this fertile coastal plain did not have far to travel.

Rising gently above the valley of the Cree to a height of 2,331 feet (710 metres), the Cairnsmore of Fleet, like the Merrick and most of the higher mountains in Galloway, is an intrusion of granite which has weath-

ered better than softer surrounding rocks. It could not, of course, resist the great Scottish ice sheets, and erratic boulders of its pale grey granite can be found across the Solway Firth in Cumbria.

Much of the scenery is moorland rather than mountain, bleak expanses of purple moor grass and heather echoing to the melancholy cries of curlew and golden plover. It was the setting for Richard Hannay's desperate attempts to elude his evil pursuers in *The Thirty-Nine Steps*. To the east, however, especially from the valley of the Big Water of Fleet, the Cairnsmore presents a far more precipitous and dramatic mountainside. Ravens, becoming rare with the decline of sheep farming in south-west Scotland, find this a good place for carrion, sometimes that of an unfortunate feral goat.

Fringing the bays and estuaries along the Firth are the areas of merse or salt marsh. Many of these are extensions of the peat bogs formed by the rise and subsequent fall of the sea level at the end of the last Ice Age, the finest example being the merse of Lochar Moss with its magnificent wildfowl reserve at Caerlaverock.

With its rocky islands and inlets, Rough Firth is a distinctive feature in the otherwise sandy coast of Dumfries and Galloway

The Caerlaverock National Nature Reserve covers over 20 square miles (50 square kilometres) of salt marsh and mud-flats at the mouth of the Nith Estuary. The 1,500-acre (60-hectare) Eastpark Wildfowl Trust Refuge is splendidly equipped for serious bird-watching. The marsh is very treacherous and nowadays access is strictly controlled, for it has become one of the most important sanctuaries in Scotland, not only as a winter wildfowl refuge, but also as a prime example of an ecological niche that is fast disappearing elsewhere.

Chief attractions among the wildfowl are the barnacle geese. Up to 10,000 of them, the summer population of Spitsbergen, migrate *en masse* to the Caerlaverock merse. There is also a small but steadily growing flock of Bewick's swan, and other species that winter in good number include whoopers, pink-feet, greylags, wigeon, pintail and teal. Birds of prey often visit the reserve in search of plump ducks and waders, and you may witness the menacing glide of a hen

147

harrier or the stuttering flight of a merlin as it hunts low over the marsh.

In summer the glasswort and manna grass on the mud-flats are bright with patches of sea pink and sea aster, which also flourish among the red fescue grass and rushes of the marsh itself. The birds that breed here, mainly gulls and oystercatchers, are not ones in any particular need of protection; more care and attention is lavished on the colony of natterjack toads.

At the western extremity of the Solway Coast lies a strange, hammer-headed peninsula called the Rhinns, from the Gaelic *Roinn*, a promontory. At its southern tip, which points out towards the Isle of Man, there is a small RSPB reserve around the colony of cliff-dwelling sea-birds. Here, at the 'Land's End of Scotland', your gaze will naturally wander out to sea. Jagged cliffs line the western side of the Rhinns which looks out across the North Channel to the Ards peninsula in County Down, while along Luce Bay on the eastern side stretches a procession of heathery dunes. In the middle of the broad bay stand the Scar Rocks, inhabited by gannets, which can often be seen fishing off the Mull.

BEFORE YOU GO
OS Landranger Series, map Nos 82, 83, 84, 85.

GETTING THERE
By car: the A75 from Gretna to Stranraer is the main east-west artery, passing through Castle Douglas, Gatehouse of Fleet, Newton Stewart and Glenluce — and providing easy access by car to most parts of the Solway coast.
By coach: regular coach services link London and Birmingham with Stranraer, stopping at principal towns and villages along this route.
By rail: trains run from Glasgow to Stranraer; Dumfries is on the Glasgow to Carlisle line.

WHERE TO STAY
This is a popular holiday area, where you are never far from accommodation. If booking in advance, send off for the south-west Scotland *Where To Stay* brochure from Dumfries and Galloway Tourist Board, Campbell House, Bankend Road, Dumfries DG1 4TH, T: (01387) 250434. The Minnigaff Youth Hostel is in Newton Stewart, T: (01671) 402211.

WHERE TO GO
Caerlaverock (SNH, NSA, SWT) and Eastpark (WWT):
signposted access from B725, 8 miles (13 km) south of Dumfries. Free access except to sanctuary area near Wildfowl and Wetlands Trust Centre. Beware of tides on the marshes and contact warden before walking over mud-flats. The WWT Centre is open daily; 3 observation towers and several hides. For further information contact the WWT Centre, Eastpark Farm, Caerlaverock, Dumfriesshire DG1 4RS, T: (01387) 770200; or the SNH Warden, T: (01387) 770275.
Criffel: rises to west of A710, 10 miles (16 km) south of Dumfries. Easiest access from north-east. Start on track to Ardwall, which leaves A710 1½ miles (2½ km) south of New Abbey. OS Landranger Series map No. 84.
Southerness Point and Mersehead Sands: 14 miles (22 km) south of Dumfries an unclassified road leads south off A710 to Southerness Point. Drive to end of road. Good viewing on all sides. Geese and waders on Mersehead Sands, immediately west of Southerness Point, can best be viewed from A710 west of Coulkerbush.
Cairnsmore of Fleet: access from unclassified road off A75, 3 miles (5 km) south-east of Newton Stewart. Path leads to
summit from Cairnsmore (OS Landranger Series, map No. 83). Access to SNH reserve unrestricted. For details and further information contact Cairnsmore Fleet NNR, Buckshead Visitor Centre, Gatehouse of Fleet, Kirkcudbrightshire DG7 2PT, T: (01557) 814435.
Mull of Galloway (RSPB Reserve): drive south from Stranraer on the A716 to Drummore, then take B7041 to the lighthouse on the headland. Unrestricted access.

FURTHER INFORMATION
Tourist information centres, from east to west: Dumfries, T: (01387) 253862; Castle Douglas, T: (01556) 502611; Kirkcudbright, T: (01557) 330494; Gatehouse of Fleet, T: (01557) 814212; Newton Stewart, T: (01671) 402431; Stranraer, T: (01776) 702595.
  Scottish Natural Heritage, Galloway Office, 23 Albert Street, Newton Stewart, Wigtownshire DG8 6EF, T: (01671) 403440.

FURTHER READING
Solway Firth Review (Solway Firth Partnership, 1996). A newsletter, *Tidelines*, is published 3 times a year; enquire at tourist information centres for details.

THE EAST COAST

Few sounds in nature can compare with the beating of ten thousand pairs of wings as a flock of geese takes off from its winter roost. It may not feel so to you, as your fingers fumble to refocus your binoculars in a biting wind, but eastern Scotland, with its wide estuaries, shallow lochs and abundance of arable land, is the Côte d'Azur to the pink-footed goose.

The coast is also a popular winter resort of seaducks, grebes and divers, bobbing like flimsy coastal craft, dwarfed by the waves of the North Sea. But to them the sea is benevolent, not cruel; it is a different story for the crews of the fishing-boats and oil rigs who seek a living from the wealth beneath the same grey waves.

From the border to the Moray Firth, the coast retains an essentially lowland character. When the sea-level rose at the end of the last glaciation and the narrow valleys in the west became flooded sea lochs, the tilt of Scotland kept the feet of her eastern mountains dry. The sea eventually settled at a less dramatic, but immensely varied coastline, subject to the same inexorable pattern of erosion and accretion that shapes the east of England.

St Abb's Head

SWT, NNR, NTS

Perched like an animated black and white frieze, thousands of guillemots, razorbills and kittiwakes nest on the cliff tops between the fishing village of St Abb's and the Bay of Pettico Wick, along with a fair number of fulmars, herring gulls and shags. The red sandstone of the Head and the offshore stacks is a volcanic intrusion thrust into the grey, gritty fabric of the Southern Uplands, and if you look at the neighbouring cliffs you can see the dramatic folds of the mountains revealed as clearly as in any geology textbook.

In the valley behind the Head an artificial lake has been created to refresh migrant waders. The edge of the lake has been planted with hawthorn and sycamore which

already shelter a growing variety of woodland flowers and attract small migrants such as yellow-browed, greenish and barred warblers. Autumn is peak viewing time for birds of passage both onshore and off, where the rival attractions, best spotted from the lighthouse, include skuas, shearwaters and terns. **Getting there** *By car:* from Coldingham, ll miles (18 km) north of Berwick-upon-Tweed, take B6438 to reserve. Walk from there along cliffs to lighthouse, or drive to car-park at NNR Reserve Centre in Northfield Farm. **Access:** unrestricted, but parties by arrangement only. **Activities:** exhibitions and a programme of guided walks in the summer. **Further information:** from Warden, Ranger's Cottage, Northfield, St Abbs, Eyemouth, Borders TD14 5QF, T: (01890) 771443. NTS leaflets at car-park.

The East Lothian Coast and The Forth Islands

Despite its proximity to Edinburgh and the paraphernalia of tourism, the shoreline at the entrance of the Firth of Forth supports an extraordinary wealth of wildlife. The landscape is dominated by North Berwick Law, a smooth cone of the same volcanic origin as the Bass Rock (see p150), whose famous gannets can be observed plummeting for fish along this stretch of coast. The Forth Islands, closer inshore to the west of North Berwick, are important breeding colonies for razorbill, guillemot, cormorant and kittiwake.
Getting there: the A198 serves most of the coastline. Good bus and train services to North Berwick.
Where to go: for bird-watching, from west to east:
Musselburgh: viewing from lagoon embankments east of River Esk. Parking west of race course off A1.
Gosford Bay: A198 runs along shore. Parking at Ferny Ness, 1 mile (1½ km) north of Longniddry on A198.
Aberlady Bay: see p150.
Gullane Point and Bay: on A198, 5 miles (8 km) west of North Berwick. Coastal car park and short walk to point.
Yellow Craig: access on minor road leading north from Dirleton, 2 miles (3 km) west of North Berwick on A198.
Tantallon Castle: on coast 3 miles (5 km) east of North Berwick. Access from A198 to Dunbar. Good coastal prospects from cliffs and castle.
Further information: TICs in North Berwick, T: (01620) 892197; Dunbar, T: (01368) 863353. East Lothian Tourist Board, T: (01620) 827422.

149

Isle of May

SNH, NNR, SSSI

A small, cliff-girt island, only 140 acres (57 ha) in area, in the mouth of the Firth of Forth. The island has been a major site for ornithological research since the early years of the 20th century and the Bird Observatory has been here since 1934. The sea-bird colonies are busy and extensive, and increasing rapidly in numbers, but it is the bird migrations that cause all the excitement. At peak migration times strong east winds cause an extraordinary number of exhausted birds from a wide range of species to make a landing on this natural aircraft carrier. One October day in 1982, for example, 15,000 goldcrest settled on the island like a very pretty locust swarm. Some of the birds are rarities for Britain: scarlet rosefinch, Lapland bunting, red-breasted flycatcher, Sabine's gull and gyr falcon to name a few. The island is quiet in winter, with the notable exception of flocks of purple sandpipers and turnstones. Grey seals breed on the north coast and many unusual butterflies are blown here at times during migration. **Getting there** *By sea:* on 1-hour boat voyage from Anstrithen, Crail or Pittenween; day trips run in summer. Contact Anstruther Tourist Office, T: (01333) 311073, for information on sailing times. **When to go:** May-July for seagull colonies; Apr-May and Aug-Sept for migrating birds. **Access:** from May to Sept. **Where to stay:** the Bird Observatory offers basic self-catering accommodation. Contact Isle of May Bookings Secretary, 2 Manse Park, Uphall, West Lothian EH52 6VX, T: (01506) 855285.

150

Bass Rock

Very small, privately owned, cliff-girt hump of rock rising to 300 feet (90 m), 3 miles (5 km) off North Berwick in the Forth Estuary. By origin an old volcanic plug, Bass Rock is famous for its gannets, 21,000 pairs of which throng the cliffs and summit of the island during the breeding season, hence the bird's Latin name; *Sula bassana*. **Getting there** *By sea:* on daily summer boat trips round the island from North Berwick — contact Bass Rock boatman, Fred Marr, 24 Victoria Road, North Berwick, T: (01620) 892838. **When to go:** May to July (weather permitting). **Access:** landing permit from Bass Rock boatman.

Aberlady Bay

Foreshore reserve of 1,439 acres (583 ha) run by East Lothian District Council

The bay is a striking example of how mud, sand and time, with the help of marram grass, glasswort and sea buckthorn, can create a whole series of new environments. The salt marshes and dunes are host to flourishing communities of plants and mosses, and over 50 species of breeding birds, the most conspicuous being the boldly patterned shelduck. As the duck is as brightly coloured as the drake, their nest must be extremely well concealed. In contrast, the eider duck with her drab speckled plumage can choose more exposed nest sites and rely on her own camouflage.

In winter, pink-footed geese and a few whooper swans roost on the flats, but to watch

seaduck it is best to go to the east end of the bay. Round the point in Gullane Bay there are always common and velvet scoter and long-tailed duck, often accompanied by red-necked and Slavonian grebe. Regular waders on autumn passage include large flocks of dunlin and knot, with good numbers of scarcer species like bar-tailed godwit. **Getting there:** Aberlady village is on the A198, 7 miles (11 km) south-west of North Berwick. Access to shoreline along footpaths. Aberlady Point to south-west; Gullane Point to north-east. Also good viewing from main road. **Activities:** key to hide from warden. Car-park ½ mile (1 km) east of village. Free permits to park from Department of Leisure, Recreation and Tourism, Brunton Hall, Musselburgh EH1 6AE. **Further information:** Ian Thompson, Warden, T: (0831) 405015.

Loch Leven

RSPB, NNR

The loch accounts for almost all the 3,946 acres (1,597 ha) of the National Nature Reserve, one of Britain's principal centres for wildfowl studies. Security is much tighter now than it was when Mary Queen of Scots escaped from Loch Leven's Castle Island. In summer there are boat trips to the ruined castle, but in the rest of the reserve strict measures are taken to prevent the public from disturbing the large population of nesting ducks.

The RSPB nature centre (with a reserve of 458 acres/185 ha) at Vane Farm is more accommodating, and if you follow their trail on the top of the Vane, you will not be disappointed. Below lies St Serf's Island, the moated refuge of mallard, tufted duck and wigeon with a noisy guard of black-headed gulls. There is also a magnificent view to the horizon beyond the loch and the roofs of Kinross, where the rounded heather-clad Ochil Hills are the last lowland range before the wilder, grander landscapes of the Highlands. **Getting there:** 12 miles (19 km) south of Perth, immediately east of Kinross. Loch is encircled by main roads: A911 to north, B996 to west, B9097 to south. But access to the shore is permitted only at Kirkgate Park, Burleigh Sands and Findatie. All are signposted. Nearest station is Lochgely or Cowdenbeath. **Activities:** RSPB car-park and

The volcanic cliffs of St Abb's Head jut ruggedly into the North Sea at the edge of the Firth of Forth

RSPB nature centre with observation room at Vane Farm. Bird hide on lochside. **Further information:** RSPB leaflet from centre. RSPB Warden, Vane Farm Nature Centre, by Loch Leven, Kinross KY13 7LX, T: (01577) 862355; or Reserve Manager SNH, The Pier, Kinross KY13 7UF, T: (01577) 864439.

The Firth of Tay

The extensive sandbanks and mud-flats of this considerable estuary, which is contiguous with Tentsmuir Point and the Eden Estuary in Fife, has long been a major place for wildfowl and waders, and the only internationally important site in Britain for eider.

Birds come here in their thousands, and successive waves of migrating geese may total 20,000 or more. But the

mud-flats are so vast that it is difficult to see birds even in these prodigious quantities, for when the tide is out, many birds at the water's edge are beyond the range of human vision. The gathering of eider for which the Tay is famous takes place at the mouth of the Firth, where the birds sit in great 'rafts' offshore from Abertay Sands, sometimes in extraordinary masses of over 15,000 birds.

The landscape and wildlife of the estuary is subject to human pressures: wildfowling, holiday development, army firing and oil pollution from ships. But the area is big enough and the birds abundant enough to absorb these pressures for the time being, and in spring and autumn the flights of incoming geese are still a wonder to be seen.

Getting there *By car:* Perth and Dundee stand to west and east

of estuary respectively. Access to north shore from A85 and B958; to south from A913. *By rail or bus:* regular services to Dundee and Perth from major Scottish cities. **Where to go:** for birds, visit Buddon Burn, a small stream entering estuary mouth from the north. Walk east along shore from Monifieth. This is MOD land. Look for warning flags or check for access with information centres at Dundee or Carnoustie. **Further information:** Carnoustie Tourist Office, High Street, T: (01241) 852258 (Apr-Sept); or Dundee Tourist Office, 4 City Square, T: (01382) 434664 (Jan-Dec).

Tentsmuir Point

SNH, FC

The sandy headland at the mouth of the Firth of Tay is one of very few sites chosen for afforestation on the East Coast. Elsewhere in Fife the land has either been mined for coal or is valuable for agriculture. It is the rapidly growing foreshore beyond Tentsmuir Forest, however, with its sands, dune heath and natural scrubby woodland that appeals more to the lover of wild places.

An enormous variety of flowers have colonized the dunes and scrub, attracting a number of attendant species of butterfly and moth. The National Nature Council Reserve includes the vast expanse of the Abertay Sands, which provide a winter roost for waders and geese and a handy resting place for common and grey seals.

Just off the sands at the entrance to the Firth of Tay you may be lucky enough to witness one of the enormous flocks of wintering eider. Through their habit of sticking together in closely packed armadas, the ducks have unfortunately been very vulnerable to oil pollution in recent years.

Getting there: an unclassified road leads east to the nature reserve from the B945, 2 miles (3 km) south of Tayport. Several FC tracks give access to point and beach. **Access:** open access. FC parking and picnic area at beach to south of reserve. **Further information:** from FE Tay Forest District, Inverpark, Dunkeld, Perthshire PH8 OJR, T: (01350) 727284.

St Cyrus

SNH, NNR

Over 300 species of wild flowers bloom along the strip of sandy beach which runs three miles (five kilometres) from the mouth of the North Esk to the headland of Milton Ness. This variety would be remarkable anywhere so far north, but is doubly so, because the reserve hardly extends any distance inland beyond the relict cliff.

On the dunes, the deep blue of the clustered bellflower is set off by cowslips and maiden pink. The grassy cliffs are equally colourful, providing

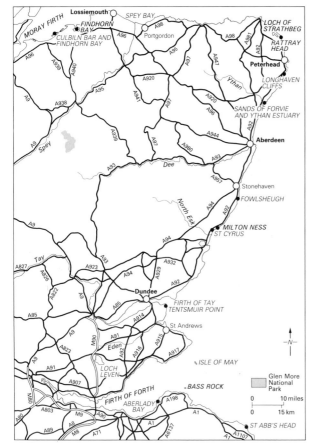

food plants for a profusion of butterflies and moths and even sites for low-level nesters such as the grasshopper warbler. The many breeding sea-birds include little tern, but their precarious colony does not enjoy the success of the herring gulls and fulmars.

Getting there: access to sands from village of St Cyrus, 5 miles (8 km) north of Montrose on A92. **Access:** south end of reserve closed during tern breeding season, May-Aug. **Further information:** contact SNH Warden, Miranda Whitcomb, Old Lifeboat Station, Nether Warberton, St Cyrus, Montrose DD10 0DG, T: (01674) 830736. Angus Tourist Board, T: (01241) 877883, F: 878550.

Fowlsheugh

Three miles south of Stonehaven, the *heugh* (a Gaelic word for cliff) reaches a height of 200 feet (60 metres) and houses a typically restless, screaming, stinking colony of sea-fowl. As at similar colonies on the Scottish coast, the two most successful breeding species are those with apparently contradictory strategies: the kittiwakes, which cement their neat nests to the cliff, and the guillemots, which build no nest at all. Other high-rise tenants are razorbills, puffins and fulmars, with a number of shag and eider duck on the lower storeys.

Getting there: from A92, 4 miles south of Stonehaven, take minor road to Crawton. Park at end of road and walk north along cliffs. **Access:** unrestricted. **Further information:** RSPB, 10 Albyn Terrace, Aberdeen AB1 1YP. Kincardine and Deeside Tourist Board, Bridge Street, Banchory, Kincardineshire AB31 3SX, T:(01330) 822000.

The Sands of Forvie and the Ythan Estuary

SNH NNR

The sight of terns hovering silently before plunging for fish gives so much more pleasure than that of gulls clamouring around mankind's refuse, yet everywhere, as man appropriates the coastline, gulls multiply and terns take fright.

Here at this 2,516-acre (1,018-ha) reserve at the mouth of the Ythan, man tries to stem the tide of his own making by encouraging Sandwich, common, arctic and little terns to breed, but it can be a heartbreaking business, especially when great and arctic skuas sabotage your good work. Another hazard is the sand, which can be blown by the wind to form new landscapes from one year to the next. The older dunes have become fixed under a cloak of heather and lichens, and in amongst them nest more eider duck than at any other site in the British Isles. You may even spot a rare king eider marking time among the non-breeding birds.

In winter the estuary is home to a flock of whooper swans, but most of the migrating geese move on southwards. Waders that can be seen feeding on the estuary usually include little stint, ruff, greenshank and spotted redshank, while large flocks of sanderling scurry back and forth at the edge of the waves.

Getting there: the A975 skirts the west bank of the River Ythan before crossing it near Newburgh, 14 miles (22 km) north of Aberdeen. Good observation points from main road. Access to sands of Forvie NNR from B9003, which leaves A975 4 miles (6 km) north of Newburgh. Forvie Centre, the NNR HQ, is on the right of road. Car-park and path to sands. **Access:** hide overlooking ternery at south end of sands, on spit to north of river mouth. Visitors are asked to keep to the footpaths in NNR. **Further information:** contact Alison Mattheson, T: (01358) 751383.

Longhaven Cliffs

SWT

These magnificent cliffs of flesh-coloured Peterhead granite stand just to the north of the Bullers of Buchan. At this famous freak of coastal erosion the sea rushes through an arch of granite into a kind of cauldron carved in the base of the cliff.

The effects of the sea's violence can also be seen at Longhaven in the shattered stacks which are a favourite nest-site for the large population of herring gulls. Guillemots and kittiwakes take up their accustomed positions on the pitted cliff face, looking down on the stoic shag below, while the grassy slopes above provide plenty of burrrows for puffins.

They also display a surprising variety of flowers, not only typical cliff-growing species such as the lovely pale-cream burnet rose, but also, in more sheltered places, incongruous spring carpets of bluebells fringed with bright clumps of primrose.

Getting there: drive south from Peterhead on A952. Access to cliffs on unclassified road about 2½ miles (4km) after turn for Boddam. **Further information:** SWT Edinburgh, T: (0131) 447 4784.

The Loch of Strathbeg

At the centre of an RSPB reserve of 2,327 acres (942 ha), this freshwater loch is the first landfall for thousands of wintering wildfowl. It was only at the beginning of the 18th century that it assumed its present shape and character; throughout the Middle Ages it had been a busy harbour, protected by a long spit of shingle. Finally the inlet from the sea near Rattray Head silted up, creating a shallow freshwater lagoon. The largest sand-dune slack in Britain, it still serves as a refuge from the rigours of the North Sea, but for geese instead of ships.

Among the incoming skeins of greylags and pink-feet in early autumn you may spot the barnacle geese which rest up here on their way to Caerlaverock. On the water of the loch, a large flock of whoopers presides nobly over the wintering mallards, tufted ducks and goldeneye, which are often joined by goosander and red-breasted merganser.

The reed-beds and willow scrub of the marshlands provide cover for small birds such as sedge-warbler and willow-warbler. Inevitably this thriving and varied community draws its share of hopeful raptors, hen harrier, sparrowhawk and merlin, and a less welcome predator in the feral mink.

Watching the sea from Rattray Head, you are far enough north to count yourself unlucky if you do not spot all three species of diver: red-throated, black-throated and the bird-spotter's holy grail, the great northern itself.

Getting there: access from village of Crimmond, half-way between Peterhead and Fraserburgh on A952. Without

154

entering the reserve one can observe loch from unclassified Rattray road, leaving A952 just south-east of Crimmond. Nearest station Aberdeen. **Access:** at all times. **Activities:** Reception building. 2 hides overlooking loch and board-walk through fen woodland. **Further information:** RSPB Manager, Stamatin Farmhouse, Crimmond, Fraserburgh, Grampian AB4 4YN.

Spey Bay

SWT

This long, shallow bay between Lossiemouth and Portgordon in Grampian holds large numbers of seaduck including common, velvet and surf scoter, scaup, goosander and eider, as well as other birds such as red-throated, black-throated and great northern divers in autumn and red-breasted merganser, purple sandpipers and commoner species. Common and arctic terns breed here, and common gulls may be seen on the beach.

Getting there: on foot along beach from Lossiemouth or Kingston, or for middle of bay drive to Speyslaw and walk to beach from there. **Access:** at all times, except for Lossie Forest at back of beach (no cars, closed at times of fire risk) and firing range to west of Kingston. **Further information:** from SWT, T: (0131) 447 4784.

Culbin Bar and Findhorn Bay

RSPB

Culbin Bar is the larger of two long spits of shingle lying off the mainland at Culbin Sands. The sands, as such, no longer exist, having been transformed into Culbin Forest. There are

those who disapprove of every conifer planted in Scotland, but at Culbin there are plenty of native Scots pine and a good sprinkling of birch.

Nor must we forget that the area was once a formidable 'desert', which had obliterated an entire community in one terrifying sand blow. Some will say that man created the desert in the first place, by pulling up the marram grass; but then again, the poor needed thatch for their houses. Conservation and social justice are often hard to reconcile.

The forest supports roe deer and birds as splendid as the capercaillie, the crested tit and the great spotted woodpecker, but true seekers of wild, natural beauty will head for the salt marshes enclosed by the bar.

This somewhat melancholy landscape is enlivened by colourful splashes of sea pink. As you would expect, bird life is more abundant in winter with the arrival of seaduck, geese and waders, but arctic and common tern breed in the area and can be seen fishing off the bar. In Findhorn Bay, you might even witness the most spectacular of all aerial fishermen, the peerless osprey. **Getting there** *Culbin Bar:* from A96 in Nairn a minor coastal road leads north-east along the dunes. Track to left in about 2 miles (3 km), at Kingsteps, leads to RSPB reserve. Be careful of tides on foreshore. *Findhorn Bay:* from Forres on A96, 10 miles (16 km) east of Nairn, take B9011, the Kinloss road; this leads along east side of the bay. **Access:** unrestricted. **Further information:** RSPB, North Scotland Office, Etive House, Beech-Wood Park, Inverness IV2 3BW, T:(01463) 715000.

Moray Tourist Board, 17 High Street, Elgin, Moray IV30 1EG, T: (01343) 543388/542666, F: 552982.

THE SOUTHERN UPLANDS

Although formed during the same episodes of titanic pressure that gave birth to the Highlands, the Southern Uplands were folded from quite different rocks, Silurian sediments of grit and greywacke. In the few places where the rocks are still exposed, grey is the predominant colour, but only in the craggy outcrops of Galloway do you feel you are in the presence of mountains, although the height of the Merrick and other surrounding peaks is largely due to intrusions of hard-wearing granite.

As you travel east, the effects of aeons of wind, rain and above all ice are clearly evident in the changing landscape. In the Lowthers and the Tweedsmuir Hills, the high moorlands are featureless tracts of grass and heather, then in the Borders you find gentle rolling hills between the dales of the streams that feed the Tweed. Although the scenery of the Borders may recall northern England, the Tweed courses through the region like a rich vein of Scottish blood.

Galloway Forest Park

SSSI FC

This is the largest forest in southern Scotland: over 250 square miles (650 sq km) run by the Forestry Commission. The conifers have not destroyed the beauty of the area's lochs and high peaks; there are also patches of unspoilt woodland and ancient peat bog.

It is easy to imagine you are a hundred miles further north when you see the Buchan Burn tumbling down its waterfall into Loch Trool and the walk along the upper glen, its narrow gorges set in woods of sycamore and sessile oak, is equally spectacular.

From Glen Trool Visitor Centre, you can follow the Gairland Burn to Loch Neldricken and Loch Enoch with their silver sands of powdered granite, then on to the extraordinary relic of glacial erosion known as the Devil's Bowling Green. The bowls are the hundreds of erratic boulders that a melting glacier left strewn on a flat clearing of ice-scarred rock. Low-lying areas in this section of the park still shelter undisturbed peat bogs or flowes, which built up when the ice had departed.

If you prefer clear mountain air to blanket bog, head north from the Bruce Monument above Loch Trool for the Range of the Awful Hand, a group of five peaks, which includes the Merrick, at 2,764 feet (842 m) the highest in southern Scotland. **Getting there:** via A712 and A714 from Dumfries. **Further information:** guide available

The Grey Mare's Tail cascades over the lip of a hanging valley on the north-west side of Moffatdale

from Forest District Office at Castle Douglas, T: (01556) 503626.

Ken-Dee Marshes

RSPB, NT
ESA, SPA, NSA, SSSI,
Ramsar

The damming of the River Dee between New Galloway and Castle Douglas in Dumfries and Galloway has created Loch Ken, and a flood plain of marshes and meadows which have become a favourite feeding and breeding place for a considerable variety of birds, notably geese.

In winter, some 300 Greenland white-fronted geese visit the valley, along with 1,000 greylags, bean geese, whooper swan and several species of duck. Hen harriers, merlins, peregrines, buzzards and sparrow-hawks hunt here; great crested grebe, redshank, curlew and goosander are among the breeding birds. The RSPB runs two reserves totalling 325 acres (132 ha) on Loch Ken, and the NTS has a 1,300-acre (526-ha) wildfowl refuge at Threave Garden and Estate on the river to the south of the loch.

Getting there: for Threave Wildfowl Refuge, turn off A75 at Kelton Mains Farm or Lodge west of Castle Douglas and continue along footpaths to 5 observation points overlooking river and marshes. RSPB reserves at Kenmure Holms and the Black Water of Dee can be viewed from A762, A713 and offshoots. **Access:** unrestricted, but no dogs. Threave Wildfowl Refuge open May-Sept only. **Further information:** from RSPB Conservation Officer, T: (01644) 430581; NTS, Ranger Office, T: (01556) 502575.

156

Ailsa Craig

An isolated, dome-shaped rock over 1,100 ft (335 m) high but only 1 mile (1½ km) in diameter in the Firth of Clyde 10 miles (16 km) off Girvan on the Ayrshire Coast, Ailsa Craig is a basal remnant of an ancient volcano composed of fine-grained granite once quarried to make curling stones. This is the Clyde's most important sea-bird station; 70,000 sea-birds nest on its 500-ft (150-m) high vertical cliffs, half of them gannets, most of them on the West Coast. The mild, damp climate supports a rich growth of wild flowers on the slopes below the cliffs, and Soay sheep and white goats run around the hills. There are adders on Ailsa Craig, and brown rats that feed on the birds' nests.

Getting there: boat trips from Girvan, on A77 south of Ayr, can be arranged with Mr McCrindle, T: (01465) 713219. These can include landing on the island. Those wishing to camp on Ailsa Craig should contact the owner, the Marquess of Ailsa, via David Gray at Cassilliss Estate, T: (01655) 882103. **Further information:** TIC, Girvan, T: (01465) 714950.

Tweedsmuir Hills

This is lowland country *par excellence*: high lowlands and nationally important moorland with long walks over peat, turf and heather. Often you will find you have only sheep and the occasional curlew or raven for company. At 2,754 foot (840 m), Broad Law is the second highest point in southern Scotland, but it is quick and undemanding to climb and can be reached easily from

Tweedsmuir, St Mary's Loch or even Loch Skeen.

If you are making for Peebles, steer north-east via Dollar Law and Dun Rig to the head of the charming valley of Glensax. There you can join the rough track that follows the burn gently down to the Tweed just to the east of your destination.
Getting there: from Tweedsmuir on A701 an unclassified road crosses hills to meet the A708 at Cappercleuch. Several tracks lead into hills from A701.
Further information: TIC, Moffat, T: (01683) 220620.

The Grey Mare's Tail and Loch Skeen

NTS

This is not the only waterfall in southern Scotland to recall the fate of Tam O'Shanter's steed, but it is by far the highest and really does hang like a silver tail. The exaggerated glacial furrow of Moffatdale left many hanging valleys along its sides; the waterfall itself is 200 foot (61 m) high, but the Tail Burn has to descend 700 foot (213 m) before it reaches Moffat Water.

Up at Loch Skeen, where the burn begins its cascade, there is another classical feature of glacial erosion, a corrie partially dammed by moraine. The whole dramatic scene can be better appreciated from the superb ridge walk between Bodesbeck and Herman's Law, south of the road.
Getting there: falls are situated west of the A708, 10 miles (16 km) north-east of Moffat. Path to falls from car-park. Steep scramble to Loch Skeen; take special care in wet weather.
Further information: NTS Lothians, Borders, Dumfries and Galloway Regional Office, T: (01721) 722502.

PRECAUTIONS FOR WALKERS

Nobody should set off into the wilds without a compass and 1:50,000 Ordnance Survey map and a knowledge of how to use them. But the true wilderness walker will also make a mental map as he or she goes:

1 At regular intervals take a sighting: in other words. visually line up three or more landmarks (conspicuous trees or rocks). This is to avoid walking in circles, which most people do because one leg takes longer strides than the other.

2 If you want to return the way you came, look back often and mark turns in the path with rocks. The same section of path looks different when seen from the opposite direction.

3 Use other senses as well as sight to mark your bearings: distinctive sounds like rushing water, the sea, church bells, cattle or sheep; and strong smells like pine forests, meadow flowers, ocean breezes.

4 Use trees to tell direction. Green moss-like algae grows on the shadier side of a tree or facing the prevailing wind. Trees growing in the open may have more leaves on the sunnier, i.e. southern, side.

What to wear
Walking boots or very strong shoes with moulded rubber soles are essential. Shoes with smooth rubber or leather soles can be lethal. Clothing should be warm and windproof – the weather in the Highlands can change

extremely rapidly and a fine day can turn almost instantly into a storm.

A hill walker dressed for the hills in summer can expect to wear: woollen jersey, warm long trousers (tweed or other wool mixture), anorak or windproof jacket, woollen socks, walking boots or shoes.

In addition you should carry a rucksack containing spare clothing consisting of extra jersey, gloves, woollen cap, cagoule (or other waterproof clothing), together with food, map and compass, rope and guide-book, torch and whistle (in case of emergency flash or whistle six times, wait one minute, then signal again), first aid kit and plastic survival bag to crawl into if you are stuck on a mountain.

The Southern Uplands Way

This 212-mile (341-km) route was dictated more by expediency than by history or the lie of the land. From Portpatrick in the Rhinns of Galloway to the Cockburnspath on the Berwickshire coast, the majority of the valleys lie across your path, and the hills are often high moorland blanketed in mist.

The way passes through the Galloway Forest Park, where it joins up with the Forestry Commission's trail along the southern side of Glen Trool; it then skirts Loch Dee and the Clatteringshaws Reservoir.

At St John's Town of Dalry you turn north-east to follow the course of the Water Ken,

but it is a tough hill walk with fine views across the valley to the Cairnsmore of Carsphairn. There follows a two-day hike across the Lowthers, from Sanquar to Beattock via Wanlockhead, the highest village in Scotland. The highest point on the way is reached at about 2,330 foot (710 m) beside the radar station on the top of Lowther Hill.

The following day you enter the basin of the Tweed on the splendid middle section of the way between Beattock and St Mary's Loch, when, after following an old drovers' pass below the threatening crags of Loch Fell, you emerge into the delightful valley of Ettrick Water. The final laps of the way allow you to take things easy, as you stroll through border country, along meandering rivers fringed with pine, birch and willow, enjoying frequent glimpses of the three peaks of Scott's beloved Eildon Hills.

Before you go: it is difficult to navigate the way by using the OS Landranger Series. Instead, buy the official guide: *The Southern Upland Way* by Roger Smith (HMSO, 1994). The route is indicated throughout with brown waymarkers carrying the CC's stylized thistle-in-a-hexagon motif. Walk from west to east to avoid getting the sun in your eyes or – more likely – the rain in your face. Unless you are a fell runner, expect to spend at least 10 days on the route. **Where to stay:** camp-sites, bed and breakfasts, hotels and hostels along the way, but book in advance. Along the route, there are 7 bothies offering basic shelter. Wild camping is not encouraged along the way and is specifically prohibited on FC property. **Further information:** Dumfries and Galloway Tourist Board, T: (01387) 253862; Scottish Borders Tourist Board, T: (01750) 20555.

CHAPTER 7

Scottish Highlands and Islands

I first entered the enchanted world of the Scottish Highlands in the company of Gavin Maxwell, an eloquent champion of wild places. He was returning to his West Highland retreat at Camusfeàrna (which he was to make famous in his idyllic *Ring of Bright Water*) after the death of his first otter. It was at Camusfeàrna that I first saw the ghostly glimmering of the Northern Lights, the *Aurora Borealis*, draped across the night sky in the direction of Greenland, and first witnessed the mysterious coming of the elvers, which arrived at the waterfall at Camusfeàrna in teeming millions after crossing the Atlantic all the way from the Sargasso Sea.

It was from here that I climbed Ben Sgreol, my first Munro (as climbers call any Highland peak over 3,000 feet/910 metres high), and from its scree-flanked summit above Camusfeàrna caught my first glimpse of the grey shapes of the Outer Hebrides far to the north-west beyond the snow-covered Cuillin of Skye. I came back to this coast often in subsequent years, once to winter here, once to sail around its lochs and islands, sometimes to revisit Camusfeàrna after the death of Maxwell and his otters.

I recall vividly my most recent return. Thick sea fog had first delayed and then diverted my flight up to Inverness. By the time I reached Camusfeàrna on the west coast it was well past midnight — but an enchanted, breathless night of

The contrast between Highland and Lowland Scotland is shown in bold relief in this sub-polar winter view from the Cairngorms

crystalline clarity. A brilliant full moon hung over the Sound of Sleat, casting a wan glow over the brooding hills of Skye and a glassy ocean that seemed to stretch motionless to the very edge of the world.

It was October, but still warm, and I flung open the shutters of the small croft by the beach to catch all the sounds and ghosts of the night — the listless flop of the waves on the sand, the distant cataract roar of the waterfall above the burn, in spate after an autumn of incessant rain, the kraak of a solitary heron stalking fish in the moonlight at the edge of the tide, a seal singing softly in the bay below the croft, the plaintive, child-like voice rising and falling like a phantom lullaby.

The next day, miraculously, was as warm and blue as high summer. I followed the tracks of the wild sea otters barefoot over the crunching shell-sand and icy shallows to the otter islands where long before I had foraged for limpets and gulls' eggs to eat, and as I stumbled over the black rock and bladder-wrack the grey seal colony gathered to stare, snorting in the sunlight, and bobbing their flippers up and down on the bottom to catch a better view. But the day after that the wind was roaring in from the sea and the rain driving horizontally across the bay, so that the burn rose two feet in an hour and the fire spat and spluttered in the chimney-piece.

The season advanced swiftly. Soon there was a first faint powder of snow on the high hills across the sound and an arrowhead skein of greylag geese came honking overhead on their southern migration, crossing swiftly from one horizon to another in a momentary vision of freedom and delight. On such days one forgot the times of discomfort and despair, when the air was saturated with salt spray and rain, and life seemed

as sour and chill as the peat. One remembered instead the miraculous beauty of sunlit days over land and water — the two essential ingredients that distinguish the landscape of the Highlands and Islands from any other in Britain.

For long the traditional haunt of the vacationing sporting gentleman, the well-to-do stalker and grouser, yachtsman and angler, the Highlands and Islands are now host to a new breed of less privileged outdoor man: the backpacker, bird-watcher and hiker, and that phenomenon of the post-industrial era, the opter-out and wilderness man, among whom in past years I would have had to number myself.

The Highlands lie to the north of the rift valley that separates them from the Lowlands and Southern Uplands of Scotland. The dividing line, known as the Highland Boundary Fault or Highland Line, runs fairly sharp and straight north-east from the Isle of Arran on the Clyde across Loch Lomond to Stonehaven on the North Sea coast. Beyond it lie some 13,000 square miles (33,670 square kilometres) of rugged, mountainous terrain; a unique and still largely unspoilt combination of loch, river, forest, moor and mountain.

The region boasts some 517 tops above 3,000 feet (910 metres), 12 above 4,000 feet (1,220 metres), 269 of them separate mountains known as Munros (after Sir Hugh Munro, a President of the Scottish Mountaineering Club, who listed them in 1891). The fantastically indented Highland coastline measures only 260 miles as the crow flies, but well over 2,000 as the seal swims, and the whole inchoate rock mass is sliced up by a series of long parallel transverse glens, of which Glen Coe and Glen Nevis are perhaps the best known, and one of which, the Great Glen, splits the Highlands diagonally into two disparate regions: the Grampians and the North-West Highlands.

More than any other part of Britain this is a region of extremes. It is possible to travel from one end to the other in comfort (if not *grande luxe*) without getting puffed or hungry or even (if you are cunning) wet, viewing the sublimest scenery from car-park look-outs or the picture windows of waterside hotels. It is also possible to backpack for days across the wilderness of moor and mountain without crossing a road or encountering another human being or habitation of any kind; or be marooned for months on an Atlantic islet with only the seals and the skuas for company and only what you have brought with

The pine marten, at home in Scotland's native pines, also thrives amid imported Sitka spruce

you for food and shelter — lost to the world in both space and time. Between these extremes of *gran turismo* and pure wilderness survival are many permutations of experience in the great Scottish outdoors. These are yours to choose.

GETTING THERE

By air: there are 5 commercial airports in this area. Inverness provides the most convenient air access. British Airways, T: (0345) 222111; Air UK (Stansted), T: (0345) 666777; and EasyJet (Luton), T: (01582) 445566, make regular daily flights, with restricted weekend services. Inverness is 80 minutes from London (Heathrow); 40 minutes from Edinburgh and Glasgow.

British Airways (operated by Loganair) flies daily (except Sun) to two airfields in the Outer Hebrides: Stornoway (Isle of Lewis) via Inverness or Glasgow and Benbecula from Glasgow. Loganair also flies to Barra in the Outer Hebrides from Glasgow daily except Sun (planes land on beach so tides affect timetable); and to Lerwick on Shetland, twice daily. Enquiries, T: (0345) 222111. The British Airways Highland Rover Pass permits 5 flights within the Scottish Network, allowing you to create your own itinerary, (excludes local flights within Orkneys and Shetland).

By sea: Caledonian MacBrayne, T: (01475) 650100, operates ferry services from Mallaig to the islands of the Inner and Outer Hebrides, including Skye.

By car: principal approach routes to the region can offer motoring as good as elsewhere in the UK, but in the mountains even the main roads tend to be narrow, winding and steep. Minor roads are often single-track, with numerous hump-backed bridges, blind corners and wandering sheep. Petrol stations are few and far between and nearly all are closed on Sun, so fill up as opportunity offers.

By rail: the east-coast route to Inverness is served by direct trains from London (Euston and King's Cross) day and night (except Saturday night), and from Edinburgh, Glasgow, Aberdeen and points *en route*. Inverness is also a direct Autoshuttle Express terminal from London. From there the slow but scenic Highland Line crosses Scotland to Kyle of Lochalsh on the West Highland coast (3 times daily, not Sun).

There is an overnight sleeper service from Euston to Mallaig via Glasgow and Fort William (change at Fort William).

Alternatively you can travel to Mallaig from Glasgow (Queen Street) via Fort William and enjoy the splendid West Highland Line by day (steam locomotives and courier-serviced observation cars in summer). There is no Autoshuttle Express on the western route; use the terminals at Edinburgh, Glasgow or Inverness. National Rail Enquiries, T: (0345) 484950.

By bus: a number of companies run express coach services to and from Scotland, and coach, bus, minibus and postbus services in the Highlands and the Islands. The *Scottish Postbus Timetable*, an invaluable companion for the remote adventurer, is available free from post offices or tourist information centres, as are 4 booklets produced by the Highland Council, T: (01463) 702695, also detailing public transport in the area. Train, Bus and Coach National Enquiries, T: (0891) 910910.

WHERE TO STAY

Hotels: high-class hotels and the wilderness experience may seem incompatible, but there are many who value their evening comforts after a rugged day on the hills.

For a complete list (over 1,600 entries) see the Scottish Tourist Board's *Where to Stay - Hotels and Guest Houses*. See also Hotels and Guest Houses listed in the following *Where to Stay* publications of the Scottish Highlands and Islands Tourist Board: *Sutherland; Ross and Cromarty; Inverness, Loch Ness and Nairn; West Highlands and Islands of Argyll; Western Isles; Isle of Skye and South West Ross*. The Scottish Tourist Board also publishes information on hotels offering shooting and stalking, and special amenities for children, the elderly and the disabled.

Bed and breakfast and self-catering: the *Where to Stay* publications listed above also include bed-and-breakfast accommodation in farms, houses and crofts, as well as self-catering accommodation in houses, crofts and purpose-built log cabins or wooden lodges. See also the complete list in the Scottish Tourist Board's *Where to Stay - Bed and Breakfast* and *Self-Catering in Scotland*.

Forest cabins: fully equipped forest cabins for self-catering holidays in Scotland's forest areas can be rented weekly from the Forestry Commission. Consult *Forestry Commission Cabins and Holiday Houses*, available from the FC, 231 Corstorphine Road, Edinburgh EH12 7AT, T: (0131) 314 6100.

Youth hostels: up to 80 are scattered throughout the Highlands and Islands. Consult *SYHA Handbook* and *Touring Map of Scotland*, from Scottish Youth Hostel Association, 7 Glebe Crescent, Stirling FK8 2JA, T: (01786) 891400.

Outdoor living: for a full list of over 350 camping, caravan and motor-home parks in the Highlands see the Scottish Tourist Board's *Camping and Caravan Parks*. Lay-bys are for meal breaks only, not overnight stops.

In remote areas there are few restrictions on wild camping. But you should always ask if you want to camp near habitation or on someone's land, and there are certain areas — in nature reserves and on Forestry Commission land, for example, or near youth hostels and certain mountaineering club huts — where camping is not allowed. It is illegal to light an open fire in the Scottish countryside without the landowner's permission. Once a fire is started it may get down into the peat and burn for years. Carry a stove and use it with care.

ACTIVITIES

See THE SCOTTISH LOWLANDS fact-pack (page 144).

FURTHER INFORMATION

Scottish Tourist Board, Central Information, 23 Ravelston Terrace, Edinburgh EH4 3EU, T: (0131) 332 2433, web-site: www.scotland.net/tourism.

Scottish Natural Heritage, 12 Hope Terrace, Edinburgh EH9 2AS, T: (0131) 447 4784.

National Trust for Scotland, 5 Charlotte Square, Edinburgh EH2 4DU, T: (0131) 226 5922, F: 243 9501.

Scottish Rights of Way Society, 10 Sunnyside, Edinburgh, T: (0131) 652 2937.

Mountaineering Council of Scotland, 4a St Catherine's Rd, Perth PH1 5SE, T: (01738) 638227.

Highlands and Islands Enterprise, Bridge House, Bridge Street, Inverness IV1 1QR, T: (01463) 234171. Runs tourist information centres in many towns.

MOUNTAIN BOTHIES

As an alternative to pitching a tent, walkers can sometimes find shelter in a mountain bothy. These old farm-workers' stone huts may either be derelict or maintained by the Mountain Bothies Association, among others. Bothies are remote and provide little else but shelter, so you have to bring everything with you.

You should respect the Bothy Code:

1 Seek the owner's permission to use a bothy.
2 Keep parties small (three or four).
3 Keep fires small.
4 Leave the bothy in better condition than you found it.
5 Leave no litter, burn or bury all rubbish.
6 Lay in fuel and kindling for the next user.
7 Add unused stores to the food cupboard — but safe from vermin.
8 Do not damage the structure.
9 Put out the fire when you leave.
10 Secure windows and doors when you leave.
11 Observe sanitary precautions and safeguard the water supply.
12 Sign the visitor's book.

For further details contact Mountain Bothies Membership Secretary, 26 Rycroft Avenue, Deeping St James, Peterborough, Cambridgeshire.

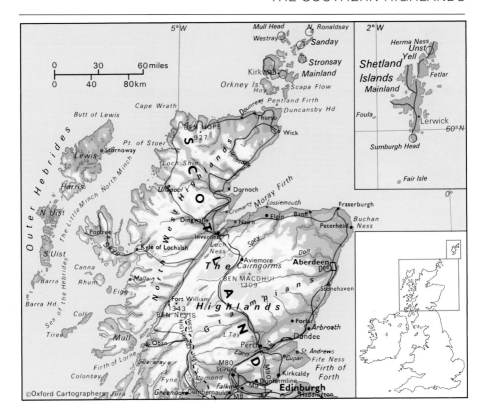

THE SOUTHERN HIGHLANDS

The Southern Highlands extend northwards from the line of the Highland Boundary Fault as far as Loch Rannoch. To the west they are bounded by the Atlantic, with its deeply riven seaboard, great sea lochs and peninsulas; and to the east by the Tay-Tummel valley, one of the two main gateways into the Highlands, the other being Loch Lomond. Along the southern edge of this region the country is lower than further north, but offers a greater variety of scenery and a more beautiful landscape of mountain, wood and water.

To the north the mountains advance towards Loch Rannoch in ranges of greater and greater height, almost reaching 4,000 feet (1,220 metres) on Ben Lawers. Seventy of the peaks are more than 3,000 feet (914 metres), 46 of them Munros, but the mountains here are mostly rounded and grassy, with few cliff faces to note except on the Cobbler at Arrochar. With its sea coast, lochs, forests, moors and accessible hills this attractive region has much to offer the wild traveller and naturalist.

Argyll Forest Park

Occupying 100 square miles (260 sq km) of rugged Highlands between Loch Eck and Loch Lomond, the Argyll Forest Park encompasses an amazing diversity of habitats, from sea-shore to mountain top. It successfully combines commercial forestry, natural history and recreational activities: anything from rock climbing to orienteering, canoeing and subaqua exploration of the underwater caves of Loch Long.

Basking shark, grey seal and sea otter frequent the Clyde sea lochs that intrude deep into the forest area, and crabs, shrimps,

163

sea scorpions, sea slugs, sea lemons, sea anemones and other creatures of the sea-shore inhabit the inter-tidal zone. Less than half the park has been afforested. Semi-natural mixed woodlands survive in the glens and along the shore of Loch Eck and in spring and summer they are full of the song of woodland birds and carpeted with primroses, bluebells, violets and wood anemones, while ferns and mosses thrive in the mild and rainy climate of the coastal area.

Above the forest line, bare hills of grassy moorland stretch upwards to a maximum height of nearly 3,000 ft (914 m) in the 'Arrochar Alps' in the north of the forest park. The crags and corries of the highest summit, Ben Arthur (2,891 ft/881 m), popularly known as the Cobbler, draw hill walkers and climbers.

Before you go *Maps:* Ordnance Survey Landranger Series, map No. 56. **Getting there** *By car:* from A83 take B828 for Loch Goll or A815 for Loch Eck and Loch Long. *By rail:* Arrochar and Tarbet, a station on the Glasgow-Fort William line, is just outside the park's north-east border. **Where to stay:** Dunoon, to the south of the park, has a wide range of serviced accommodation. See the Dunoon and Cowal Peninsula Tourist Board brochure, available from the information centre, 7 Alexandra Parade, Dunoon, Argyll, T: (01369) 703785. The Forestry Commission, T: (01546) 602518, runs the Ardgartan camp-site, by the A83, 2 miles (3 km) south-west of Arrochar. **Further information:** *Argyll Forest Park Guide* from FC offices or nearby tourist information centres in Dunoon, T: (01369) 703755 and Tarbet, T: (01301) 702260.

164

Loch Lomond

NSA, SNH NNR

The largest freshwater lake in Britain, Loch Lomond occupies a deep channel gouged by glacial ice. At Balmaha near its southern end, it is bisected by the Highland Boundary Fault, which marks the beginning of the Highland region. North of this fault the loch narrows and deepens like a fjord, crowded in by mountains to north, east and west.

To look up Loch Lomond from the southern end is to stare at one of Scotland's scenic glories: a shining ribbon of water that disappears among the distant mountains, luring you onwards towards an interior promising magic and mystery. The eastern shore is the less spoilt; there is no road beyond Rowardennan, and to continue north you must take the West Highland Way (see page 189) into the Craigroyston hills and beyond.

Alternatively the walker can strike out east over one of the wooded trails that crosses the vast Queen Elizabeth Forest Park to Aberfoyle and the Trossachs, or take the track that leads to the summit of Ben Lomond. The most southerly Munro in Scotland, Ben Lomond is an easy, popular climb offering from its summit a tremendous panorama over Loch Lomond, Ailsa Craig and the Arran Hills, the Paps of Jura, Ben More on Mull, Ben Nevis and Ben Lawers.

The national nature reserve is situated in the south-west corner of Loch Lomond, where it occupies more than 1,000 acres (405 ha) of wood, water, shore and fen on five islands and marsh on the mainland. Fine oak-wood flora and fauna, unusual fishes such as a freshwater herring called the powan, swamp and fen with rich wetland vegetation round the mouth of the River Endrick, and wintering wildfowl and waders in a cast of thousands.

Before you go *Maps:* Ordnance Survey Landranger Series, map No. 56, OS Outdoor Leisure Series, map No. 39. **Getting there** *By sea:* steamer from Balloch to Inversnaid and other points, T: (01389) 752069. Ferry from Inverbeg to Rowardennan. *By car:* the A82, which clings to Loch Lomond's west bank, is the main Glasgow-Inverness road. Access to the quieter east bank is on the B837 from village of Drymen. This road stops half-way along the loch. The B829 from Aberfoyle leads to Inversnaid at the north-east end of the loch. *By rail:* trains from Glasgow to Balloch; stations on Glasgow-Fort William line (from south to north) at Arrochar, Tarbet and Ardlui. *By bus:* regular coach service between Glasgow and Inverness. Postbus operates daily between Aberfoyle and Inversnaid. **Where to stay:** *Where to stay* brochure from Argyll, the Isles, Loch Lomond, Stirling and Trossachs Tourist Board, Albany Street, Oban, Argyll PA34 4AN, T: (01631) 563059. TICs at Balloch, T: (01389) 753533, and Tarbet, T: (01301) 702260. *Youth hostels:* at Loch Lomond, T: (01389) 850226, and Rowardennan T: (01360) 870259. **Activities** *Fishing:* permits for Loch Lomond and its rivers available locally from boat-yards and many hotels. Fishing map from Loch Lomond Angling Improvement Association, T: (01506) 633033. *Boating:* boat hire from Balmaha, Lush, Balloch, Drumkinnon and Ardlui. *Canoeing:* Rowardennan Youth

Hostel is centre for Scottish Hostellers' canoe club, T: (01360) 870259. **Further information:** excellent map of the loch (4 inches to the mile) from Cuillins Yacht Charters, T: (01301) 704244; includes useful information on travel and recreation in the area.

Inversnaid

RSPB Reserve

North-east of Loch Lomond the ground rises steeply through deciduous woods to a rocky ridge and moorland beyond. The loch is a migration route for wildfowl and waders, making this an ideal site for the RSPB reserve. Buzzards nest in the woods and crags; blackcock on the slopes; dipper, grey wagtails and common sandpiper along the shore of the loch and the burns. The 'wildness and wet' of Inversnaid was celebrated by Gerard Manley Hopkins in a marvellous poem of that name. **Getting there** *By sea:* ferry from Inveruglas on west bank, T: (01877) 386223. *By car:* B829 west from Aberfoyle, then minor road north to reserve. **Access:** at all times. **Further information:** RSPB Warden (Mike Trubridge), West Garage House, Gribloch, Kippen, Stirling FK8 3HS.

Ben Lui

Includes SNH NNR

Ben Lui is at its most beautiful under bright winter snow. It rises to an elegant, 3,708-ft (1,130-m) conical summit north of Loch Lomond, the main peak of a group of four Munros on the Perthshire-Argyll & Bute border. Its high

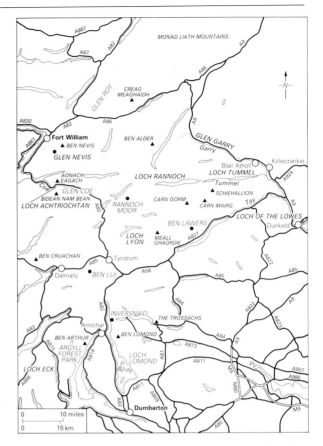

north-east corrie offers serious mountaineers a classic climb, while gentler souls can accomplish a satisfying traverse of all four mountains in about 10 hours on a horseshoe route of moderate difficulty between Tyndrum and Dalmally.
  From the summit of Ben Lui you can see across to Ben Nevis and all the way to Ben More on Mull. The northern cliffs of Ben Lui are outstanding for their rich mountain flora and an area of some 5,199 acres (2,104 ha) is now a national nature reserve.
Before you go *Maps:* Ordnance Survey Landranger Series, map No. 50. *Guide-books:* Scottish Mountaineering Trust Guide: *The Southern Highlands* (SMT

is affiliated to Mountaineering Council Of Scotland). **Getting there** *By car:* Ben Lui rises above the A82 between Crianlarich and Dalmally. *By rail:* Tyndrum and Crianlarich are stations on the Glasgow-Fort William line; Dalmally is on the Oban line. *By bus:* good service along A82. **Activities** *Walking:* the most popular ascent of Ben Lui leaves the A82 1½ miles (2½ km) east of Tyndrum. Follow the rough track to where it ends past Canonish Farm. Then head along one of the ridges to the summit. This is a moderately strenuous climb of about 6 miles (9 km). A shorter, rougher ascent can be made from the north-west, near

Dalmally. **Where to stay:** Dalmally, Tyndrum, Crianlarich. Accommodation listed in *Holidays* brochure published by Argyll, the Isles, Loch Lomond, Stirling and Trossachs Area Tourist Board, T: (01369) 701000. Youth hostel in Crianlarich, T: (01838) 300260. **Further information:** SNH, T: (01631) 567228. TIC, Tyndrum, T: (01838) 400246.

Ben Lawers

NTS Reserve, SNH NNR

At 3,984 ft (1,214 m), Ben Lawers is the highest mountain in Britain south of Ben Nevis, and so nearly 4,000 ft (1,219 m) high that in the late-19th century a cairn was built on the summit to enable climbers to scramble up to this magic number.

In winter its long, easy, southern slopes make it good for skiing (fortunately without the usual commercial damage). There are good long walks to be had over Ben Lawers and the neighbouring Tarmachans and its lime-rich metamorphic schists make it Britain's finest mountain for flowers, especially post-glacial arctic-alpines. The moles of Ben Lawers, incidentally, are particularly hardy and adventurous, burrowing upwards to ever greater heights.

Before you go *Maps:* Ordnance Survey Landranger Series, map No. 51. **Getting there** *By car:* via unclassified road leaving A827 5 miles (8 km) north-east of Killin. Car-park and visitor centre 2 miles (3 km) along this road. **Where to stay:** youth hostel at Killin, T: (01567) 820546. **Access:** open access to

all NT land, mainly south of principal summits. **Activities:** nature trail, audio-visual programme, ranger service. **Further information:** booklet and leaflets from Ben Lawers Visitor Centre, T: (01567) 820397, or NTS Office, Lynedoch, Main Street, Killin FK21 8UW, T: (01567) 820988.

Atholl

NSA, including SWT Reserve, RSPB Reserve

Atholl is the name of the large, elongated area that stretches along the line of the River Tay from south of Dunkeld, where the Lowlands give way to the Highlands, northwards to beyond Blair Atholl, hereditary seat of the Dukes of Atholl, lairds of this domain for more than seven centuries.

Three rivers flow down this valley through the hills: the Garry, the Tummel and the Tay. Both the Garry and the Tummel have been badly affected by hydroelectric development, but on the inaccessible higher slopes lie areas of interest to the naturalist and the hill walker. From the large estate at Blair Atholl right-of-way tracks lead through Glen Tilt across wild country to Deeside and through Glen Bruar across no less wild country to Speyside: major expeditions requiring proper gear and true grit.

There are two important reserves in the area. The SWT Reserve at Loch of the Lowes covers 242 acres (98 ha) of loch with fringing woodland and marsh in a hilly Highland setting east of Dunkeld. The loch is most famous for its ospreys, which have nested here

off and on since 1969, and can be seen between early April and August; and also for its grebes.

The RSPB reserve at Killiecrankie stretches from the gorge of the River Garry through oak woods, pasture and birch woods to crags and heather moorland nearly 1,000 ft (300 m) above. Woodland birds include redstart, crossbill and wood warbler, while black grouse, buzzard, sparrow-hawk and whinchat inhabit the moorland, and raven the crags. With luck you might see golden eagle and peregrine, too. The wooded gorge of the adjacent Pass of Killiecrankie (part of the Loch Tummel National Scenic Area) is NTS land, and worth visiting for its birds, flowers and geology.

Before you go *Maps:* Ordnance Survey Landranger Series, map Nos. 43, 44, 52, 53. **Getting there** *By car:* the main road through Atholl is the A9 from Perth. For Loch of the Lowes, turn off A9 at Dunkeld and take A923 in direction of Blairgowrie. For Killiecrankie, turn off A9 just north of Pitlochry and continue on B8079. **Access:** at Loch of the Lowes, restricted to south shore, bird hide, visitor centre (Apr-Sept) and car-park at west end. Free access at all times to Killiecrankie RSPB reserve, but on way-marked trail only. Access to NTS property is unrestricted. **Further information:** RSPB Warden (Martin Robinson), Balrobbie Farm, Killiecrankie, Pitlochry PH16 5LJ. NTS Killiecrankie Visitor Centre, T: (01796) 473233. Leaflet and handbooks from SWT Loch of the Lowes Visitor Centre, Dunkeld, Tayside, T: (01350) 727337 (open Easter to September).

Rest and Be Thankful, a quaintly named pass at the head of Glen Coe, is far from restful in winter when fierce winds tear through it

Glen Lyon

Part of the Loch Rannoch-Glen Lyon NSA

Glen Lyon is deeply entrenched between the high mountains of Meall Ghaordie (3,410 ft/1,039 m) and Ben Lawers (3,984 ft/1,214 m) to the south and Carn Gorm (3,377 ft/1,029 m) and Carn Mairg (3,419 ft/1,042 m) to the north.

Loch Lyon descends through wild, bare mountain country to Meggernie Castle, where the landscape becomes gentler and more sylvan. Every bend in the river offers a fresh view of water, wood, mountain and meadow. At the Pass of Lyon, the river hurls itself through a rocky, beech-screened gorge before opening out to the civilized world around Fortingall.

Before you go *Guide-books:* Scottish Mountaineering Trust Guide: *The Southern Highlands.* **Getting there** *By car:* from B846, 5 miles (8 km) west of Aberfeldy, an unclassified road leads the full length of Glen Lyon to the power station at Loch Lyon. *By bus:* a daily 11-seater postbus goes up the glen as far as Gallin. **Where to stay:** youth hostel at Killin, 7 miles (11 km) south of glen, T: (01567) 820546. **Further information:** tourist information centres at Killin, T: (01567) 820254, and Aberfeldy, T: (01887) 820276.

Rannoch Moor

SNH NNR

Rannoch Moor is a 1,000-ft (300-m) high plateau whose rotted granite was ground flat by the last batch of Ice Age

glaciers to leave 60 square miles (150 sq km) of nothing but peat bogs, lochans, pools, puddles and blanket bog.

But Rannoch Moor is far from lifeless. There is wildlife all around you: red and roe deer, dunlins, greenshanks, ducks, divers, plovers and other birds of moorland and water, and a luxuriant spread of boggy plants like bog myrtle, bog asphodel, cotton grass and sphagnum moss.

Rising like islands on the watery horizon lie the surrounding mountains: stand by Loch Ba in the west and you can stare eastward across one of the wildest terrains in Scotland, all the way to the exquisite cone of Schiehallion, which rises to 3,547 feet (1,081 m) in the far distance like some sheer volcanic islet on the ocean's rim.

To the north lies Loch Rannoch, with Rannoch Forest on its northern flank and the Black Wood of Rannoch on its southern slopes. In this important remnant of the old native pine woods of Scotland, the last wolf in Britain met its end. Now it is a forest nature reserve of nearly 6,000 acres (2,430 ha) where pine marten, wildcat, capercaillie and golden eagle still thrive.

Before you go *Maps:* Ordnance Survey Landranger Series, map Nos. 41, 51. **Getting there** *By car:* A82 Callander-Ballachulish road flanks the west of the moor and the B846 runs between Rannoch station and Aberfeldy. *By rail:* Rannoch, to the east of the moor, is a station on the Glasgow-Fort William line. *By bus:* services to Rannoch station from Pitlochry. **Where to stay:** hotel at Rannoch station. Limited bed-and-breakfast accommodation in immediate vicinity. Information centre at Aberfeldy will assist, T: (01887) 820276. Youth

hostel at Loch Ossian, 9 miles (14 km) north-east of Rannoch Station, T: (01397) 732207. Kilvrecht camp-site (FC) 4 miles west of Kinloch Rannoch in Rannoch Forest. **Where to go:** Rannoch Forest: access from unclassified road leaving B846 at Kinloch Rannoch and following south side of Loch Rannoch. 3 picnic sites. Way-marked walks. Fishing and boating on Loch Rannoch. **Access:** restricted access to deer-stalking estate; contact Andrew Gordon, Blackmount Estate, T: (01796) 481355. In Rannoch Forest keep to forest tracks. Access to SNH reserve is unrestricted. **Further information:** for SNH reserve contact the Battleby office, T: (01738) 444177. FC information from Tay Forest District Office, T: (01350) 727284/5. Tourist information from Fort William and Lochaber Tourist Board, T: (01397) 703781.

Loch Tummel

NSA

Stretching westward from the Pass of Killiekrankie and presenting upland sylvan scenes rather than a wild mountain landscape, the famous Queen's View (a favourite spot for Queen Victoria) enjoys a marvellous outlook over Loch Tummel westward to the cone of Schiehallion (3,547 ft/1,081 m). The Forestry Commission owns an area of 10,032 acres (4,060 ha) of mixed woodland and lochs on the north side of Loch Tummel, Tayside. Woodland birds include capercaillie and goldcrest. **Getting there** *By car:* south of the B8019, 3 miles (5 km) west of its junction with A9 at Garry

Bridge in the Pass of Killiekrankie. An unclassified road from Pitlochry runs along the southern shore of the loch.
Where to stay: youth hostel, Pitlochry, T: (01796) 472308.
Where to go: Queen's View: on B8019, 4 miles (6½ km) west of Garry Bridge. Linn of Tummel: NTS wooded valley. Car-park on B8019 at Garry Bridge. Forest of Tummel: mainly to north of loch. Way-marked walks and picnic places.
Activities: FC visitor centre at Queen's View, T: (01796) 473123. Exhibits and slide shows. Open from Easter until the end of October. Nature trail at Linn of Tummel. **Further information:** leaflet from FC, T: (0131) 334 0303. Booklet from Killiecrankie visitor centre (NTS) on B8019, T: (01796) 473233.

The sea eagle, until recently extinct in the British Isles, has now been reintroduced on Rum

THE CENTRAL HIGHLANDS

The Central Highlands, which are confined by the Great Glen to the north and west, Strath Spey and Glen Garry to the east and Rannoch to the south, cover a smaller area than the Southern Highlands but contain double the number of mountain tops: the Black Mount Hills, Ben Alder, Creag Meaghaidh, Ben Cruachan, the Monadh Liath mountains and Ben Nevis, the tallest of the British peaks. These massive lumps, with their sensational corries and enormous cliffs, offer some of the best rock-, snow- and ice-climbing, and (on the Glen Coe hills, the Mamores and the Grey Corries of Lochaber) the finest ridge-walking in Britain. Magnificent glens such as Glen Nevis, Glen Coe and Glen Etive thread through this mountainous region, with extensive wilderness areas in the hinterland.

Glen Coe

NTS, SNH NNR, NSA

Glen Coe is a spectacular mountain wilderness of precipitous summits, towering, cloud-hung rock faces and deep gullies. A tourist road runs through the bottom of the glen bearing its teeming hordes of summer holiday-makers, but up in the wilds of the surrounding hills, Glen Coe is not a place to be trifled with. Only the foolhardy would venture out to walk or climb without proper preparation; the local mountain rescue team is one of the most experienced in Britain.

The visitor from the south approaches the Glen by way of Black Mount, with the desolation of Rannoch Moor stretching far to the east. Viewed from the moor, the mountain of Buchaille Etive Mor (3,353 ft/1,022 m) dominates the landscape to the north-west. A rocky gateway called the Study forms the entrance to the Glen, an ice-worn valley lying between the 6-mile (9½-km) ridge of Aonach Eagach and the spurs of Bidean nam Bian, which, at 3,766 ft (1,148 km), is the highest mountain in Argyll.

Between sheer walls of volcanic rock, the River Coe rushes westward over foaming cataracts and through limpid pools to the stiller waters of Loch Achtriochtan. Precipices and waterfalls tower above the flats of the lower glen; this is climbing country *par excellence.*

Glen Coe was the appropriately spectacular location of the notorious massacre of the Macdonalds by Campbell of Glen Lyon in 1692. There is little shelter for wildlife here, though red deer, golden eagle and peregrine can occasionally be seen, and there is a rich mountain flora on the most inaccessible cliffs. **Before you go** *Maps:* Ordnance Survey Landranger Series, map No. 41; OS Outdoor Leisure Series, map No. 38. **Getting there** *By car:* via A82 Glasgow-Fort William road, which runs through glen. *By bus:* good coach service along same route. **Where to stay:** Clachaig Hotel is in the glen and welcomes campers on surrounding land. Bed and breakfast in Glencoe village. Youth hostel between village and glen, T: (01855) 811219. **Further information:** nearest tourist information centre in Ballachulish, T: (01855) 811296. NTS information centre, T: (01855) 811307 (summer only), or, (01855) 811729.

Ben Nevis

NSA

Ben Nevis, as almost everyone knows, is the highest mountain in Britain, heaving its great bulk up to 4,406 ft (1,343 m) above Fort William at the western end of the Great Glen. It is essentially a granite mountain ground down by ice and time, and displays many of the typical features of a granite-mountain landscape, including enormous corries with sheer cliffs that fall vertically for as much as 2,000 ft (610 m).

Walkers toil up to the summit in droves along the easy pony track way in summer — easy, that is, in terms of technical difficulty, but arduous in terms of fitness and stamina, for it is a long, 7-hour haul. With a mean monthly temperature below freezing, snow can fall on any day of the year and icy, howling winds buffet about the place most of the time.

If you are lucky and the cloud clears for a moment, and it will usually be only a moment, you will glimpse the ultimate mountain view in Britain, right across to the Irish hills 120 miles (193 km) away, to the Hebridean Isle of Rum 50 miles (80 km) away, the Cuillin of Skye beyond it and, 77 miles (124 km) away to the west, the Paps of Jura, not to mention other heights nearer to hand: Torridon, the Cairngorms, Ben Lawers and the Glen Coe peaks.

There are many other ways up Ben Nevis, most of them much more difficult. By far the best is by way of Glen Nevis, one of the most beautiful glens in Scotland. The middle section of this approach is almost Himalayan in character, with the river running clear and swift and the waterfalls streaming down from the cliffs above. From this glen you can stare up a continuous slope through 4,000 ft (1,220 m) of evolving landscape, up past alpine-like meadows to moor and rock. All you have to do is persuade your feet to follow where your eyes have gone — it's worth it.

Glen Coe is best remembered for the massacre of 1692; today, its rugged beauty attracts more sporting visitors

Before you go *Maps:* Ordnance Survey Landranger Series, map No. 41, OS Outdoor Leisure Series, map No. 38. *Guidebooks:* SMT Climbers' Guide: *Ben Nevis*. **Getting there** *By car:* Fort William is on the A82, 65 miles (104 km) south-west of Inverness. From the south side of Nevis Bridge, close to the centre of town, an unclassified road leads along Glen Nevis. To the north of Bridge another road is signposted to Ben Nevis Path. *By rail:* Fort William, the base for any exploration of the area, is on the Glasgow-Mallaig railway line. *By bus:* Fort William is a principal stop for coaches from Edinburgh,

Glasgow and Inverness. **Where to stay:** all ranges of accommodation at Fort William. Ben Nevis Bunkhouse, T: (01397) 702240, is at the start of Ben Nevis footpath, 1 mile from Fort William. **Further information:** the Highlands and Islands Tourist Board, Cameron Square, Fort William PH33 6AJ, T: (01397) 703781.

Glen Roy

SNH NNR

Nearly 3,000 acres (1,214 ha) in extent, the reserve occupies the

mountainous country between Glen Spean and Glen Mor. It is of primary importance for earth scientists on account of its series of Ice-Age geological features, above all the so-called 'Parallel Roads of Glen Roy', which mark the successive shoreline of an ancient ice-blocked lake.
Getting there *By car:* from Roybridge, 3 miles (5 km) east of Spean Bridge on the A86, take unclassified road north along Glen Roy. Good viewing of Parallel Roads in about 3 miles. **Access:** open all year round. **Further information:** the Highlands and Islands Tourist Board, T: (01397) 703781.

THE CAIRNGORMS AND EAST GRAMPIANS

This enormous mountain group comprises the whole of the north-east Highlands between the rivers Tay and Spey, some 2,200 square miles (5,700 sq km) of high, wild, mountainous country. From the Pass of Drumochter in Glen Garry in the west, the main Grampian range stretches for some hundred miles to the coastal lowlands above Aberdeen to the east. About 20 miles (30 km) east of Drumochter this range sends out a northern spur, a high granite range occupying 400 square miles (1,000 sq km) of high mountain country north of the River Dee. This is the Cairngorms. To the south of the River Dee lies a semi-circle of high mountains which are usually referred to as the East Grampians, with Lochnagar (2,789 feet/850 metres) in the Royal Forest of Balmoral taking pride of place.

The high plateau of the Cairngorms is dominated by the broad 4,000-foot (1,220-metre) summits of Cairn Gorm, Cairn Toul, Braeriach and Ben MacDui, at 4,296 feet (1,309 m) the second highest mountain in Scotland.

Cairngorm National Nature Reserve

SNH NNR, NSA

Over 100 square miles (260 sq km) of the Cairngorms is now a

huge national nature reserve, the largest in Britain. The reserve straddles the Lairig Ghru and reaches to north and south of the high tops down to the pine woods of the low ground. It thus presents to the visitor not only the grandeur and almost polar isolation of its awesome landscape but a wide range of Highland wildlife

in a variety of habitats.

On the wind-swept, nearly arctic summits, the few flowering plants that can survive the climate of the region include moss campion and wood rush. The high corries shelter highly localized plants such as mountain rock-cress, alpine speedwell and a few very rare plants such as arctic mouse-ear and hare's-foot sedge. The moorland slopes are dominated by heather and deergrass; lower down are the native Scots pine woods.

Most of the area has long been managed as deer forest. Roe deer frequent the woods and lower moors in small family groups, and reindeer, red squirrel, blue or mountain hare and all the carnivorous animals of Scotland except the pine marten can be found here, among them the otter in the streams and lochs. Breeding birds of the pine forest include black grouse, capercaillie, crossbill, siskin and crested tit, while golden eagle and peregrine nest on the cliffs, and osprey have returned to breed after many years' absence.
Before you go *Maps:* Ordnance

Survey Landranger Series, map Nos. 36, 43. **Getting there** *By car:* the A9, A93 and A939 roughly define the perimeter of the Cairngorms. Within there are many tracks but little opportunity for the motorist to penetrate more than 2 or 3 miles into the mountains. *By rail:* the Perth-Inverness railway stops at Kingussie and Aviemore. *By bus:* coaches between Edinburgh and Inverness serve Aviemore and other centres along the A9. There are also services between Aberdeen and Braemar. **Where to stay:** accommodation of all kinds is easy to spot, but booking is essential in peak periods. For places on the main tourist route along the A9 to the north of the region, contact the Aviemore and Spey Valley Tourist Board, T: (01479) 810363, who will supply *Where to Stay* brochures and more information. *Youth hostels:* at Aviemore, T: (01479) 810345, and Braemar, T: (01339) 741649. *Outdoor living:* there are several mountain bothies in the area. Their location is clearly indicated on OS maps. The FC has a convenient camp-site near Loch Morlich in Glenmore Forest. **Further information:** from SNH wardens at Achnagoichan, T: (01479) 810477. Glenmore Forest Park Visitor Centre, T: (01479) 861220.

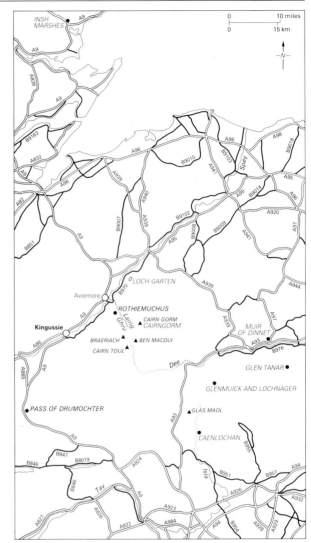

Insh Marshes

RSPB Reserve

These 2,000 acres (800 ha) of wetland fen are situated in the flood plain of the upper River Spey between the Monadhliath and Cairngorm mountains. They are of international importance for wintering whooper swans, as well as large numbers of greylag geese on passage. An impressive range of birds of prey has been seen here: buzzard, sparrow-hawk, hen harrier, osprey, golden eagle, goshawk, marsh harrier, peregrine, kestrel and the occasional merlin.

Other fauna include 17 species of butterfly (the Scotch argus most notably), 200 species of moth (Rannoch sprawler, Kentish glory, elephant hawk-moth), several species of dragonfly, the one and only bee beetle and roe deer, otter, badger and fox.

Getting there *By car:* off B970 to Insh village 2 miles (3 km) south-east of Kingussie. **Access:** open daily. **Activities** *Walking:* guided walks at 2pm on Thursdays (Apr-Aug). Reception centre and car-park. **Further information:** RSPB Warden, Ivy Cottage, Insh, Kingussie, Highland PH21 1NT, T: (01540) 661518.

Rothiemurchus

SNH NNR, FC, SSSI

This enormous private estate covers more than 30 square miles (75 square kilometres) of lochs and hill ground between the Spey Valley and Braeriach in the middle of the Cairngorms. It contains very fine stands of native pine, as well as moorland and wetland with a good range of characteristic flora and fauna.

The beautiful Loch an Eilein (otters, brown trout, pike, eel, crossbills, buzzards and osprey) is also part of the estate and can be explored along the nature trail. A large part of the estate lies within the boundary of the Cairngorm National Nature Reserve and 85% of the land is protected as Sites of Special Scientific Interest. **Getting there** *By car:* visitor centre on B970 south of Aviemore. **Access:** all year, but in forest keep to way-marked paths; open access to Cairngorms above tree line except during period of deer cull (Sept-Oct) and calving (May-Jun), when visitors should keep to specified hill routes. **Further information:** leaflets from Rothiemurchus Estate Office, Dell of Rothiemurchus, by Aviemore, Inverness-shire PH22 1QH, T: (01479) 810858.

Loch Garten

RSPB Reserve

This reserve in Speyside, Highland, occupies nearly 3,000 acres (1,200 ha) of the

Abernethy Forest, a remnant of the ancient Caledonian Forest and now the largest area of natural woodland in Britain. These great old northern pine woods are a national heritage, but it is Loch Garten's famous ospreys that are one of the great conservation success stories. After half a century's absence from Scotland a single pair of ospreys came to Loch Garten in the 1950s to breed. Every spring since then ospreys have returned from their winter quarters in Africa to nest in their Loch Garten eyrie and have gradually spread out to other sites.

Seventy-two other birds breed here and a remarkable total of 144 species have been recorded (some of them extremely rare). 26 moths, 18 butterflies, 11 dragonflies; and otter, wildcat, pine marten, red deer, red squirrel, badger, fox, and a wide variety of northern pine-wood plants. **Getting there** *By car:* turn off B970 at Boat of Garten and follow signpost to reserve at Loch Garten. **Access:** ospreys are in Statutory Bird Sanctuary; access confined to way-marked paths leading to observation post (open mid-Apr-Aug). Rest of reserve accessible at all times. **Further information:** for booklet, send a self-addressed envelope to the Warden (R. Thaxton), Grianan, Nethy Bridge, Highland PH25 3EF, or contact RSPB North Scotland Office, T: (01463) 715000.

Glen Tanar

SNH NNR

Occupying over 10,000 acres (4,000 ha) of woodland and moorland on the Glen Tanar Estate south of the River Dee,

this is the finest and most easterly remnant of the ancient Caledonian Forest, with large spreads of splendid native Scots pine of great age, and natural regeneration on an extensive scale. Typical pine-wood fauna includes crossbill, siskin and capercaillie, red squirrel, wildcat, fox and mink. **Getting there** *By car:* to Glen Tanar Estate at Braeloine, south of B976, almost 6 miles (9½ km) east of Ballater. **Access:** at any time on way-marked paths on old drove roads. Access off paths by permit only; apply Glen Tanar Estate Office. Visitor centre open Apr-Sept. Summer ranger service. **Further information:** SNH, Grampians Area, 16/17 Rubislaw Terrace, Aberdeen AB1 1XE, T: (01224) 642863, F: 635020; or Glen Tanar Estate Office, Braeloine, nr Ballater, Grampian, T: (01339) 886451.

Glenmuick and Lochnagar

The reserve covers 6,355 acres (2,572 ha) of mountainous terrain and lochs, with the stark, boulder-strewn slopes of Lochnagar rising abruptly from the shores of Loch Muick: the highest point of a range of hills forming an almost continuous 9-mile (14-km) plateau. Lochnagar is remarkable for the sheer granite cliffs of its gigantic, ice-sculptured corries and the vast expanse of purple heather on its hillsides in August.

This is wild country by any standards, the world of running deer, soaring eagles, swooping peregrine. In winter it feels like Alaska, but in summer you can see adders and lizards basking

by the trail on sunny days. The luxuriant flowers of the corries are the region's scientific treasure: globe-flower, alpine willow-herb, alpine sow-thistle and various saxifrages, as well as alpine lady fern and parsley fern. You might also see rare birds such as honey buzzard and wry neck.

Before you go *Maps:* Ordnance Survey Landranger Series, map No. 44. **Getting there** *By car:* turn off the B976 at Bridge of Muick and follow road to Spittal of Glenmuick. Proceed from car-park on foot. **Where to stay:** good range of accommodation in Braemar, including youth hostel, T: (01339) 741659 (open all year). **Access:** at all times. Best time: May-Sept for birds and flowers, Nov for deer. **Activities:** visitor centre and ranger service at Spittal; a variety of trails, some rough, some easy, lead from here to Loch Muick, Lochnagar and Glen Clova. **Further information:** contact Balmoral Estates Office, T: (01339) 742334.

Caenlochan

SNH NNR

The reserve covers 9,100 acres (3,680 ha) of wild mountain country centring on the head of the River Isla and stretching east as far as the Glen Clova mountains. This is a difficult place to get to and involves some rough walking in rugged terrain. But it is the real McCoy — who was McCoy? — with red deer in great numbers on the corries and summits, and blue hare and foxes, and golden eagles wheeling over the glens, and many ptarmigan, golden plover, dunlin and ring ouzel.

Before you go *Maps:* Ordnance Survey Landranger Series, map Nos. 43, 44. **Getting there** *By car:* Glas Maol (3,502 ft/1,067 m), the area's highest mountain, rises to the east of A93 — in the Cairnwell Pass —

Sunlight plays on the Grampian moor between Clattering Bridge and Bridge of Dye

between Blairgowrie and Braemar. Climb it from the highest point on the main road. The area has an attractive back door at the head of Glen Clova, reached on the B955 north from Kirriemuir. *By bus:* there is a daily (except Sun) service along the B955. **Where to stay:** tourist information centre in Kirriemuir will assist with accommodation, T: (01575) 574097. Glendoll Youth Hostel at head of Glen Clova, T: (01575) 550236 (open 20th Mar-1st Nov). **Access:** restricted to nature reserve June-20 Oct. **Further information:** contact SNH, Grampians Area, 16/17 Rubislaw Terrace, Aberdeen AB1 1XE, T: (01224) 642863, F: 635020. Alternatively, contact Kincardine and Deeside Tourist Board, Bridge Street, Banchory, Kincardineshire AB31 3SX, T: (01330) 822000, F: 825126.

THE NORTH-WEST HIGHLANDS

The cataclysmic landslip of the Great Glen cleanly slashes Scotland in two. This flooded fault stretches diagonally from Inverness on the east coast to the Isle of Mull on the west. Incorporating the deep waters of Loch Ness in its 76-mile (107-km) course, the Great Glen is the most stupendous geological feature in Britain. Beyond it lies the wild world of rock and water of north-west Scotland; the wettest, windiest, oldest and least populated part of Britain. It is also a very complex region. From Moidart to Cape Wrath the west coast is a confused mixture of old rocks and new volcanic ones, a wild jumble of ancient gneiss, old sandstone and the weathered lava flows and eroded granites of the volcanoes. The Torridonian mountains of Wester Ross jut 3,000 feet (914 metres) straight out of the sea. The wastes of west Sutherland, a so-called 'wet desert' scoured bare by the Ice Age, stretch soilless and treeless to the edge of vision.

The coast, where the Atlantic rollers thunder against the sheer cliffs and offshore islands with an impact measured at three tons per square foot, is wild and indented, and fiercely glaciated sea lochs like giant fjords gnaw deep into the heart of the rocky landscape. Amid this grandeur and desolation signs of human settlement are few: only here or there an isolated cottage where a crofter wrests a living from the meagre soil.

SCOTTISH PLACE NAMES

Aber *river mouth*	Eilean *island*
Aird, ard *height,*	Fionne, fyne *white, shining*
promontory	Garbh *rough*
Allt *stream*	Inch, innis *island*
Aonach *ridge*	Inver *river mouth*
Auch, ach *field*	Kil *church, burial place*
Ban *white*	Knock *knoll*
Beallach *pass*	Kyle *firth, strait*
Beg, beag *little*	Lairig *pass*
Ben, beinn, bheinn	Liath *grey*
mountain	Linn, linne *pool*
Breac, vrackie *speckled*	Meall, mheall *rounded hill*
Cairn, carn *hill*	Mor, more *big*
Cnoc *hill, knoll*	Na, nam, an *the, of, of the*
Coire, corrie *mountain*	Ru, rhu, row, rudha *point*
valley, hollow	Sgurr *peak*
Creag *crag, rock*	Stob *peak*
Dearg *red*	Strath *broad valley*
Druim, drum *ridge*	Tarbet *isthmus*
Dubh *dark, black*	Uamh *cave*
Eaglais *church*	Voe *narrow bay*

Ardnamurchan, Moidart and Morar

NSA

These three west Highland peninsulas overlook the Small Isles, forming a coastal landscape of tremendous variety and interest. To the south lies Loch Sunart and the remote Morvern peninsula, whose interior consists entirely of moorland and low hills; to the north the wild, uninhabited mountain country of the Morar peninsula is split almost in two by the trackless 10-mile (16-km) length of Loch Morar, the deepest inland water in Britain (1,067 ft/325 m down).

The coastal fringe is made up of several subsidiary areas, each different in character but complementary to the others: the rocky, indented coastline of northern Ardnamurchan; the sandy bays and moss of Kentra; Loch Moidart's sheltered, intimate landscape of wooded islands, sand, rock and water; the wooded shores, rocky promontories and heather-covered islets of Loch Ailort and Loch nan Uamh; and the silver sand beaches of Morar, backed by five miles (eight kilometres) of machair overlooking the Sound of Arisaig and the Isle of Eigg.

It was on the beach where the Borrodale Burn flows into the Loch nan Llamh that Bonnie Prince Charlie landed in July 1745 to raise his rebellion, and hence he departed 14 months later after its failure. With its looming hills and mountains, its ever-changing western light, its gigantic flaming sunsets behind the isles, this is a magical part of the Highland world, inaccessible by road, but a joy on foot.

There is an SNH-FC reserve of native woodland on two sides of Loch Sunart — oak on the north bank, ash wood on the south. The main scientific interest is the range of rare and local species of mosses, lichens and leafy liverworts which flourish luxuriantly in the high humidity of the area.

Lacking really high and dramatic peaks, this area attracts few climbers and hill walkers. However, the traverse of the Rois Bheinn ridge of Moidart from Rois Bheinn (2,895 ft/882 m) across the mountains of Loch Shiel to Glenfinnan, a high-level walk of 18 miles (29 km) across a rough and trackless wilderness, must count as one of the finest hill walks in Britain, offering considerable variety and marvellous views. An experienced walker should allow nine hours, and be prepared for wind and rain. **Before you go** *Maps:* Ordnance Survey Landranger Series, map Nos. 40, 47, 49. See also *The Knoydart and Morar Passes*, a map produced by the Scottish Rights of Way Society, T: (0131) 652 2937. *Guide-books:* for route details of climbs in the area consult *The North West Highlands* by the Scottish Mountaineering Trust, T: (01738) 638227. **Getting there** *By car:* A861 leaves the A830 18 miles (29 km) south of Mallaig at Lochailort in South Morar, giving access to Loch Ailort and Loch Moidart. At Salen it turns east, keeping to the north shore of Loch Sunart. The B8007, which leaves the A861 at Salen, gives access to the Ardnamurchan peninsula. *By rail:* Lochailort is a station on the Fort William to Mallaig line. **Where to stay:** bed and breakfast and hotels at Loch Ailort, Arisaig, Morar and Mallaig. *Where to Stay* brochure from Fort William and Lochaber Tourist Board, Fort William, T: (01397) 703781. **Where to go:** Loch Sunart NNR: access to Ariundle Wood from A861 north of Loch Sunart. Travelling west, turn right at Strontian, then right again after 1 mile at sign for Ariundle. Nature trail. Fine waterfall. Leaflet from FC office at Fort William, T: (01397) 702184. Access to Glen Cripesdale section of reserve is by permit only. Apply SNH. Rois Bheinn Ridge: access to Rois Bheinn along west slope from Roshven on A861, at mouth of Loch Ailort. **Further information:** TICs at Strontian, T: (01967) 402131, and Kilchoan, T: (01972) 510222. SNH West Highland Office, T: (01397) 704716.

Knoydart

NSA

The first time I set eyes on Knoydart was from nearly 3,200 feet (975 m) up on the top of Ben Sgreol one blindingly frosty, sun-lit, blue day in midwinter. I had climbed up the mountain in Wellington rubber boots and a peat-digger's donkey jacket, starting literally at sea level on the beach at Sandaig Bay and following the line of a very steep burn for much of the way. When I eventually got to the top, and looked about me in that dry, crystal light, the view took me completely by surprise.

Skye, and the whale-backed hump of Rum, and the blue shapes of the Outer Isles; all that I had expected. But I was quite unprepared for the view over the mountains of the hinterland. To north, east and south stretched a seemingly limitless wilderness devoid of human habitation; under its cover of pristine snow it looked more like a mountain range in Siberia, certainly unlike anything I had seen in Britain up to that time.

Much of this wild and crackling landscape I saw from Ben Sgreol belonged to a remote region called Knoydart, which stretched away from the far shores of the deep, dark loch called Loch Hourn below me. I was intrigued by this unexpected wilderness, and I resolved to set foot there as soon as the opportunity offered.

So one still, early spring day in late March I launched the dinghy into Glenelg Bay, and after picking up a friend from the south at Glenelg jetty, set course for the Knoydart shore. My friend had brought a bottle of excellent Glenfiddich malt whisky to help the voyage along, so to speak, and we steered a giddy course down the Sound of Sleat, before abruptly grounding on the boulder shore by the Croulin Burn on the north side of Knoydart.

I teetered ashore. It was a very hallucinatory sort of day. Above the high spring tide-line lay an abandoned croft whose owner, an old and reclusive fisherman, had recently died. Now there were deer in the overgrown garden, two hinds in his tumbledown parlour and a very proud, heavily antlered, seriously lame stag out on the rough track that led over the hill and far away. I followed the limping stag into the silent interior over the rough, bouldered ground, and at length stood alone in a bowl of rocks, above which wheeled the silhouette of a buzzard on stiff, flared wings, and beyond which soared a horseshoe of summits, with a high, extremely precipitous, solitary peak behind them: Ladhar Beinn (3,343 feet/1,019 metres).

I was so mesmerized by the curiously primordial magic of this wild place that in subsequent years I tried to buy some sort of dwelling there: croft or bothy or ruin, I didn't mind. Only much later did I discover that Knoydart was ruled by a very autocratic and feudal pro-Nazi laird who rigorously repelled all intruders; and this was one reason why Knoydart had remained for so long a wilderness backwater, unvisited, unknown and unsung. All this quickly changed, however, following the death of the laird; now, with the creation of the Knoydart Foundation, the residents have all been given a share in the land.

The Rough Bounds of Knoydart is the old name for this wild and isolated peninsula of mountains and glens, lying to the north of Morar between Loch Nevis and Loch Hourn. It is an apt name, for though strictly speaking it refers only to the coast, which is both trackless and exceedingly rough-going on foot, it could serve just as well for the interior, where no road goes and precious few people either.

Loch Hourn, on Knoydart's northern frontier, is one of the most gaunt and melancholy of all Scottish sea lochs, and so hemmed in on both sides by mountains above 3,000 feet (914 m) that it is virtually sunless — hence, perhaps, its name, which means Hell Loch. By contrast, Loch Nevis (Loch of Heaven), bounding Knoydart to the south, has an open and sunny aspect, but like Loch Hourn it penetrates deep into

The typically Highland scenery of Loch Blain lies at the landward end of Ardnamurchan

the mountains, and together these two sea lochs serve to emphasize Knoydart's sense of remoteness and separateness.

Five main glens and passes open up Knoydart to the wild traveller. Shepherds' and stalkers' tracks lead through these glens, and you would be well advised to stick to them as far as possible, because away from them Knoydart is rugged indeed. The tracks, which are rights of way, provide convenient access to Knoydart's three Munros: Ladhar Bheinn (pronounced Larven; 3,343 feet/1,019 metres), the most westerly Munro on the British mainland, with a spectacular corrie ringed by 100-foot (30-metre) vertical cliffs; and to the east the peaks of Luinne Bheinn (3,083 feet/939 metres) and Meall Buidhe (3,107 feet/946 metres).

The only two settlements on Knoydart are at Barrisdale Bay on Loch Hourn and at Inverie on Loch Nevis. There is a good long walk you can do across the rugged and mountainous country between the two via Ladhar Bheinn — distance: 22 miles (35 kilometres), time: 11 hours — but you will have to try to connect with the evening mail boat from Inverie to Mallaig or you will be stranded for the night.

BEFORE YOU GO
Maps: Ordnance Survey, Landranger Series, map No. 33. *The Knoydart and Morar Passes*, published by the Scottish Rights of Way Society, T: (0131) 652 2937.
Guide-book: *The North-West Highlands*, produced by the Scottish Mountaineering Trust, T: (01738) 638227.

GETTING THERE
By sea: thrice-weekly mail boats from Mallaig (Mon, Wed, Fri) stop at Inverie and Tarbet, hamlets on Loch Nevis. Contact Bruce Watt Cruises, The Pier, Mallaig, T: (01687) 462233, or 'Western Isles', East Bay, Mallaig, T: (01687) 462320.
By car: the determined motorist can penetrate a part of this remote area from the A87 on two winding and precipitous unclassified roads. One leaves the main road at Loch Garry, 5 miles (8 km) west of Invergarry, ending at the head of Loch Hourn (Kinloch Hourn). The other leaves the A87 at Shiel Bridge by the head of Loch Duich and goes via Glenelg to Corran on Loch Hourn.
By bus: a 4-seater postbus runs daily (except Sun) to Arnisdale on Loch Hourn from Kyle of Lochalsh. Another postbus service links Invergarry with Kinloch Hourn 3 times a week.

WHERE TO STAY
Bed and breakfast at Mallaig. Hotel at Tomdoun, 20 miles (32 km) east of Loch Hourn. *Youth hostel:* Ratagan, near Shiel Bridge, T: (01599) 511243. Two tourist boards produce *Where to Stay* brochures for the region: Fort William and Lochaber (south and central), T: (01397) 703781, and the Isle of Skye and South West Ross (north), T: (01478) 612137. Four self-catering houses and an inexpensive walkers' hostel on the estate. Inverie House takes bookings for parties of 7 or more. Enquiries to Knoydart Estate Office, Mallaig, T: (01687) 462243.

ACCESS
Most of this area is 'deer forest'. In late summer or autumn enquire whether deer stalking is in progress.

ACTIVITIES
Walking: there is rough, trackless going across the peninsula's beautiful mountains. Ladhar Bheinn (3,343 ft/1,019 m) is accessible from Inverie on north shore of Loch Nevis. On any excursion into this remote region, carry an authoritative guide-book.
Stalking: the changes in ownership have altered the face of Knoydart. From an unknown wilderness, it is rapidly becoming an up-market, high-profile wilderness, with the cost of killing a deer about the same as a new car.
Fishing: is excellent and slightly less expensive than stalking (enquiries to Estate Office).

FURTHER INFORMATION
TICs at Shiel Bridge, T: (01599) 511264; and Mallaig, T: (01687) 462170.

Loch Arkaig to Loch Quoich

Inland from Knoydart, between the national scenic areas of Kintail to the north and Loch Shiel to the south, lies a vast tract of uninhabited mountain country that must count as one of the wildest and least tamed areas in Britain. It has no name, this rugged, almost trackless muddle of peaks and glens, but it is bounded immediately to the west by the wild lands of Knoydart and Morar, and far to the east by the definitive divide of the Great Glen, and it incorporates the lonely inland lochs of Arkaig and Quoich (pronounced Kooich), and between them one of Scotland's most remote and most dramatic mountains, Sgurr na Ciche, rising in sharp and perfect symmetry on all sides to a height of 3,410 ft (1,039 m).

This exciting wilderness has one other distinction: it is one of the wettest places in the British Isles, with an average annual rainfall of up to 159 in (4,040 mm) recorded at Kinlochquoich, and fine days counted on the fingers of your hands. This makes an expedition to the interior a more than unusually serious undertaking, for not only are there no roads, but there are no bridges either, and as the burns can rise extremely rapidly in sudden floods, and entire hillsides stream with water, you may have to make long detours — thus adding considerably to your allotted time, and even leaving you stranded in the wilds overnight.

The trek from Arkaig to Quoich takes you cross-country from south to north. But five rights of way radiate through the mountains from Strathan, the stalker's cottage at the head of Loch Arkaig, and instead of following Glen Dessarry towards the north, you could follow Bonnie Prince Charlie's escape route eastward down the boggy track through Glen Pean to Morar (and the Hebrides), thus accomplishing an east-west crossing of this Highland outback. But in such a free-ranging landscape, where the skyline's the limit, you can head off in any direction you like, an ocean voyager over the peat and rock and the morained and hummocked ground, where your Ordnance Survey is your lodestone and evening star.
Before you go *Maps:* Ordnance Survey Landranger Series, map Nos. 33, 34. **Getting there** *By car:* this wild area lies immediately west of the A82 between Spean Bridge and

Invergarry. For Loch Quoich, take the A87 from Invergarry. A minor road to the left in about 5 miles (8 km) follows Glen Garry and leads to the north shore of Loch Quoich. For Loch Arkaig leave the A82 at Spean Bridge. The B8004 and B8005 lead to a minor road that clings to the north shore of Loch Arkaig. *By rail:* Spean Bridge is a station on the Glasgow-Fort William line. *By bus:* a 4-seater postbus operates Mon, Wed and Fri from Invergarry to Kinloch Hourn, passing Loch Quoich. **Where to stay:** accommodation at Spean Bridge, Invergarry and Fort Augustus. Hotel at Tomdoun, 6 miles (10 km) east of Loch Quoich. *Where to Stay* brochure from Fort William and Lochaber Tourist Board, Cameron Centre, Cameron Square, Fort William PH33 6AJ, T: (01397) 703781. Youth hostel at Loch Lochy, 3 miles (5 km) south of Invergarry, T: (01809) 501239. **Activities:** Sgurr na Ciche (3,410 ft/1,039 m), the area's highest mountain, requires a long hike up Glen Dessarry from the end of the road at the west end of Loch Arkaig. **Further information:** tourist information centre at Fort Augustus, 7 miles (11 km) north of Invergarry, T: (01320) 366367.

Kintail

From Gaelic *Caen da Shaill*, 'the head of two seas'

NTS, NSA

To the north of the wild areas of Knoydart, Loch Quoich and Loch Arkaig and immediately to the south-west of Glen Affric lies another superb piece of the wild, West Highland jigsaw puzzle. This is the national scenic area of Kintail, consisting of three long mountain ranges terminating round the head of Loch Duich: Beinn Fhada, the Five Sisters of Kintail and the Cluanie Forest, which culminates in the summit known as the Saddle.

All these ranges have peaks in excess of 3,300 ft (1,000 m), and Sgurr Fhuaran (one of the Five Sisters) is over 3,500 ft (1,070 m). Together they present a mountain scene of imposing grandeur, with the pinnacles of the Saddle dominating Glen Shiel and the beautifully elegant peaks of the Five Sisters — among the sheerest grassy mountains in Scotland — forming a majestic background to the head of

The wildcat is one of Scotland's most elusive predators

Loch Duich.

These mountains, only a few miles from the western sea, form the watershed of mainland Scotland, and the glens which thread between them from Loch Duich are short, steep and deep, with rivers and burns which tumble headlong from the ridges and corries of their upper reaches over waterfalls and through alder-fringed pools down to the green pastures of the lower glens.

Thus one of the highest waterfalls in Britain, the spectacular Falls of Glomach, plunges nearly 350 ft (110 m) down a narrow ravine into a savage cauldron in wild, rugged and remote mountain country above Loch na Leitreach.

Kintail is the epitome of the West Highland scene, and for naturalist and hill walker alike it is a land of delights. Herds of red deer and wild goats roam through the area and the varied flora on its grass slopes includes such notable species as fragrant orchid, butterfly orchid, pale butterwort and mountain azalea. The area offers three very fine long mountain walks. The first, a 14-mile (22-km) traverse of moderate difficulty along the Five Sisters Ridge, starting at the Cluanie Inn and ending about 10 hours later near Shiel Bridge, takes up most of a long and arduous day but offers from the top of Sgurr Fhuaran one of the finest views in all Scotland, with the whole of the Inner Hebrides, all the Outer Hebrides between Harris and Barra Head, and the mainland peaks between Assynt and Ben Alder laid out around you. The second walk is along the South Kintail Ridge, which runs parallel to but further west than the first, and contains no less than seven Munros in 8 miles (13 km) — a delightful, relatively easy traverse of about 182

7-8 hours starting at the Cluanie Inn and ending at the battlefield of Glen Shiel, where the Redcoats fought the Jacobites in 1719. The third walk is over the Saddle of Glen Shiel, starting and ending at Shiel Bridge. This walk takes about 7 hours and is very fine, but since it entails crossing rocky and exposed sections, it is not recommended for the inexperienced.

Before you go *Maps:* Ordnance Survey Landranger Series, map No. 33. **Getting there** *By car:* easy access to Loch Duich and to the mountains along both sides of Glenshiel from the A87, the Invergarry to Kyle of Lochalsh road, which bisects this scenic area. *By bus:* buses from Edinburgh, Glasgow and Inverness, bound for Skye, run along the A87. **Where to stay:** accommodation at Shiel Bridge and Dornie. Inn at west end of Loch Cluanie. Morvich caravan and camp-site on River Croe near Loch Duich, T: (01599) 511354. *Youth hostel:* Ratagan, Kyle, 1 mile from Shiel Bridge, T: (01599) 511243. *Where to Stay* brochure from Isle of Skye and South West Ross Tourist Board, Portree IV51 9BZ, T: (01478) 612137. **Activities:** NTS Countryside Centre at Morvich Farm, off A87 3 miles (5 km) north-east of Shiel Bridge. Resident ranger/naturalist. Guided walk service. **Further information:** NTS ranger/naturalist, Willie Fraser, Morvich Farm, T: (01599) 511231.

Glen Affric

NSA, FC Reserve

Glen Affric is a long glacial valley with steep sides and a broad floor containing a

roaring river and two substantial lochs. The lower slopes of the hills are covered by one of the most beautiful of all the remnants of the native Caledonian Forest, with many fine old trees, a good sprinkling of birch and rowan and a canopy open enough to allow heather and bilberry to carpet the hummocky ground.

By contrast, the high ground of the upper glen is stark moor and mountain, and it is here you may see the red deer which have been banished from the pine woods as part of a forest regeneration programme. A few deer still inhabit the woods, along with the pine marten, wildcat, badger and fox. There is a thriving population of crossbill, capercaillie and black grouse; and fungi galore.

A walk along the high mountain ridge which forms the northern boundary of Glen Affric National Scenic Area takes you across Scotland's main watershed from east to west via Carn Eige, the highest mountain north of the Great Glen. You begin at Loch Beinn a'Mheadhoin, not far from Affric Lodge, and end at the Allt Beithe Youth Hostel at the western end of Glen Affric, or at the Cluanie Inn if you prefer. It is a very long, tough mountain traverse of some 26 miles (42 km), including 6 Munros, and it will take a fit and experienced mountain walker up to 14 hours hard slog — albeit in some of the wildest and most remote and most wonderful Highland scenery in Scotland.

Before you go *Maps:* Ordnance Survey Landranger Series, map Nos. 25, 33. **Getting there** *By car:* from the village of Cannich on A831, 27 miles south-west of Inverness by road, an unclassified road is signposted to Glen Affric. *By bus:* sparse bus service to Cannich from Beauly and Inverness. *By foot:*

access from Cluanie Inn on A87, to south of Glen Affric, or from Croe Bridge to west. **Where to stay:** bed and breakfast and hotel at Cannich. Remote youth hostel at Allt Beithe in Glen Affric (book through Central Reservation Service, T: (0541) 553255) and at Cannich, T: (01456) 415244. Accommodation brochure from tourist board (see below). **Activities** *Walking:* long ridge walk to north of Loch Affric, including twin peaks of Carn Eighe (3,877 ft/1,182 m) and Mam Sodhail (3,862 ft/1,177 m), the highest mountains in North-West Highlands. Access on track from north shore of Loch Beneveian. Distance to Cluanie Inn — end of traverse — 26 miles (42 km). A' Chralaig (3,673 ft/1,120 m) and Sgurr nan Conbhairean (3,634 ft/1,108 m) — mountains to south-west of Glen Affric — are short climbs from A87 east of Cluanie. Full details in Scottish Mountaineering Trust's *The North-West Highlands*. Most of Glen is in Affric Forest (FC). 4 car-parks, picnic sites beside river and lochs. Short way-marked walks start from picnic areas. *Fishing:* permits available from FC office. **Further information:** Inverness, Loch Ness and Nairn Tourist Board, 23 Church Street, Inverness IV1 1EZ, T: (01463) 234353. FC guidebook from Forest Office Cannich, Beauly, Inverness-shire.

Strathfarrar

NTS, SNH NNR, NSA

Glen Affric is the most southerly of the great glens which feed into Strathglass and the Beauly River. The other

An eerie mist settles on Glen Affric, obscuring the view of Loch Beinn a'Mheadoin

two, Glen Cannich in the centre and Glen Strathfarrar to the north, have been spoilt in part by hydroelectric schemes, with the exception of the lower middle stretch of Strathfarrar. The reserve covers some 10,000 acres (4,000 ha) of native Scots pine wood: the largest surviving remnant of the ancient Caledonian Forest in this part of Scotland. The best pine stands are on the south side of the River Farrar at Coille

Garbh, where some massive specimens may be up to 300 years old. To ensure the continuation of these pine woods a regeneration programme is under way which is scheduled to last one hundred years.
Before you go *Maps:* Ordnance Survey Landranger Series, map No. 33. **Getting there** *By car:* easy access to Loch Duich and to the mountains along both sides of Glenshiel from the A87. *By bus:* services from Edinburgh, Glasgow and Inverness, bound for Skye, run

along the A87 — the Invergarry to Kyle of Lochalsh road — which bisects this scenic area. **Where to stay:** accommodation at Shiel Bridge and Dornie. Cluanie Inn at west end of Loch Cluanie. Morvich caravan and camp-site (NTS) on River Croe near Loch Duich, open Mar-Oct, T: (01599) 511354. *Youth Hostel:* Ratagan, Kyle, 1 mile from Shiel Bridge, T: (01599) 511243. *Where to Stay* brochure from tourist board (see below). **Activities** *Walking:* the Five Sisters of Kintail, a ridge to north of Glen Shiel, may be walked in one long traverse (14 miles/23 km) from Cluanie Inn to Shiel Bridge. Access to the Falls of Glomach (NTS) involves a 4-mile (6½-km) walk from the FC car park at Dorusduain. Turn north at west end of Loch Duich viaduct on A87. NTS guide-book gives directions for this walk and others in the Kintail region. NTS visitor centre at Morvich farm, off A87 3 miles (5 km) north-east of Shiel Bridge. Resident ranger naturalist. Guided walk service. *Climbing:* highest point, Sgurr Fhuaran (3,505 ft/1,068 m) is a steep but straightforward climb directly from A87 1½ miles (2 km) east of Shiel Bridge. For this and other climbs see *The North West Highlands* by the Scottish Mountaineering Trust. *Fishing:* in River Croe; permits from NTS visitor centre. **Further information:** Isle of Skye and South West Ross Tourist Board, Portree IV51

'Human beings need primeval nature to re-establish contact now and then with their biological origins; a sense of continuity with the past and with the rest of creation is probably essential to the long-range sanity of the human species.'

Rene Dubos:
So Human An Animal

9BZ, T: (01478) 612137. NTS ranger, Willie Fraser, Morvich Farm, T: (01599) 511231. TIC, Shiel Bridge, T: (01599) 511264.

Wester Ross

NSA

North of Glen Carron the landscape undergoes an abrupt change from West Highland character to Northern Highland. Between Applecross and Assynt in Wester Ross there are sandstone mountains of immense antiquity and extraordinary shape; between Assynt and Cape Wrath in Sutherland a vast and desolate wilderness of rolling moor from which scattered mountains rear like monoliths. In Wester Ross you will find some of the sublimest sea, loch and mountain landscapes in the Highlands, and extensive pockets of wilderness as remote and pristine as any in Britain.

To traverse the whole length of this superb back of beyond, from the lowering crags and vertiginous corries of the Applecross Forest in the south-west to the piranha-teeth ridges of An Teallach in the north-east, is to explore a cross section of mountain scenery which can be rivalled in few other parts of the British Isles: Ben Damph, Beinn Eighe, the Torridon group and especially Liathac,

'the most soaring mountain in the north', Ben Alligin, Slioch, A'Mhaighdean, Mullach Coire Mhic Fhearchair, Beinn Lair, Ben Dearg Mhor and An Teallach, whose eastern corrie is one of the greatest of the natural sights of Scotland.

The area has much else to offer beside the rugged grandeur of the highest peaks: gentler, more lush parts, where woods of oak, birch and Scots pine soften the lower slopes around inland lochs of serene and breathless beauty. Going south to north the main components are the Applecross Forest, the Ben Damph Forest, the Torridon Mountains, Loch Maree, the Letterewe Forest, the Fisherfield Forest, the Strathnasheallag Forest (where An Teallach rises) and along the coast the sea lochs of Torridon, Gairloch and Ewe and the broader expanse of the beautiful Gruinard Bay, with their beaches, headlands, isles, inlets and wooded slopes, their incomparable views across the water to Skye and the Outer Hebrides, their marvellous synthesis with the mountains that soar from the vast hinterland lying behind them.

From Loch Torridon to Loch Maree stretches a truly vast, truly wild expanse of mountain territory. Few roads penetrate the interior of this peninsula, and there are few signs of human habitation; this is a trackless refuge for rare and sensitive species such as the peregrine and golden eagle. Most of the area lies within the Gairloch Conservation Unit, a landowners' co-operative for the management of the large herds of red deer which roam these parts. Much of this land is privately owned, with restricted access during the stalking season between September and November, but two major areas — Torridon and Beinn Eighe — are held for the nation by the National Trust for Scotland.

Torridon is the huge wilderness either side of Glen Torridon and Upper Loch Torridon, offering some of the oldest mountains on earth, with 18 tops above 3,000 feet (910 metres), six of them Munros. To the south, in the wild country of the Ben Damph and Coulin Forests between Glen Carron and Glen Torridon, where the going is almost as rough as Knoydart, rise some dozen mountains to which access can be gained from Achnashellach or Annat along a network of old stalking tracks.

To the north of Glen Torridon lies the Torridon range proper, with its fine triplet of peaks: Ben Dearg (2,995 feet/913 metres); Ben Alligin (3,232 feet/985 metres), with its vast views down the coast between Capes Wrath and Ardnamurchan; and the 3,456-foot (1,053-metre) mass of ancient sandstone known as Liathac (pronounced Leeagach), a narrow five-mile (8-km) long ridge bearing no less than eight tops including two Munros in its short length.

Beinn Eighe has seven summits. The highest — Ruadh Stac Mor (3,314 feet/1,010 metres) and Sail Mhor (3,218 feet/981 metres) — are just on the boundary of the reserve. The remaining four — the highest is Sgurr Ban (3,188 feet/972 metres) — lie on the long jagged ridge which dominates the southern half of the reserve. This fine mountain and moorland habitat is rich in associated fauna: pine marten, wildcat, fox, red and roe deer, golden eagle, peregrine, merlin and buzzard can all be found here. The mountain tops are clothed with a fine carpet of alpine vegetation and there is a spectacular high-altitude traverse for climbers as well as good low-altitude trails for ramblers.

BEFORE YOU GO
Maps: Ordnance Survey Landranger Series, map Nos. 19, 24, 25; OS Outdoor Leisure Series, map No. 8.
Guide-book: SMT Guide, *The North-West Highlands.*

GETTING THERE
By car: one main road winds through Wester Ross. Starting as the A896 on Loch Carron, it cuts north to Shieldaig on Loch Torridon, then angles northeast past the Torridon Forest and Beinn Eighe. At Kinlochewe it becomes the A832, veering north-west along the shore of Loch Maree, then changing direction again at Gairloch as it circles clockwise past Loch Ewe, Little Loch Broom and An Teallach to join the A835 12 miles (19 km) south of Ullapool. A few roads lead off this north-south artery towards tiny communities on the coast.

By rail: Kyle of Lochalsh, directly south of Wester Ross, is the nearest station, linking the area by rail with Inverness.

WHERE TO STAY
Gairloch is the principal centre for accommodation, but there are plenty of hotels and guest houses in the region as well as self-catering accommodation . Write for the *Where to Stay* brochure from Ross and Cromarty Tourist Board, Information Centre, North Kessock, Ross-shire IV1 1XB, T: (01463) 731505.
Youth hostels: at Craig (very remote, on north shore of Loch Torridon), which can be booked through Central Reservation Service, T: (0541) 553255, and Carn Dearg, near Gairloch, T: (01445) 712219.

FURTHER INFORMATION
Tourist Information Centre, Gairloch, T: (01445) 712130.

Ben Wyvis

SNH NNR

If you have slogged over the superb wilderness areas of Wester Ross and still have an appetite, you can always try Easter Ross. Here Ben Wyvis, an isolated plateau measuring 6 miles by 3 (10 km by 5), sprouts nine tops above 3,000 feet (910 m) in an ocean of moor. The national nature reserve is outstanding for its continuous carpet of moss heath, the most extensive in Britain.

Before you go *Maps:* Ordnance Survey Landranger Series, map Nos. 20, 21, 26. **Getting there** *By car:* the A836, running north from Inverness, crosses the eastern edge of this region; the A832/835 from Inverness to

Ullapool skirts the south. No main roads reach the interior but a few minor roads and tracks provide useful access. **Where to stay:** accommodation is in Strathpeffer. Strathpeffer youth hostel, T: (01997) 421532. **Activities** *Climbing:* Ben Wyvis — 6½ miles (10½ km) due north of Strathpeffer — can be climbed from the A835 to the west (about 4 miles/6 km) or from Loch Glass to the north-east. **Further information:** leaflet from SNH, 17 Poltenny Street, Ullapool, Ross-shire IV26 2UP, T: (01854) 613418.

Coigach to Assynt

NSA

In the northernmost corner of Ross and Cromarty, between Little Loch Broom and Eddrachillis Bay, lies a rugged and spectacular landscape the like of which cannot be found elsewhere in Britain: a vast, flat, hummocky sea of gneiss, from which rise a few steep, widely scattered sandstone peaks. Because they soar in such angular and eccentric relief out of a relatively uniform lowland of hillocky moor and peaty hollows, moraines, tarns and lochans, these remarkable mountains give the impression they are higher than they really are. Ben More Coigach, for example, is only 2,438 ft (743 m) above sea level, while Stac Polly, its summit ridge shattered into little pinnacles and great cascades of scree like some geological Armageddon, barely clears 2,000 ft (610 m). Even the extraordinary sugar loaf of Suilven is dwarfed by many less celebrated peaks in the Highlands.

All these peaks are made in

whole or in part of old Torridonian sandstone and hugely shaped by erosion. Coigach, in the north of the area, is almost entirely sandstone; Quinag, in the far north, has a bed of gneiss up to 2,000 ft (610 m), but seven sandstone tops, the highest 2,651 ft (808 m) above the sea. Ben More Assynt (3,273 ft/998 m), across in Sutherland to the east, is composed largely of gneiss, with great caverns in its limestone lower slopes.

Further north lie two other natural attractions. The first are the falls of Eas a' Chual Aluinn, the highest in Britain, where a little burn drops 658 feet (201 metres) off a mountain, four times the height of Niagara. The second is the sea stack of the Old Man of Stoer, a sheer sandstone needle thought unclimbable till Don Whillans got to the top in 1966. **Before you go** *Maps:* Ordnance Survey Landranger Series, map Nos. 15, 19. *Guide-book:* SMT guide *The North-West Highlands.* **Getting there** *By car:* the A835 heads north-east from Ullapool, then joins the A837 and curves around west to Lochinver on the coast. Most of the Coigach/Assynt hills are encircled by this 35-mile (56-km) loop of highway; only Quinag, to the north, and Ben More Assynt, to the east, lie outside it. *By bus:* buses run daily from Lairg to Lochinver and infrequently — summer only — from Lochinver to Ullapool. Another daily service connects Fiag Bridge with Kylesku. **Where to stay:** Ullapool, immediately south of this region, and Lochinver to the north are the major centres for serviced accommodation, but there are bed and breakfasts and hotels scattered throughout. Information centres at Ullapool, T: (01854) 612135, and Lochinver, T: (01571) 844330, will assist.

Youth hostels: at Ullapool, T: (01854) 612254; Achininver, nr Achiltibuie, T: (01854) 622254; Achmelvich, nr Lochinver, T: (01571) 844480. **Further information:** Ross and Cromarty Tourist Board, Information Centre, North Kessock, Ross-shire IV1 1XB, T: (01463) 731505; Sutherland Tourist Board, The Square, Dornoch, Sutherland IV25 3SD, T: (01862) 810400.

Ben More Coigach

SWT Reserve

Set amid the spectacular mountains of Coigach and overlooking the Summer Isles at the mouth of Loch Broom, this is a huge wild place of rock, bog and rolling moorland. It rises in the south from sea level to the summit ridge of Ben More at 2,438 ft (743 m); in the north it is bounded by a chain of large lochs, beyond which lies Inverpolly National Nature Reserve.

Typical north-west Highland fauna to be found here includes red deer, pine marten, wildcat, badger, otter and seals; golden eagle, peregrine, raven, black grouse, greenshank, eider, red and black-throated divers and barnacle geese. **Before you go** *Maps:* Ordnance Survey Landranger Series, map No. 15. **Getting there** *By car:* minor road to Achiltibuie leaves the A835 at the Old Drumrunie Lodge, 9½ miles (15 km) north of Ullapool. The road runs along the north-east boundary of the reserve, but a chain of lochs and burns makes access difficult from here. Continue on this road, which leads through Achiltibuie and

The summit of Suilven is a popular goal for backpackers setting out from nearby Lochinver

Polglass, to gain access to the reserve — and to Ben More Coigach itself — from the south-west. *By bus:* a daily minibus service runs between Ullapool and Achiltibuie. **Where to stay:** bed-and-breakfast and self-catering accommodation in Achiltibuie. Tourist information centres in Ullapool, T: (01854) 612135, or Lochinver, T: (01571) 844480, will assist. **Further information:** leaflet from SWT Ground Officer, 132 Polglass, Achiltibuie-by-Ullapool, Ross and Cromarty. Ross and Cromarty Tourist Board, Information Centre, North Kessock, Ross-shire IV1 1XB, T: (01463) 731505, F: 731701. Sutherland Tourist Board, Dornoch, T: (01862) 810400.

Inverpolly

SNH NNR

This enormous, uninhabited wilderness covers some 27,000 acres (11,000 ha) of magnificent moor, mountain, woodland, lochs, bogs, seashore and islands, and contains the spectacular sandstone peaks of Stac Polly, Cul Mor (2,786 ft/844 m) and Cul Beag (2,523 ft/769 m). No roads enter Inverpolly and few tracks cross the undulating gneiss plateau of wet moorland and blanket peat.

Red deer, otter, wildcat, pine marten and badger inhabit these wilds; 104 species of birds have been recorded here; and in the scattered fragments of surviving birch-hazel woodland

a rich ground cover thrives. But Inverpolly is best known for the rocks at Knochan Cliff, a classic geological site.

Before you go *Maps:* Ordnance Survey Landranger Series, map No. 15. **Getting there** *By car:* reserve is bounded to the east by A835. A minor road, which leaves the A835 at Drumrunie, gives access to Stac Polly and the south of the reserve; another unclassified road leads north to Lochinver along the reserve's western boundary. **Where to stay:** Lochinver, Achiltibuie and Ullapool provide serviced accommodation. Youth hostels at Achininver, nr Achiltibuie, T: (01854) 622254, and Achmelvich, nr Lochinver, T: (01571) 844480. No camping on reserve. **Further information:** leaflet from SNH Office, T: (01854) 613418; TIC, Lochinver, T: (01571) 844330.

Inchnadamph

SNH NNR

Covering 3,200 acres (1,300 ha) of moorland and limestone plateau, between Loch Assynt and Ben More Assynt, the reserve is famous for its caves, swallow holes, underground streams and the best limestone pavements in Scotland. The caves above Allt nan Uamh have revealed the bones of brown bear, arctic fox, reindeer, lynx and lemming which inhabited this part of Scotland at the end of the last Ice Age, as well as evidence of Stone Age occupation.

Today, of course, the fauna is much reduced: red deer, wild cat and mountain hare; red grouse, ring ouzel and twite. But the reserve is well known for its rich and varied flora: mountain avens, holly fern, globe flower and serrated wintergreen, which flourish on the limestone outcrop. The willow scrub found here includes three species (whortle-leaved, creeping and eared).

Before you go *Maps:* Ordnance Survey Landranger Series, map No. 15. **Getting there** *By car:* reserve lies to east of A837, just south of Inchnadamph Hotel. *By bus:* Daily Lairg-Lochinver bus service passes reserve. **Where to stay:** all ranges of accommodation in Lochinver. Hotel at Inchnadamph. Youth hostel at Achmelvich, nr Lochinver, T: (01571) 844480. No camping on reserve. **Where to go:** Ben More Assynt (just north of reserve): access from Inchnadamph Hotel, then cross-country up Glen Dubh. Various routes to summit. Return trip 6-7 hours. **Access:** contact SNH, Ullapool, T: (01854) 613418. **Further information:** leaflet from SNH. TIC, Lochinver, T: (01571) 844330.

North-West Sutherland

A huge, empty and rugged region of more than 2,000 square miles (5,000 sq km) but less than 20,000 people, containing 2 NSAs

This is a remarkable wet and windy part of the world, and arctic in appearance in winter, and I remember vividly how I was blown backwards by fierce winds from Cape Wrath when I tried to fly along the craggy northern coast of Sutherland in a light air-craft out of Orkney.

Much of the interior is a marvellous, un-inhabited tundra of moorland and bog. Partly forested in ancient times, it is now spattered by innumerable lochs and lochans and criss-crossed by a complex network of peaty streams. This is the land called the Flow Country, which stretches all the way to Caithness in the east and contains much of the world's surviving bog-land.

No less exciting are the peripheries of this British Lapland. In north-west Sutherland you can see the highest cliffs in mainland Britain (921 feet/281 metres) at Clo Mor, near Cape Wrath, the great caves of Smoo, magnificent sea lochs such as Eriboll (the deepest natural anchorage in Britain) and the silted Kyles of Tongue and Durness.

Isolated peaks such as Ben Hope (3,040 feet/927 metres) and Ben Loyal (2,504 feet/763 metres) in the north, and Foinaven (2,980 feet/908 metres), Ben Arkle (2,580 feet/786 metres) and Ben Stack (2,356 feet/718 metres), which soar majestically out of the wilderness of the Reay Forest in the north-west, provide superb climbs for hill walkers and refuge for the golden eagle, ptarmigan, dotterel, snow bunting, and blue hare. From the tip of Foinaven, you can look west over 120 square miles (310 square kilo-metres) of absolute desolation containing hundreds of glittering lochans.

Cape Wrath, the north-west corner of mainland Britain, enjoys no formal status, though it probably attracts more people than most places in the region by reason of the grandeur of its location.

A long, rough but exciting coastal walk has been devised between Cape Wrath and Kinlochbervie to the south. Sixteen miles (26 kilometres) in length and about eight hours in duration, it crosses sheer granite cliffs, skerries and stacks, wide bays of gold-en sand such as the mile-long Sandwood Bay, and trackless heather moorland and peat, rarely out of sight or sound of the screaming birds and the booming Atlantic rollers crashing on to the shore.

BEFORE YOU GO
Maps: Ordnance Survey Landranger Series, map Nos. 9, 10.
Guide-book: full details of the routes mentioned here in SMT guide: *The North-West Highlands.*

GETTING THERE
By car: from Ullapool take the A835 and A894; the A838 then leads up and around the north-west corner.
By rail: nearest station is Lairg.
By bus: buses from Inverness connect with services to most towns.

WHERE TO STAY
Despite its remoteness, this is a popular tourist area. Write for *Where to Stay* brochure from Sutherland Tourist Board (see below).
Youth hostels: Durness, T: (01971) 511244; and Tongue, T: (01847) 661301.

FURTHER INFORMATION
The Sutherland Tourist Board, The Square, Dornach, Sutherland IV25 3SD, T: (01862) 810400.
Tourist information centres in Durness, T: (01971) 511259; and Bettyhill, T: (01641) 521342. Reserve leaflets from SNH, North Highland Office, T: (01408) 633604, F: 633071.

Handa

SNH

A very high island of 766 acres (310 ha) a few hundred yards off the Sutherland coast in the North-West Highlands, bounded on three sides by vertical sandstone cliffs rising to over 400 ft (120 m). These cliffs have weathered in layers to produce ideal nesting ledges for sea-birds and in the breeding season Handa is like a spectacular multi-storey bird-park, a wild, guano-white tenement block of busy, unruly, noisy, squalor-inclined guillemots, black guillemots, fulmars, razorbills, kittiwakes, puffins, shags and gulls — most easily and impressively seen on the Great Stack of Handa.

The interior of the island consists of rough pasture, heather moor, peat bogs and six lochans. The moorland has been colonized by arctic and great skua, and the moorland flora is enlivened in the damper parts by orchids, bog asphodel, pale butterwort and royal fern. Red-throated diver, shelduck and eider breed on Handa. Grey seal and various species of whale and dolphin can sometimes be seen offshore.
Getting there *By sea:* boat service operates daily (except Sun) from Tarbet on the mainland opposite. Contact Steve MacCleod, T: (01971) 502340, Apr-Sept. **Access:** at all times, but keep to the way-marked path and take extra care on the cliff-top. **Where to stay:** no accommodation except for one bothy on the island.
Further information: contact Neil Willcox at SWT, Cramond House, Cramond Glebe Road, Edinburgh EH4 6NS, T: (0131) 334 0303.

West Highland Way

Scotland's finest national long-distance path starts in Milngarvie, north-west of Glasgow, and runs for 95 miles (152 km) across the increasingly wild and rugged interior of the Southern and Central Highlands to Fort William below Ben Nevis. The way follows the eastern side to Loch Lomond, goes over the slopes of Ben Lomond to Crianlarich, then across the western side of Rannoch Moor and past the mouths of Glen Etive and Glen Coe to Kinlochleven, whence it follows an old military road over the slopes of the Mamores and across wild country in the Ben Nevis range to its journey's end. A terrific walk, but tough at times.
Before you go *Maps:* Ordnance Survey Landranger Series, map Nos. 64, 57, 56, 50, 41. *Guide-books:* the official guide is published by HMSO, and comes with a separate 1:50,000 map. Alternatively use Tom Hunter, *A Guide to the West Highland Way* (Constable, 1995). **Getting there** *By car and rail:* Glasgow and Fort William, the end points of the route, are linked by the A82 and the Glasgow-Mallaig railway. One or other of these arteries follow the path for much of the way, providing opportunities to join or leave the route at various places along the way. **Where to stay:** the West Highland Way calls for careful preparation since there is little chance of finding a pub for shelter, a shop for a loaf of bread or a farmhouse for unbooked accommodation. *Youth hostels:* only 2 along the way, at Rowardennan, T: (01360) 870259, and Crianlarich, T: (01838) 300260, as well as one at each end — Glasgow, T: (0141) 332 3004, and Glen Nevis, in Fort William, T: (01397) 702336. Budget-minded walkers should be prepared to camp. Accommodation details are included in the invaluable free leaflet available from the West Highland Way Path Manager (South), Balloch Castle, Balloch, West Dumbartonshire, T: (01389) 758216.

Scotland: The Islands

At one time when I was travelling the West Highland coast, I was told a story about Squeaky Harris, a Hebridean steamer ferry skipper, now long dead, who was renowned throughout the islands as one of the truly eccentric salts of the sea.

It seems that on one memorable voyage through the channel of the little Minch separating Skye from the outer Hebrides, Squeaky's little ship was overtaken by a particularly thick Hebridean sea fog. Though Squeaky's navigational aids were rudimentary, he knew these waters like the back of his whisky locker, and his old tub juddered onwards at full-ahead, straining at every rivet — to the mounting alarm of a naval Admiral who happened to be a passenger on board.

At length, unable to conceal his anxiety any longer, the Admiral decided to go up to the bridge and check the situation for himself. Squeaky was profoundly unimpressed by the sudden appearance of all this gold braid in the middle of his holy of holies.

'Get off my ploody pridge, you ploody pugger,' he squeaked in his high-pitched Hebridean voice.

The Admiral explained as tactfully as he could that he was merely interested in the course they were steering and would love to have a peep at the charts.

'Well, if it's charts you're after, Admiral, I've got some somewhere here or hereabouts,' squeaked Squeaky. He finally found a dog-eared pile of old sea maps, and laid them out for the Admiral's perusal: the South China Sea, the Malacca Straits, the Mozambique Channel, and at last the Minch. The Admiral stared in horror at the chart and, pointing with quivering finger at a cluster of black dots strewn right across the steamer's bow, loudly exclaimed: 'What on earth are *those*?'

Squeaky peered at the chart, first with one eye, and then with another, and after due deliberation declared: 'Well, Admiral, if those are rocks we're buggered for sure. But if they are what I think they are, which is fly shit, then we'll be as right as rain.'

And he gave a great puff and blew away the fly shit rocks and the sand banks of accumulated dust and reefs of old tobacco ash and gave a great hoot on the ship's siren as his battered old tramp ploughed on through the fog at an unabated full-ahead amid the scream of seagulls.

This story tells us a lot about the isles. About the island weather, for instance, and the preoccupation with the sea; about the exoticness of travel in those parts (clearly we are not off Bournemouth, or even Cromer), and the sheer hazardousness of adventuring into this wild, watery North West Frontier of the European continent.

What the story does not convey is the sheer magic of Scottish island-going, the sorcery these places work on all those who venture among them. There is the ever-changing beauty of those vast skies and long, empty seas, and the wonderful pellucid light which has been compared with the light on the Greek islands. And there is the extraordinary aural clarity: for miles across the water I have heard the stags roaring from among the hills of Skye, and from far out in the bays the snort of a grey seal surfacing to breathe.

There is, too, the sense of primordiality: those soaring basalt cliffs, the winter hurricanes, the Northern Lights, the gunshot boom of the ocean swell exploding in the sea caves. I recall, almost with terror, my first sight of the great black fin of a killer whale cruising off Canna. I recall, too, the long, marvellous skeins of geese migrating out over Eilean Bhan at the first dust of snow on the Cuillin of Skye; the time I was thrown across the galley of a boat when we ran full tilt into the dreaded maelstrom of the Corryvreckan off the Isle of Jura; flying backwards before a storm-force westerly when I tried in vain to fly out of Orkney by light aircraft; and sleeping rough on a tiny island beach one spring, listening in the dark to the crooning of the seals and the murmuring of the surf and the strange cries of the distant birds in the vast, starlit, mind-expanding Hebridean night.

Sandaig Bay, on the edge of the Sound of Sleat that separates Skye from the mainland, looks out towards Eigg and the Western Isles

THE INNER HEBRIDES

The wind-swept islands of the Hebrides, the half-sub-merged edge of the continent of Europe, consist of about 550 islands divided into two parallel archipelagoes called the Inner and Outer Hebrides, which stretch for 240 miles (386 km) along the western coast of Scotland. Fewer than 70 of them are inhabited, some of them only by light-house keepers. The total population of the Hebrides amounts to little more than 30,000, making this one of the most deserted regions in Europe. Some of these islands are mere pin-pricks in the ocean; others are more substantial places, such as the islands of Islay, Jura, Mull and Skye in the Inner Hebrides.

Islay

Pronounced 'Eye-la'

A large island off the south-west coast of Jura, and the most southerly island of the Inner Hebrides. Though the Paps of Islay struggle up to more than 1,600 ft (490 m) in the south-eastern corner, the island is mostly low-lying and the scenery rather tame. However, Islay has a lavish variety of habitats: woods, scrub, moorland, cliffs, dunes, machair, sea- and freshwater lochs, rivers, marshes and farming land — and this is good for the birds.

The RSPB has a big reserve at Loch Gruinart in the north of the island, but that is not the only place to watch some spectacular species; along the cliffs of the Oa in the south, for example, you may see golden eagle, peregrine and chough by the cliffs of the Rinns in the west. But it is the geese which have pride of place, and for these you go to Loch Gruinart. **Before you go** *Maps:* Ordnance Survey Landranger Series, map No. 60. **Getting there** *By air:* daily (not Sun) flights from Glasgow run by Loganair, T: (0345) 222111. *By sea:* daily car ferries from Kennacraig on Kintyre to Port Ellen and Port Askaig. Contact Caledonian

MacBrayne Ltd, Kennacraig, T: (01880) 730253. **Where to stay:** accommodation brochure from tourist board (see below). **Further information:** TIC, Bowmore, Isle of Islay, T: (01496) 810254. West Highlands and Islands of Argyll Tourist Board, Albany Street, Oban, Argyll PA34 4AR, T: (01631) 563122.

Jura

From the Gaelic meaning 'deer island'

NSA

A large, mountainous island (and national scenic area) to the south of Mull, 28 miles (45 km) long and 8 miles (13 km) wide, for the most part barren and uninhabited, and overrun by red deer, which outnumber the human population of 200 by ten to one. Unlike lava-layered Mull, Jura is made of hard quartzite rock which rises dramatically in the south of the island to form the three attractive but desolate peaks of the Paps of Jura, which as their name suggests resemble three teat-tipped breasts, each bosoming the sky to a height of

more than 2,400 ft (732 m). Much of the island is trackless, and much of the interior consists of bog and scattered lochans, which makes exploration of Jura's remarkable west coast no task for faint hearts and tenderfoots. **Getting there** *By sea:* a regular car ferry leaves Kennacraig on Kintyre for Port Askaig on Islay; journey time: 2 hrs. Contact Caledonian MacBrayne Ltd, Kennacraig, T: (01880) 730253. From Port Askaig take the short car-ferry crossing to Feolin in Jura on Western Ferries (Argyll) Ltd, Kennacraig, Argyll, T: (0141) 332 9766. **Further information:** TICs at Tarbert, T: (01880) 820429, and Bowmore, Isle of Islay, T: (01496) 810254.

Scarba, Lunga and the Garvellachs

NSA, SSSI, World Heritage Site

Lying off the north coast of Jura, the small, rocky, conical island of Scarba is part of a national scenic area which includes the neighbouring islets of Lunga and the Garvellachs (the holy 'Isles of the Sea' or 'Rough Islands'). Tidal races rip between these islands with considerable velocity, notably through the narrow sound between Scarba and Jura — the Gulf of Corryvreckan — where the funnelling of the fierce, nine-knot, Atlantic tide over the uneven sea bed produces a celebrated whirlpool which can give small boats a nasty time (as I discovered when my boat ran into it with an impact that threw me and a pan of baked beans from one side of the galley to the other).

The tiny uninhabited Garvellachs, which blaze with wild flowers in summer, are the site of the earliest Christian settlement in Britain, dating from AD542 — two decades before St Columba reached Iona.

Getting there *By sea:* boat trips to the islands leave from Cullipool on the Isle of Luing. Access to Luing by road from the A816. The boatman, Dave Ainsley, Dunaverty, Easdale, Oban will take passengers around Scarba and the Garvellachs. Boat trips to the Garvellachs are run by Farsain Cruises in Craobh Haven, T: (01852) 500644. **Access:** the crossing is dangerous on even the calmest day and should not be attempted without an experienced local pilot. **Where to stay:** strictly no camping without prior permission: contact Major Torquil Johnson-Ferguson, T: (01387) 372240, for Lunga; Shane Cadrow, T: (01852) 314334, for Scarba; and Smiths Gore, T: (0131) 555 1200, for the Garvellachs. **Further information:** TIC, Oban, T: (01631) 563122.

Mull

A large, rainy, beautiful island, part Hebridean in character, part West-Highland. Mull was the centre of violent and prolonged volcanic activity in the tertiary period. For millions of years vast waves of lava poured out and settled in layers, which at one time were up to 6,000 ft (1,830 m) thick. These layers weathered into the terraced landscape which is characteristic of much of Mull today. Mull is fertile and forested, but has plenty of wild places — mainly south of the narrow neck of land between Salen and Loch na Keal.

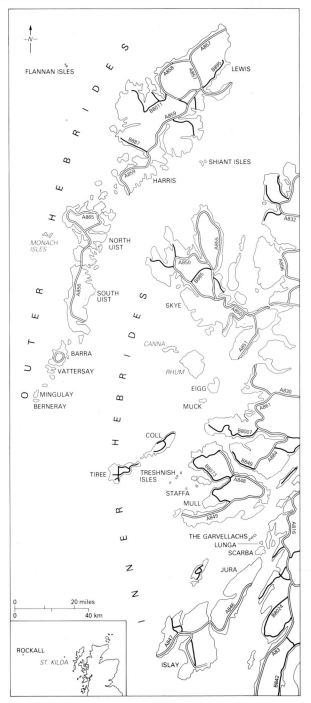

A winter stag party of red deer forage amicably, the rivalry of the rut forgotten until next autumn

The west coast is very striking, being deeply indented with lochs and spattered with rocks and islets, while inland the high table land rises to 3,169 ft (967 m) on Ben More, the highest mountain in the Hebrides outside of Skye and the haunt of red deer, blue hare and golden eagle. The ascent of the Ben More ridge takes about four hours of relatively straightforward, airy going with fabulous views as far as the Barra Head light, 60 miles (96 km) away.

More mountains rise up in the south-east, while to the south-west of Ben More, in the hinterland north of Loch Scridain, lies the wilderness of the Ardmeanach peninsula, which can be explored only on foot. At the seaward tip, embedded in the basalt cliffs of Rubha nah-Uamha, stands the cast of a 40-ft (12-m) fossil tree: 'McCulloch's Tree', engulfed by lava 50 million years ago and visible only at low tide.

Along the southern shore of the island's longest peninsula,

194

the Ross of Mull, stretches a wild, little-visited sea coast of columnar basalt cliffs and numerous caves where no road goes. This is a fine island for the wild traveller, offering plenty of wildlife interest, too: dolphins and basking shark offshore, otters on the sea-lochs, sea-birds along the coast, and fascinating rocks and fossils for the geologist and petrologist.

Before you go *Maps:* Ordnance Survey Landranger Series, map Nos. 47, 48, 49. **Getting there** *By sea:* year-round car ferry from Oban to Craignure and Kilchoan to Tobermory (Sun only in the summer) run by Caledonian MacBrayne Ltd, Oban, T: (01631) 566688. **Where to stay:** list from tourist board (see below). **Activities** *Climbing:* Ben More is most frequently climbed along its north-west ridge. Access from B8035 south-west of Salen. See *Islands of Scotland (including Skye)* by SMT. **Further information:** TICs at Oban, T: (01631) 563122; Tobermory, T: (01688) 302182. West Highlands and Islands of Argyll Tourist Board, Oban, T: (01631) 563122.

Staffa

NTS

Tiny lava island like a tilted black block 6 miles (10 km) off the west coast of Mull. Staffa is famous for the rock formations at the entrance to Fingal's Cave, a huge gap in the cliffs, 60 ft (18 m) high and over 200 ft (60 m) deep, where the basalt lava has cooled and cracked into perfect hexagonal columns similar to those at the Giant's Causeway in Northern Ireland. When rough seas pound into the cave, the roar reverberates all over the island; it inspired the motif for Mendelssohn's *Hebridean Overture*.

Before you go *By sea:* daily boat trips from Oban to Iona and Staffa. Contact Caledonian MacBrayne, T: (01475) 650100. For sailings from Iona and Fionnphort, contact Gordon Grant Marine Ltd, T: (01681) 562842; or David Kirkpatrick, T: (01681) 700358. Also trips from Ulva Ferry, Isle of Mull; contact Iain Morrison, T: (01688) 400242. **Further information:** TIC, Tobermory, T: (01688) 302182.

Rum

From the Gaelic *I-Dhruim*, 'Isle of the ridge'

SNH NNR, Biosphere Reserve

I first came to this great, whale-backed lump of an island on a MacBrayne steamer one wild and storm-tossed day in March half a lifetime ago, when gannets were hurtling about the sky like flying crucifixes and floating 'rafts' of Manx shearwaters rose and fell in the sea swell like flotsam from a mid-Atlantic wreck.

The impression of Rum from the sea on such a day was daunting: huge cliffs girt the island's wild coast; volcanic mountains, pyramidal and black, rose straight from the sea; and an extraordinary turreted Gothic edifice, an incongruous red in colour, stood four-square on the shore.

When I enquired if I could land I was informed that the island was a strictly private estate where no uninvited visitors were allowed to set foot. Today all that has changed for the better. The island now belongs to Scottish Natural Heritage, and is used for wildlife conservation and ecological research. Visitors are welcome provided they respect these aims.

The island sparkles best in summer. Winters are mild but fiercely windy, relentlessly rainy and, with only eight resident families, screamingly lonely. There are no public roads or public transport on Rum, so all journeys round the island have to be made on foot. Four valleys radiate from the island's low-lying centre and rough tracks follow each of the valleys to former settlements, all, except Kinloch, in ruins. One track leads north over heather-clad moors to the sands of Kilmory, another east down the nature trail to Kinloch, another south-west to the storm beach at Harris Bay and another west to the long green slopes of Guirdil.

There are also pony trails from the Harris track to the massive scree buttress of Bloodstone Hill above the west coast and from Kinloch southwards past the great 666-foot

(203-metre) sea cliff of Welshman's Rock to the canyon of the Dibidil River and Papadil Loch, the southernmost point of the island, where bare treeless slopes are dominated by the great towering cones and peaks of the Cuillin of Rum.

The Rum Cuillin, the weathered teeth of an extinct volcano, provide some of the best ridge-walking in Britain. All the peaks but one have evocative Norse names bestowed in the days when they served as landmarks for passing Viking ships: pyramid-shaped Askival (the highest at 2,663 feet/812 metres), Hallival, Barkeval, Trollaval, Ainshval, Ruinsival. The exception is Sgurr nan Gillean, a Gaelic name. All can be climbed by non-climbers with a modicum of puff and willpower. The reward is a vast panoramic view over the Outer Isles and the Cuillin of Skye — one of the finest in the Hebrides.

Rum's striking landscape of glens, lochs, corries and razor-ridged mountains was shaped by the Ice Age. The native forest that followed the Ice Age was largely felled by early settlers, but the vegetation and wildlife of the cliffs and mountain summits has been little disturbed.

The flora thrives in a rich and fascinating variety due to the island's oceanic position and wide range of soil types and growing conditions. Specialized plant communities exist in a series of distinct ecological systems: alpine, moorland, woodland, grassland, wetland and coastal. Rum is an island full of flowers, and a total of 427 species has been counted there. Across the brilliant summer machair one can wade knee-deep in them. Relict native woodland of stunted birch, rowan, holly, hazel, aspen and oak survives in ravines and crags and protects a woodland flora of wood sorrel, wood anemone, wild hyacinth, ferns and other shade-loving plants.

Bird life is abundant on Rum, where around 200 species have been recorded. A huge and uniquely high-altitude breeding colony of over 60,000 pairs of Manx shearwaters is one of the island's ornithological specialities. The birds make their nesting burrows in the loose soil on the highest terraces of Askival and Hallival, whence the flightless fledglings must shuffle down the mountain sides and hurl themselves off the cliffs to reach the open sea, where they will spend the rest of their lives.

Another speciality is the convocation of eagles: several pairs of golden eagles breed regularly on Rum, and in 1981 a pair of sea eagles, reintroduced from Norway, occupied a nest site for the first time since the species became extinct on the island in the early part of the 20th century. The reintroduction of the sea eagle to Britain has been a resounding success: in 1996 a total number of 55 wild sea eagles fledged in Scotland. Significant colonies of guillemots, razorbills, fulmars and kittiwakes can also be found nesting on the southern cliffs, and common and arctic terns, black-backed and herring gulls, puffins, black guillemots and shags on scattered promontories.

The wild animals most commonly seen on Rum are the red deer, numbering about 1,500 in large free-ranging herds on the open hill ranges. Other wild animals include the feral goat, grey seal, common seal, otter, brown rat, pygmy shrew, pipistrelle bat and Rum mouse. The wealth of butterflies makes the island a lepidopterist's paradise.

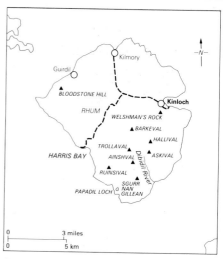

BEFORE YOU GO
Maps: Ordnance Survey Landranger Series, map No. 39.
Guide-book: Scottish Mountaineering Trust Guide, *The Islands of Scotland (including Skye)*.

GETTING THERE
By sea: a year-round scheduled passenger and mail ferry service from Mallaig to Rum and the other Small Isles is provided by Caledonian MacBrayne (Mon-Sat, journey time: 3hrs). Advance bookings from Ferry Terminal, Mallaig, T: (01687) 462403.
By rail: services to Mallaig from Glasgow and Fort William connect with the ferry.

WHERE TO STAY
Accommodation on Rum is limited and consists of a hostel in Kinloch Castle; four bothies and a camp-site in Kinloch. The Castle Bistro is open to all (Apr-Sept) for breakfasts, packed lunches and evening meals. Apply for information and bookings to the Castle Co-ordinator for the hostel, T: (01687) 462037; or the Reserve Office for the bothies or camp-site, T: (01687) 462026.

ACCESS AND CLOSURES
No cars may be taken on to the island. Dogs may be brought on to the island if they are kept on a lead, but cannot stay overnight. Visitors wishing to stay must make prior arrangements with the Castle Co-ordinator or the Reserve Office. As Rum is a national nature reserve, some areas may be restricted from time to time. The red deer area at Kilmory is open to the public only at weekends. During June and October the area is closed completely. There is a part-time post office and general store stocking groceries, fresh produce and alcohol. Orders can be made and delivered to the hostel or bothies before arrival; contact the Post Office, Isle of Rum PH43 4RR, T: (01687) 462026.

ACTIVITIES
Climbing: applications for rock climbing must be made in advance, by climbing club secretaries, to the Reserve Office. There is no rescue service on the island, so parties should not number less than 4 and must be prepared to carry out their own rescue operation in the event of an accident.
Fishing: during the angling season permits are available for Kinloch River and some of the hill lochs. Contact the Reserve Office.

FURTHER INFORMATION
The Reserve Manager, The Reserve Office, The White House, Isle of Rum PH43 4RR, T: (01687) 462026.
Fort William and Lochaber Tourism, Cameron Centre, Cameron Square, Fort William, Inverness-shire PH33 6AJ, T: (01397) 703781, F: 705184.

Muck

From the Gaelic for 'pig'
(meaning sea-pig or
porpoise)

SSSI at Camas Mor

The most southerly of the
Small Isles, Muck is a small,
low, green island, covering only
2½ square miles (6½ sq km);
nearly treeless and very
exposed. Like Eigg, however, it
enjoys some of the most fertile
soils in the Hebrides. A mass of
black volcanic rock dykes
swarm up the west coast. The
whole island is run by Mr and
Mrs Laurence MacEwen and
provides an interesting insight
into communal Hebridean
living, as well as an excellent,
relatively untrodden island
platform from which to admire
the beauties of the sea of the
Hebrides and all its denizens.
Getting there *By sea:* on
Caledonian MacBrayne ferry
from Mallaig, T: (01687)
462403. *By car:* There is a 1-
mile road — Muck 1 — from
Port Mor across to the Atlantic
coast. **Access:** at all times.
Where to stay: guest house, T:
(01687) 462365; holiday
cottages, T: (01687) 462362;
bed and breakfast, T: (01687)
462371; The Bunkhouse
Hostel, T: (01687) 462042; or
camping near sandy beach on
west coast. Bring your own
supplies. **Further information:**
Mr Laurence MacEwen,
Gallnach, Isle of Muck, T:
(01687) 462362.

Canna

NTS Reserve

The most westerly of the Small
Isles, Canna is inhabited by
about 30 people, covers 3,785
acres (1,532 ha) and is largely
given over to farming; it has
been referred to as 'The
Garden of the Hebrides'. There
are good walks along the cliffs,
where you can see breeding sea-
birds such as puffins, razorbills
and Manx shearwaters, and
various birds of prey, including
the sea eagle from nearby Rum.
  Both Canna and its subsidiary
island of Sanday are made up
of ancient lava flows which can
be clearly seen in the 400-ft
(122-m), columnar, basalt cliff
face in the northern part of the
island and in the basalt reefs
and platforms along the coast.
The rich iron deposits in
Compass Hill deflect the
compasses of passing ships.
Getting there *By sea:* on
Caledonian MacBrayne ferry
from Mallaig, T: (01475)
650100. **Access:** at all times.
Not safe between cliffs and
shore. Access to Sanday at low
tide or by footbridge. **Where to
stay:** camping only. No shop.
Further information: leaflets
from NTS, T: (01687) 462466.

Eigg

SWT Reserve, SSSI

Eigg is a naturalist's paradise.
This small, privately owned and
actively crofted island 12 miles
(19 km) from the mainland and
to the south-east of Rum
measures only 5½ by 4 miles (9
by 6 km), yet it contains no less
than seven SSSIs and three
nature reserves run by the
SWT.
  Like many islands of the Inner
Hebrides, Eigg is overlaid by
sheets of lava which poured
from volcanic eruptions on
nearby Rum and other places
in tertiary times. A large part of
the island consists of a plateau
of basalt over a platform of
Jurassic limestone, edged by
high escarpment cliffs. The
exception is the Sgurr, at 1,300
ft (396 m) the highest point and
dominating feature of the
island, a volcanic outcrop of
black pitchstone which cooled
to form hexagonal columns.
The narrow ridge of the Sgurr
extends for 2 miles (3 km) to
the north-west across rough
country containing two lochs
and 11 lochans, and from the
summit on a clear day you can
look out over Rum, the Cuillin
of Skye, the Outer Hebrides,
Muck, Coll, Tiree, Mull and
Ardnamurchan.
  Much of the hinterland is
heather moor, but woodland,
bog, marsh, loch, flower
meadow, sea-shore and cliff
face provide a variety of
alternative habitats for a wealth
of island wildlife; 68 species of
bird breed on Eigg, including
golden eagle, long-eared owl,
short-eared owl, red-throated
diver, raven, buzzard and Manx
shearwater.
Getting there *By sea:* on
Caledonian MacBrayne ferry
from Mallaig, T: (01475)
650100. Arisaig Marine Ltd
also runs Hebridean island
cruises, T: (01687) 450224. *By
car:* there is only one road, a
Land Rover track from the port
of Galmisdale to the small
village of Cleadale. Local
'taxis' available; enquire at pier
tea shop. **Access:** at all times to
the island. Best time: May-July.
Where to stay: bed and
breakfast and guest houses;
wild camping possible by the
Singing Sands. Only one store,
in Cleadale; open irregularly, so
bring your own supplies.
Further information: contact
Neil Willcox, SWT Edinburgh,
T: (0131) 312 7765. Fort
William and Lochaber
Tourism, Cameron Centre,
Cameron Square, Fort William,
Inverness-shire PH33 6AJ, T:
(01397) 703781, F: 705184.

197

Skye
From the Norse *Sku-o*, 'Island of Cloud'

Skye is the largest and most northerly of the islands of the Inner Hebrides. Measuring 60 miles (96 kilometres) in length and covering some 670 square miles (1,735 square kilometres), Skye retains its island character in spite of the rolling expanse of high moorland and the mass of ridge-backed Cuillin mountains that give its hinterland something of a Highland flavour. It is one of the most heavily crofted areas in the Highlands and Islands, with crofted land along much of the coast and much of the high ground inland given over to rough grazing for livestock.

Nowhere on Skye are you ever more than five miles (eight kilometres) from the sea, for a dozen or so sea lochs reach deep into the land, bringing their share of the sea creatures for which these waters are famous: the killer whale and basking shark, porpoise and dolphin, grey seal and sea otter, and sea-birds of great variety, from the Manx shearwater that skim an inch or two above the waves to the great sea eagle on a visit from neighbouring Rum, gliding and soaring in leisurely orbit high above the water on its huge raptor wings.

The mountains of Skye are wild and grand. There are three main groups: the Black and Red Cuillin in the south of the island, and the Trotternish in the north. The Cuillin are essentially ramparts of granite and gabbro, the Trotternish a huge heap of solidified lavas. Cuillin is a Norse word meaning keel-shaped ridge, and the main ridge of the Black Cuillin — the highest and most rugged of the Skye hills — forms a spectacularly pinnacled seven-mile (11-kilometre) horseshoe around Loch Coruisk. Reaching 3,257 feet (993 metres) at its highest point on Sgurr Alasdair, it offers the mountain walker a challenging climb in a landscape of immense diversity.

Fortunately the highest peak with the grandest views, Sgurr Alasdair, can be reached relatively easily by ordinary walkers from Glen Brittle via the Great Stone Shoot of Coire Lagan. But the real magic of these hills lies in their infinite changes of mood in capricious weather, from stormy Wagnerian melodrama to ethereal mist-hung mystery.

By contrast, the Red Cuillin, to the north and east of the Black Cuillin, are composed of granite — hence their name. They are considerably lower than their black neighbours, and their highest summits, Glamaig and Beinn na Caillich, reach only 2,542 and 2,403 feet (775 and 732 metres) respectively. For the most part these are rounded, scree-covered hills, offering next to no opportunities for rock-climbing.

The rocks of the Trotternish hills, on the other hand, assume fantastical shapes that require fantastical climbs. The basalt lava of this part of Skye has slipped and eroded to form a castellated landscape of towers and spires. Round the rim of a corrie unique in Scotland the 160-foot (50-metre) pinnacle of the Old Man of Storr rises weirdly from a rock plinth in the company of a number of lesser pinnacles. At the north of the Trotternish group a natural rock fortress called the Quiraing, guarded by a hundred-foot high natural obelisk called the Needle, looms out of the mist and rain like the ramparts of an ancient lost city.

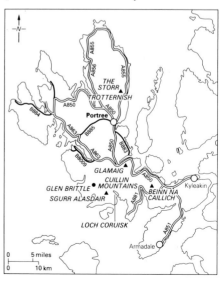

The jagged basalt pinnacles of the Storr on Skye have been a landmark since the first prehistoric settlers ventured to the Hebrides

BEFORE YOU GO
Maps: Ordnance Survey Landranger Series, map Nos. 23, 24, 32, 33.
Guide-books: serious hill walkers should consult *The Islands of Scotland (including Skye)* by the Scottish Mountaineering Trust.

GETTING THERE
By sea: car ferries leave the mainland port of Mallaig for Armadale on Skye (a 25-minute trip). Contact Caledonian MacBrayne, Armadale, T: (01471) 844248.
By car: the A87 toll bridge connects Skye to the mainland between Kyle of Lochalsh and Kyleakin.
By rail: take the West Highland line from Glasgow to Mallaig or the beautiful Kyle line from Inverness to Kyle of Lochalsh.
By bus: daily services from Glasgow.

WHERE TO STAY
Complete listing in the Isle of Skye and South West Ross *Where to Stay*, available from tourist information centres.
Youth hostels: at Armadale, T: (01471) 844260; Broadford, T: (01471) 822442; Glenbrittle (for the Cuillin), T: (01478) 640278; Kyleakin, T: (01599) 534585; and Uig, T: (01470) 542211.

WHERE TO GO
Two regions of Skye have been designated as national scenic areas. These are the Cuillin Hills in the south-west and the Trotternish peninsula in the north-east. The Cuillin Hills are most easily approached from the junction of the A863 and A850, at the Sligachan Hotel 9½ miles (15 km) south of Portree, or from Glen Brittle on a minor road leaving the B8009 1 mile (2 km) south-east of Carbost.

The Old Man of Storr is a short walk from a car-park on the A855 7 miles (11 km) north of Portree; 10 miles (16 km) farther north along the A855 the remarkable pinnacles of the Quirang overlook Staffin Bay. Quick access from a minor road that cuts across the peninsula to Uig.

ACTIVITIES
Walking: walkers looking for something challenging but low could try one of Britain's most

unusual long-distance walks: the circumambulation of the coast of Skye, which, with all its ins and outs, measures between 600 and 1,000 miles (960 and 1,600 km)

FURTHER INFORMATION
General inquiries by post to Isle of Skye and South West Ross Tourist Board, Meall House, Portree IV51 9BZ, T: (01478) 612137, F: 612137. Year-round tourist information centre at Portree, T: (01478) 612137. Other centres (May-Sep) at Broadford, T: (01471) 822361; Kyle of Lochalsh, T: (01599) 534276, and Shielbridge, T: (01599) 511264.

The sturdy Soay sheep is found on several Hebridean islands

THE OUTER HEBRIDES

Stretching from Barra Head in the south to the Butt of Lewis in the north, the Outer Hebrides or Western Isles lie 50 miles (80 kilometres) from the West Highland coast. These outer islands wear two faces. Their windward western sides are fringed with dazzling white beaches of shell sand that stretch, island after island, for a hundred miles and are lapped in fine weather by a crystalline sea of exquisite peacock colours. Behind the beaches lie the sand dunes, and behind the dunes the machair that is the Western Isles' greatest glory. In spring and summer it is carpeted with a marvellous multi-coloured tapestry of wild flowers, whose scent is so strong that it can be smelt on ships far out at sea. Their eastern sides are a total contrast, covered by infertile peat bogs up to 20 feet (32 m) deep and dotted with rocks and innumerable lochans of brown acid peat.

The Hebridean sea is the haunt of marine creatures of all kinds, from the giant killer whale, dolphin and basking shark of the open sea to the grey, Atlantic and common seals of the great nurseries on the Treshnish Islands and the humble acorn barnacles, sand mason worms and hermit crabs of the tidal rock pools.

Barra

Only two of the 20 islands at the southern end of the Outer Hebridean chain are still inhabited: Barra and Vatersay (the latter only tenuously). Barra itself, the main island of the group, noted for its sand beaches and rich machair, is now a focus of tourism, and its machair has suffered considerable degeneration.

South of Barra, however, you will find some of the loveliest, loneliest desert islands in the British Isles, and some of the most wondrous seascapes in the Hebrides. One of the largest, Mingulay, a mere one mile by two, was inhabited until the early years of the 20th century, but is now the realm of the puffins, kittiwakes and guillemots that crowd its soaring 800-foot (240-m) cliffs. The southernmost of them all, Berneray, which sprouts a lighthouse 580 feet (177 m) up on the sheer cliffs of land's end at Barra Head, is the anvil for some of North Atlantic's most punishing hammer blows — seas that can toss fish on to the very top of the high headland, and roll a 42-ton block of solid gneiss several feet.

Before you go *Maps:* Ordnance Survey Landranger Series, map No. 31. **Getting there** *By air:* BA flights from Glasgow to Barra, T: (0345) 222111. *By sea:* Caledonian MacBrayne, T: (01631) 566688, operates car ferries between Oban and Castlebay on Barra. No regular service to Mingulay but excursions can be arranged from Castlebay with Barra boatmen, including Mr Maclean, T: (01871) 810339. **Further information:** TIC, Castlebay, T: (01871) 810336.

North and South Uist

SNH NNR, NSA

The Uists have much to offer the wild traveller and itinerant naturalist. These islands are as yet relatively unspoilt by modern tourism, and possess two nature reserves of importance. The long, white, shell-sand beaches of the Atlantic coast, and the sweetly perfumed summer machair behind them, are one of the glories of the Western Isles, and the machair supports the densest population of breeding waders in Britain.

The beautiful machair coast of South Uist stretching down the western side of the island from Stilligarry to the southern tip is as fine as anything in the Outer Hebrides and has won accolades as a national scenic area. The eastern side, by contrast, is peaty and mountainous, and the highest peak, Beinn Mhor, rears its summit more than 2,000 ft (610 m) above the sparkling (or, as often as not, darkening) sea. Beneath the southern slopes of Beinn Mhor, which is a good place to watch out for golden eagles, lies the national nature reserve of Loch Druidibeg, famous for its breeding greylag geese.

North Uist is a large, low, virtually treeless island of lochs and marshes, machair and sea-shore. The east coast of North Uist (and of Benbecula beyond) is a littoral (and literal) chaos, a maze of channels, skerries and islands, almost inaccessible except by boat, and almost uninhabited except for the small ferry port of Lochmaddy — the whole wild bomb-burst scene a classic example of land drowned by the sea when the ice cap thawed at the end of the last Ice Age. Only in its north-west corner does the North Uist coast rise significantly above the level of the sea. Between Griminish Point and Balranald there are cliffs and geos and great rock arches, as well as more of those dazzling white shell-sand beaches and peacock-coloured, clear-water bays that are so characteristic of the western shores of the Hebridean islands. North Uist is an important place for wintering and migrating birds, and at Balranald there is a nature reserve, one of the two reserves in the main Outer Hebrides island chain.

Before you go *Maps:* Ordnance Survey Landranger Series, map Nos. 18, 22, 31.

Getting there *By air:* BA has daily (except Sun) service from Glasgow to Benbecula, T: (0345) 222111. *By sea:* car ferries operate between Oban and Lochboisdale in South Uist. Another car ferry runs a triangular route between Lochmaddy in North Uist, Tarbert in Harris and Uig in Skye. Contact Caledonian MacBrayne Ltd, Ferry Terminal, Lochmaddy, T: (01876) 500337. *By car:* the A865 connects North Uist, Benbecular and South Uist across 2 causeways, which have made travel between the islands much more practical.

Where to stay: *Where to Stay* brochure available from tourist board (see below). *Youth hostel:* Lochmaddy, North Uist, T: (01876) 500368.

Further information: tourist information centres at Lochmaddy, North Uist, T: (01876) 500321, and Lochboisdale, South Uist, T: (01878) 700286. Western Isles Tourist Board, 26 Cromwell Street, Stornoway, Isle of Lewis PA87 2DD, T: (01851) 703088.

Monach Isles

SNH NNR

A group of small, low-lying islets of sand-swamped reef, eight miles (13 km) south-west of Hougarry Point, North Uist, the Monachs are remarkable for their wealth of machair wild flowers and an important grey-seal nursery. Barnacle and white-fronted geese winter on the islands, and a variety of wading birds can be seen on the sandy shores.

Inhabited till 1942, the Monachs now provide a night stop for passing lobster fishermen and summer grazing for sheep. A thriving population of feral cats keeps down the less thriving population of breeding terns.

Getting there *By sea:* by small boat; enquire at Grimsay Post Office, North Uist. **Access:** restricted. Contact SNH, South Uist, T: (01870) 620238.

Lewis and Harris

NSA

Lewis is the largest and most northerly of the Outer Hebrides. The southern half is known as Harris, separated from the main bulk of the island by a line of bare hills and a wilderness of moors, lochans and deer forest. North Harris is joined to South Harris — almost an island in its own right — by a narrow isthmus, no more than half a mile (1 km) wide.

Though Lewis and Harris, sometimes collectively called the Long Island, share the same continuous coastline, they present very different faces to the world. Lewis is for the most part bare, treeless and flat, a wasteland of featureless blanket bog where the peat is up to 13 ft (4 m) thick in places. The wild traveller can squelch for miles over the island's peaty horizons without encountering another soul.

The coast is an almost perfect reverse image of the moorland interior: a splatter of innumerable sea rocks and islets strewn across a waste of water, a haunt of birds and sea creatures, at its finest at Loch Roag and the Great Bernera peninsula and between Valtos and Mangersta. To traverse this coast on foot, from, say, the north-west roadhead at Brenish in Lewis to the south-west roadhead at Hushinish in North Harris, is no mean feat of Hebridean exploration, for there is no formal route, indeed no track at all, and you pick your own way across the wilds, pushed far inland by the long sea lochs of Tamanavay and Resort.

Harris is more spectacular than Lewis. The hills of North Harris are the highest in the Outer Hebrides, reaching 2,622 ft (800 m) on the peak of Clisham. Though hardly comparing in grandeur with the loftier crags of Skye, the high ground of Harris is well endowed with space and solitude, and yields rewarding views towards Cape Wrath in the north-east and the Cuillin in the south-east and the dramatically massed outlines of St Kilda, 50 miles (80 km) away on the distant western horizon.

The interior of Harris is badland: dead, empty, infertile. But its coast is a gem. The south-east side overlooking the Little Minch is rocky and deeply indented, a steep gneiss desert with 20 bays in a 12-mile stretch between Tarbert (the chief port and town of Harris) 202

and Renish Point, and densely populated little clachans at the heads of the inlets.

The north-west coast of South Harris is a gentler, more exquisite place: a succession of sandy bays and white, deserted beaches backed by grassy dunes and a flower-scented machair, dominated by the high hill of Chaipaval on Toe Head. From the 1,200-ft (366-m) summit of Chaipaval one can look out over the shallow, green and turquoise, island-scattered channel of the Sound of Harris, which separates Lewis and Harris from the rest of the Outer Hebrides, the Uists and Benbecula. At Callanish, near the west coast of Lewis, stands the finest prehistoric monument in the Hebrides, a stone circle of great gneiss monoliths with a Neolithic burial cave in the centre.

Before you go *Maps:* Ordnance Survey Landranger Series, map Nos. 8, 13, 14, 18. **Getting there** *By air:* daily BA flights (except Sun) link Stornoway, Isle of Lewis, with Benbecula, Inverness and Glasgow. For details, T: (0345) 222111. *By sea:* Caledonian MacBrayne operates a daily car ferry service (except Sun) between Ullapool and Stornoway, Isle of Lewis. There is also a vehicle ferry from Uig on Skye to Tarbert, Isle of Harris. Contact Caledonian MacBrayne, T: (01475) 650100. Local offices: Stornoway, T: (01851) 702361, and Tarbert, T: (01859) 502444. **Where to stay:** most serviced accommodation to be found in Tarbert, Isle of Harris, or Stornoway, Isle of Lewis. Both towns have tourist information centres that will assist. Alternatively, write for the *Where to Stay* brochure from the tourist board (see below). *Youth hostel:* in Stockinish, Isle of Harris, T: (01859) 530373; 7 miles (11 km) from Tarbert. **Further information:** TICs at

Stornoway, Isle of Lewis, T: (01851) 703088, and Tarbert, Isle of Harris, T: (01859) 502011. Western Isles Tourist Board, 26 Cromwell Street, Stornoway, Isle of Lewis PA87 2DD, T: (01851) 703088.

The Shiant Isles

The Shiants, a group of small islands five miles (8 km) off the south-east coast of Lewis, are the northern outposts of Scotland's youngest rocks. The hexagonal columns of solidified basalt on the northern face of the Garbh Eilean are the most impressive examples of this curious rock formation in Scotland. Flowery and lush, with a large puffin colony and substantial seal nursery — and a lot of brown rats.

Getting there *By sea:* boat trips in the summer from Tarbert and Scalpay, Isle of Harris. Contact Malcolm MacLeod, T: (01851) 870537, or Western Edge, Aberdeen, T: (01224) 210564. **Further information:** Western Isles Tourist Board, Stornoway, T: (01851) 703088.

Flannan Islands

SSSI

These seven small islands, also known as the Seven Hunters, and numerous skerries lie 17 miles (27 km) west-north-west of Gallan Head on the west side of Lewis. All the islands are cliff-bound and rise sheer from the sea. The largest, Eilean Mor, is 39 acres (14 ha) in area and 228 ft (70 m) at its highest point. The islands are a favourite spot for grey seals and for a large variety of sea-birds, most importantly Leach's petrel, which breeds in holes on the grassy top of Eilean Mor.

The lighthouse on Eilean Mor is one of the most remote in the world. In 1900 all three lighthouse-keepers mysteriously vanished in circumstances resembling the disappearance of the crew of the *Marie Celeste*. They were in all probability swept away by a freak wave.

Getting there *By sea:* no regular boat service, and landing is difficult except at the lighthouse jetty. Prospective visitors should make their own arrangements for boat hire on Lewis. Cruises advertised in SWT and RSPB magazines. **Access:** can be restricted during sea-birds' breeding season (May-July). **Where to stay:** no accommodation on the islands. **Further information:** SNH, Stornoway, T: (01851) 705258.

Callanish on Lewis is set amid a classic Hebridean landscape of water and weathered stone

North Rona
From the Old Norse *Roy-y*, 'seal island'

SNH NNR

A green island, one mile square, 44 miles (70 km) north-east of the Butt of Lewis and the same distance north-west of Cape Wrath. With Sula Sgeir it forms the northern termination of the Outer Hebrides and is one of the most remote British islands ever to have been regularly inhabited. Continuous habitation finally ended in 1844 but the ruins of the old settlement can still be seen. Today the men of Ness bring their sheep to graze on the island every summer.

North Rona is one of the most important breeding colonies in the world for the grey Atlantic seal: about one-seventh of the world's population congregates on the island, and some 2,000 pups are born here each year.

The seal nursery is located on the only low, level ground along the coast, for the rest of it is cliff-bound, pierced by huge caverns and fringed by many stacks and rock arches and hidden skerries and reefs. The air is full of the booming of the great Atlantic rollers and the screaming of the innumerable gulls. North Rona boasts major colonies of Leach's and storm petrel, uncommon birds which only ever come ashore to breed. **Getting there** *By sea:* by private charter with boatmen at Ness, Lewis. Mr McDonald, 1 Eirstadh, Uig, Isle of Lewis charters the *M. V. Cuma* to North Rona. See SWT and RSPB magazines for cruises around the island. **Access:** restricted during Oct (seal breeding) and from May-July for breeding sea-birds. **Further information:** SNH, Stornoway, T: (01851) 705258. Western Isles Tourist Board, 26 Cromwell Street, Stornoway, Isle of Lewis PA87 2DD, T: (01851) 703088, F: 705244.

ORKNEY

Only six miles (ten kilometres) from the Scottish mainland lie the Orkneys, some 67 islands, of which 21 are inhabited. Their intricate outline of firths and peninsulas is the consequence of the rise in the sea-level following the melting of the Ice Age ice cap: if the present sea-level fell by 120 feet (37 metres) Orkney would become a single island again. The land is for the most part low-lying, with the notable exception of the island of Hoy, where a great wall of red sandstone cliffs rises sheer to 1,140 feet (348 m), and in front of it a spectacular geological freak, a perpendicular pillar of rock 450 feet (137 m) high, which is known as the Old Man of Hoy.

Like Shetland, the Orkneys are strung out along the main bird route between Scotland and Scandinavia, and birds swarm over the islands in numbers worthy of Genesis. Two special groups of birds are attracted to these islands: the Atlantic birds, the ocean wanderers that breed on the islands' cliffs in prodigious colonies; and the Scandinavian land birds, the passage migrants that use the islands as vital stepping stones on their great aerial voyages between north and south.

Mainland

RSPB Reserve

Mainland is the principal and most developed island of Orkney. Much of the interior moorland has been reclaimed for farming, especially cattle pasture, but sizeable areas still remain, along with their associated marshes, lochs and streams; and much of the coast, which includes the great naval anchorage and seaduck haven of Scapa Flow, is in as pristine a condition as ever.

The RSPB have established several reserves on Mainland. Birsay Moors and Cottasgarth, in the north of the island, consist of rough, rolling heather moorland, with blanket bogs, marshes, lochans and streams. They are the home of two Orkney specialities that both need wide open spaces in which to hunt: the hen harrier

and short-eared owl. Merlin occasionally nest in the heather. At the Loons, in north-west Mainland, the reserve occupies a marsh bordered by the Loch of Isbister. Marwick Head reserve runs along a mile of sheer cliffs on the north-west Mainland coast. The sea-bird colonies are the most spectacular on Mainland and the easiest to see anywhere in Orkney. The most numerous birds are guillemots (35,000) and kittiwake (10,000 pairs) and razorbill, fulmar, a few puffin, rock dove, raven and peregrine also nest here, while great and arctic skua maraud up and down offshore. Look out for thrift, sea campion and spring squill, and grey and common seals, too. Lord Kitchener was drowned off Marwick Head in 1916 when his cruiser struck a German mine. A memorial stone stands on the cliff-top, overlooking the wheeling, shrieking birds.

The Hobbister reserve, by

Waulkmill Bay overlooking Scapa Flow, incorporates heather moorland, bogs and fen, low sea cliffs and salt marsh. The diversity of habitat has produced a corresponding diversity of breeding bird species, including hen harrier, short-eared owl, merlin, red grouse, curlew, snipe, red-throated diver, discreet little twite and many more.

Before you go *Maps:* Ordnance Survey Landranger Series, map Nos. 5, 6, 7. *Guide-books:* For a list of maps, guides and general literature about Orkney, write to the tourist board (see below). **Getting there** *By air:* Mainland is the first port of call for most visitors to the Orkneys. British Airways operate a direct service to Kirkwall Airport on Mainland from Aberdeen, Glasgow and Inverness, with connecting services from London, Birmingham and Manchester, every day (except Fri), T: (0345) 222111. *By sea:* P&O car ferries sail daily (except Sun) from Scrabster, near Thurso, to the Mainland port of Stromness; journey time: 1 hour, 45 minutes. Contact P&O, Stromness, T: (01856) 850655. A pedestrian ferry operates daily between John O'Groats and Burwick, May-Sep; journey time: 40 minutes, T: (01955) 611353. **Where to stay:** the Orkney Tourist Board publishes a full list. Youth hostels are at Stromness, T: (01856) 850589 and Kirkwall, T: (01856) 872243. **Further information:** Tourist Information Centre, Kirkwall, T: (01856) 872856, and Ferry Terminal, Stromness, T: (01856) 850655. Orkney Tourist Board, 6 Broad Street, Kirkwall, Orkney KW15 1NX. For information about RSPB reserves, contact RSPB Managing Warden, Orkney: Keith Fairclough, T: (01856) 872210.

Hoy

From the Old Norse
meaning 'high island'

RSPB Reserve

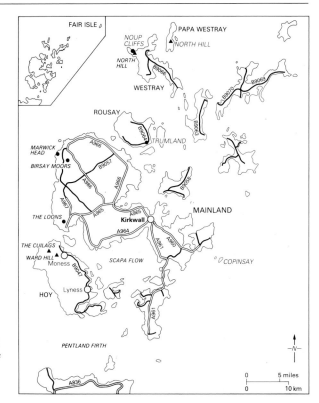

Hoy is the largest island in
Orkney after Mainland; it is
also the highest, rising to 1,570
ft (479 m) at Ward Hill and
1,420 ft (433 m) in the Cuilags.
While most of the Orkney
islands are green and
cultivated, Hoy is wild, rugged
moorland with an even wilder,
more rugged coast. The cliffs
soar sheer from the sea to great
heights: 1,140 ft (348 m) at St
John's Head for example, and
450 ft (137 m) at the immense
detached pillar of rock called
the Old Man of Hoy.

Between Hoy and the
mainland of northern Scotland
swirl the fearsome waters of the
Pentland Firth, the worst tidal
race in the British Isles, where
Atlantic and North Sea meet,
sometimes with turbulence
severe enough to send a boat to
the bottom.

A very extensive RSPB reserve
occupies the north-west part of
Hoy around Ward Hill. Large
populations of great and arctic
skuas breed on this moorland
plateau; kittiwake, shag, raven
and peregrine nest on the cliffs,
with a small colony of Manx
shearwater not far away.
Between Ward Hill and the
Cuilags you may be lucky
enough to sight a golden eagle;
you should certainly see
mountain hare.

Getting there *By sea:* daily
passenger ferry from Stromness
(Mainland) to Moness (Hoy),
T: (01856) 850655, or by car
ferry from Houton to Lyness,
T: (01856) 811397. Taxis or hire
cars available; enquire at pier.
Access: at all times. **Where to
stay:** Hoy Inn at Moness.

Hostels at Rackwick and
outside Moness; contact
number for both, T: (01856)
873535. **Further information:**
RSPB Warden (T. Prescott),
Ley House, North Hoy,
Orkney, T: (01856) 791298.

Copinsay

*RSPB, James Fisher
Memorial Sea-Bird Reserve*

Small, grassy island off the
west coast of Mainland, with
nearly a mile of vertical cliffs
where large colonies of
kittiwake, guillemots, razorbill,
fulmar and other sea-birds
breed. On the north coast,
where the old red sandstone

cliffs have been eroded into a
jigsaw of geos, stacks and
headlands, the plant life is
luxuriant.

Several little holms nearby,
accessible at low tide, are also
part of the reserve: a small
colony of arctic tern and an
abundant spread of oyster
plant have established
themselves on Corn Holm.
Cormorants have taken over
the Horse of Copinsay as a
nesting site, and puffins can be
seen on Black Holm as well as
Corn Holm.

Getting there *By sea:* on day
trip from Skaill in Deerness,
weather permitting. Prior
arrangement necessary; contact
S. Foubister, T: (01856) 874252.
Access: unrestricted at all times.
Where to stay: rudimentary
self-catering accommodation in
converted farmhouse, which

also serves as RSPB information centre. **Further information:** RSPB Senior Site Manager at Copinsay, T: (01856) 721121.

Noup Cliffs (Westray)

RSPB Reserve

Perched high on the sandstone cliffs running south from Noup Head at the north-west extremity of the island of Westray, the reserve is just a section of the five-mile (eight-km) stretch of cliffs between Noup Head and Inga Ness which houses a huge number of sea-birds in spectacularly overcrowded slum conditions.

In one of the largest sea-bird colonies in the British Isles, 60,000 pairs of kittiwakes, 60,000 guillemots and many other sea-birds pack the rock ledges in a state of frenzied perpetual motion. The noise, smell, personal habits and sea-bird expertise of these birds will never fail to astonish and amuse. Peregrine and raven hunt about the cliffs at Noup Head, arctic skua and arctic tern breed on the heathland behind, and grey seal, porpoises and dolphins can sometimes be seen.

Getting there *By air:* on Loganair flight from Kirkwall, T: (01856) 872494. *By sea:* daily passenger ferry to Westray from Kirkwall, T: (01856) 872044. *By car:* to get to the cliffs at Noup Head take the minor road from Pierowall to Noup Farm and then walk along the track to the lighthouse (map ref. HY 392500). **Access:** unrestricted to both cliffs and moorland. Best time: May-July. Please take extreme care on cliffs and close all gates behind you. No dogs or other pets. **Where to stay:** bed-and-breakfast, self-catering and farmhouse accommodation is available on Westray. **Further information:** RSPB Orkney Officer, T: (01856) 721210; and Westray and Papa Tourist Association; contact Mr P. Needham, T: (01875) 677404.

North Hill (Papa Westray)

RSPB Reserve

Papa Westray (known in Orkney as 'Papay') is one of the smaller, more intensively crofted islands. The reserve, situated at its uncultivated northern end, consists mainly of maritime heath, a relatively unusual habitat in Britain, of which this is the finest example in northern Scotland. One of the three largest arctic tern colonies in Britain is located here. The terns are constantly rising from their nests in noisy commotion, sometimes because of marauding skuas, who harry the terns as they return with fish and gobble up any undefended chicks. Great black-backed, lesser black-backed, herring and common gulls also nest here, as do eider, ringed plover, dunlin and oystercatcher. A substantial colony of cliff-nesting birds occupy the modest sea cliffs at Fowl Craig on the east side of the reserve: one of the last breeding sites in Britain of the now-extinct great auk.

Getting there *By sea:* passenger ferry to Papa Westray, T: (01856) 872044. *By car:* enter the reserve from the northern end of the island's principal road. Contact the RSPB summer warden at Rose Cottage on arrival. **Access:** at all times, but visits should be arranged in advance with the warden, who will escort you round the nesting colonies. Best time: mid-May-July. **Where to stay:** self-catering and guest-house accommodation available on the island; contact the Co-op Shop, Papa Westray, Orkney, T: (01857) 644267, for details. **Further information:** Contact RSPB warden, c/o Rose Cottage, Papa Westray, Orkney KW17 2BU, T: (01857) 644240, or RSPB Orkney Officer, (01856) 721210.

Trumland (Rousay)

RSPB Reserve

Most of the island of Rousay is moorland, and the Trumland reserve at its southern end is no exception. The heather moor above Trumland House rises to 800 ft (240 m), and its otherwise monotonous expanse is enlivened by several small valleys, a lochan and a few crags. The range of birds is considerable: red-throated diver, hen harrier, short-eared owl, merlin, raven, both kinds of skua and four kinds of gull. Sea-birds nest on the cliffs at the north of the island, and are easy to see; not so those other noted denizens of Rousay: the otter and the Orkney vole, who do their best to evade humankind, naturalists included.

Getting there *By sea:* from Tingwall (off A966, Mainland); contact Tingwall Terminal in Evie (Mainland), T: (01856) 751360. *By car:* by B9064 to Trumland at south end of island. **Where to stay:** some

Herma Ness in Shetland, the most northerly land in Britain, provides perfect sites for colonies of gannets and puffins

hotel and bed-and-breakfast accommodation available on island. **Access:** at all times. Best time: May-July.
Further information: RSPB Summer Warden, Lower Cottage, Trumland, Rousay, T: (01856) 721210.

Fair Isle
From the Old Norse *Fridarey*, the 'peaceful isle'

NTS Reserve, NSA, European Diploma

Situated half way between the Orkneys and the Shetland Islands, where the waters of the North Sea and the Atlantic

Ocean meet, Fair Isle is 25 miles (40 km) from the nearest land, which makes it the most remote continuously inhabited island in Britain. It also lies at a crossroads for many migrant bird species in the northern hemisphere and has been the site of a world-renowned bird observatory since 1948.

Every spring and autumn hundreds of thousands of migrating birds use the island as a staging post, including exotics such as the American kestrel, Siberian ruby throat, Greenland redpoll and red-flanked bluetail from as far away as Siberia, Central Asia, North America and Brazil, as well as huge 'falls' of commoner species: 65,000 redwing in one day alone.

In addition, 18 species of sea-bird (including storm petrels) breed in their thousands on the shelves and ledges of the majestic 600-foot (180-m) sandstone cliffs. The Fair Isle

wren, which is larger and darker than the mainland version, is the only British species listed in the *Red Data Book of Endangered Species*.

Fair Isle also sports a wide and luxuriant range of flowering plants (over 238 recorded species) in habitats as diverse as heather moorland, hill bog, sea cliff, burn side, meadow land and cultivated ground, and you can find orchids growing wild here, and Britain's smallest-flowered plant, the allseed, as well as arctic-alpine species such as dwarf willow and alpine bistort.

By contrast, you have only to lift your eyes up towards the sea to stand a fair chance of spotting a grey seal or basking shark, killer whale, pilot whale or white-beaked dolphin. Land animals, on the other hand, are few, though Fair Isle does produce the largest house mice in the world.

People have lived on Fair Isle since earliest times. Stone Age houses, Bronze Age sites and an Iron Age fort can still be seen here. The Vikings left their place names and dialect; the Norse colonists used it as a stepping stone on the long, hard voyage between Iceland and Scandinavia; and 300 Spanish Armada survivors of the shipwrecked *El Gran Grifon* found sanctuary here amid a populace one-fifth their number.

Today Fair Isle's 70 residents live in the more verdant southern half of the island. It is a thriving, buoyant community — a rare thing these days on an island as remote as this — which is world-famous for its patterned knitwear and has pursued the most successful and ambitious crofting programme in Scotland.

Getting there *By air:* Loganair runs daily inter-island flights calling at Fair Isle, T: (01595) 840246. For flights from the mainland, call BA Express, T: (0345) 222111. *By sea:* The *Good Shepherd IV* boat runs between Fair Isle and Shetland (Grutness). The voyage takes about 2½ hours and operates on Tues, Thurs and Sat. Advance bookings, T: (01595) 760222. **Access:** Unrestricted access all year. Best times: May and Sept-Oct for bird migrations; May-July for breeding birds. **Where to stay:** Full board at Fair Isle Lodge and Bird Observatory from mid-Mar to late-Oct. Apply Bookings Dept, Fair Isle Lodge and Bird Observatory, Fair Isle, Shetland ZE2 9JU, T: (01595) 760258. **Further information:** Fair Isle Bird Observatory Trust, 21 Regent Terrace, Edinburgh EH7 5BT. Orkney Tourist Board, 6 Broad Street, Kirkwall, Orkney KW15 1NX, T: (01856) 872856, F: 875056, for leaflets and further details about the islands.

208

SHETLAND

Only six degrees south of the Arctic Circle, the Shetland Islands are further north than St Petersburg or Stockholm. In these latitudes, you can read a book at midnight in summer, when the sun shines for nearly 19 hours out of 24; but in winter there are barely 5½ hours of light a day, and conditions can be stark.

The highly fragmented Shetland archipelago is made up of 117 islands, of which only 13 are inhabited. The islands of Mainland, Yell and Unst form the core of the Shetlands; the coastline is a labyrinthine complex of peninsulas and voes (or long sea-channels) with tremendous cliffs more than a thousand feet high in places. The sea-birds are reason enough to visit Britain's northernmost islands: so are the marvellous cliff landscapes and thundering waves, the sense of standing at one of wild Europe's most dramatic ocean frontiers.

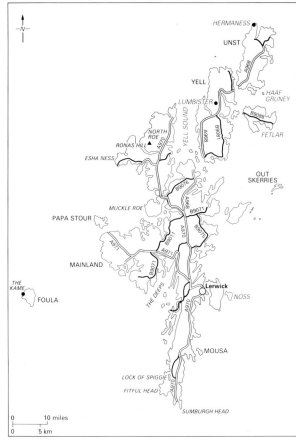

Mainland

NSA, RSPB Reserve

Mainland is the largest of the Shetland Isles; its port of Lerwick is the first landfall for most visitors. The stretch of coastline between Fitful Head and the Deeps, and the peninsulas of Muckle Roe, Esha Ness and North Roe have been designated National Scenic Areas.

The island has been inhabited since prehistoric times. On the sea-shore at Jarlshof near Sumburgh Head, the island's southernmost tip, excavations have revealed Bronze Age, Iron Age and Viking settlements. The Shetlanders of today are a hardy folk of Norse origin who have traditionally earned their livelihood from fishing and crofting, now substantially augmented by North Sea oil.

Ronas Hill in north Mainland is the most extensive wilderness area in Shetland, and at 1,475 ft (450 m), the highest. The 'Hill' is made of a large, dome-shaped mass of granite, smoothed by ice and exposed to gales reaching 170 mph (270 kph). The effect of the winds is a dwarf-shrub heath of wild azalea, bearberry, blackberry and dwarf willow. In places large unbroken carpets, a few inches deep, of woolly hair moss cover huge tracts. The country is very rough, with great sea cliffs extending 15 miles (24 km) around Esha Ness to the west, and arctic-alpine habitats on the higher ground. Snowy owls, snow buntings and dotterel can be seen here. The area has been little explored, so now is your chance.

The RSPB has a reserve at Loch of Spiggie in southern Mainland. These 284 acres (115 ha) of freshwater loch and marshland near the sea are the most important freshwater site in Shetland for wintering wildfowl. Some 300 whooper swans regularly spend their winters here and a variety of sea-birds (skuas and arctic terns), wildfowl and waders variously breed, moult, display or merely bathe; including 50 long-tailed duck who come each spring to moult prior to migration.

Before you go *Maps:* Ordnance Survey Landranger Series, map Nos. 1, 2, 3, 4. The Shetland Tourist Organization, Lerwick, Shetland ZE1 0LU stocks a wide range of books, maps and guides available by post.

Getting there *By air:* BA operates frequent direct flights to Shetland's Sumburgh airport from Aberdeen, Glasgow and Edinburgh; for details, T: (0345) 222111. Convenient connections from most UK airports as well as from Bergen, Oslo, Copenhagen, Paris, Amsterdam and Dublin. *By sea:* P&O car ferries operate five times a week between Aberdeen and Lerwick throughout the year; journey time 14 hrs. A Shetland services brochure is available from P&O Scottish Ferries, PO Box 5, Jamieson's Quay, Aberdeen AB9 8DL, T: (01224) 572615.

Where to stay: the Shetland Tourist Organization's *Accommodation and Services* brochure lists all types of accommodation. Youth hostel at Islesburgh House, Lerwick ZE1 0EQ, T: (01595) 692114.

Further information: tourist information centre, Lerwick, T: (01595) 693434. For information on Loch of Spiggie reserve, contact RSPB Shetland Officer, Peter Ellis, 'Seaview', Sandwick, Shetland ZE2 9HP, T: (01950) 460800, or Summer Warden (by the boat shed at the northern end of the loch).

Foula

From the Norse *Fugl ey*, meaning 'bird island'

One of the most spectacular islands in Shetland, 3,540 acres (1,430 ha) in extent, Foula is situated 14 miles (23 km) west of Mainland. Its precipitous cliffs rise sheer out of the ocean to a height of 1,220 ft (372 m) at Kame. A sea-bird island of international importance, it has one of the biggest breeding populations in the North Atlantic.

Altogether 16 species of sea-bird nest on the island's prodigious rock faces — some 125,000 pairs in all, including nearly one-third of all the great skuas breeding in the northern hemisphere, as well as Manx shearwater and Leach's and storm petrel. The interior of the island is high, peat-covered ground sloping down to the scattering of crofts on the east coast.

Getting there *By air:* flight details from J. Leasle & Son, Lerwick, T: (01595) 696644, or Loganair, T: (01595) 840246. *By sea:* ferry from Walls in west Mainland or Scalloway, every Tues, Thurs and Sat, weather permitting, T: (01595) 753232. **Access:** at all times. Best time: May-July for breeding birds. **Where to stay:** Foula has little accommodation. For bed and breakfast contact Mrs M. Taylor, T: (01595) 753226.

Mousa

A low, grassy, uninhabited 450-acre (182-ha) island half a mile off the east coast of Mainland, with the best preserved Pictish broch (or fort) in Britain. It has withstood a thousand years of

209

winter storms and storm petrels nesting within its walls. Other breeding sea-birds include great and arctic skua, arctic terns and black guillemots. Common and grey seals frequent the shore, the former breeding here in good numbers.

Getting there *By sea:* from Sand Lodge, Sandwick (on Mainland). Contact TIC, Lerwick (see below). **Access:** unrestricted, except by weather. Best time: May to July. **Where to stay:** to see the storm petrels you have to stay overnight; contact TIC, Lerwick. **Further information:** TIC, Lerwick, T: (01595) 693434.

Noss

From the old Norse Nøs, 'a point of rock'

SNH NNR

Noss is basically a wedge of old red sandstone separated from the inhabited island of Bressay by a narrow channel. It is small, green and uninhabited, covers 774 acres (313 ha) and rises to nearly 600 ft (180 m) at the Noup sea cliffs. When a south wind sends rollers crashing on to the island's rocky shore, making landing impossible, Noss is cut off from the world.

Noss was permanently inhabited for over 1,000 years until the last islanders left in 1939. It is still grazed by sheep, but its main claim to fame is its bird population. The towering sandstone cliffs to the east and south of the island house a vertical bird city containing more than 100,000 breeding birds of 12 different species, including nearly 7,000 pairs of gannet, 65,000 guillemots, 10,000 fulmar and 20,000

210

kittiwakes. Arctic and great skuas, known here by their Shetland name of 'bonxie', breed on the moorland interior.

Noss is overrun by rabbits which not even the feral cats can keep down. Otters are relatively common and come ashore to sleep and breed, and seals, mostly grey Atlantic ones, can often be seen in the water or hauled out on to the rocks to bask. Porpoises are often sighted in Noss Sound.

Getting there *By sea:* car ferry from Lerwick to Bressay, then by SNH inflatable dinghy across Noss Sound (10am-5pm) every day except Mon and Thurs, May-Aug. Check with TIC, Lerwick, T: (01595) 693434, before setting out in case Noss ferry has been cancelled. A red flag is flown on Noss if island is closed. **Access:** unrestricted 10am-5pm, May-Aug. Please keep to cliff path so as not to disturb inland skua grounds. No pets allowed. Warden present on island all year round. **Where to stay:** SYHA have a hostel in Lerwick, T: (01595) 692114. **Further information:** SNH, Lerwick, T: (01595) 693345.

Papa Stour

A small island off the west coast of Mainland, with spectacular sea-bird cliffs and enormous sea caves. The largest arctic tern colony in Shetland is to be found here, as well as arctic skuas and a variety of wildfowl and waders on the small inland lochs. The wild flowers are so abundant that sailors were said to have taken bearings by their scent.

Getting there *By air:* Loganair runs daily inter-island flights stopping on Papa Stour, T: (01595) 840246. *By sea:* passenger ferry from West

Burrafirth, weather permitting, T: (01595) 810460. **Access:** unrestricted. **Further information:** TIC, Lerwick, T: (01595) 693434.

Yell Sound

RSPB Reserves

A group of six small uninhabited bird islands in the sound between Yell and Mainland: Gruney, Ramma Stacks, Unyarey, Fish Holm, Muckle Holm and Samphrey. Some 15 species of sea-bird are found on these islands, as well as both species of British seal (which breed on Gruney and Muckle Holm) and otter (which breed on Samphrey). **Getting there** *By sea:* small boat by special arrangement. Call TIC, Lerwick, T: (01595) 693434. **Access:** permit only. Best time: May-July. **Further information:** RSPB Shetland Officer, T: (01950) 460800.

Lumbister (Yell)

RSPB Reserve

The reserve at Lumbister occupies 4,000 acres (1,619 ha) of peat moors, lochans and sea cliffs in the south-west corner of Yell, the second largest island in Shetland.

The low hills of Yell are covered in blanket bog and are not wildly beautiful to look at, though they make fine walking. But there are plenty of birds to be seen: red-throated diver, red-breasted merganser and eider breed on the lochs, arctic and great skuas and golden plover, curlew, durlin and twite breed on the moorland as well as raven, rock dove, puffin and

black guillemot.

Lumbister is one of the few places in Britain where otters can legitimately be described as common; common and grey seals are common too.

Getting there *By sea:* car ferry from Mainland to Yell, T: (01957) 722259. Reserve is best entered from the lay-by 4 miles (6 km) north of Mid Yell on the A968. **Access:** unrestricted, but take care not to disturb the breeding birds. Best time: May to mid-July. **Further information:** from RSPB Shetland, T: (01950) 460800.

Fetlar

RSPB Reserve

The smallest of the three inhabited northern islands of Shetland with an RSPB reserve

and statutory bird sanctuary of 1,727 acres (699 ha) in the northern part — an area of grassy moorland interspersed with lochans and marshes. A breeding bird population of international importance and the only place in Britain where snowy owls are known to have bred (between 1967 and 1975). Female snowy owls can still be seen on the island, as can Fetlar specialities such as whimbek and red-necked phalarope.

Getting there *By sea:* car ferry from Yell, T: (01957) 722259. **Access:** unrestricted, but the reserve and sanctuary may be entered only in summer (mid-May to late-July) by arrangement with the warden. **Where to stay:** self-catering, T: (01595) 695718/760250; bed and breakfast or camping, T: (01957) 733227. **Further information:** RSPB Shetland Officer, T: (01950) 460800.

The vertiginous bird cliffs of St Kilda, the most far-flung island of Britain, soar out of the Atlantic

Haaf Gruney

SNH NNR

Small, low, uninhabited inshore island off south-east coast of Unst. Storm petrel and black guillemot breed on the boulder beach, and common and grey seals haul out on the rocks.

Getting there *By sea:* small boat in calm weather only. Contact Lerwick Tourist Information Centre, T: (01595) 693434. **Access:** unrestricted except by weather. Best time: May-July. **Further information:** leaflet from SNH, Lerwick Office, T: (01595) 693345, or from Lerwick Tourist Information Centre, T: (01595) 693434.

Out Skerries

SNH NNR

A group of very small and very rocky islands at the easternmost point of Shetland, beyond which there is no land until Norway. Because of their remote position, the Out Skerries attract a remarkable number of rare birds looking for dry land on which to rest up during passage; more species than in any other part of Shetland except Fair Isle. **Getting there** *By air:* Loganair's inter-island service stops here daily, T: (01595) 840246. *By sea:* ferry from Lerwick (Tue and Thur), or from East Mainland (Mon, Fri, Sat and Sun), T: (01806) 515226. **Further information:** TIC, Lerwick, T: (01595) 693434.

Hermaness

SNH NNR

The reserve on the Hermaness peninsula of Unst is the most northerly tip of Britain. Beyond the offshore rocks of Muckle Flugga and Out Stack there is no more land till you reach Siberia on the other side of the North Pole.

Hermaness is one of the principal bird stations in Europe: 14 species of sea-bird breed here, including 10,000 pairs of gannets which you can look down on from the top of the cliffs, tens of thousands of puffins in burrows on the grass slopes and a sizeable population of great and arctic skuas on the moorland. **Getting there** *By air:* on daily inter-island Loganair flights, T:

(01595) 840246. *By sea:* car ferry to Yell and Unst, T: (01957) 722259. *By car:* on B9086, then on foot. **Access:** unrestricted except breeding season, when visitors are asked to keep to marked paths and the cliff-tops in order to minimize disturbance to birds. Best time: May-July. **Where to**

stay: Britain's most northerly hotel, Baltasound Hotel, T: (01957) 711334; Clingera Guest House, T: (01957) 71157; bed and breakfast, Mrs S. J. Firmin, T: (01957) 755234; Gardiesfauld Hostel, T: (01957) 755311. **Further information:** SNH, Lerwick office, T: (01595) 693345.

THE OUTLIERS

O ff the West Highland and Hebridean coasts lie a small number of remote islands and rocks. None are very large, but they have a wildlife importance out of all proportion to their size; many of them teem with unbelievable numbers of sea-birds. In their island isolation, some of the birds have evolved into forms found nowhere else in the world.

They are exciting and romantic places, these wave-wrapped outliers of the North Atlantic and Hebridean Sea. A few of them, like St Kilda, are as fabulous as any wild place in the world; some are very difficult to get to or land on; all provide an unforgettable adventure in island-going.

St Kilda

A corruption of the Old Norse *Hirtir* meaning 'stags'

NTS, SNH NNR, World Heritage Site

To say that St Kilda is spectacular is to clutch at verbal straws; it has a stark grandeur, an awesome magic almost without parallel in Europe. No one who has ever approached St Kilda from the sea will forget the first distant glimpse of the islands: massive blue shapes looming on the skyline like cathedrals towed out to sea, then nearer to hand the dizzying whirl of the sea-birds, drowning all thought. If I were to be rationed to one wild part of Britain, it would, I think, be this one.

This isolated group of seven wild and precipitous islands and stacks lies 45 miles (72 km) west of Griminish Point, North Uist, the last gigantic rock paroxysm of the continent of Europe. Hirta, the main island, was the most remote inhabited island in British waters, and its sea cliffs, which at Conachair leap vertically out of the sea to the prodigious height of 1,397 ft (426 m), are the highest in Great Britain. Stac an Armin, where the last great auk in Britain was killed in 1840, boasts the highest rock stack in Britain, 627 ft (191 m) above the thundering sea.

St Kilda is the leading sea-bird station in Britain, with the largest gannetry in the world, the largest and oldest fulmar colony in Britain and nationally important colonies of puffins and petrels. It is also home to three unique sub-species; a wren, a field mouse and the wild Soay sheep, and over 130 species of flowering plants (but not a single tree or shrub). At Village Bay on the southern shore of Hirta, virtually the only place on St Kilda suitable for human habitation, lie the poignant remains of a curving line of cottages known as the Street. These were once the homes of a remarkable community; well into the age of intercontinental flight and experimental television these secluded citizens of the United Kingdom eked out a living on their remote island homeland by harvesting the birds from St Kilda's terrifying cliffs. Tragically, the St Kildans were forced by recurrent epidemics, successive crop failures and the demoralization that set in when they realized they were impoverished anachronisms in the modern world, to evacuate the island in 1930, never to return again.

In 1957 the National Trust for Scotland became owners of the island. The Trust then leased the entire archipelago to the Nature Conservancy Council (now Scottish Natural Heritage) as a National Nature Reserve, and the Conservancy Council in turn sub-leased a small area of Hirta to the Ministry of Defence as an Army rocket-tracking station. For some years annual groups of volunteers have been restoring the remains of the unique settlement in Village Bay. This is still almost the only way the ordinary civilian can get to stay for any period of time on this loneliest, stormiest, most spectacular and unforgettable of all the British Isles. **Getting there** *By air:* the Army runs regular helicopter flights out from the mainland, but you would need to have a *very* good reason to persuade them to take you. *By sea:* the NTS run cruises and circumnavigations

round the islands which may provide a few hours ashore. Several charter companies run short excursions to St Kilda, but you sleep on board, not on the island. Private charters are expensive. For details of working holidays on Hirta, which are the best way to spend a fortnight there if you don't mind working a 24-hour week doing restoration work, contact NTS Argyll, Lochaber & the Western Isles Regional Office, T: (01631) 570000. **Access:** anyone wishing to stay on Hirta must first obtain permission from the NTS. Please inform the NTS even if you propose only a temporary landing. Landing on other islands or stacks is virtually impossible. **Where to stay:** if you are visiting by boat, you normally sleep on the boat anchored in Village Bay, Hirta. Accommodation on land at Village Bay is available for members of NTS work parties. There is also a camp-site. Apply NTS or SNH, (see below). **Further information:** SNH, 135 Stilligarry, South Uist HS8 5RS, T: (01870) 620238. NTS Agyll, Lochaber & the Western Isles, Regional Office, Oban, T: (01631) 570000. **Further reading:** David A. Quine, *St. Kilda* (1994); Bob Charnley, *Last Greetings from St. Kilda* (1989); T. Steel, *The Life and Death of St Kilda* (1988).

Sule Skerry

A flat reef some 40 miles (64 km) north of Loch Eriboll on the north coast of Scotland, half a mile (1 km) long, 35 acres (14 ha) in extent, 45 ft (14 m) at its highest point. Home to one of Britain's largest puffin colonies. Lighthouse.

Sule Stack

Small islet, a few miles south-west of Sule Skerry, 6 acres (2.5 ha) in extent, 130 ft (40 m) high. Small gannetry. Rather steep, exposed and inaccessible — only four naturalists have been able to get ashore in 50 years.

Rockall

A 70-ft (21-m) high, 83-ft (25-m) wide rock far out in the North Atlantic, 191 miles (305 km) due west of St Kilda, Rockall is the remotest part of Great Britain and the only British land beyond the continental shelf. Rockall was landed on in 1810, 1887, 1888, 1921, 1955 and 1985. The island was recently at the centre of a dispute between Greenpeace and the British government over plans for oil exploration in the area. Greenpeace's 48-day occupation of Rockall in 1997 is the longest ever and has led them to declare the island capital of 'Waveland', the new Greenpeace 'state'. **Getting there:** no known means. **Accommodation:** none. **Further information:** none.

'Yet three score miles - rocks - surge - uninhabited - uncouth landing places: how to get to it, and upon it - that is a question!'

T. S. Muir:
Ecclesiological
Notes on the
Islands of Scotland

GLOSSARY

AONB, Area of Outstanding Natural Beauty. Landscape designation covering large sites identified on aesthetic grounds by the Countryside Commission.

Biosphere Reserve, a site included in the UNESCO Man and the Biosphere (MAB) programme, which aims to develop reserves of sustainable biodiversity and promote interdisciplinary research and training. This conservation project began in 1971 and by April 1996 covered 337 sites in 85 countries.

CCW, Countryside Council for Wales. Government agency set up to notify SSSIs and manage NNRs in Wales and to advise on Welsh wildlife and countryside matters.

EC, European Council. A summit of Heads of State, meeting at least twice a year as part of the Council of the European Union.

European Diploma, EC award given for good management of protected areas.

EN, English Nature. Government agency set up to notify SSSIs and manage NNRs in England and to advise the government on English wildlife and countryside matters.

ESA, Environmentally Sensitive Area. Designation covering landscape, wildlife and historic sites, under which landowners voluntarily undertake land management duties agreed with the Ministry of Agriculture.

FC, Forestry Commission. National organization with offices throughout England, Scotland and Wales. Set up to manage, protect and expand the nation's woodland.

Heritage Coast, landscape designation covering coastal sites.

NNR, National Nature Reserve. Wildlife designation covering SSSIs which are managed, usually by government agencies, to demonstrate correct procedures for protecting wildlife sites..

NP, National Park. Principal landscape designation covering large areas of England and Wales.

NPA, National Park Authority. In the 1995 Environment Act, National Park Authorities were established to oversee the management of the parks.

NSA, National Scenic Area. Scottish version of the NP designation.

NT, The National Trust. Registered charity founded in 1895 to preserve the nation's countryside and buildings.

NTS, The National Trust for Scotland. Largest charitable conservation body in Scotland, established in 1931.

Ramsar, wildlife designation providing protection under international law for wetlands, particularly those used by wintering wildfowl and wading birds. Sites around the world provide a network of areas for migrating birds. Ramsar is the Iranian town where this convention was adopted in 1971.

SAC, Special Area of Conservation. Wildlife designation, established in response to the 1992 EC Habitats Directive, covering habitat types and populations of species (other than birds) whose survival in Europe is under threat.

SNH, Scottish Natural Heritage. Government agency set up to notify SSSIs and manage NNRs in Scotland and to advise on Scottish wildlife and countryside matters.

SPA, Special Protection Area. Wildlife designation, established in response to the 1979 EC Birds Directive, covering bird populations of European importance.

SSSI, Site of Special Scientific Interest. Principal government wildlife designation, on which all other wildlife designations are based, covering sites of biological or geological importance.

TIC, Tourist Information Centre.

USEFUL ADDRESSES

The following organizations provide useful information and assistance for those interested in exploring wild Britain and in learning about its flora and fauna. Several of them are mentioned throughout this book, often in abbreviated form. Where this is the case, the abbreviations used are given in brackets.

British Tourist Authority, Thames Tower, Blacks Road, Hammersmith, W6 9EL. T:(0181) 846 9000, F: 563 0302.

British Mountaineering Council, 177-179 Burton Road, Manchester, M20 2BB. T:(0161) 445 4747, F: 445 4500.

Campaign for the Protection of Rural Wales, Ty Gwyn, 31 High Street, Welshpool, Powys, SY21 7YD. T:(01938) 552525.

Council for National Parks, 246 Lavender Hill, London, SW11 1LJ. T:(0171) 924 4077, F: 924 5761.

Council for the Protection of Rural England, Warwick House, 25 Buckingham Palace Road, London, SW1P OPP. T:(0171) 976 6433.

Countryside Commission (CC), John Dower House, Crescent Place, Cheltenham, Gloucestershire, GL50 3RA. T:(01242) 521381, F: 584270.

Countryside Council for Wales (CCW), Plas Penrhos, Penrhos Road, Bangor, Gwynedd, LL57 2LQ. T:(01284) 370444.

Cyclists' Touring Club, Godalming, Surrey. T:(01483) 412217, F: 426994, e-mail: cycling@ctc.org.uk and www.ctc.org.uk.

Dartmoor National Park Authority, Parke, Maytor Road, Bovey Tracey, Newton Abbot, Devon, TQ13 9JQ. T:(01626) 832093, web-site: www.dartmoor.npa.gov.uk.

Edinburgh and Scotland Information Centre, 3 Princes Street, Edinburgh, EH2 2QP. T:(0131) 557 1700, F: 557 5118.

English Nature (EN), Northminster House, Peterborough, PE1 1UA. T:(01733) 455000.

Field Studies Council, Preston Montford, Montford Bridge, Shrewsbury, SY4 1HW. T:(01743) 850674, F: 850178.

Forestry Commission (FC), 231 Corstorphine Road, Edinburgh, EH12 7AT. T:(0131) 334 0066.

Highlands and Islands Enterprise, Bridge House, 20 Bridge Street, Inverness, IV1 1QR. T:(01463) 244435, F: 244241, e-mail: du.bryden@hient.co.uk.

Highlands of Scotland Tourist Board, Cameron Square, Fort William, PH33 6AJ. T:(01397) 703781, F: 705184, web-site: www.host.co.uk.

Landmark Trust, Shottesbrooke, Maidenhead, Berkshire, SL6 3SW. T:(01628) 825920.

Lincolnshire Trust for Nature Conservation (LTNC), Banovllum House, Horncastle, Lincolnshire, LN9 5HF. T:(01507) 526667, F: 525732, e-mail: lincstrust@cix. compulink.co.uk and www.enterprise.net/wildlife/ lincstrust.

Long Distance Walkers Association, 29 Appledown Close, Alresford, Hampshire, SO24 9ND.

National Trust (NT), 36 Queen Anne's Gate, London, SW1H 9AS. T:(0171) 447 6749, F: 233 3037.

National Trust for Scotland (NTS), 5 Charlotte Square, Edinburgh, EH2 4DU. T:(0131) 226 5922.

Norfolk Ornithologists' Association (NOA), Broadwalk Road, Holme next the sea, Hunstanton, Norfolk, PE36 6LQ. T:(01485) 525406.

Ordnance Survey (OS) Customer Information Helpline, Romsey Road, Southampton SO16 4GU. T: (08456) 05 05 05, e-mail: custinfo@ordsvy.gov.uk and www.o-s.co.uk.

Orkney Tourist Board, 6 Broad Street, Kirkwall, Orkney, KW15 1NX. T:(01856) 872856, F: 875056.

Outdoor Trust (The), Windy Gyle Belford, Northumberland, NE70 7QE. T/F:(01668) 213289, e-mail: trust@outdoor.demon.co.uk and www.outdoor.demon.co.uk.

Peak District National Authority, Aldern House, Baslow Road, Bakewell, Derbyshire, DE45 1AE. T:(01629) 816200, F: 816310, e-mail: Aldern@PeakDistrict.org.

Ramblers Association, 1-5 Wandsworth Road, London, SW8 2XX. T:(0171) 339 8500, F: 339 8501.

Royal Society for the Protection of Birds (RSPB), The Lodge, Sandy, Bedfordshire, SG19

2DL. T:(01767) 680551.

RSPB Orkney Officer, Smyril, Stenness, Stromness, Orkney, KW16 3JY. T:(01856) 850176.

RSPB Scottish Officer, 17 Regent Terrace, Edinburgh, EH7 5BN. T:(0131) 311 6500.

RSPB Shetland Officer, The Baelans, Fetlar, Shetland, ZE2 9RJ. T:(01957) 733246.

RSPB Wales Officer, Bryn Isel, The Bank, Newtown, Powys, SY16 2AB. T:(01686) 626678.

Royal Scottish Forestry Society, 62 Queen St, Edinburgh, EH2 4NA. T:(0131) 225 8142.

Scilly Isles Tourist Information Centre, Wesleyan Chapel, Well Lane, St Mary's, Isles of Scilly, TR21 OH2. T:(01720) 422536.

Scottish Countryside Activities Council, 11 West Craigs Crescent, Edinburgh, EH12 8NB. T/F:(0131) 339 7014.

Scottish Natural Heritage (SNH), 12 Hope Terrace, Edinburgh, EH9 2AS. T:(0131) 4474784, web-site: www.snh.org.uk.

Scottish Tourist Board, 23 Ravelston Terrace, Edinburgh, EH4 3EU. T:(0131) 3322433.

Shetland Islands Tourism, Market Cross, Lerwick, Shetland, ZE1 OLU. T:(01595) 693434, F: 695807, e-mail and web-site: shetland.tourism@zetnet.co.uk www.shetland-tourism.co.uk.

South West Way Association, Secretary, 'Windlestraw', Penquit, Ermington, Devon, PL21 OLU. T/F:(01752) 896237.

Wales Tourist Board (UK), 1

Regent Street, London, SW1Y 4NS. T:(0171) 8083838, F: 8083830. (Wales), Brunel House, 2 Fitzallen Road, Cardiff, CF2 1UY. T:(01222) 499909.

Wildfowl and Wetlands Trust (WWT), Slimbridge, Gloucester, GL2 7BT. T:(01453) 890333, F: 890827.

Wildlife Trust (WT), National Office (UK), The Green, Witham Park, Waterside South, Lincoln, LN5 7JR. T:(01522) 544400, F: 511616.

Devon Wildlife Trust (DWT), Shirehampton House, 35-37 St David's Hill, Exeter, Devon, EX4 4DA. T:(01392) 279244, F: 433221.

Cornwall Wildlife Trust, Five Acres, Allet, Truro, Cornwall, TR4 9DJ. T:(01872) 73939, F: 225476.

Cumbria Wildlife Trust, Brockhole, Windermere, Cumbria, LA23 1LJ. T:(015394) 48280, F: 48281.

Glamorgan Wildlife Trust (GWT), Fountain Road, Tondu, Bridgend, CF32 0EH. T:(01656) 724100, F: 729880.

Hampshire Wildlife Trust (HWT), 8 Ramsey Road, Eastleigh, Hampshire, SO50 9AL. T:(01703) 613636/613737, F: 612233.

Kent Wildlife Trust (KWT), Tyland Barn, Sandling, Maidstone, Kent, ME14 3BD. T:(01622) 662012, F: 671390.

Norfolk Wildlife Trust (NWT), 72 Cathedral Close, Norwich, NR1 4DF. T:(01603) 625540, F:630593.

Scottish Wildlife Trust (SWT), Cramond House, Cramond

Glebe Road, Edinburgh, EH4 6NS. T:(0131) 312 7765.

Scottish Youth Hostels Association, 7 Glebe Crescent, Stirling, FK8 2JA. T:(01786) 891400, F: 891333.

Suffolk Wildlife Trust, Brooke House, The Green, Ashbocking, Ipswich, IP6 9JY. T:(01473) 890089, F: 890165, e-mail: suffolkwt@cix.compulink.co.uk.

Yorkshire Wildlife Trust, 10 Toft Green, York, YO1 1JT. T:(01904) 659570, F: 613469.

Yorkshire Dales National Park Authority, Colvend, Hebden Road, Grassington, Skipton, N. Yorks, BD23 5LB. T:(01756) 752748, F: 752745.

Yorkshire Tourist Board, 312 Tadcaster Road, York, YO24 1GS. T:(01904) 707961, F: 701414, e-mail: ytb@yorkshire-tourist-board.org.uk

Youth Hostels Association (YHA), Trevelyan House, 8 St Stephen's Hill, St Albans, Hertfordshire, AL1 2DY. T:(01727) 845047.

INDEX

Species are indexed only where information is provided in addition to location, and where they are illustrated; page references in *italics* refer to illustrations.

PICTURE CREDITS

Jacket Front Cover - John
Cleare/Mountain Camera, Jacket
Back Cover - Harry Williams. 10, 11
- Colin Molyneux. 19, 22 - John
Cleare/Mountain Camera. 27 - Dr.
Alan Beaumont. 31 - Colin
Molyneux. 35 - John
Cleare/Mountain Camera. 38 - Dr.
Alan Beaumont. 42, 43 - Michael
Freeman. 47, 50, 51, 54, 55 - Dr.
Alan Beaumont. 59 - Michael
Freeman. 62, 63 - John
Cleare/Mountain Camera. 70 - John
Heseltine. 75 - Simon Warner. 78,
83 - John Cleare/Mountain Camera.
87, 90, 91 - Douglas Botting. 98 -
Roger Scruton. 103 - John
Cleare/Mountain Camera. 107 - Dr.
Alan Beaumont. 110, 111 - Colin
Molyneux. 119 - Kim Taylor, Bruce
Coleman Ltd. 122 - John
224

Cleare/Mountain Camera. 127 -
Colin Molyneux. 130 - John
Cleare/Mountain Camera. 134, 135
- Colin Molyneux. 138, 139, 142,
143 - John Cleare/Mountain
Camera. 147 - Derek G.
Widdicombe. 151 - Jermey Young,
Landscape Only. 155, 158, 159 -
John Cleare/Mountain Camera. 175
- Colin Molyneux. 178, 179 - Archie
Miles. 183 - Alistair Scott. 187 -
John Cleare/Mountain Camera. 191
- Douglas Botting. 194 - Gordon
Langsbury, Bruce Coleman Ltd.
199 - Michael Feeman. 203 -
Alistair Scott. 207 - Robert
Burton/Bruce Coleman Ltd. 211 -
John Cleare/Mountain Camera.

ACKNOWEDGEMENTS

The author and editors wish to
extend special thanks to James

Millar Watt for his hospitality at
Sandaig, Wester Ross; Anthony
Smith of Bamburgh,
Northumberland for hospitality and
amenities; to Bud Young for
hospitality and amenities on
Dartmoor and in the New Forest.
  Grateful thanks are also due to:
Kevin Baverstock, Dr David
Boddington, Roger Boulanger,
Louise Brown, Andrew Campbell,
Valerie Chandler, Peter Ellis,
Franky Eyron, Verena Gnatsy, Tony
Hare, Shane Harris, Judith Harte,
Stephen Lee, Debbi Loth, Scott
Maclean, Anthony Mason, Rob
Mitchell, Christine Noble, Olivier
Occelli, Sonal Patel, Matt Phillips,
Tracey Stead, Lee Twomey and Neil
Willcox.